Daniel Hale Williams

NEGRO SURGEON

Daniel Hale Williams, M.D., M.S., LL.D., F.A.C.S.

DANIEL HALE WILLIAMS

Negro Surgeon

BY

HELEN BUCKLER

Pitman Publishing Corporation

NEW YORK   TORONTO   LONDON

THE AUTHOR wishes to thank the following for permission to reprint certain material: Harvard University Press for lines from "Red Iron Ore" from *Ballads and Songs of the Shantyboy*, collected and edited by Franz Fickaby. Copyright 1926, 1954. Portia Washington Pittman for quotations from the letters of her father, Booker T. Washington.

to the memory of
MY FATHER AND MY MOTHER
who taught me the meaning
of brotherhood

The only way you can succeed is to override the obstacles in your way. By the power that is within you, do what you hope to do.

— Frederick Douglass to Daniel Hale Williams, 1894

Acknowledgments

PROPER thanks can be but imperfectly voiced here to the many persons who contributed to the making of this book. The late Dr. Louis T. Wright suggested the matter. A list of those who submitted, often at inconvenience to themselves, to interviews and the patient answering of correspondence is found on page 362. Included there are members of the Williams and Price families who were more than generous with letters, mementos, and photographs. I am grateful even to those two or three relatives who refused me the door; their implacability made clear what Daniel Hale Williams had suffered.

I wish to express appreciation for the unfailing courtesy and care with which assistance was given by officers and staffs of the Hall of Records, Annapolis; the National Archives; the American Medical Association; the American College of Surgeons; the Janesville, Wisconsin, *Gazette;* Provident Hospital, Chicago; the libraries of the New York Academy of Medicine, Northwestern University Medical School, Fisk University, Franklin and Marshall College, Atlanta University, and Howard University; the Library of Congress; the public libraries of New York City, Chicago, the State of Pennsylvania, the State of Illinois, of Janesville, Wisconsin, and of Rockford, Illinois; the registrars of Northwestern University Medical School, Howard University, University of Wisconsin, Milton College, Wilberforce University, and Meharry Medical College; the Courthouse officials of Anne Arundel County, Maryland, of Blair, Cambria, Dauphin, Lancaster, Mifflin and York Counties in Pennsylvania, and of Cook County in Illinois; the Historical Societies of Maryland, Pennsylvania, Wisconsin, New York and Chicago, as well as of Mifflin, Blair, Dauphin, Lancaster and York Counties in Pennsylvania, and the Antiquarian Society of Worcester, Massachusetts. Special mention should be made of the cheerful assistance outside of regular hours of Phil Waters, Librarian of the Johnstown, Pennsylvania, *Tribune*, and of Ella Snowberger and Floyd Hoenstine of the Blair County Historical Society.

From his invalid quarters the late Dr. Carl Glennis Roberts encouraged and assisted the research for five years. Dr. Ulysses Grant Dailey took time out of a busy life to review the manuscript in its medical and surgical aspects, as did Dr. Roberts. Various friends and colleagues contributed their criticisms as the manuscript progressed. Marquis James read an early draft and made useful suggestions. For proposals as to the final form of the book and their sympathetic yet uncompromising editorial pencils, I am indebted to Jeannette and Dudley Cloud. And finally to my sister, Mrs. Lyman Ball Johnson, I owe thanks for the drudgery of typing.

The hospitality of Davis House, interracial hostel of the Religious Society of Friends, in Washington, made possible the prolonged research needed in the capital and nearby. And to Pendle Hill, that rare Quaker community of work and worship, study and creation, retreat and fellowship, I owe the year's shelter, spiritual and physical, that enabled me to do the final writing.

Any errors, as well as matters of judgment and opinion upon the controversial material herein presented, are, of course, my responsibility.

H. B.

Foreword

TEN years ago when I was working on a magazine article, I came across the statement that the first man in the world to operate successfully on the human heart was an American Negro, Daniel Hale Williams. Dr. Williams performed this feat in 1893, said my information, only thirty years after Emancipation.

Surprised, and a good deal interested, I soon began the long search that finally revealed the story told in these pages. That search led me through fourteen states, and involved interviews with some two hundred and thirty individuals, and correspondence, often prolonged, with fifty more. I talked with doctors, both black and white, many of whom Dr. Williams had trained, to nurses who owed their profession to him, to patients whose lives he had saved, to a man whose heart still beat vigorously because forty-five years previously Dr. Dan had "sewed it up."

I followed the trail to cellars and attics, to old courthouses and government archives, to yellowed newspapers, some of them muddied by flood waters, to creased, brittle letters, to cracked photographs, tintypes, ambrotypes, to carefully folded away marriage records — all the fascinating memorabilia that lure the biographer. I found an almost unbelievable story.

Daniel Hale Williams was a great American surgeon, accorded top rank by his contemporary colleagues, white as well as black. After his first heart operation in 1893 in Chicago, he went on to perform other history-making operations. He was a charter member of the American College of Surgeons and one of the founders and first vice president of the Negro National Medical Association. He founded Provident Hospital in Chicago, the first interracial hospital in the United States and progenitor of a hundred such institutions today. He introduced the training of colored nurses and internes and was appointed by President Cleveland head of Freedmen's Hospital in Washington. He became nationally and internationally known. Why he has slipped into oblivion is the story of these pages.

Dr. Dan was a handsome man, fair-skinned with red hair, and he could have passed for white as some of his relatives and forebears had. But he called himself a Negro and all his life he worked for the advancement of the Negro race. His life was a stormy one, filled with controversy, with struggle and remarkable achievement. His story is a heartening chapter in the development of American surgery and throws new light on the history of the Negro in this country.

On my search I encountered and penetrated the "black velvet curtain" for the first time in my segregated white life. I visited Negro campuses and Negro summer resorts. Through a thin summer-hotel partition I listened to a long evening bull session of colored young people, in which one lone student tried passionately, but without much success, to convince a roomful of skeptics that not all white people are insincere. "We mustn't condemn a whole race," she cried, "for the sins of the majority. I myself know a very nice white woman and I'm sure she's all right!"

I was assured by a seventy-year-old colored gentlewoman that *she* had no race prejudice and she would continue to attend her class reunions at the white college where she had been graduated and continue to speak to white audiences when asked even though her friends condemned her for it.

It was good for me to hear these things, to feel the shoe on the unaccustomed foot, though sometimes a very kind person would inadvertently administer a very sharp stab. An elderly colored gentleman patted my hand as I left him after a long interview and said: "My dear, you haven't a single colored characteristic left. *You* could go *anywhere!*" I went from his door with aching heart, aching because of his revelation of what he had suffered, aching because he assumed that only one with colored blood would have interest enough to ask about Dr. Williams.

After some time in a Negro community, I being the only white person there, I met a woman one day who said, "Oh, so you're a writer. I thought when I noticed you staying here that you must be either a writer or a social worker." This implication that only a professional, not a personal, interest could bring a white person among colored was another sad commentary on the state of affairs in this country.

How little we peoples know each other and how much enjoyment we miss! There are qualities of life in the Negro ghetto that few whites have dreamed of. I have stepped off miserable streets into houses of wealth and taste, into homes whose old walnut and mahogany, china and crystal came from generations back, whose books and paintings invited acquaintance. I remember a reception room, a jewel of a room, exquisite in its restraint. It was a small room, circular in shape; under my feet, a rare carpet from old China; for my waiting a carved chair of some dark wood; to feast my eyes, a lucent marble bust of a woman, a Donatello-like woman, on a slim Florentine column.

I remember an old lady, fragile as Dresden, with snowy hair and bright blue eyes, in whose veins flowed, so I had been told, some of the "best" blood America had ever known, but who refused to tell her nieces the story and hoped the painful past might be forgotten when she died. I remember another old lady, one of Oberlin's first graduates, who spoke seven languages fluently.

There were so many fascinating trails, but I was concerned with only one — Dr. Dan's. For the most part, as I pursued this elusive fact, then that, I was received hospitably on my quest. People were ungrudging of their time and patient in their attention beyond anything I had a right to expect. But once I sat up all night on a local train to reach a distant town in Ohio and then was denied an interview. "He wanted to be white," said

Dr. Dan's cousin through the merest crack in her door. "He wanted to be white, then let him be it." No persuasion availed. Though Dr. Dan had been dead a dozen years, this woman's hatred of one she believed to be a traitor was still a live thing. Her face worked with emotion, her hand trembled, as she closed her door firmly against me.

At the opposite extreme from this experience, a colored man risked his life and received me a few days after he had suffered a severe coronary occlusion. An oxygen tank stood ready by his pillow. But Dr. Carl Roberts was determined to assist, if he could, in restoring this great and forgotten surgeon to what he believed was his rightful place in history.

So controversial a figure was the hero of this story, I soon found, that I had always to weigh any evidence by the partisanship, pro as well as con, of the witness. Then, too, I was of an alien race and I had always to discount what was told me by this unhappy fact. The truth was what I wanted, but it was difficult to come by. All the more so since the curse hurled at this man by his enemy had proved only too effective. "I'll punish him worse than God ever will," his opponent had cried. "I'll see he's forgotten before he's ever dead." The means used to bring this malediction to eventuality, the obscuring of facts by the passage of time, the death of so many who had been party to the drama — all made discovery of the true tale a slow and sometimes discouraging process.

The surprises in the story were many. It turned out to bear little resemblance to the usual Negro story. There are no slave cabins, no cotton fields, no city slums, no lynchings — only the slow crucifixion of the spirit. And who knows of the Negro who was "always free"? Yet he existed in numbers both North and South from earliest times — propertied, cultured, of global outlook. Who knows of the many white women who chose to marry darker husbands and lived happily ever after? But more especially, who knows the Negro not as a type but as an individual, not as victim, or as conqueror, but as an infinitely varied, infinitely interesting mixture of strength and weakness, even as you and I?

And who knows how bitter is the struggle, not between Negro and white, but between Negro and Negro, inside the segregation camp of racial discrimination?

Each discovery brought another question. If Daniel Hale Williams looked white, and he did, then why did he *feel* like a Negro? And what drives were in him that would not let him rest on his own hard-won success, but made him try to carry his "race" forward with him? And why, in the end, after he had become an inspiration to colored people everywhere, after he had made the greatest contribution of his day to the progress of the Negro people, why was he cursed for disloyalty, driven into obscurity, forced out of colored medicine, out of the hospital he founded and spent twenty years building? And then, after this treatment and after another twenty years on the staff of an important white hospital, after having been a charter member of the American College of Surgeons, how explain that his heart was still with Negroes? Why did he, despite everything, send his library to a Negro hospital and make a will giving the bulk of his money to two Negro medical schools and the National Association for the Advancement of Colored People?

My search for fact in the end became a search for motivation. And motives of course are always open to question. No one of us can ever know another entirely. This is the story as it has seemed to me.

In the nine years I have lived with this story I feel I have come to know few persons as well as I now know Dr. Dan — his aspirations, his disappointments, and his success — this sensitive, almost shrinking human being, left so ill equipped by fortune for the rough-and-tumble of the life that was his, and yet a human being who could summon up a magnificent courage, a courage far beyond the modicum required by thicker-skinned individuals.

I might have met Dr. Dan face to face in 1920–1921, for I was then a patient for some months in St. Luke's Hospital and he was still active on the staff. I did watch operations, for my malady was chronic rather than acute and my surgeon sought to save me from boredom by sometimes allowing me to follow him about at his work. I might have watched instead some of Dr. Dan's operations, some of those here described from his own notes. But Fate ruled otherwise. Perhaps it is as well. I was young then, and inexperienced. Perhaps I should have been put off by the façade he had built between himself and the world. Perhaps I know Dr. Dan better now than if I had met him in the halls of St. Luke's years ago.

HELEN BUCKLER

Pendle Hill
Wallingford, Pennsylvania
June 1953

Foreword to the Second Edition

TIME has never passed more swiftly than in the fifteen years since this volume first appeared. Scarcely a phase of life, at home or abroad, has not known metamorphosis. Heart operations to which Daniel Hale Williams dared open the door seventy-five years ago have become actual heart transplants, though still occasioning outcries against this disrespect for "the seat of the soule."

The black community to which he gave his loyalty, love, and leadership has changed too. The goal is not yet reached; the struggle goes on. But the community has changed. It has changed its vocabulary. It no longer calls itself colored, but black. As Doctor Dan did at Camp Funston, it speaks out more. It no longer bows to the dictates or waits upon the wishes of one political overlord.

In vain Dr. Williams tried to persuade Booker Washington to allow him to open a surgical clinic at Tuskegee where he could save black lives and teach black surgeons. "There is nothing," he assured Washington, "that our people cannot do once given the chance. They make the best soldiers; they could make the best surgeons too." Washington turned him down and the black South, the whole country, was the loser.

Today we can only read about what might have been and hope

that the inspiration from this brave life may help the black men and women, the black boys and girls, of the urban ghetto and the forgotten rural slum "override the obstacles." As Frederick Douglass urged Doctor Dan, "By the power that is within you, do what you hope to do."

HELEN BUCKLER

Boerum Hill
Brooklyn, New York
June, 1968

Contents

Illustrations

Daniel Hale Williams

NEGRO SURGEON

CHAPTER I

The Wandering Barber Finds a Home

ON freezing nights in the winter of 1877 a young man might be seen struggling down an unlighted side street, buffeting the wind and often a blinding snow, in the little Wisconsin town of Janesville. To any passer-by his battle with the fury hurled from the Great Lakes must have seemed a losing one for a person of his thin frame — thin-seeming despite enveloping coat, thick scarf, and cap and earlaps of fur. Frequently he carried a covered bass viol in mittened hands, weaving the unwieldy instrument about to keep it safe as he slipped and slid on the plank sidewalk.

On such a night, undoubtedly his one thought was to get home quickly. At this time Daniel Hale Williams had dreams of bettering himself, but no well-defined plans for his future. He spent his days working several hours as a barber in Charles Henry Anderson's Tonsorial Parlor and Bathing Rooms and the rest of the time attending classes at the Janesville Classical Academy. Half his evenings he spent practicing or playing with Anderson's popular string band. His studying he squeezed in where he could.

It was a full schedule, but it seemed normal enough to Dan. Every man in Janesville hustled from morning to night, and every woman too. There was so much to be done in an expanding country trying still to make up for the long stagnation and drain of the War Between the States. The urge was in everyone to be busy, never let up, and Dan felt the urge with the rest.

Dan boarded at the Anderson home. Harry Anderson, more a friend than an employer, had several years ago invited his new assistant to move in with him and his family in the comfortable two-story white frame house on Glen Street. There Dan, a lonely lad, adrift in a strange town, had found a warm welcome. Harry's wife Ellen mothered him, as she mothered her stepson George and her own children — the pretty, talented Traviata, usually called Vytie (Dan said 'Viata), frail Tessie and little Alfie who was crippled, and finally the new baby, Daniel Herbert, named for Dan but called Bertie.

Ellen Anderson was a generous, loving woman, well content with her life in this bustling, growing Western town. Perhaps her family back in County Cork had found it strange when she wrote some eighteen years ago that she was marrying a mulatto in the New World. But who else could be so fine, so kind, so openhanded as Charles Henry Anderson? That he was a widower with a little brown boy to bring up had appealed to her warm sympathies and she had never regretted her choice. She was proud of her olive-skinned children. She was proud, too, of George, her stepson, twenty-two now, darker-skinned than her husband and with rounded African features and crinkly hair.

And she was proud of Dan, eager, red-haired, quick as a young pacer and as graceful. Dan had needed her care and affection as much as the others. His pale handsome face held contradictions. There was intelligence in the fine forehead and shapely nose and strength in the square-cut jaw and firm chin. But a dimple gave that chin a womanish look and the thin, curving mouth was too sensitive, the dark brown eyes too melancholy to promise much happiness for their owner. No one would have guessed that the pale, red-haired Dan had African blood in his veins, or Indian blood. But Dan proudly claimed both.

Daniel Hale Williams had been born in Hollidaysburg, Pennsylvania, on January 18, 1856. He was the fifth child of Daniel Williams, Jr., and Sarah Price Williams. His father was descended from early pious German folk who had settled, long before the

Revolution, in the territory that became York County, and had intermarried with the peace-loving Shawnee and Delaware Indians. Their descendants had intermarried sometimes with Negro and sometimes with Welsh, Scotch and Irish families until Dan's father showed, except for some crinkle in his hair, the contours of his high cheekbones, and his erect dignified bearing, but little physical indication of the racial mixture that was his.

The Williamses were a proud, independent, God-fearing clan. Farmers, small businessmen, barbers, all owned property and many preached the word of God on Sunday. A few had disappeared back into the white race out of which their forebears came. These were the exceptions that only made more invincible the passionate loyalty of the free Williamses to the interests and welfare of their enslaved African brothers. They and others of like blood and like views had by their own unflagging zeal encouraged Benjamin Lundy, William Lloyd Garrison and the rest of the white Abolitionists to greater and greater effort. The Williamses and their friends held state and national conventions, made speeches, published pamphlets, worked on committees, traveled back and forth, got protests into the white newspapers. Each generation of sons and daughters received the imprint of this intrepid devotion.

Though Dan's grandfather had married a white woman, Dan's father married a girl darker than himself, a girl of the same three racial strains as his own. When Sarah Price, a fifteen-year-old bride, tied her bonnet over her straight black Indian tresses, placed her hand trustfully in that of her tall twenty-three-year-old husband and turned her face westward to the wild Alleghenies, she left behind on Church Circle in Annapolis a comfortable, pleasant home. The Prices, like the Williamses, were a free family, a family that could, even in the South, enter into wedlock. It made all the difference. Sarah's grandfather Smith Price had owned a small estate called Greenhill outside the town gates and a shop and house in the city. Her father, the Reverend Henry Price, canny in real estate matters, educated, fearless, was respected by whites as well as by colored.

Dan's father prospered in Hollidaysburg, the boom town at

the head of the Pennsylvania State Canal. He bought property in town and land rich in iron ore on Brush Mountain. After Dan, two more children were born, to swell the number to seven. When Dan was eleven and the Civil War was over, the family at last could go to visit his mother's ancestral home in Annapolis. While they were there, his father fell victim to quick consumption and died. Undoubtedly his arduous traveling and speaking for the Equal Rights League had contributed to his early death.

For a time Sarah stayed on with her widowed mother. But she was restless and uncertain. Her elder son Price, already a grown man of twenty, went off on his own up North, teaching school and studying law. Sarah wanted to go back West. With reckless disregard for her purse, she placed two girls in an expensive convent school, left the youngest with her mother, and, with Annie and Sally, now in their late teens, she set off for Rockford, Illinois. There the three of them would live with some Williams cousins and learn the hair goods trade. Dan she took out of school and apprenticed to a shoemaker in Baltimore.

Poor young Dan, bereft so suddenly of all that had made his childhood happy, asked to sit still all day, pushing a needle through ill-smelling hides, must have felt miserable. Often he must have asked himself why his mother had abandoned him. One day when he could stand his fate no longer, he bundled up his clothes, went to a railroad man who had known his father and asked for a pass to go West.

When twelve-year-old Dan suddenly appeared in Rockford, his mother was startled. But she only laughed her easy laugh, Dan years later told his niece, and said that with all that spunk Dan could take care of himself. Soon her restless spirit would drive her back East again. She took her eldest daughter with her, but again left Dan behind, this time with his sister Sally and his cousins. Dan made his own way, working sometimes in barbershops, sometimes on the lake boats — at whatever he could get.

But the Rock River valley drew him. At seventeen he was running his own small barbershop in the little village of Edgerton,

Daniel Williams, Jr.,
father of Daniel Hale Williams

Sarah Price Williams,
mother of Daniel Hale Williams

Young Dan at about age 6

Wisconsin, but soon he moved to the larger Janesville, a few miles away. His sister Sally was with him. Sally at once found a job in the hair goods trade, making the popular Saratoga frizzes, chignons and waterfalls, and hair jewelry too. Dan went to Harry Anderson and asked for work in his Tonsorial Parlor and Bathing Rooms. Anderson's six-chair establishment was the biggest and best in town, patronized by the best people, and offered a plumbingless population warm baths at all hours, as well as fashionable trimming of beards and mustaches, haircuts, and shaves for the few smooth-faced men who wanted them.

Dan was well-mannered, neat and clean, and he was nimble with scissors and blade. Anderson could use him. Barbers were a nomad lot and Anderson had to exercise some ingenuity to keep enough help. Good board was a lure and he had taken Dan to the house on Glen Street to board, and with him his sister Sally.

More than anything else Dan wanted an education. Although he had been only eleven when his father died, he remembered his father had said over and over again, "We colored people must cultivate the mind." Dan could support himself by working in Anderson's barbershop only part-time and that way he was able to attend the Jefferson High School.

It was a fine school, much better than the old shanty set aside for colored children in Hollidaysburg, or even the new but segregated Stanton School of the Freedmen's Bureau he had attended for a few months near his grandmother's home in Maryland.

But Sally soon married and went north to live in Portage. Undoubtedly Dan again felt abandoned. He continued his high school work a while, but he suffered frequent heavy chest colds and finally left high school without being graduated.

One day Harry Anderson discovered Dan could strum a guitar and sing in a very passable tenor. Perhaps he overheard him singing to the children:

> Come all ye bold sailors that follow the Lakes
> On an iron ore vessel your living to make;
> I shipp'd in Chicago, bid adieu to the shore,

Bound away to Escanaba for red iron ore.
Der-ry down, down, down derry down!

Dan, usually reticent, disclosed he had followed the Lakes for
a time, playing and singing, though he just played by ear. He
wasn't as good as his uncle who had an orchestra back in Harrisburg. His uncle, his mother's brother, used to go into a music store
and look at the music, not to buy it, just to whistle it off under
his breath. Then he would go home and play it all, without missing a note. In contrast to this glamorous uncle, Dan depreciated his
own abilities, but Anderson evidently thought Dan had the mak-
ings of a note-reader in him. At any rate the young barber started
going to the bandrooms after work. He learned to play the big
bull fiddle and became a member of Anderson's famous string
band, accompanying celebrities who came to the Meyer Opera
House, Modjeska among them, playing for the important entertainments at Apollo Hall, the frequent square dances at the Grange
Hall, and traveling all over Wisconsin and sometimes outside
the state.

Among Janesville's citizenry of 10,000 were many strong, venturesome men who had left New York State and New England
in the depressions of the '30s and '50s and come out to sparsely
settled Wisconsin in search of new opportunities. They had found
them in the unusual beauty and riches of the Rock River valley.
The fertile prairies carpeted with luxuriant grasses needed no
clearing to yield the farmer his return, and the wide clear stream
flowing over a limestone bottom provided water power for a
variety of industries — woolen and cotton mills, manufacture of
boots and shoes, of fine buggies and carriages, sleighs and cutters,
and the much-needed farm machinery.

These early settlers were men of vision and faith. Not a few
were college-trained. It mattered little what their business or profession, they were all civic-minded and put as much effort into
the affairs of Janesville as they put into their own affairs: W. T.
Van Kirk, the grocer; Orrin Guernsey, the insurance man; Henry

Palmer, the physician. Palmer was on the boards of the pickle factory and the savings bank, of a commercial college and the new cotton mill. These men held town office and went to the state legislature.

Coming in to Anderson's barbershop for a haircut or to have their beards trimmed, these settlers from the East who had brought with them their books, their Abolitionism, their passion for betterment, stayed on to argue all sorts of matters. They argued the virtues of free trade, the need for resuming specie payments, Darwin's theories of evolution, the way Hayes was handing the South back to its old leaders.

To young Dan Williams, snipping away with agile fingers, listening to all that was said, the barbershop was a kind of school, and between customers, it was a good place to get some reading done.

"You like to read?" Orrin Guernsey asked the youth one day, seeing him put aside a book as he jumped up to serve him. Yes, Dan answered, he did, whenever he could get hold of a book.

Guernsey was sympathetic. Janesville ought to have a library, but he reminded Dan that they did have books at the reading rooms of the Young Men's Association.

"I've read all those," Dan replied, "all I like, I've read."

Encouraged to say what he did like, Dan mentioned history and great lives, and Guernsey promptly began bringing the boy books to read from his own library.

But Dan was not satisfied with this life. What he really wanted was to enter college. To do that he must have a high school diploma or pass examinations that were beyond him.

Under the stimulation of Guernsey's books and his own yearning to make something of himself, he arranged for special tutoring in the Classical Academy. Principal Haire's fees were within his reach — seventy-five cents a week for Latin and the higher studies. Anderson agreed to let him go back on a part-time basis at the shop, and apparently never referred to any difficulties the new arrangement might cause him. The least a colored man could do was help an ambitious lad of his race get on, especially a lad you had come to love like your own son.

The day after Dan had attended his first classes at the Academy, Dr. Haire received two callers in his office. The first was the beautiful Minerva Guernsey, eighteen-year-old daughter of Dan's kindly lender of books. Already Minnie was Janesville's favorite elocutionist, and not without reason, for in time Minnie would bring sophisticated audiences of Boston and New York to her feet. Just now, however, she was preparing at the Academy for her college entrance examinations. She still remembered, when she was an old lady, how upset she was as she stood before the tall, thin, bald-headed principal.

"Oh, Professor Haire," she cried, "Maggie Hullihan says her father won't have Dan Williams in this school. She says her father will make you put him out. Just because he has colored blood!" Her young bosom heaved and her eyes were bright with unshed tears as her Abolition inheritance and her flair for the dramatic combined to urge her on.

"Professor Haire," she cried, "if you put Dan out of this school, I'll — I'll *leave*, that's what I'll do!"

"Please control yourself, Miss Guernsey," replied the unperturbed principal. "We have no intention of dismissing Mr. Williams from our school."

Scarcely had Minnie departed than Maggie Hullihan's father, an oculist and former North Carolinian, climbed the stairs to the principal's office.

"I'm told one of those young barbers of Anderson's is in attendance here. Is that true?" he demanded.

"If you mean Daniel Williams, sir," John Haire answered, "it is. He's a very good student."

"Good student or not," Hullihan shouted, "he can't go to school with my daughter! Don't you know he's got Negro blood in him? Maybe he does look white, but he's a Negro all the same."

"Yes, I know Mr. Williams has an African strain, Mr. Hullihan," the principal replied as he unlocked a small drawer in his roll-top desk. Out of it he took three silver dollars and handed them to his caller. "Here is Miss Maggie's tuition, sir. I believe you had paid one month in advance? Quite so." As the outraged father picked up his hat, the unruffled principal added soothingly, "This is Wisconsin, not North Carolina. I fear you do not realize that fact, Mr. Hullihan."

If the Hullihans expected other families to follow their example, they were disappointed. None did. But somehow Dan learned what had happened. Dan who could well remember his sister Ida's leading him past the white children's fine brick school back East and on to the shabby frame shack where the colored children received their second-rate education, Dan thanked his principal by redoubling his time with his books.

Despite the spotlight focused on him, his demeanor remained apparently unruffled as he pursued his serious quiet way. When the girls discussed the new boy in the cloakroom Mara Franc Edwards gave it as her opinion — and she repeated it when she was ninety-two — that "He's just like everybody else," and since Frankie's opinion counted, that settled the matter.

Janesville in the '70s offered much to arouse and encourage those disposed to accept it. Professor Haire conducted Home Forums on Tuesday evenings, and on Wednesday evenings Literary Round Tables were led by blind, talented John Van Cleve. A spirit of search and inquiry, a passion for learning and improvement was in the air.

Janesville was not ingrown. The great men and women who were stirring other parts of the country were invited to come to Janesville. Henry Ward Beecher came, and Elizabeth Cady Stanton, and the challenging Colonel Robert Ingersoll.

Dan came away from Ingersoll's lecture excited and elated. The man's words sparkled in his consciousness like an invasion of meteors from another planet: "When people read, they begin to reason, and when they reason, they progress." He was reading, so perhaps he was progressing after all. What else had Ingersoll said? "Every library is an arsenal, filled with the weapons and ammunition of Progress, and every fact is a Monitor with sides of iron and a turret of steel . . . the life of a lie is simply a question of time. Nothing but truth is immortal." That gave you hope.

At this time, Dan had the good fortune to come under the influence of the pastor of All Souls Unitarian Church. By rights Dan should have attended the Methodist Church. His own father had been an ardent worker in the Methodist Church and both his grandfathers had been devout Methodist preachers. The Andersons, too, went to the Methodist Church. But Dan became a Unitarian.

The Reverend Jenkin Lloyd Jones, pastor of All Souls, spearheaded much of the intellectual and moral ferment of Janesville. He was always startling people, saying women ought to vote, that Negroes should be treated as equals, and announcing flatly that, although he had fought in the Civil War, he would never don uniform again.

He organized a Mutual Improvement Club for the young people. Into its programs he brought a wide range of interests — scientific, civic, and philanthropic as well as literary. And to balance this serious hour he added an hour of square dancing to follow and invited Anderson, George and Dan to come and play for it.

Dan played at All Souls, too, for the dime entertainments of the Sunday School and for the church services on Sunday. One way and another, he saw a good deal of the inspiring preacher with the advanced ideas. The Welshman's influence upon the impressionable, aspiring youth was important.

While Dan was playing bass fiddle, barbering and attending. classes, two years had slipped quickly by. Now he was twenty-one. Soon he would have his diploma from the Academy and another decision would lie ahead of him. He must do something, get ahead, but how?

That spring of 1877 Dan had another problem. Despite himself, he was caught in a flirtation, an invasion of all his careful program for work and study — an invasion of the wall between himself and white persons, a wall behind which he had proudly withdrawn. It was blonde, apple-cheeked Ida Williams, by chance of his same name, by fate of another race,. who had breached it. It all started by chance. Various men in the orchestra stepped out at times for a dance or two, and all the girls at the Academy loved to dance with Dan; he had a true musician's grace and rhythm. But Ida, pert, popular Ida, used to having her own way, had pushed the matter beyond chance. It was not Dan's doing, at least not in the beginning. Minnie Guernsey and Frankie Edwards were positive about that. But soon he was dancing with no one else.

"Ida's got a terrific crush on Dan Williams!" The word buzzed around. It could be confirmed at any party. Sooner or later the high-spirited Ida would be found in a set right under the nose of the orchestra. And sooner or later Dan would be found on the dance floor following Ida's white Paris muslin frock through the mazes of circle left and circle right and ladies' chain to the grand finale, when he turned with thumping heart and caught her hands in his as Harry Anderson called out: *"S-w-i-n-g the girl behind you!"*

Dan might well have been disturbed to find himself thus perched on the brink of so unwanted a situation. Some Williams men had loved and married white women. His grandfather had chosen a Scotch-Irish bride, his grandfather's cousin a German one. Harry Anderson had married Ellen and it was a happy marriage. It was all right, Dan could suppose, if a woman was ready to place her loyalties where yours were, to stick out everything, through thick and thin. His own father, however, had married a girl darker than himself. And if Dan had thought of matrimony at all, he doubtless had thought that of course he would do as his father had done. Not many months later he wrote Anderson: "I might have had thousands for liesure, but I would not marry a white girl." But Ida's father solved his problem.

Gossip of the flirtation inevitably reached the ears of John P. Williams, the town's leading basso, soloist in all the local cantatas, as popular in adult circles as his daughter was in younger circles. He understood his willful offspring rather well. He took her aside for a frank talk, Ida confessed to Frankie Edwards, and suggested he was thinking of sending her to public school along with her stepsister, Carrie Jacobs.

Ida wanted to stay on at the Academy. So she decided to be more circumspect. Soon she was seen setting her cap for Blanche Burdick's fiancé Jim Lord.

And Dan, how could he make amends to Ida? It was a sweet debt, and he did not forget it. Years later, when the widowed Ida Williams Lord brought her ailing son to the famous Dr. Williams for an operation, he performed it and sent no bill. And many years later still, when he sat down to write his will, he bequeathed, in the middle of a long list, a sum to Ida Lord, because, he wrote, it had been her father who had first encouraged him to study medicine.

A strange explanation. Though old Simeon Lord was in fact a doctor and had several daughters, Ida was only his daughter-in-law. Moreover, not Dr. Lord but another Rock County physician was to encourage Dan Williams to study medicine.

CHAPTER II

A Medical Apprentice in 1878

GRADUATION Day at the Academy came and went and still Dan had made no decision as to his future.

Preaching had been the ardent, sincere pursuit of many of his devout forebears. Both his grandfathers had preached on Sundays, not to make a livelihood, but out of a dedicated spirit, offering their people faith and hope and the love of God to carry them through. But remembering the iconoclastic Ingersoll and the Unitarian Jenkin Lloyd Jones, Dan could no longer accept the theology of his ancestors.

Teaching should be possible, now that he had a diploma. Especially if he took a country school. But he was far too shy to face a roomful of big strapping boys intent on worsting him.

Then there was the law. His brother Price, ten years older than he, was a successful lawyer and politician, flitting from Philadelphia to New York and back again to Washington. Daring, voluble, Price was their mother's favorite. Now that Dan had his diploma, why couldn't he read law like Price? He could keep books and do clerical work for a lawyer, and read law while he was doing it. Dan knew a white Congressman, a leading member of the Janesville bar, who had delivered an eloquent address on Emancipation Day. It would be easy enough to speak to the man the next time he came into the barbershop.

So it came about that Dan Williams, destined to be a doctor,

spent the winter turning the dusty pages of Littleton and Blackstone and grew ever more miserable. He had not yet found his
true bent.

There is no one to tell us today just how Dan's interest was
first caught by medicine. His growing distaste for law — in after-
life he said law was making money out of people's quarrels and
he always shrank from quarrels — made him look around for some
more congenial profession. Medicine and surgery were spread
graphically before him in almost every issue of the local paper.
The *Gazette* liked nothing better, apparently, than to describe the
doings of the town's most prominent doctor and ex-mayor. If
Henry Palmer was not snowbound, forced to abandon his horse
and buggy, and trudging on foot to care for his patients — "Show
us the man," cried the *Gazette*, "that says the doctor has not got
sand!" — then he was amputating a child's leg, crushed when
the boy clambered up on a moving freight car. Or he was probing
to no avail for the bullet that had lodged somewhere in the body
of the victim of a drunken brawl.

The gunshot case was reported on regularly for several issues.
One bullet had passed clear through the body, another was se-
creted where it could not be found. Was the liver injured? Dr.
Palmer could not tell. It was not the most hopeful sort of case,
though sometimes bodies did heal with bullets inside them. Everyone would have to wait and see what turn affairs took. Five or
six days might tell . . .

It was enough to stir an imagination far less vivid than Dan's.
His inquiring mind would understandably lead him to ask questions of the doctor when he encountered him as he had constant
occasion to do — in the barbershop where he had found a friend in
Orrin Guernsey, at the Art Association reception where Dr. Palmer's interest in pictures would bring him and where Dan played
with Anderson's band, at Dr. Palmer's silver wedding anniversary
where again Dan played, or, perhaps, on the country road. Dan
used to take the Anderson buggy and drive Ellen's friend, Mrs.
Benjamin Hall — another white woman married to a mulatto —
when she had carpet rags ready to go to the weaver at Mt. Zion.

When buggies pulled out to pass on country roads, folk stopped a while to exchange news and rest their horses. But whether on such an occasion or some other, Dan had every opportunity in a small friendly town to talk with Dr. Palmer.

And eventually the talk led to his entering Dr. Palmer's busy office as an apprentice. Dr. Palmer's daughter, Elizabeth Palmer Taylor, then a little girl, remembers only that Dan came about the time or shortly before her brother Will left for medical college when her father needed another apprentice.

She recalls that her father did not accept Dan as an apprentice right off. He made Dan go home and think it over, not once, but several times. Young men should not be forever switching about, the doctor pointed out. Did Dan want to throw away those months he had put in at law? And was he strong enough for long and irregular hours, for cold buggy rides on dark, stormy nights? Was he prepared for the wear and tear of constant dealing with pain and suffering and for being unable, sometimes, to do anything whatever about it?

The red-haired, quicksilver Dan was made to do some sober, solid thinking. But the more he thought, the more desirable medicine became. In the end he convinced Palmer and was allowed to take a place beside Will in the doctor's busy office in the Smith Block, at the corner of Main and East Milwaukee Streets.

Now at last Dan began to be his own man. Now he could put all his energy into his vocation — for he was certain that medicine was his vocation — instead of dissipating half of it in inner bewilderment and rebellion. The change in him was startling. His health improved. His step quickened until he fairly ran.

No one could beat Dan when it came to driving himself in hard work. And fortunately he had the dictionary habit. He buckled down to learning the strange new vocabulary. His Latin was a help, and his German. Soon he was turning the dog-eared pages of Palmer's books — Gray's *Anatomy* and *The National Dispensatory* — with twice the avidity he had employed in reading Littleton's *Tenures* or Blackstone's *Commentaries*.

Reading medicine in some doctor's office was the method in

1878 for beginning a medical career. Still earlier, apprenticeship had been the sole means of acquiring a medical education. But now, in Dan's youth, a student began with a practicing doctor as his preceptor and, when the doctor was ready to give him credentials, he went on to attend one or two terms of lectures at some medical school. Dan could begin his medical education, therefore, without any financial outlay. Later he would have to find ways and means to complete his training.

The apprentice system was as good as the individuals involved. If the student was eager and hard-working, if the preceptor was both a skilled practitioner and a good teacher, then the results were good. The actual contact with cases gave a reality to the affair that was lost in the later system of purely didactic schooling and not regained until the establishment of interneships. If Dan had to sweep out the office, care for Palmer's horse and phaeton, and help keep accounts, he also helped set fractures and dress wounds. He put up powders and that gave him a knowledge of the properties of drugs, their appearance, taste and feel, along with the conditions for which they were used, and the dosage. He became skillful in making a urinalysis. Above all he saw disease and did not just read about it.

Dan was fortunate in his preceptor. Henry Palmer was fifty, at the height of his powers, when Dan began studying with him. For his day Palmer was unusually qualified. His short formal education had been preceded by two years' apprenticeship with two eminent physicians and professors of medicine in Albany, New York, and followed by two years as resident surgeon of an infirmary in Troy. Thus qualified he had come out to Janesville in one of the early immigrant waves from the East and had had almost ten years' experience before the Civil War broke out. Volunteering then as a surgeon, he had come out of those arduous, bloody years a seasoned, daring operator, and the director, as well, of the largest military hospital of the war.

Palmer's horizons were not at any time confined to the Rock River valley, nor was his reputation. He was active in the new American Medical Association and served a term as vice-president.

He held the office of Surgeon General of Wisconsin for ten years and, when the College of Physicians and Surgeons was founded in Chicago, he was called not to one chair but to several — operative surgery, surgical pathology, clinical surgery.

Dr. Palmer was cool, quick of eye, and dexterous. People trusted him. Supported by a strong will and great powers of endurance, he performed some of the most dangerous operations under the difficult conditions of the preantiseptic era. Surgery was rough then and often brutal. You made up your mind what had to be done and did it quickly. There was no such thing as preoperative preparation either of patient or of instruments. Postoperative infection was the expected thing. Internal surgery was almost never tried. No opening the body to find lost bullets or to inspect or remove diseased parts. Cases were confined to the necessities of accident injuries. The new railroads, the agricultural machines, and runaway horses sent many patients to Dr. Palmer's office. Tobogganing on Janesville's hills brought in some cases, too.

Broken noses were common affairs. The doctor would poke his finger swiftly up one nostril, then up the other, slap on the plaster Dan handed him, and say:

"Go on home now and go to bed, son. In a week you'll be ready to go rooting again."

It was not the techniques learned from Dr. Palmer that were to take Dan so far, but, what was more important, a certain courageous promptness and dispatch.

Henry Palmer was a ripe scholar and a man of culture. He found time while on a trip inspecting the hospitalization of wounded in the Russo-Turkish War to make the best art collection known to Southern Wisconsin. On his return he had lectured to his fellow townsmen and they packed the Baptist Church to hear him. He went to other towns, when he could find time, and repeated the lecture. He was part and parcel of important civic enterprises, an indefatigable worker of broad interests. Association with such a man left its inevitable mark on his apprentices. Dan knew he was fortunate to be where he was.

In the spring of 1879 Palmer accepted another apprentice, Frank Pember, a year younger than Dan, who had spent three years at Milton College eight miles away. And in the fall of 1879, when his son Will went off to medical college, Palmer accepted yet another, James S. Mills, four years Dan's senior, also from Milton, a sober mature young Scot who after ten years of alternate study and teaching had finally won his A.B. With three apprentices on shift, Palmer could announce that his office was open day and night.

Out of the association of these three young men came mutual respect and lasting friendship. Pember gave Dan his autographed photograph. "To my associate in study," he wrote, and Dan put it alongside a photograph of Dr. Palmer's big brick house, keeping them both in a leather-bound album of his friends, girls and young men, colored and white.

In the late spring of 1880 Palmer told his apprentices that by fall he would be ready to give them credentials for medical college. The time had come for Dan to leave Janesville. It promised to be easier for Dan than he might once have found it, for everyone else seemed to be leaving Janesville too. The Reverend Jenkin Lloyd Jones was moving on to wider fields and All Souls Church must find a new pastor. Mrs. Haire had died and her husband had closed the Academy. The Andersons were moving from Glen Street. Harry Anderson had fitted up living quarters over his barbershop, "in fine style," the *Gazette* said, and was installing his family there. Dan's friends from the Academy were scattered. Minerva Guernsey, after good notices in Boston, was preparing for her New York City debut. Ida Williams's father had died and she had gone to Madison to live.

When Pember and Mills made up their minds to go to Chicago to finish their training, Dan determined to go with them, though where the money was coming from he scarcely knew. He had always made what money he could on the side; he had barbered for Anderson and he played in the orchestra. Now he added another occupation, stringing up wires for the new telephone ex-

change — there were sixteen subscribers — and the new electric
street lights. Henry Palmer's capital and energy were, of course,
behind both ventures and through him Dan secured the work.

Dan managed to save enough money to buy some necessities
and the new suit with the braid-bound cutaway without which
he did not feel he could face a strange new world. He grew a
drooping silky mustache. But he still lacked a good part of the
hundred dollars or more he would need for fees and books.

Harry Anderson had been enormously pleased with Dan's
change from law to medicine, pleased with the new vim it had
put into the young man, and pleased that his race, in the person
of Dan, should thus be making progress. Secretly he cherished the
hope that this restless, aspiring young man would someday marry
his daughter Vytie, though he had to admit it was only a hope.
So he suggested to Dan that he borrow the money he needed at
the bank; he said he would gladly go on his note.

There remained then the matter of living expenses. Dan felt
he might well get help from his mother. His grandfather Price
had died during the war, his grandmother in 1876. The Price
estate was now being settled between his mother and her brother's
widow, Mary. In July some Harrisburg property had been
awarded by the courts to Mary Price, and the home place in
Annapolis, together with a smaller property, had been assigned
to Sarah Williams. There remained two other small pieces of real
estate and twenty shares of bank stock, with dividends accumulated during thirteen years, to be sold and divided between the
two women. All Sarah's older children were now married and
settled. The two younger were in their twenties and making their
own way, Alice by sewing and Florence in office work. There
seemed no reason why Dan should not now receive some help
from his mother.

She was slow in answering his plea, but on the strength of this
hope he wrote an old family friend, the elderly Mrs. John Jones,
who lived in Chicago near the college he hoped to attend. He
asked her if she would take him to board. Mrs. Jones would not

commit herself in advance to boarding Dan, but she did write him to come and see her when he got to Chicago.

When Dr. Palmer's three apprentices went to Chicago to complete their training, mushroom medical schools, faddists and unchartered diploma mills were at their height. Homeopaths and Eclectics were two of the more sober in a galaxy of medical sects that ranged from the Botanic school to the Thompsonian. Some self-styled colleges required only twelve or sixteen weeks' attendance before they granted the degree of Doctor of Medicine. Many were but a step or two ahead of the preceptor, if, indeed, they were not behind him. Ill-prepared practitioners came in to brush up. They were put in classes with boys of no educational background. All attended the same set of lectures — an identical daily dosage ladled out to all alike. The *sine qua non* was anatomy and for this study dissecting material was essential. The inability to secure cadavers by grave robbing or otherwise was often the event that ended more than one of these hastily established and short-lived educational institutions. Often irate citizens ended the venture with a shotgun.

Out of this array the serious student had but two real choices in Chicago, Rush Medical College and Chicago Medical College — for the College of Physicians and Surgeons had not yet been founded. Rush was the older, had four hundred students, twice as many as Chicago Medical, and boasted a newer, larger building. It stood at the corner of Wood and Harrison Streets, across from Cook County Hospital. In contrast the gabled, turreted, gingerbread-trimmed quarters of its rival at Prairie Avenue and 26th Street seemed old and shabby. But Chicago Medical had more important advantages and it was these which had made it Henry Palmer's choice for his son and for his apprentices. In fact, in all the country, impecunious Dan Williams could not have hit upon any better school.

Founded twenty years before as the medical department of the defunct Lind University and now affiliated with Northwestern University, Chicago Medical was not just another proprietary school run for the profit of its owners. It had operated from the first in a university setting. Its express mission was to carry out the long-propounded reforms of that great educational innovator, Nathan Smith Davis, one of the founders of the American Medical Association. Courageously those ideals had been put into practice: better preliminary education, a graded curriculum, more and longer terms, direct clinical instruction. Not even the Eastern schools had gone so far, nor did they for a dozen years after Chicago Medical was founded.

In the fall of 1880 when Dan went to Chicago, Rush required two terms of five months each. But Chicago Medical required three terms of six months. In the face of such competition, the standards of Chicago Medical were heroically high. Students who failed to pass their first-year examinations at Chicago Medical could and did go over to Rush, pass their examinations, and be graduated at the end of the second year, a whole year ahead of those with whom they had entered college. Chicago Medical students had to draw their satisfaction from the fact their school went in for quality, not quantity.

As soon as they arrived in the city, Dan and his companions had but one thought, to register and unburden their pockets of unusual wealth before it was lost or stolen. As quickly as possible they made their way, by horse car and on foot, to Prairie Avenue and 26th Street. With some relief they saw the neighborhood was superior. It was clean, which most of Chicago was not, with paved streets and, along the borders, trees.

Entering the college building, they found it empty and echoing. They were a week early and there was no one to greet them but a middle-aged janitor. This was a chilling welcome, but the janitor was amiable about showing new students around.

Dan, Pember and Mills eagerly followed him from room to room, feasting their eyes on the cabinet of drugs in the museum, on the casts and models and skeletons, including the mounted skeleton of an elephant. At last they tore themselves away from the museum, took a quick look into the chemical laboratory with its stained tables, scattered bottles and strange odors, then followed their guide to the two amphitheaters. Chicago Medical could give lectures to two classes simultaneously.

The young men looked down the descending tiers of cramped seats. Far below in the dim funneled light they saw the lecture platform, where operations sometimes were performed. The janitor warned them not under any circumstances to try to sit in the lower seats. First-year men did well to know their place and that was not in the seats with the best view.

Grateful for the warning, the three then toured the dispensary rooms. Through its eight departments passed a thousand patients a month, more than they saw in many times that period in Dr. Palmer's office. One door in the basement was not opened to them. "That's the dead house," explained the janitor.

The dissection room was Chicago Medical's particular pride. The *Announcement* declared that "special facilities for the preservation of material are such that the supply is absolutely unfailing." The young men wished to see these special facilities and, hopefully, some of the "material," but they had to be content with the janitor's description. The room, he said, had a double wall of logs. Into the space between, tons of ice were poured each season. What he did not tell them and what they must wait to find out for themselves was that the logs became moist, soft, rotten and moldy — and the cadavers did too, often reaching the students soft from decomposition or dry and leathery, and in either case sure to be covered with long green moss. It was a hardy soul who pursued his anatomical studies beyond the minimum requirements of dissection of "three parts of the body."

In blissful ignorance of what lay ahead of them, the neophytes followed the janitor upstairs. They thanked him for his kindness and went next door to take a look at the exterior of the great Mercy Hospital on the corner of 26th Street and Calumet Avenue. This "elegant structure," or so the *Announcement* styled it, was staffed entirely by members of the college faculty and used exclusively by Chicago Medical for the bedside instruction of advanced students. It was no mean asset at a time when Mercy and

Cook County were the only hospitals of consequence in Chicago. Cook County, although next door to Rush, was not at the exclusive disposal of Rush, but necessarily as a public institution was open to all medical students in the city, unless the politicians closed its doors completely against any students, as they occasionally did. St. Luke's was but a modest frame building in Hell's Half Acre of poverty and violence. On the North Side were two or three Catholic institutions. That was all that boastful, thriving Chicago provided for the medical care of its 400,000 inhabitants.

The Janesville trio walked slowly around two sides of the famous red brick structure, twin of the college building. They knew there were as many as 175 patients in Mercy Hospital, but not for another year would they be permitted to go inside.

While Mills and Pember set out to make their living arrangements, Dan went to call on Mrs. Jones. Walking south on Prairie Avenue past the fantastic stone mansions of Millionaire Row, he turned east on Ray Avenue, three blocks below the college, and stopped at No. 43.

Mrs. Jones's home was a substantial white frame structure of dignified classical lines. John Jones had built it in the suburbs, only to have the spreading city engulf his property. It was the mushrooming city and some shrewd real estate investments, coupled with a conscientiously built tailoring business, that had enabled John Jones, at his decease the previous year, to leave his widow and daughters a fortune. He left them as well a name outstanding both in colored and white Chicago, for he had been a leader in many civil rights reforms and was twice elected County Commissioner. When Dan called on Mrs. Jones her husband's portrait hung over the mantel in her walnut and horsehair parlor; later it would go to the Chicago Historical Society.

If Dan felt no timidity in approaching this imperious old lady, social arbiter and wealthiest of Chicago's colored elite, it was because his own family standing was the equal of that of Mary and John Jones. John Jones might have died rich, but he had started poor, and the Prices and the Williamses had been comfortably well-to-do for many generations. And if the Joneses were of free, mixed blood, the Prices and the Williamses had enjoyed that status back to the Revolution and before.

John Jones and Dan's relatives had been through the long fight for Emancipation together. Side by side with his Rockford cousins in the state conventions of free colored people, and with his father and other Williamses in the national conventions, Jones and all of them had fought — fought to keep up the hope of their despairing brothers below the border, to organize and sustain the resistance of their fellows in the North, to spur on the white Abolitionists. It had been a fight that had called for men of like character, men of courage and singleness of purpose, men who never gave up. The friendships forged in those years were of a strength that outlasted more than one generation.

Mrs. Jones was happy to receive the son of her husband's old friend. She saw his purpose was serious and found his manners correct, so she told Dan readily enough that he might come to live in her home. He breathed a sigh of relief.

It was a feminine household, she told him, consisting of herself, her widowed daughter, Lavinia Lee, and her adopted daughter, Sarah Raynie Petit, still unmarried. Both the younger women were in their middle thirties. There was also a nine-year-old granddaughter, Theodora Lee. And Theodora's poodle. Rather a nuisance, but it seemed children had to have pets. Thedy was perhaps a little spoiled, said the old lady dryly. Now what could Dan tell her of his father's cousin, Samuel Williams, who had gone to Liberia in the days of the exodus before the Civil War? What had happened to him? Did he ever come back?

"That was before my time, ma'am," Dan answered, "but of course I know the story," and he told her how Samuel Williams had grown sick and tired of discrimination and had sold all his considerable property in Johnstown and bought much equipment, including a sawmill, and transported it with all his family and thirty friends to Liberia. The sawmill had failed because he could not get the logs down the swampy rivers, and his wife and his old mother had died of the fever. However, Samuel lived to make several trips back and forth between the two continents. "He wrote a book about his experiences," Dan wound up.

"I'd like to read it," said Mrs. Jones and regaled Dan with accounts of visits to her home by John Brown. In short the two got on famously.

CHAPTER III

Dan Goes to Medical School

ALL the medical colleges opened with fanfare and a public lecture on the same evening. Each vied with the other to entertain the laity and impress the new student by jocular accounts of the ignorance of the medical past and complacent references to those who "have purged the profession of its errors and brought it to its present perfection." Audiences responded first with gratifying laughter and then with applause. The customary benediction followed.

Next morning the serious work of the year began. Dan hesitated to set out. Even late in life, when he was famous, his friends revealed he would sometimes have this reluctance to meet new white people. He couldn't blurt out the facts of his mixed blood, he wanted no one who discovered it later to think he was trading on his appearance, and especially he wanted no one to turn against Pember and Mills because they were seen with him. But Pember and Mills had long ago forgotten he was a Negro. They included him in Chicago as they had in Janesville.

Dan sat between his two friends, high up in the amphitheater, holding his bowler on his knees. Dean Davis stood before them, deadly serious. His piercing eyes under shaggy white brows rested on first this one, then that, dominating them each in turn by the forcefulness of his personality as he delivered his opening remarks. "Gentlemen, you are at the threshold of a great profession. . . .

Be worthy of your choice." The sonorous voice floated up to them: ". . . conservators of the bodies of men . . . moral and spiritual menders of the minds of weak humanity. . . . Favor not the fleshpots of the wealthy, but serve alike the rich, the poor, and yes, the sordid. . . . Be ready for hardships. . . ." To control his emotion, for opening days always stirred him, the dean pinched his nose with a gesture they would all come to recognize. The young men before him relieved their feelings by shuffling their feet and clearing their throats.

Finally Dean Davis concluded his opening oratory and settled down to a plain talk on the importance of industry. Much hard work lay ahead of them. . . .

Two days after college opened, a slightly homesick Dan sat down and wrote to Janesville. Taking a pencil and a ruled tablet, he inscribed "*Chicago, Ill.*" with a great flourish at the top of the page as if to convince himself he really was an inhabitant of the fourth largest city in the country. But after he had written "Mr. C. H. Anderson, My Dear Friend," with proper formality, he was done with flourishes and opened his heart at once: "Many times since I left your home," he wrote, "and come here to further my end in life, have I realized your true interest and friendship. When I get among strangers and observe there actions I can well appretiate your fatherly interest in me." Though Professor Haire's Classical Academy had not been able to make up for early neglect in matters of spelling and grammar, Dan did not have to be taught gratitude. "I hope," he wrote, "that I will never do anything that will for an instant cause you to regret the part you have taken in my career.

"I have been, and am happy to say, successful in obtaining board and care in the Jones family. I know you are sure I could not do better. I am faring better and have cheaper board than any student in the college. Not even those that board themselves scantily and live in cold cheerless rooms, live as cheaply as I do. Mrs. Jones never has had a boarder and said she would take me as one of the family. Gave me a nice room, bath tub, gas, heat and 1st class board and they do try to make it pleasant for me. She charges me $3.75, which I think is very reasonable. Do you? I could not do better. If I hunt Chicago over. I am only three blocks from the college and am well satisfied. I feel that I will do a good winters work."

And then the big question they would not ask and he would answer but indirectly: was he encountering any race prejudice? "I get along nicely," he wrote, "with everyone and can see the bright side for once in my life."

"I keep account of my expenses," he added next, "and will render you account from time to time. Enclosed find itemized account of the money I received from bank. You will observe that I have carefully laid out my money. There is once in a while that I or any one has to spend a few cents without much benefit to themselves." Had he perhaps gone to see Goodwin's Froliques at the Grand Opera House on Clark Street, or Josh Whitcomb at McVicker's?

Once more he assured them, for he knew the letter would be read by the whole family, of his determined optimism: "I like the College and live in hopes of graduating a satisfaction to you and all concerned." Then he ended: "With a fond hope that you and family are well I remain Yours Obediently and Truly, D. H. W. 43 Ray Ave — "

Everything was better than he had dared hope for. Dan set to work with vigor. Then word came from his mother that she had no cash to give him, she had been making some loans. Instead she sent him notes and suggested he collect on them. He saw at once they were of questionable value. Once more Sarah Williams had failed her son in a critical moment.

There was his board to pay. He must have shivered when he thought of Mrs. Jones. If only he had been franker when first he made his arrangements with her. But Price pride and youthful timorousness had ruled him. Dressed in his new clothes, he had said nothing to her to counteract his appearance of prosperity. If he had, his way would have been easier now. Wealthy Mrs. Jones

Dan at age 14

Charles Henry (Harry)
and Ellen Byron Anderson

Daniel Williams as a medical student in 1880

had not always been rich; no one would have been more sympathetic to his plight than she. But Dan had felt he must meet her as an equal. He had got into her home, he saw now, under false pretenses. What could he say to her?

In his extremity he threw himself on Harry Anderson, on the man who was father to him. Anderson sent money for his immediate emergency, but asked for enlightenment. Wouldn't Dan get something when the Price home was sold? And if that was delayed, would not Mrs. Jones, who certainly did not need the money, wait until his inheritance came through? In a tangle of emotions, Dan sat down to try to explain.

"I was delighted yesterday to receive my first letter from you," he wrote Anderson. "Not what it contained, but to know that you would write me once in a while. Of course I was in need of its contents, but am getting along nicely." He swung back and forth between resigning himself to extreme despair and lulling himself into a false sense of security. In neither did he come to grips with his situation. Finally he took a big breath and plunged in:

"I laid aside today to write and tell you everything. You know just how I am fixed. The question is what can I do, situated as I am. I can do nothing. Its hard for you to support your family, meet your expenses and educate me."

Even as he wrote the words, Dan knew the obvious answer was that his own family should help him, not Anderson. But he had to acknowledge that he could not count on his family: "I have written and appealed to them for means but it seems without avail." He tried to soften the harsh words, and added: "I know they have not got it. If Mother had it, she would send it." Evidently he could not bring himself to mention the extravagances, bad judgment, and indifference that explained why Sarah Williams had seemed never to have any money despite her substantial inheritance. Instead he hastened to talk about the valueless notes she had sent him: "Nor can I get a dollar out of that fellow I have the notes on. I wrote to Mother and she is going to try and get some money on them for me." Anxious to show her in the best light he could, he said: "You will see by the telegram which I received last night that Mother is trying to help me. She wants me to send the notes so that she can make some arrangements with some one to get some money on them."

Now came the hardest part of all. "You ask me if I made arrangements with Mrs. Jones to pay her when I get the money. I did not dare tell her I was so poor. I really don't think she would have taken me and not for such a small price. She took me on the strength of knowing my relatives, etc."

It must have seemed to Dan as he sat in his comfortable room, with classes under way a scant three weeks, that all his dreams were dissolving in his hands. "I get so discouraged," he wrote Anderson, "that I can't make much progress. I know that I have a good friend in you and here I find myself when I sit down to think it over. The question comes to me. What will I do. What can I do. I can only do the best I can. I could quit for a year or so and resume my studies again. But I am afraid that if I stop now that I will never commence again. . . . I have been up town but three times since I've been here. . . . I don't go anywhere but from house to the College. . . . I will write another letter, one you can show to Viata and folks."

So Dan agonized over his dilemma, when he should have been devoting all his energy to his difficult new studies. On a Sunday early in November he again wrote Anderson; there was bitterness in almost every word: "Today being my day to write, if I had any, I thought I would drop you a line. The money you sent me of course you know I received. I am not in need of any money today, though I have but 35 cents. But before another Sunday I shall be. The money which you were so kind to send me, I paid to Mrs. Jones for board. I paid her $8.75 and kept $1.25 for sundries. I board by the month and she wants everything straight on 1st of each month. So do I, for she is rather of the old coon style, if she is John Jones wife. I mean she is one of the old school — like Aunt Charlotte of Annapolis fame. They are very particular about everything. It will do me good, it will learn me to think before I act and say."

The answer from Wisconsin was more satisfactory than that from Maryland. Dan was touched. He filled his letters with expressions of appreciation. "I think of your genuine fatherly interest in doing as much for me as you would for your own children."

And so he stayed on in Chicago, though on an unsatisfactory precarious footing. Each month brought its board bill and with it the ordeal of making another appeal for funds. If there were wash bills, it was necessary to ask for a little extra change. Any delay seemed to produce agonies of guilt in the hypersensitive self-conscious boarder. "My board I want to pay for as soon as convenient to you. They have not said anything about it, but I know they think."

School itself, when Dan could concentrate on it, was all that could be desired, a dream come true. "Everything is going along nicely and we all bid fair to progress in our studies" — such was the prim report. And again: "I am making fair progress, I think. It is hard work and much study, but I am up in the front rank and keep neck and neck with the leaders."

Dan's curriculum that first year was formidable: descriptive anatomy, physiology, histology, materia medica and general chemistry. There was no clinical work before the second year. Meanwhile Dan attended three lectures a day and burned the gas far into the night.

Of the original Chicago Medical faculty, five men remained on the staff of thirteen when Dan entered school. They were notable men, dedicated to their profession. Like other practitioners of their own youth, they still wore the distinctive garb of their calling, a long-tailed black broadcloth frock coat buttoned to the chin over a standing collar. They were never seen without it in classroom or at operating table. Rush professors relented so far as to wear turned-down collars, but Chicago Medical faculty stuck to formality and discomfort. Dean Davis and James S. Jewell, Professor of Nervous and Mental Diseases, wore full evening dress all day long.

Despite this formality of attire, Dan soon found these men were warmly interested in their students. He forgot the fears and shyness of that first day and relaxed into the easy naturalness of his Janesville days. Pember and Mills and new friends too dropped in at Mrs. Jones's to study and discuss and argue in Dan's comfortable heated room.

In materia medica, Dan sat under William E. Quine, the little giant with the high-pitched voice. Quine hammered away continually at his thesis that materia medica overshadowed every other subject in importance. So persuasive was he, or so effective were the oratorical fireworks he brought to bear, that his classes would terminate the hour with vociferous applause. The thunder followed him as he entered his carriage.

Anatomy was Dan's favorite subject. He was fortunate to study it under the tutelage of Robert Laughlin Rea whose equal as a teacher of descriptive human anatomy perhaps never has stood before a medical class. Rea was new at Chicago Medical that year. He had a passion for order and for punctiliousness, and was never late for a class. Dan learned to take his seat well before the scheduled time. Professor Rea always came early. He would pace the narrow limits of the waiting room and, at the last stroke of the bell, stand before his class, a majestic figure, over six feet tall, with burning eyes deep set under a classic brow, a man aglow with the fires of his own enthusiasm. There would be a moment of dignified silence, then Rea would begin his fascinating discourse. Unlike Quine, no rhetorical embellishment, no oratorical effort dimmed the lucidity of Rea's presentations. He had no use for anecdote and innuendo, neither time nor tolerance for humor. Always he kept the unadorned subject before his students.

If the didactic method of teaching anatomy has since become largely obsolete, it was a method, nevertheless, that the older generation could use with masterly effect. Rea, in the united opinion of his contemporaries, was one of the most masterly of his time. "For the sluggish student he was a kindly goad, for the dishonest and indifferent student a walking terror, for those of better endowment and studious bent a flaming inspiration." Dan caught fire at once. He made Rea his pattern, even to his dress and manner of speech, and never relinquished his ideal afterwards.

While Dan had to study physiology without benefit of laboratory work, in histology he had the help of a newly enlarged microscopic laboratory, recently refitted with excellent microscopes. The practical usefulness of that instrument was just beginning to be appreciated. The great Christian Fenger, newly come to Chicago from Denmark, was making pathology the fashion, though bacteriology was not yet taught. Men continued for a long time, however, to pontificate from the naked-eye appearance of a specimen.

It can be said with some justice that at a time when even a clinical thermometer was still a curiosity and had to be read before it was removed from the mouth, men had a certain right to pride themselves upon a diagnostic judgment empirically acquired. The Palmers could tell body temperature by dryness or moisture of the skin, by respiration, appearance of the pupils of the eye, and more particularly by some sixth sense born of long experience. They learned by close observation the significance of a change of pulse, an expression of the face, and the movements of the hands. Observation of the mouth showed them signposts of diseases of wide variety and location. The limitations of early science had forced the development of medicine as an art and there were its gifted exponents who gave their patients something more than sympathy and moral support after a long cold buggy ride. Dan and his fellow students were a bit inclined to belittle this fact as they excitedly embraced the new laboratory and the new instruments.

After a while a hint of homesickness crept into Dan's letters to Janesville. "How much company are you going to have Christmas?" he asked. Within a few days he was writing again: "When Christmas comes, I should like to come home. Are you to have company Christmas?"

Halfway through December, after a lonely Sunday afternoon,

Dan again wrote Anderson. Instead of his usual casual pencil, he took up pen and with it put an extra formality into his opening. "C. H. A., Dear Sir," he wrote, "I was sitting down this afternoon thinking about the approach of Christmas and matters in general and concluded that I would write you today as there is only one more Sunday before I be Home." Gathering his courage he approached his point. "I want to ask you," he said, "that when you send me, would you send me a few dollars extra. You know I do not spend one dollar foolishly. What I want with it is to buy a few little trinkets. The folks all give me something and I want to have a little something to give them. I would rather that they would not give me anything, but you know I can't control that. I don't want you to think I am fooling your money away. I think you will understand me and my situation."

It was not an easy letter for the proud Dan Williams to write, but it would not have been easy to go home empty-handed either. Having got it down on paper, he restored his self-respect by adding: "I have made splendid progress so far this winter and feel that I am twice the man I was one year ago. . . . I have a nibble of a chance to a position in Cook County Hospital. With Respect and Gratitude, I am Yours Truly, D. W. H."

Back from Janesville after the holidays, the Cook County Hospital job failed to materialize and Dan's financial situation became even worse than it had been. Anderson was shorthanded in the barbershop, his income was cut, and he did not send any money for a couple of months. The board bill went unpaid and Dan dared not have any washing done. When finally some money came from Anderson he admitted that "I have not had but a tencent piece since I came back. I kept that ten cents and if any one would say money, I would show it up."

Being able to pay the board bill lifted Dan's spirits enormously and he could end his letter on an unwontedly lighthearted note: "I hear you travel," he said, "to Baraboo with 'The Great Light Guard Quadrille Orchestra Colored Band.' How does Severance [one of Anderson's competitors] like that? I must go to study.

Good night, love and health." After which sudden warm note, he took his usual formal leave with "Yours Truly, D. H. W."

Late in November one of the internes on his rounds in the Mercy Home, behind the hospital and connected with it by a corridor, had discovered a suspicious case of illness. It proved to be smallpox. Chicago, just over a scourge of 20,000 typhoid fever cases, was plunged into an epidemic of smallpox that lasted all winter. Although Jenner had discovered the principles of vaccination over eighty years before, the practice was still far from established. Soon the city pesthouse was crowded beyond capacity. The Health Department consented to the opening of an extra quarantine ward in the attic of Mercy Hospital, and even that overflowed. As the weeks passed, more than a hundred patients at a time were within the walls where the college students passed daily. Patients who entered for other ailments contracted the disease and died.

Dan was forced to take to his bed the middle of March. To make matters worse, it was final examination week. He stayed in bed a few days and then sent for Dr. Marcus Hatfield, his friendly chemistry professor. Hatfield said the case looked suspicious; he thought he could tell for certain by the next day.

As he lay waiting the verdict, Dan unburdened himself in a long letter to Anderson. He owed a month's board, 60 cents at the college, and $2.80 he had borrowed. He had looked forward to earning a goodly sum during the vacation months and had applied for a job in Springfield, Illinois, where he might expect to earn as much as $75 a month, with passes there and return. But dared he take such a job in his present state of health? "I am a little anxious about my condition, though I'm not scared," he confided to Anderson. Fortunately before he mailed the letter on Monday he was able to add a postscript saying Hatfield had decided that what he had was varioloid. He was immensely relieved. He could say now, "I was pretty well scared yesterday. I thought my time had come. I want to get away for a rest."

Immediately letters came back from both Harry Anderson and

Traviata — warm affectionate letters full of hospitality and eagerness to see him. They had missed him every bit as much as he
had missed them, and they would not hear of his going to Springfield.

Dan was overcome by this combined tenderness of father and
daughter. He huddled in his room and penned his foster father
a shaking, distorted, blotted letter:

"My dear Friend, Just as was leaving the house your welcome,
kind and fatherly letter was handed to me. Childish as it may seem
to you I had to spend my morning lecture hour in quiet to my self
and gratitude to you. . . . I will do as I promised. I will not remain the summer in Springfield. . . . It seems like a burden for
me to remain with you. It seems like imposing on your good heart
and kindness to me." At the end of the letter he added: "Aunt
Charlotte is dead and bad news comes from the east, which however does not disturb Yours Most Gratefully and Respectfully,
D. H. Williams."

The bad news from the East was that he would never get any
of his inheritance. The home place was sold, but it was found that
Sarah had mortgaged it to the hilt. Every cent of the sales price
would have to go to pay off the debts she had contracted through
the years. The patrimony of the Prices, built up through the
generations and held intact for the sake of the children, was now
dissipated.

Somehow Dan struggled through his examinations. While he
managed to pass every subject, he did so with no more than a
low average grade, he who had started out neck and neck with
the leaders. He found little comfort in the fact that twenty per
cent of his class failed altogether.

As he slowly regained his strength that summer in Janesville,
aided by Ellen Anderson's gentle mothering and Dr. Palmer's
medicines, Dan must have felt discouraged. The six months in
Chicago had cost so much in so many ways, and he had so little
to show for it. Perhaps in dark moments he thought of his
brother Price, stocky, robust, self-assured, so patently successful
in all he attempted. Recently Price had added two newspaper

ventures to his legal work, putting out *The Pilot* in Philadelphia and, with the future Congressman Louis B. Anderson, *The Star* in Washington. But by fall Dan was in better health and more optimistic. The only indications of his recent illness were a couple of varioloid pockmarks on his handsome nose.

The Barber Becomes a Doctor

DAN had become so much a member of the Jones household he returned there as a matter of course his second year. Mrs. Jones saw that he had his favorite milk toast. He repaired her green-shaded lamp. On the way from classes he would pick up young Theodora at her school and see that she got home safely.

A second-year man came back with a certain ease born of familiarity with the college and its ways. Dan had twice as much vigor to put into his work. His middle-year program included general pathology and pathological anatomy under the professorship of the scholarly John H. Hollister, one of the original faculty. Professor Hollister taught a Bible class at Plymouth Church on Sundays and proved his religion was genuine by showing charitableness to all races, creeds and nationalities on weekdays. Dan liked him, liked his ample figure, pleasant face and hearty voice. The fact that he wore his hair almost as long as he wore his beard was an old-fashioned peccadillo you accepted with a tolerance born of affection.

In therapeutics and hygiene Dan again had William E. Quine; in nervous and mental diseases, James S. Jewell of the flapping black coattails; and in medical chemistry and medical jurisprudence, his old friend and personal physician, Marcus Hatfield. Some students did not like Hatfield, but Dan got on well with him. To complete his program, Dan was concluding anatomy with

Robert Laughlin Rea, and he was fortunate to do so, for Rea would leave Chicago Medical the next year.

The great excitement of middle year, however, was launching into clinical work. "This is the essence of instruction," he wrote Anderson, ". . . any amount of bedside instruction and practical teaching." In small groups of a half dozen, the students alternated between the wards of Mercy Hospital and the South Side Dispensary in the basement of the college building. Altogether they spent two weeks in each of the eight dispensary departments. Sometimes a patient mistakenly called a student "Doctor" and the appellation would be so pleasant the temptation was not to correct the error.

During the year Chicago Medical acquired additional clinical privileges at St. Luke's Hospital. St. Luke's was small and crowded, but its location in Hell's Half Acre brought it numerous accident cases, useful for observation. Clinics for eye and ear diseases were instituted at the Illinois Charitable Eye and Ear Infirmary. These were important aids to the program since the politics-ridden Cook County Hospital had again frivolously closed its wards to class teaching.

The most engrossing were the surgical clinics held Tuesdays and Saturdays at two. Edmund Andrews, another of the original faculty and next to Dean Davis in importance, was in charge. Andrews discussed problems with his students as simply and directly as though they were his peers. Dan was tremendously stimulated by the man, as were they all. When his great hulking figure shuffled into the amphitheater at Mercy Hospital, the room burst into applause. Everything about him was big — his frame, his bewhiskered head, his kindly blue eyes, his generous mouth. Now in his middle fifties, Andrews was insisting upon experimenting with the new antiseptic surgery.

Fortunately for Dan, modern surgery came in during his college days. Before he came to Chicago there had been little variety in surgery outside of accident cases and drainage of infections. Superficial tumors and cysts were removed. Sometimes an emergency stomach operation was performed as a last resort when a gastric ulcer perforated or the pylorus was obstructed. A strangulated hernia would bring about a similar attempt. Only very rarely was there a surgical approach to the gall bladder, the liver, spleen or kidney. Tuberculous glands were sometimes attacked. Ligation of diseased veins and arteries was fairly common. While Ephraim McDowell had removed an ovarian cyst with success some decades earlier, few had been bold enough to repeat that attempt *in extremis*. And rightly so. Every entry into the abdominal cavity brought almost inevitable infection and the patient's survival depended upon his ability to throw it off. Students who were graduated in the year Dan had entered Chicago Medical had seen six abdominal operations in the course of their three years and every patient had died.

But in one year's time a revolution had taken place. The theories of the English Quaker, Joseph Lister, had reached Chicago. Dan and his classmates never forgot the first operation they attended. A Mercy Hospital nun sat at a high table at the end of the room manipulating the new carbolic steam spray and filling the place with a benumbing, asphyxiating cloud that rendered the occupants and everything else all but invisible. Although the patient had been anesthetized before she was wheeled in, ether continued to be freely administered — it seemed in almost equal quantities to the students and patient alike.

Dan was soaked to the skin. His eyes smarted and he breathed with difficulty. But everyone else was in the same condition; they must bear it like heroes. This was the only way, Lister said, to ward off the microbes that filled the air. Dan strained forward to watch what was going on. He could see disappointingly little. The mountainous figure of Dr. Andrews and his chief assistant were moving about enveloped in big oiled-silk aprons over their frock coats. Everyone else, the anesthetist, the spongers, the orderlies, the visitors, all wore ordinary street clothes. Small tables held a basin of sea sponges in carbolic solution, pans of instruments, a small basin of silk ligatures. No longer were ligatures conveniently worn in the operator's buttonhole to be pulled out as needed.

Andrews used carbolic solution lavishly in preparing the site of the operation, then consulted freely with his assistants and visitors as to the best place to make the incision and how deep to make it. These were responsibilities surgeons were glad to share when everyone, even the best of them, was just learning. At long last the wound was closed, more carbolic solution was administered and dressings soaked in carbolic solution were applied. The patient was wheeled away. Dan was glad to get out into the air.

The question was, Would pus develop in the wound? Already during the past few months Chicago Medical staff had had several successes in achieving healing "by first intention," without any of the usual suppuration. But they could not count on it. Every operation was an experiment. Elaborate routines were adopted, only to be dropped for something that might prove better. All over the city and all over the country, thinking men were questioning old methods and searching out new ones.

A stumbling block to progress at first was the failure to see the danger of infection by contact while attempting valiantly to keep out infection by air. All the time trouble was being invited by unsterilized hands, instruments and clothing. When the presence of bacteria on everything was finally recognized, a frantic search began for methods of sterilization by solutions. Carbolic solutions and bichloride of mercury were tried and eventually given up for the less irritating normal salt and boric acid solutions.

The difference between esthetic and antiseptic cleanliness was hard for the old-time operator to grasp. Only slowly was the marine sponge relinquished for gauze sponges. A surgeon would dip his hands in an antiseptic solution preparatory to examining or operating and then touch his face, rub his nose thoughtlessly or even shake hands with a visiting colleague who of course came into the room just as he was. It became the duty of the interne to remind him after each such dereliction to "please disinfect your hands, sir."

Nor did the visiting colleague take kindly to being refused

the customary privilege of poking an exploratory finger, un-sterilized, into the wound. Old-timers had washed their hands after the operation, not before. And it was hard not to lift the dressings and peek at the incision to see how things were going. Lister had expressly ordered that "as long as there is no fever or hemorrhage, leave the dressings undisturbed." Most operators were not certain enough to follow this advice more than part way.

But Andrews stubbornly persisted, trying one technique after another. Slowly his successes grew more numerous, as did those of others. Temperatures remained normal, wounds remained dry, and when, after the proper interval, stitches were removed, even they were found to be free of any pus whatever. Almost any operation might be attempted now. Exciting vistas opened to faculty and students alike. Dan and his fellows walked in an atmosphere surcharged with wonder, possibility, and violent differences of opinion. Bitter controversy raged in classrooms and corridors and spilled over into rooming houses.

Dan had returned to college with no better financial arrangement than to call on Harry Anderson from time to time for amounts of ten and fifteen dollars. Each time the sum was exhausted he had to go through the painful process of asking for another amount. "You will not think hard of me," he would plead, "you know I do not wast a penny." Frequently the money was tardy in arriving. Anderson had invested in a road show, *Escaped from Slavery*, and in a touring organization called the Nashville Colored Church Choir. These were taking all his spare cash. He became more disposed to question every item.

Dan had to wait to start his precious clinical instruction while letters passed back and forth and he impatiently tried to explain what the "hospital ticket" was and why he had to pay six dollars to get it. Then Anderson felt Dan need not buy medical books, he could borrow them. Dr. Palmer had provided books for his apprentices, why should not the Chicago doctors do the same? Finally Anderson sent the money and Dan was grateful. "You are the only true friend I have," he wrote.

Dan wanted Anderson to come up to Chicago for the spring festival, but Anderson did not get there. "It was too rich," wrote the growing sophisticate, "for most of them to understand." Other Janesville visitors made Dan homesick. "When I went to the train with Henry Doty friday P.M. I felt as though I'd like to go home with him, but I knew I could not." Traviata and her friend, Alice Smith of Oconomowoc, an exotic girl with Indian tresses, also spent some time in Chicago. Alice had a fascination, Dan admitted to himself — and to Alice's sister years later — that the exuberant 'Viata, for all her warmth, lacked. He invited his college friends to meet the two and entertained for them at tea at Mrs. Jones's home. The girls were a great success. " 'Viata is enjoying her visit very much I imagine," Dan wrote her father, "she has every attention shown her." Dan felt no pique, only complacency, at seeing 'Viata surrounded by suitors. He was as proud of her as any brother would be. Later when the Andersons did come to Chicago for a visit, Mrs. Jones enjoyed Ellen's gay Irish wit and remarked how fond Dan was of his little namesake, Bertie.

When his middle year ended, and it did so with better grades than his first year, Dan decided to stay on in Chicago for the spring and summer to gain some experience in Mercy Hospital. Ordinarily he would have had to wait until his senior year for any chance at ward duty. But the overburdened senior internes sometimes relinquished part of their work to students, and Dan and Frank Pember had been quick to snatch so fruitful an opportunity.

Dan arranged with Mrs. Jones to care for her horse and buggy in payment of his board during this time. When he wrote Anderson these plans, Anderson, always in need of a barber and feeling somewhat ill used, did not answer. He did not reply to a second letter either, and Dan tried a third time to explain why he must seize upon this opening.

"I have thought it best," he wrote, with more fluency and better spelling than were once his to command, "for me to remain here as long as I can. I can learn and see more in one week than I could in Janesville in six months."

"You know," he added, with growing wisdom, "talk and success are widely different. Men may talk what they can and will do, but it takes knowledge and experience to accomplish much. I might stay in Janesville in Dr. Palmer's office ten years and never see a case of childbirth. Here I can see ten to twenty cases a week and have charge of all in Mercy Hospital if I will attend them." Honesty compelled him to modify this exaggeration and he added: "Frank Pember and I attend them between us." His effort to persuade Anderson made him say: "I have chances in operative surgery every week, doing some operation." What if the "operation" were only lancing an abscess? It meant handling a knife and involved dressings. Dan gave the affair all the glamour he could.

"We have hospitals," he told Anderson, and "Post Mortem examinations to keep our attention on our life work. In Janesville, when they did have post mortem examinations, it was only a few could come in. Down here we all go to Dead house where there assemble from fifty to one hundred doctors and everything is opened before us and understood."

Carried away perhaps by his own eloquence, Dan allowed a slightly patronizing tone to creep into his letter: "You will not probably recognize the scope of a physician, but you must know that where there are more sick and dead there is better field for investigation and study."

But at heart Dan was deeply loyal to his old friends. He added, "I want to come up some time in June and stay a few days at least. . . . How is George getting? I shall hope to hear from you Soon. Regards to all."

The summer was long and hot and the Mercy Hospital obstetrics ward always full. Dan and Pember learned to work almost continuously through the lengthy nights. They did not complain, for here were the riches of experience, free for the taking. Sometimes, however, they were embarrassed when a private watchman from nearby Millionaire Row would appear and object that through the open windows of the maternity ward their patients were disturbing the peace of Prairie Avenue with their cries and groans.

In the fall Dan again needed a weekly sum for room and board. Unfortunately, when he wrote to Anderson expecting the old arrangement to continue, Anderson said he had no ready cash to loan. Couldn't Dan continue to work for Mrs. Jones and get along? But Dan had already relinquished his stable job in anticipation of term opening and Mrs. Jones had hired a boy to take his place. He was panic-stricken. He must not be stopped now, with his goal so near.

With that same desperation with which as a boy he had wrenched himself out of shoemaking, and as a youth had flung off barbering, Dan now clutched at medicine. He wrote Anderson with some assertiveness. "I received your letter. I know when a man is not making money it is hard to spend it. No one realizes your position more than I do." But there was no real difficulty, he went on to say. Why could Anderson, with his "unlimited credit," not borrow the money to loan him? "It is going to take comparatively little to take me through," he argued, "not more than $150.00. . . . You can't but see that the current will be in your direction before many months."

"It is my final struggle for an education," he cried, "and while I am at work I can't spare the time to go seek here and there for money to pay my living expenses." It was a tone he should have used long ago with his mother. Failing that, he used it now with his foster parent. "It is not pleasant for me," he said, "any more than it is for you. I hate to ask you for it, but what am I to do? . . . If you were giving this money, it would be different. You are not. You will get your money back and interest thereon. I shall await to hear from you."

Anderson did not fail him and Dan stayed on in school.

As Dan had progressed in his training, Chicago Medical had grown. Six professors had been added to the faculty, making the total nineteen in Dan's last year. Among them was Oscar DeWolf for a course in Public Health. DeWolf, Chicago's first health commissioner, was determined to rid the city of its filth — the city which "has her wash-pot, her chamber-pot and her drinking cup in the great lake at her feet." E. C. Dudley came that year too and Dan profited in his course in gynecology — then such a fast-developing field — by Dudley's curiosity, his daring and with it all his careful weighing of evidence.

But Dan's greatest stroke of luck was the acquisition of the noted Danish scientist Christian Fenger. It was too late for Dan to take his pathology course, but he attended Fenger's lectures and sat in his clinics. Looking back, men said it was from the coming of Fenger that Chicago slowly but surely developed as an important medical center. There were plenty, however, in 1882 who mocked this apostle from the great European clinics, carrying his homely green carpetbag with the initials embroidered by his sister. But there were others, Dan among them, who worshiped him, absorbed his wisdom, and in their turn made medical history because they had known him.

Shortly before the end of their last term, the seniors went through the ordeal of competing for the few interneships available. Frank Pember won a place at Mercy, but Dan, like the majority, was not successful. Fortunately he had already worked as a volunteer in the Mercy Hospital wards.

Finally the last week in March, 1883 rolled around and with it Commencement Day. Exercises had outgrown the Plymouth Church and this year were held in the Grand Opera House downtown. Solemnly the three dozen men followed the faculty down the aisle, Dan among them, sporting a new-grown full beard trimmed exactly like that of his first-year anatomy professor, Robert Laughlin Rea. Dan must have wished his father could see him, that his mother were present.

The program unfolded, pleasantly interspersed with music. The secretary read a long report of the year's work and then the prizes were announced, sixteen in all, but neither Dan nor Pember won one. Mills carried off a prize for general excellence, as befitted one who had entered medical college with an A.B. degree. One of the prize winners read the valedictory and then the president of Northwestern University handed out the ribbon-tied diplomas, conferring on each man as he did so the proud new degree.

Doctor Daniel Hale Williams! Daniel Hale Williams, M.D. As he walked down the aisle, phrases of the Hippocratic Oath perhaps flashed through Dan's mind: ". . . to reckon him who taught me this Art equally dear to me as my parents . . . by precept, lecture and every other mode of instruction I will impart a knowledge of the Art to my own sons . . . and to disciples . . . may it be granted to me to enjoy life and the practice of the Art, respected by all men, in all times."

CHAPTER V

Operating in a Dining Room

AS soon as Dan's diploma was in his hand, he applied for a license to practice in the District of Columbia. Apparently his one thought was to return to his mother, now that his success would ensure her welcome.

But when the license came, he found that the nebulous, un-realized ties of family did not pull him half as much as the ties he had made in Chicago. He was twenty-seven and he had a life of his own. He made another application, this time for an Illinois license.

The new-fledged Dr. Daniel Hale Williams began his practice of medicine in a time of economic depression amounting to panic. It was tough going, but there was something to be said for start-ing out in a big place. His friend William E. Morgan, graduate of the Class of '82, had first set up an office in his home town, Madi-son, Wisconsin. In three months he saw not one patient. He had in the end come back to Chicago and opened an office at State and 32nd Streets. Another good friend, Frank Billings, '81, was at 31st and State. Dan found a small suite not far from his colleagues, at 31st Street and Michigan Avenue, on the northwest corner, 3034 Michigan Avenue. The neighborhood was well-to-do, as much white as colored, and white doctors had the adjoining suites.

When Dan opened his office, there was no Black Belt. The

Negro population numbered around 10,000 and colored families were scattered through white areas. White people knew colored people at first hand, recognized their individual differences and did not have the common disposition born of separation to regard all Negroes as alike and the likeness one of inferiority, mental and moral. Since the neighborhood was well-to-do, the colored people in it were well-to-do too. They were also mostly of mixed blood, since these were the Negroes who had been the earliest to attain freedom and to establish themselves. In such a neighborhood Dan from the first drew his patients from both races.

Two colored physicians had practiced in Chicago before the Civil War and before licensing was required. When Dan started, there were three colored doctors, two of them with the less highly regarded Eclectic diploma. All three had their offices in other neighborhoods and none of them was his competitor.

Dan continued his professional contacts with the men he had known in his student days. Professor Marcus Hatfield, looking toward his retirement as staff physician of the Protestant Orphan Asylum, secured Dan an appointment as attending physician. The orphanage was only nine blocks north of Dan's office on Michigan Avenue. While the job was unpaid and rather trying, especially when all 250 children came down at once with measles, still it offered experience and prestige.

Dan's office hours were 9 to 10 every morning, 3:30 to 5 in the afternoons, and 7 to 8 in the evenings. Home calls and orphanage calls had to be sandwiched in between. But he was used to hard work and he was happy. He had entered upon a distinguished profession and he had status, though it was only the status of a beginner.

Among his earliest private patients were the personal friends he had made in Mrs. Jones's home. A young untried man is not always acceptable in a professional capacity to those who have long known him, at least not until he has proved himself. But Dan could have no better sponsor than John Jones's widow, and she continued to be his sponsor even when he felt he should assume a more independent position and took a room on Boston Place near Halsted. Mrs. Jones was inordinately proud of him. His parted chin whiskers, she insisted, were just like John Brown's. And she added, with an old lady's plain-spokenness, "Dan sits on more brains than other men have in their heads." Everyone knew that she chose Dan to be Thedy's godfather when the child was taken to St. Thomas's African Episcopal Church for baptism. After that event, if for no other reason, Dan's position was solid.

Julia LeBeau was organist and choir leader of St. Thomas's. When her mother fell ill, she called Dr. Williams, even though he was but a few months out of medical school. The diagnosis was uncomplicated; it was hemorrhoids. But the patient demurred when Dan told her they must be cut out.

"I won't go to a hospital," she declared flatly. Dan bowed to her dictum readily enough. Few hospitals in the city had accommodations that would appeal to the private patient, and times were scarcely past when to go to the hospital was to go to the grave.

"I'll do it right here," Dan assured his patient. "We'll take down the lace curtains and scrub everything, walls as well as floors. Julia can help me."

Scrub her home! The proud old lady bristled at the imputation her house was not already immaculate. Dan had his hands full, explaining and placating. Finally he won her over and a time was set.

Dan neglected nothing to make Mrs. LeBeau's dining room as antiseptic as possible. He scrubbed and fumigated and sprayed valiantly. The wash boiler on the kitchen stove was his sterilizer, the kitchen pans his receptacles for sponges and instruments. He gave the anesthetic himself and then excised the hemorrhoids as quickly and deftly as could be. The old lady's recovery was prompt, her new comfort magical. She told all her friends what a smart fellow her doctor was and they at once took note of his address.

Those who had known him as Dan could not call him Dr. Williams. They compromised with "Dr. Dan." This title of affection coupled with respect clung as his practice widened and all and sundry knew him as Dr. Dan. Patients who came to him once seldom left him. He who had suffered so much himself was very gentle with those who came seeking his aid. Patients felt the sincerity of his interest in them and they were warmed by it. They liked his dignity, too, his well-proportioned figure — he was about five feet eight — his immaculate grooming, his alert, handsome face. They liked his air of certainty; they could see at once that he knew his business. The day came when patients packed the little waiting room at 3034 Michigan Avenue.

All the time Dan was doing more and more surgery. Surgeons developed those days as cases were thrust upon them by self-evident diagnosis. A man either had to shirk a case and decline the responsibility or accept it. If he accepted it, he then had to nerve himself to tackle it and do his best, learning his techniques as he operated; there was no other way.

His friends, Frank Billings and Franklin Martin and others, were doing as Dan was doing, operating in private homes, in kitchens and dining rooms. Billings went into the slums and amputated a tubercular leg. There were so few hospitals in Chicago and all were as tightly organized as a personal club. Staffs were small and they did not welcome newcomers. The younger men usually chose Sunday mornings for their home forays into surgery. Friends served each other as anesthetists and orderlies and suppliers of moral support.

Dr. Dan was more fortunate than some. He found an opportunity to perform minor operations regularly by securing an appointment to the surgical staff of the South Side Dispensary. As he operated he gave clinical instruction to Chicago Medical students. He also served as one of the demonstrators of anatomy.

Teaching was not easy in a day when medical students were much given to bantering, to stealing fingers, toes and sometimes even a whole hand from the dissecting table to be dropped into the pocket of some unsuspecting freshman. Dan's seriousness would have been an invitation to horseplay, but his enthusiasm carried students along. They found themselves caught up despite themselves. His good judgment and shrewd diagnoses won their respect and they recognized his ability was above that of the usual dispensary instructor. He who had found it so hard to express himself now used an excellent vocabulary, and his voice, rather penetrating, with an individual timbre, the timbre of a singer, attracted and held attention. He enjoyed his teaching and his students enjoyed him — among them Charlie Mayo and, later, Coleman Buford and Andy Hall.

Dr. Dan followed every lead. He got a job as surgeon to the City Railway Company, where E. Wyllys Andrews, son of his former professor in surgery, served in a similar capacity. Young Andrews was in the courtroom one day when Dan had to appear as an expert witness in an accident case. Coming out of the courtroom afterward, Andrews patted his colleague on the back and told him he certainly had his data well in hand; even the judge could understand it!

The name of Dr. Daniel H. Williams appeared frequently now in the Negro newspaper, the *Conservator*. He was attending this case or that one, or he was a guest here or a guest there. The handsome bachelor who was forging ahead so fast was noticed by thoughtful mothers with marriageable daughters. And the daughters and the sons and the young married couples flocked around him whenever his schedule permitted him to appear at a party.

"Here's Dr. Dan!" they would cry and thrust a guitar into his hand. Dan, with every vestige of self-consciousness cleared away in this sunshine of popularity, would put a well-polished shoe up on whatever was handy, the nickel fender of the parlor stove or a convenient hassock, rest the guitar on his knee, and sound forth in an acceptable tenor. Soon the whole room would be rollicking to his gay rhythms.

During this time Dan kept up his letters to Harry Anderson, paying him back money as he could. These were sad times for the Anderson family. Soon after Dan's graduation, frail, loving Tessie had died at seventeen. A few months later her mother suddenly and unaccountably died, too. The double blow left all of them benumbed, Dan included. Tessie had been a beloved younger sister and Ellen's warmth and gaiety and frequent subtle guidance had carried him along through the difficult years when the courage often oozed out of him.

With Ellen gone, Harry Anderson could not bear to stay on in Janesville. His road shows were prospering and he moved his family to Chicago to an apartment at the corner of State and Van Buren. Traviata managed the household and mothered Alfred and Bertie while she continued her study with the internationally famous organist, Clarence Eddy. One of the young singers in Anderson's road show was Charles E. Bentley. He was a fine tenor and Dan had known him when he was a guest in the Anderson home in Janesville. Bentley continued to call on the Andersons in Chicago and soon proposed to 'Viata. She accepted him, and when they were married Bentley moved in with the family. He gave up singing and on funds supplied by Harry Anderson enrolled in the Chicago College of Dental Surgery. Anderson still had his heart set on seeing his Vytie the wife of a professional man.

People asked Traviata why she had not married Dr. Dan. "Dan?" she replied with the greatest candor, "Why I couldn't *marry* Dan! He's just the same as a brother."

As for Dan, he seemed relieved to have matters thus taken out of his hands. 'Viata would always occupy a big place in his heart, and he was pleased to see her happy. He liked Charles Bentley enormously; he was a keen, intelligent fellow, interesting to be with. Dan visited the Anderson-Bentley home constantly.

Dan had a passion for friendship. Cut off from his family, he clung to his friends. Though he had spent but a short time in his boyhood at his grandmother's in Annapolis, he had never completely lost touch with a friend he made then, and now, with money in his pocket, began to visit again.

Hutchins Bishop came of a family as old as the Prices and likewise of free, mixed blood. The Bishops lived on Church Circle, just across from the Prices. The two little boys in their brass-buttoned waist-length jackets and ankle-length baggy pantaloons had trudged off together to the Freedmen's Bureau school each morning, first pulling down hard on the visors of their kepi caps. There was always a gantlet of white hoodlums before you got there. But, hand in hand, head ducked down and shielded by a bent arm, the boys arrived with no more than an occasional bruise from a thrown rock.

That handclasp had held across the miles and years. While Dan was learning to save bodies, Hutchins, as fair-skinned as Dan and equally imbued with a desire to help his race, was studying at the General Theological Seminary in New York, learning to save souls. He wanted to go back to Maryland to take a parish, but the Southern Episcopal Church would not accept a man of African descent for the Lord's service. Hutchins received ordination finally in Albany through the help of Dan's cousin, Sadie Williams Topp, who succeeded in bringing the matter to the attention of Bishop William Croswell Doane.

At Hutchins's insistence, Dr. Dan made a flying visit to Albany, saw his chum ordained and then accompanied him to Charleston and served as best man at his wedding. Six years later Dr. Dan was appearing as godfather in St. Philip's, now his friend's charge in New York City, for Hutchins's second child, a son, whom he named Shelton Hale Bishop to honor the young doctor. This was Dr. Dan's third godchild and second namesake, Bertie Anderson being the first. But it was not the last, for soon he was standing godfather constantly for a stream of little Daniels and Hales who proudly bore a name that appeared more and more in the Negro press across the country.

These trips East to see Hutchins turned out to be important to Dr. Dan. In Albany there was a considerable colored colony of wealth and culture — families who had settled there in earliest times, intermarried with the Dutch and other white settlers, and later worked against slavery in those same Negro conventions in which the Williams clan had labored. Dr. Dan's cousin had married into the Topp family. Other names equally prominent were the Benjamins, the Van Vrankens, the Pauls, the Lattimores, the Blakes, the Olcotts, the Mathewses.

There was a gay winter season in Albany and a gay summer

season at Saratoga Springs. On one of his visits, Dr. Dan was dancing in a hotel at Saratoga Springs with the fair-skinned but nevertheless "Negro" Nina Pinchback, when officialdom asked them to leave the floor. Colored society all over the country was outraged. Nina Pinchback was the daughter of the honored P. B. S. Pinchback, lieutenant governor of Louisiana in Reconstruction days. What did freedom mean if a lieutenant governor's daughter could not dance where she chose?

The incident probably did not bother Dr. Dan. Slights from white people were usual. But another blow came to him in Albany which did shatter him. Against blows from people of color, his mother's color — against these, he showed again and again that he had no defense.

Dr. Dan inevitably met in Albany Kittie May Blake, lovely daughter of Mr. and Mrs. Adam Blake. The Blake daughters were the belles of colored Albany. Bismark Pinchback, Nina's brother, was in love with one daughter. Dr. Dan fell head over heels in love with Kittie May. She was not only an exquisite girl with the fair skin and hair of her Dutch and Yankee ancestors and the charm and grace of her African forebears, but she had been most carefully nurtured. From childhood she had attended St. Agnes Convent School. Year after year she had been awarded the banner as the most beautiful girl in the white school. Bishop Doane, people said, "loved her like his own daughter." After a year's finishing in New York City she had been taken to Europe for a final round of polishing. These were the exterior things; her spirit was sweet and gentle, as lovely as the outer body that clothed it.

Dan was carried headlong into an adoration that made him forget himself completely, left him with all his defenses down. He no longer hesitated as he had with other girls, but exposed his heart in all its tender, quivering honesty. He left himself no loophole, no avenue of escape. He loved her, he told her, with all his being. Would she marry him?

Kittie May answered with quiet dignity: Yes, she said, she would marry him. He was the ideal she had dreamed of, the

Prince Charming she had hoped would come someday — handsome, tender, serious, gifted. Dr. Dan's heart must have swelled to the point of bursting.

It was Mrs. Blake, nee Benjamin, who shattered the idyll. She had no intention of allowing her darling to marry a man identified with colored people. Kittie May with her beauty and her wealth could marry anyone she chose and if Kittie May did not know where to choose, her mother would choose for her.

If Kittie May had not been so gently nurtured, she might have had more spine; she might have stood up and demanded the right to live her own life. If Dr. Dan had been charged with anything but his race, he might have striven to change it. Poverty? He could win riches. Obscurity? He would win honor. But race? He could more easily cut off his right hand, his surgeon's hand, than deny his people. He could not imagine himself for a moment as anything but Negro, loyal to Negroes everywhere.

If looks had been all, he could have passed to the white side long before. In his milieu there were those who did so every year — someone whose elderly parents had died and who felt free to embrace an easier path; someone who was marrying across the line; someone with little children who wanted an easier life for them than colored children could hope for. They went to Mexico, Brazil, France or just to another state. While he sympathized with their reasons, Dr. Dan had only pity for those who "passed." It was a possibility he could not for a second entertain, even to win Kitty May.

He went back to Chicago and threw himself into a passion of work.

Kittie May dutifully married the white lawyer her parents selected for her. But from friends in Albany Dr. Dan learned that her brightness was quenched; she drooped and had little interest in life.

Dr. Dan grimly worked on. Every hour he could snatch from his patients he spent in the anatomical laboratory, dissecting cadavers. With sharp blade in supple fingers he attacked the inert flesh — cutting, retaliating, reaching those inmost recesses as life had reached him, at the raw center, at the quick. Unconscious of the double motive that impelled him, glorying in his natural manual dexterity, fostered during those years in barbering, he must have found a release in the use of the knife at the same time that he found knowledge.

People wondered why the steadily advancing young doctor whose practice had grown so well, who drove a horse worthy of Janesville's best traditions, who owned a four-story brick flat building on Dearborn Street, did not marry. Mothers with marriageable daughters hopefully set their caps for him. But though he was pleasant, courteous, and charming, he eluded them all.

In September 1887, Dr. Dan decided to go to Washington to attend the International Medical Congress; he could at the same time have a short visit with his mother and sisters and look into their finances which, it seemed, were forever needing his assistance, although when he had needed theirs it had not been available.

There had been no meeting of the world medical body since the one in Copenhagen in 1884 and the event was eagerly awaited by American doctors who would play host for the first time. Dr. Dan's old preceptor Henry Palmer was going and his former dean was secretary general of the Congress. Franklin Martin was to contribute to the gynecological section. Nicholas Senn of Milwaukee would read an important paper on intestinal surgery. With the work of these men Dr. Dan was already familiar. It was the others he especially wanted to hear. Mills had spent a summer in European hospitals, but Dr. Dan had not been able to go. Now Europe was coming here and he embraced the opportunity.

The five days were packed with an exchange of ideas, discoveries, theories. The strides being made everywhere under antisepsis, asepsis, and the new bacteriology were extremely stimulating — sometimes to the point of irritation and bitterness when the new school lost patience with the old.

Senn, Milwaukee's patient vivisectionist, argued for two hours that death from hemorrhage or septic peritonitis was not necessary if surgeons would only dare to operate on the abdomen. A buzz of excitement followed his paper. The vigorous-minded were elated. The cautious held back, making virtue of their "conservatism." The volatile John B. Murphy of Chicago was furious. If you waited as long as the "conservatives" demanded, you were performing a post mortem, not an operation. Anyone who did clean surgery could enter the abdomen any time — for exploration and diagnosis as much as for any other reason.

It was apparent the old days were not yet entirely gone. The discussion on the use of the Caesarean section revealed that of 153 cases in the United States to date, only 56 had recovered. This long-known method of delivering a child when normal birth proved impossible was still called into use only as a last resort and usually too late. The representative from Bellevue Hospital Medical College, no convert to Listerism, felt that "when performed in a 'healthy locality' away from 'infected hospitals,' the technique had a fair measure of success."

Dr. Dan saw that many old fogy notions still persisted. He was beginning to raise his head above the sea of textbook detail in which his timidity had once buried him. He would not be as cautious as many at the congress. He agreed with Murphy; it was not caution, it was cowardice. All you needed was knowledge. He returned to his dissecting.

While Dr. Dan plugged away, change went on around him in the ever-growing city and in his circle of friends. The new "commercial" and "elevator" buildings shot up here and there — simple, almost functional structures, ten stories high, frankly American, shorn of European pretense. The new plate glass was letting in light on Victorian stuffiness and many things were no longer the same.

Nothing was more surprising than that George Anderson should suddenly throw off his lethargy and at thirty-five enter dental school. Or that Theodora Lee should appear one day a young lady of sixteen come to tell her godfather good-by before going off to Rockford College. Dr. Dan made her promise not to use face powder until she was at least eighteen. There would be a gift then, he assured her, if she kept her promise.

Somehow Thedy expected at least a diamond ring for such a sacrifice and when Dr. Dan presented her instead with long-handled, pearl-inlaid opera glasses, Thedy was outraged. "He's always trying to *improve* me," she stormed to her mother.

It did not occur to Dr. Dan that everyone was not as enchanted with opera as he was. Ever since the old Exposition Building had been converted into a vast playhouse for the presentation of opera in Chicago, he had found surcease there during such times of relaxation as he permitted himself. And when in December 1889 the ambitious new rival Auditorium on Michigan Avenue was dedicated in the presence of the governor of the state and the President of the United States, Dr. Dan was among the first to secure a ticket.

He had a double interest. Of course he wanted to hear Adelina Patti sing "Home, Sweet Home." And since it was Traviata's teacher, Clarence Eddy, who would play the organ, he wanted to hear him too. But piquancy was added to both events because Eddy, coming to the famed prima donna's rescue when her regular accompanist fell ill, had brought no one else than 'Viata to accompany the famous soprano on one or two occasions. It had been a great feather in their beloved Vytie's cap and all the Anderson-Bentley clan rejoiced, Dr. Dan with them.

To walk down the street with Dr. Dan in the late '80s was to take inventory of the man's riches in popularity. He knew everyone's name, had a friendly word or question for all — in short, he was the pleasantest person you could ever want to meet. Plain folk liked him; he isn't stuck up, they said, he's just Dr. Dan every time you see him.

He was no longer the young man who had to be helped. Thanks to hard work, simple ways, and that same canny sense for real estate values of his Grandfather Price, he was now owner of several pieces of property and a substantial member of the community, one to whom others turned for help and advice. Widows asked him how to invest their money, and young men how to get ahead. He encouraged men to venture, to learn skills that would be lifetime assets.

"If you don't aim at something," he told young James Gordon, "you may go hunting, but you'll come back without a thing." On Dr. Dan's urging, Gordon learned mechanics and later went into contract hauling of machinery. He stopped at Dr. Dan's office one day to tell him how he was getting along. The busy physician dropped everything and patted the tall thin fellow on the back.

"So you've gone into business for yourself," Dr. Dan cried. "I told you so!" Gordon went out proud and full of courage.

Dr. Dan was generous in support of all worthy Negro enterprises. At a time when a mechanic earned $1.75 a day and a woman cleaned floors all week for three dollars, people gasped with awe and delight to see their Dr. Dan put a five-dollar bill on the collection plate at Old Bethel. He attended no one church, but visited and helped to support them all. His own preference, when he followed it, was to attend All Souls Unitarian Church on Oakwood Avenue and Langley Boulevard, where Jenkin Lloyd Jones, his Janesville friend and mentor, had come to be minister and where the congregation was forward-looking, and black and white sat side by side.

When a vacancy occurred in the Illinois State Board of Health in the spring of 1889, Joseph W. Fifer, then governor and a Republican, appointed the promising Dr. Daniel Hale Williams of Chicago. Dr. Dan's membership in the powerful Hamilton Club, a Republican organization with few Negro members, but into which he probably came under the aegis of John Jones's name, undoubtedly helped secure his appointment.

At that time the Illinois Board of Health, in existence but a dozen years, was making its way more tolerated than favored by a purse-tight legislature. It had on it, however, some considerable men. One was the patriarchal Newton Bateman, eminent author and educator, friend of Abraham Lincoln and now president of Knox College at Galesburg. Dr. W. A. Haskett of Alton was the Board's president. Its secretary, guiding spirit and enthusiastic dynamo was Dr. John R. Rauch. Rauch envisaged public health on nothing less than a global scale. These men, leaders from other cities and some of them from other walks in life, were stimulating confreres to the rapidly developing Dr. Dan.

Those were the days when devastating epidemics hit the population like a scourge of the Lord. Communities bowed helpless before the blast, buried their dead, and grimly waited for the fatal visitation to burn itself out. Diphtheria and scarlet fever came and went with the seasons. Typhoid struck whole families simultaneously. Yellow fever broke out periodically in the lower Mississippi Valley, and frightened Illinois. Cholera and smallpox recurred with each wave of immigration. Against such holocausts the only public health measures were to regulate drains, sewage and plumbing. The Board wrote many "Rules and Regulations" in Dr. Dan's day. It did not issue diphtheria antitoxin until two years after he left.

Dr. Dan had studied public health under Oscar DeWolf, who, as Commissioner of Health in Chicago, had instituted the placarding of scarlet fever despite denouncement for "waste of cards and tacks." Dr. Dan had learned antisepsis, too, under Edmund Andrews. He had a vision of other means than sanitation to curb disease. Possibly other men on the Board, too, understood something of the germ theory of disease. But the Board was limited as to funds, all members served without pay, and even the travel fund could not be stretched over more than four meetings a year, with an occasional special meeting at the time of some epidemic. The work of the Board, therefore, devolved largely upon its secretary and as long as Rauch remained in office, which he did until 1891, his burning ambition was to mop up all wet spots, to sanitate and to vaccinate the whole state.

One valuable function the overworked, underfinanced State Board of Health did perform during Dr. Dan's incumbency: that was the elevation and strict enforcement of medical practice standards. The first meeting of the Board Dr. Dan attended in late June 1889 was typical. The secretary asked the Board that day for authorization to proceed against Blue Mountain Joe of the Oregon Indian Medicine Company. The concern was operating wholesale in the towns of northern Illinois, giving free consultation to the sick, prescribing medicine during the day and at night lecturing in public halls. While his outfit staged operatic performances, Blue Mountain Joe sold such "Indian" concoctions as Modoc Oil, Worm Eradicator, and something called Katouka.

In the previous two years, twenty-two itinerant showmen and mountebanks, enjoying sales estimated at $2000 daily, had been run out of the state. But Blue Mountain Joe was inclined to persist in his lucrative business and had appealed to the courts. A penny-foolish committee of the legislature was casting lingering glances after the $11,400 formerly collected in license fees from these itinerants. The Board had all it could do to protect the Medical Practices Act and at the same time force out the Blue Mountain Joes. Five suits had to be brought against "Doctor" Oregon Charley and four against "Colonel" T. A. Edwards before the Oregon Indian Medicine Company was put out of business.

The matter of diploma mills was constantly before the Board. At its February 1890 meeting — Dr. Dan never failed in attendance — the Chicago Correspondence University was investigated. This self-styled university had been incorporated by a board of six directors: a printer, a laborer, a teamster, a lawyer, a bookkeeper, and a stove repairman. No doctor whatever brought dull reality into its affairs. But every time some such flimsy institution was outlawed, "graduates" would come squealing to the State Board of Health that their opportunities of earning a living were being ruined. So individuals not having diplomas from accredited medical schools were allowed the opportunity of taking examinations given by the unsalaried doctors of the Board.

Reappointed in 1891, Dr. Dan continued to be a faithful attendant at all meetings of the Board, whether held in Chicago or Springfield. During the four years of his incumbency he received none of the plums; he was never, for instance, a delegate to the various meetings of the American Public Health Association. Frequently he was the man who moved that someone else be sent. He would not place them in the predicament of not being able to send a Negro. And it was usually the punctilious, gracious Dr. Dan who proposed resolutions of appreciation for some member leaving the Board. If any of the old timidity remained, it was apparently buried past resurrection.

With the defeat of Joseph W. Fifer by the Democrat Altgeld, in the gubernatorial campaign, the entire Board went out. Dr. Dan was succeeded by the elderly William E. Quine, once his professor in materia medica.

Coming back to his bachelor room one evening after a long day of hard work, Dr. Dan found a letter from the East. Kittie May had escaped from her unbearable life. Her illness had not been long, but she had showed no wish to get well. Despite all efforts made for her, she had just quietly died.

After that Dr. Dan worked harder, if possible, than ever. A few knew how great a blow had fallen upon him. Years later one said, "He took it hard," and another added, "His heart was broken."

CHAPTER VI

First Interracial Hospital, 1891

ONE blustery day in December 1890 Dr. Dan received a note
from the Reverend Louis H. Reynolds, pastor of St. Stephen's
African Methodist Church, asking him to come over that evening
and discuss a problem. It was another of those requests for help
which came to him frequently from local pastors. That evening,
after his last house call, he drove through heavily falling snow to
the parsonage over on the West Side of Chicago. Years later
James Gordon remembered every detail, remembered Dan's covering his horse with a blanket. The Reverend Mr. Reynolds
greeted him eagerly and introduced him to his sister Emma. Dan
listened intently to the story they unfolded.

Emma Reynolds was educated and ambitious. She had come on
from Kansas City to join her brother, hoping to get into one
of the new nurses' training courses. Every training school in Chicago had turned her down. No Negroes accepted. Her brother
thought perhaps Dr. Dan with his connections might be able
to help.

"Well," said Dr. Dan when they had finished, "here we are,
only twenty-six years since Emancipation!" He frowned and
shook his head, biting at his mustache. As a matter of fact he had
been mulling over an idea for a long time. Perhaps now the moment had come for action.

The trained nurse was a recent arrival on the Chicago medical scene. Inevitably antisepsis, asepsis and bacteriology must end the bedside regime of both the devoted servant and the religious Samaritan. As doctors adopted the new techniques they required nurses able to understand and abide by their instructions. The change came slowly, just as the new surgery came slowly. There was inertia to be overcome and determined opposition in some quarters where the spoils system persisted.

Dr. Dan was among those who welcomed the increasing number of trained nurses. But he went further. As soon as he saw this new profession taking form, he saw what an opportunity it was for the energies and capabilities of colored women — a means of self-expression, of earning a living, of raising health standards among the uneducated of the race. He longed to see them enter this newly open door abreast of white women. But even before Emma Reynolds appealed to him, he had realized that the reluctant acceptance, if it could be won, of one colored student here and another there would not open the door wide enough or soon enough.

The matter had its daily practical side for Dr. Dan. Old Aunty Babcock was too sick to be left alone. She must have a nurse. But where could he find a nurse Aunty would trust, who would not add to her worries and tensions, however unwittingly? Aunty would never feel at ease with a white woman around. And here was another problem: Mrs. Danvers must have an hysterectomy, but how to get her a private hospital room? That proud, cultivated woman must not be shoved into a charity ward, as Negroes invariably were. Dr. Dan wanted to operate on her himself. But what hospital would allow him the privilege? That operation could not be done on a dining room table.

It was hopeless, waiting to get on a hospital staff. If William Morgan, a full professor now, couldn't get a regular staff appointment, who could? And these younger colored doctors, colored doctors of darker hue, one or two more of them coming out of medical school each year. What of them? Where were they to get interneships or find a theater for their professional work?

Unless Negroes founded a hospital of their own, the whole

progress of the race in medicine and nursing, in health care and health education would be slowed down for years to come. You couldn't wait for white people to see the light. You had to tackle things yourself.

All these things Dr. Dan had been turning over in his mind for months before he sat talking with the Reverend Mr. Reynolds and his sister in their lamplit parlor that stormy December evening. In his more optimistic moments he told himself a Negro hospital was not an impossibility. Weren't there now some two hundred Negro enterprises in Chicago, in twenty-seven different fields? And enough Negroes to sustain twenty churches, a dozen or so lodges, three weekly newspapers. Why not a hospital?

But it should not be a hospital for Negroes only. It must be interracial, open to all, regardless of race or creed — owned, operated and staffed by white and black together. It must be a hospital that would not only solve the medical problems of the Negro, but point the way to new and better interracial understanding and interracial co-operation.

While he was working on the Illinois State Board of Health, Dr. Dan saw the need for more hospitals, not only for the colored, but for everybody. Hospitals were the only safe place for proper care of the sick; they were a demonstration of proper hygiene and diet; they were the necessary teaching laboratory for internes and nurses alike.

For long months these ideas had kept teasing his mind. Now at last, here in the Reverend Mr. Reynolds's parlor, he was confronted with an immediate, concrete need. It was no longer a question of his own plan, but of Emma Reynolds's dilemma — and beyond her all the others: young colored women, colored doctors, colored patients. With that shift his dream was focused, his energies were released.

"No," he said to Louis and Emma Reynolds, but he said it smiling, "I don't think I'll try to get Miss Reynolds into a training course. We'll do something better. We'll start a hospital of our own and we'll train dozens and dozens of nurses!"

Like a southern Wisconsin windstorm, Dr. Dan swung into

action. Within a matter of days he had swept dozens of his friends, black and white, onto committees and put them to work.

He asked his friend Lloyd Wheeler to arrange rallies all over the West and South sides. This was a master stroke, for Lloyd Wheeler — whom he had once taken with him to spend a Christmas in Janesville — had married Mrs. Jones's adopted daughter, Raynie Petit, and become manager of all the Jones business interests. He was heir, in a way, to John Jones's prestige. Known as "a good dresser," "an elegant mixer," and a man able to talk on any subject, the popular Wheeler made every meeting tingle with enthusiasm.

Another of Dr. Dan's closest friends, James Madden, first colored bookkeeper to work in a Chicago white firm, constituted himself auditor and "never missed a duty and kept every detail straight." The preachers of the community gave their moral support to Dr. Dan's venture as he had given financial support to theirs. They turned over their churches for meetings and they served on his boards and committees: two bishops, John M. Brown and B. F. Arnett, and a half dozen pastors — George W. Gaines, Louis H. Reynolds, of course, J. F. Thomas, R. E. Knight, and the educated, eloquent John T. Jenifer whose daughter was another of Dr. Dan's growing list of godchildren. White pastors helped too: Dr. Dan's old friend, Jenkin Lloyd Jones, and the famous writer, liberal lecturer and minister of Plymouth Congregational Church, F. W. Gunsaulus.

Many other persons whose names are cherished in Chicago Negro history joined the undertaking. Captain John R. Marshall of Company A, later to be colonel when Company A was expanded into the Illinois 8th Regiment, and later still to be first colored deputy sheriff in Chicago, was an ardent supporter. He brought in the brilliant Franklin A. Denison, valedictorian of his class at the Union College of Law and recently appointed assistant city prosecuting attorney. The businessmen came in too: Theodore Wellington Jones, born among the Negro refugees in Canada and, now nearing forty, the successful owner of a furniture transit company and soon to be a member of the Board of Commissioners of Cook County. Mr. Jones represented South Side business interests. From the West Side colony came R. M. Hancock, colored foreman of the big Allis Chalmers Machine Shop, who did honor to his position by always appearing on Sundays in a plug hat, a Prince Albert coat, and shiny speckless boots. When Mr. Hancock presided at one of the rallies for Dr. Dan's Hospital, his very presence gave tone to the proceedings.

Tirelessly Dr. Dan travelled from group to group, putting the situation before them. Like his father, preferring deeds to words, he spoke simply, quietly, rapidly, without emotional appeal. He laid it before them — the need among the poor, the great opportunity for colored young women and colored doctors, the way it could be worked out. They'd have to start small, of course. But what Chicago hospital had not started small? Mercy Hospital, he told them, had had only a dozen beds at first; Wesley, but six. St. Luke's had begun in a small frame house. He thought the three-story brick flat building on the southwest corner of Dearborn and 29th Streets would do nicely for a start. There was room for twelve beds, and they ought not to tackle more at first.

He reported that his friends at Chicago Medical College and at Mercy Hospital were interested and would help service the new venture; the new hospital would have the best men in the city on its staff. Eventually they might open a dispensary and handle even more cases without much more overhead. Of course it would take some capital. He himself would give two hundred dollars and P. D. Armour of F. W. Gunsaulus's congregation would give an equal amount! At this point pandemonium broke out and Lloyd Wheeler pounded in vain for silence.

Every meeting — some of them were held in the flat of Mrs. J. C. Plummer on the southwest corner of Dearborn and 30th Streets, some in the Bethel African Methodist Episcopal Church on the southeast corner, and others elsewhere — every meeting ended more enthusiastically than the last. A hospital where Negroes would be received on an equal basis, a hospital Negroes would run! It was thrilling to think of it; it drew the whole neighborhood together in mutual hope and fellowship. At every supper table, from the home of the Reverend Jenkin Lloyd Jones to that of Jesse Binga, the vegetable huckster, Dr. Dan's hospital was the main subject of conversation.

And then word got around that there were dissenters. At the next meeting the opposition came out into the open. John G. Jones, head of the colored Masons, called for the floor. "Mr. Chairman," he cried, "are we self-respecting people, or aren't we?"

Jones was an able lawyer, would go to the state legislature, but he was a man of negative turn. "Indignation" Jones they called him. He was against a great many things, particularly those in which he had not been consulted from the start. Dr. Dan had failed to approach the man earlier and now he was against Dr. Dan's hospital because, according to him, it was going to be a segregated hospital.

"I'd let colored people die in the streets," he shouted, "and be eaten up by flies before I'd put them in a separate hospital!"

Murmurs of approval could be heard here and there. The committee hastened to explain that all sick and suffering would be admitted to Dr. Dan's hospital, all, no matter what color of skin, what nationality or what religion.

"What about the nurses?" challenged Jones.

The battle was on then between the theorists and the realists. It lasted a long time and grew more and more legalistic. Finally Fannie Barrier Williams, wife of the up-and-coming colored lawyer, S. Laing Williams, another of Jenkin Lloyd Jones's congregation, rose to her feet. Mrs. Williams was a lecturer and journalist in her own right; moreover, she was pretty. Years before, during the Civil War, her father had sat beside Dr. Dan's father at the National Convention of Free Colored Men in Syracuse. She was shoulder to shoulder with Dr. Dan now — persuasive, intelligent, a woman ahead of her time.

"But don't you see," she said, with all the appeal of voice and smile she could bring to bear, "there are other training schools for white women, but none at all for colored women. Why let white women take any of the few places we'll have open, at least at the start?"

While this was sinking in, she deftly set them laughing by pointing to Charles Bentley. "Dr. Bentley has to have teeth to work on or he can't be a dentist," she said, "and our nurses will have to have patients to train on or they can't become nurses." She reminded them that the patients would be white as well as colored and that the doctors would be colored as well as white. This was so reasonable that the opposition seemed to be dying out when Edward H. Morris, another lawyer, arose. Morris, elected the previous year to the state legislature, had built a three-story flat building at Dearborn and 27th Streets.

"I'm not against the hospital," he said, "I'm just against the location."

Mr. Morris wanted to know what a house full of sick and dying was going to do to property values. "Some of us have heavy investments in that neighborhood," he said, "and look what happened when that undertaking place opened up . . ."

Laughter burst forth and Lloyd Wheeler took the opportunity to point out that after all Dr. Dan would be on the job and everyone wasn't going to die. If folks would send their sick to the hospital before they got too bad, they'd have a better chance of being cured. Then he asked, "Dr. Dan, don't you own some property yourself in that neighborhood?"

The contrary Jones had one more try. He declared it cost money to run a hospital and challenged anyone to show him one hospital in the whole country supported by colored people. Dr. Dan could not stand this defeatism. He jumped up with eyes blazing.

"It's about time then!" he cried. "Look at the foreigners in this country. I don't care how poor they are, how uneducated. They have the humanitarian spirit to provide for their own sick and injured. Every single nationality has done so. And they don't number one tenth of us colored people." Words poured from him. For once his calm had deserted him; he pounded the table passionately. "A people who don't make provision for their own sick and suffering," he said, "are not worthy of civilization."

The hall burst into cheers. John G. Jones was completely

silenced, and organization now proceeded apace. Two ladies'
auxiliaries were formed — one on the West Side under the presidency of Mrs. Mollie Green, another on the South Side headed
by Mrs. Connie Curl. The ladies held ice cream socials and potato-
collecting parties to raise funds. Dr. Dan found time to attend
every affair. He was the brains behind every committee, he was
the dynamo that kept them all going. With P. D. Armour's gift
to cite and Jenkin Lloyd Jones to back him up, he approached
others on Millionaire Row. H. H. Kohlsaat gave another $200, as
did Miss Florence Pullman of the sleeping-car interests — just now
being defied by Clarence Darrow on behalf of the workers. Dr.
F. C. Greene gave still another $200. Rabbi Emil Hirsch, pleased
with the interracial aspect of the project, influenced the Young
Men's Hebrew Association to contribute $100.

There was one gift of $75 and four of $50 and that was the
extent of the larger contributions. The rest was collected bit by
bit, a task to which Fannie Barrier Williams lent her charm and
her capabilities. Donations came from both white and colored and
mostly in comparable amounts. The Sunday School of the Third
Presbyterian Church gave $41.41; Bethel Church took up a special
collection of $7 and there was a Christmas collection of $11.25.
In such small amounts and even smaller was the total of $2,114.03
finally achieved. It would take twice that much to buy a minimum
of equipment and meet current expenses the first year. But most
of the community was now supporting the project and there were
promises to continue contributions throughout the year, month
by month.

On January 23, 1891, articles of incorporation were drawn up
in the name of the Provident Hospital and Training School Association. Dr. Dan himself insisted on the impersonal name, but many
people continued to call it Dr. Dan's Hospital for a long time.
Those who signed the historic document — birth certificate of the
institution that was to be a beacon in the wilderness of Negro
medical care and education, progenitor and pattern for a hundred
such institutions today — were all colored and all ministers except Madden. The top line was left blank and never filled in. The

busy Dr. Dan, after writing out the document, was called away before he could sign it.

The endeavor grew by leaps and bounds. An advisory board of white people was formed. It included the Honorable Walter Q. Gresham, former Postmaster General, member of the Hamilton Club and frequently spoken of as Presidential timber; the Reverend F. W. Gunsaulus; and two doctors from Chicago Medical College, Frank S. Johnson and Ralph N. Isham. This white board, however, was purely advisory. The trustees, the executive committee and the finance committee, on whom fell the real burden of the enterprise, all were colored. The genius of the whole affair lay in the fact that behind these committees and officers was a large membership organization, the Provident Hospital Association, of which every donor was a member. That meant almost everybody who was anybody in colored Chicago and a great many white people besides.

There was much to do in the three months that intervened before the hospital could open. While Dr. Dan secured the equipment, the neighborhood poured in their gifts. Practically every household donated something. Mrs. Lloyd Wheeler gave a parlor stove, Mrs. David McGowan a clothes wringer; Mrs. Austin M. Curtis, six yards of chiffon lace for the nurses' caps. The S. Laing Williamses presented a portrait in crayon of Herman H. Kohlsaat, already beloved in the community for his gift of a library to the colored people. The Williamses sent books too, *Half Hours With Great Authors, Looking Backward,* and some others.

One day as willing hands were scrubbing and painting and putting the flat building into final shape, a commotion occurred at the door. On the high stoop stood old Preacher Calloway, waving his arms and crying: "May the Lord lay His curse on this work of evil!" Preacher Calloway was as negative about new things as "Indignation" Jones and much more indignant.

Laughter rang out in answer, yet trailed off a little nervously when the infuriated man shouted next: "May the whole place burn to the ground before sunrise! A-men!" The building, however, still stood intact the next day and the Reverend Mr. Calloway had made the mistake of putting himself on record a little too explicitly.

At last all was in readiness and Provident Hospital threw wide its doors. The whole South Side poured in for the grand opening benefit party on May 4, 1891, only eighteen months after Emma Reynolds had sought a hospital where she might learn nursing. Every one was in a happy, expansive mood — all Dr. Dan's old friends, all who had worked so hard on the committees. Among them was pretty Alice Smith, now Mrs. Jackson, the Indian girl from Oconomowoc, who had come with Traviata to visit when Dr. Dan was a struggling student. Mrs. Jackson took charge of the American booth. Colorfully bedecked booths of all countries turned the first floor into an international parade ground gay with streamers, flags and bunting. Countless homemade cakes and gallons of ice cream sold out as soon as they were placed in view.

In the crowd wandered J. M. Johnson. He had once been a porter in a boot and shoe emporium and had risen to become a well-to-do boot and shoe merchant. But he had never been able to throw off the frugality which had enabled him to make that transition. Suddenly Mr. Johnson was impelled to do a strange thing. He led two elderly ladies up to a booth and bought them dishes of ice cream. When James Gordon saw that he rushed over and told Dr. Dan a new era had indeed started.

After the opening, scores of families kept up month-by-month contributions from their own stores: sheets, beds, a bundle of old linen, sugar, soap, blackcurrant jelly, and loaves of bread on baking day. The ladies' auxiliaries remained faithful. From time to time, Charles H. Smiley, the fashionable caterer, sent a can of assorted French ices, remainder of some gala event on the Gold Coast. Every evening Huckster Binga, one day to be a banker and contributor of more worldly goods, brought his leftover potatoes and vegetables and donated them to the hospital larder.

In all the long lists of donors and their gifts, only one item carried a money valuation: "Hall: Japanese screen, worth $6.50."

Whatever Dr. Dan's hospital lacked in the way of space and equipment was made up for by the galaxy of medical and surgical names with which he was able to embellish its staff. There were few higher in Chicago. Busy men lent their names and, when needed, gave advice. Frank Billings, now full professor of physical diagnosis and secretary of Chicago Medical College, was chief consulting physician. The great Christian Fenger was consulting surgeon. Ralph N. Isham at sixty, so generous with his services as unpaid professor at Chicago Medical, gave both money and time to his former student's project. He and Dr. Dan were the attending surgeons. Then there were W. W. Jaggard and Henry T. Byford of the Chicago Medical faculty, and Horace Starkey who taught alongside Dr. Dan in the South Side Dispensary; these were consulting obstetrician, gynecologist and oculist-aurist, respectively.

When it came to adding Negroes to the staff, Dr. Dan had difficulty. His standards were unrelentingly high, like those of the men with whom he had studied and been associated. It was important to himself as a serious professional man, to his position on the Illinois State Board of Health, to those who had consented to lend their names to his project, and above all, he felt, for the honor of the Negro race that everyone connected with this venture should be soundly trained and properly qualified to serve the sick. All the more so since the Negro in the eyes of many would be on trial here. He wanted to use Negroes on the staff as soon as they were ready for it, but not before. And here he ran into some difficulties.

There was no question about Traviata's husband, Charles Bentley. He was eminently fitted to be their oral surgeon. He had been a clinician for three years in the Rush Dispensary, had recently accepted a full professorship in oral surgery at Harvey Medical College, and was credited with being the first dentist in Chicago to use cocaine as a local anesthetic. There was ample recognition of Bentley's ability in the fact he had just served as president of the city-wide Odontographic Society.

Another highly qualified colored man was Allen A. Wesley, who had been on the faculty of Fisk University before he entered Chicago Medical College. Both before and after taking his M. D., he had been clinical assistant to Dr. Walter Hay as well as to Isham. With Byford in consultation, Wesley could be very safely relied upon for the gynecological cases.

For the one interneship to be filled there was Austin M. Curtis, just being graduated at Chicago Medical. Curtis was intelligent and willing, not reluctant to spend the night, if need be, with Dr. Dan in scrubbing the walls and floor of the small bedroom that served as operating room in order to be ready for an early morning operation. And as soon as Curtis could complete his interneship, Elmer E. Barr would be through Rush and ready to step into his shoes.

Another Negro applied for a place on the staff. He was George C. Hall, the man who had given the hospital a screen worth $6.50. Hall had been practicing medicine about two years, mainly in the red light district. His medical degree came from an Eclectic school. He was not well trained. From Dr. Dan's point of view he was not qualified. Others on the Board, more sentimental, eager to have another Negro on the roster, perhaps liking Hall's affable ways, urged his appointment. Dr. Dan finally compromised by allowing Hall to be appointed to the children's department.

He made no compromises about the nurses' school. The training period was set for eighteen months, as long as any in the city. The instruction, Dr. Dan insisted, must be "most rigid," including all details of antiseptic preparation and nursing for surgery as well as care of serious medical cases. After a year he could say the advantages to students "are equal to those of any training school in the Northwest." All applicants had to be "fairly educated" and exhibit punctuality, personal neatness, general order, a gentle voice and manner, and a patient temper. "Let the nurse cultivate these qualities," said Dr. Dan, "together with a Christian, loving spirit." After the initial weeding-out process none was encouraged to remain who did not exhibit real aptitude for the work. Seven young women enrolled in that historic first class, including of course Emma Reynolds.

Conservative Dr. Dan had thought it best to begin cautiously with a twelve-bed establishment. But so great was the response to the new hospital that within a few months it became necessary to move the student nurses into rented quarters nearby in order to make room for the influx of patients. At the end of the first year, Dr. Dan made a public report of the work. Of 189 sick and injured, 23 had improved, he said, 3 had not, 22 died, and 141 recovered entirely. It was a ratio of which any hospital could be proud, especially in a time when only the most desperate cases were taken to a hospital. While the majority of patients served were Afro-American the interracial policy was maintained and 12 Irish, 6 Germans and Swedes, and 17 "others" were cared for.

"Although we lacked means and proper equipment," Dr. Dan said, "through the generosity of friends we have been able to give perfect care and treatment to such patients as our limited capacity permitted." As for the nurses' training school, many of the most influential persons of the city had inspected it and had given "their unqualified approval for its practical workings." What was needed now, especially in view of the approaching World's Fair, was enlarged facilities. "We sincerely trust," Dr. Dan said, "that before the close of another year a new and more modern building with most approved appointments will enable us to accomplish everything required of a modern hospital."

This dream could be brought about, he continued, in many ways. "You can not only make bequests," he enumerated, "and help endow beds, but you can subscribe a certain sum monthly on the cards distributed by the Auxiliary Societies . . . collect funds among your acquaintances . . . send jellies and fruit from your tables . . . arnica, Pond's Extract, Brown's Ginger, plasters, camphor from your medicine chests . . . old rags from your linen closets."

He made them feel there was nothing they could not do for their hospital. "If you live in the country," he said, "beg from the farmers potatoes, butter, eggs and vegetables of all kinds." And then he reminded them, "You can speak a good word for the hospital when you are among strangers, and you can pray for it."

People did pray for Provident Hospital, and they danced for it too. The Chicago colored group's first full-dress affair was a charity ball held in the 2nd Regiment Armory on the evening of February 25, 1892. The event was not only a gala one whose memory some preserved for fifty years in a creased, yellowed invitation with flourishing script reading "Yourself and ladies are invited . . ." but, what was more to the point, it netted the new hospital $231.15, and reduced the first year's deficit, on outlay for equipment, to only $795.78. This could easily be absorbed in the second year's operation.

Three fourths of the cases coming to the new hospital were surgical. Some were accident cases from the stockyards and the railways. Others were Dr. Dan's personal patients. His interest in surgery was growing more and more and he decided to do some special study in abdominal and pelvic anatomy with F. Byron Robinson, just back from six months spent in England with the great experimenter, Lawson Tait.

While Robinson taught in various of the inferior schools and published in the less fashionable firms, the discerning recognized his caliber. Christian Fenger said his research on the peritoneum was a classic. Another gave Robinson credit for changing the entire aspect of abdominal surgery. A third, while he considered Robinson the best man in Chicago with whom to study gynecology, added, "Provided you can keep from killing him after you have endured him for a week."

However much Dr. Dan may have been troubled by Robinson's rude manners, he admired the man's fever for work and passion for dissection. Robinson signally helped Dr. Dan to move out of the confines of internal medicine and into surgery.

About this time Chicago Medical College effected a closer union with Northwestern University and, dropping the old name entirely, moved to new and larger quarters on Dearborn between 24th and 25th Streets. The move brought about an expansion of postgraduate opportunities and Dr. Dan, now ten years out of medical college and determined not to drop behind in the march of science, promptly enrolled in a course in bacteriology. The subject, still so nebulous in his own college days, had by now assumed a form and stature he felt demanded study. He could squeeze it in; it was only a quick walk of four blocks from his hospital to the university.

His small hospital demanded constant attention. Still he found time in this busy year to prepare his first medical paper. He wrote it despite lack of encouragement.

Dr. Dan had not been asked to join the exclusive South Side Medico-Social Society founded by a small group of his college contemporaries in the year of his graduation. This circle, secret at the time, enjoyed making each meeting a white-tie-and-tails affair. They ate an expensive dinner together in a South Side hotel and then listened to each other's papers preparatory to getting themselves "suggested" at one of the larger medical societies where they all duly appeared to "discuss" the paper and enhance each other's reputations. At least five of these men were Dr. Dan's personal friends — Franklin Martin, Frank Billings, L. L. McArthur, Otto Schmidt, and E. Wyllys Andrews. But they were not a majority in the social club and Dr. Dan was not included.

So, with no logrolling, but with Fenger's blessing, Dr. Dan presented his maiden effort before the Gynecological Society on a March night in 1893 when a strong lake wind beat upon the windows and rattled a loose sash. The noise competed unsuccessfully, however, with Dr. Dan's well-schooled voice and manner. He had faced rowdy classrooms and had aroused the interest of bored indifferent claims courts. He knew how to get and to hold attention.

His paper was a short one on appendicitis and supplementary to a longer discussion of that subject which Fenger was to read the same evening.

Appendicitis was a highly controversial subject just then. Dr. Reginald Heber Fitz had read his famous paper in 1886 establishing the responsibility of an inflamed appendix for the condition previously defined vaguely as inflammation of the bowels, cholera morbus, or, later, perityphlitis. Fitz had urged that procedure in such cases be radical: if the symptoms did not subside within twenty-four hours, he declared the surgeon should remove the offending appendix at once. But Fitz was not immediately convincing.

The conservatives and the progressives drew up in two battle lines that stretched clear across the country. A bitter contest waged between them for years and nowhere was the engagement hotter than in the Middle West. In the spring of 1888 Will Mayo reported nine cases to the Minnesota State Medical Society and urged a waiting period before operating. In 1889 John B. Murphy appeared before the Chicago Medical Society with thirteen case histories and insisted unequivocally upon early surgical intervention. He was shouted down. Now four years later, the internal medicine men were still stubborn about yielding the field to the surgeons. Fenger was among those who held back and Dr. Dan held back too.

He presented two cases of successful delayed operations, one case of fatality where operation had been refused by the patient, and five cases of which four had recovered without operation. He had employed catharsis, he said, and local heat — both of which have since gone into the discard — and he wrongly deduced a possible infection of the appendix from the caecum, instead of vice versa.

The members present, who had braved the inclement weather to come, on the whole agreed with him. Robinson, who was there, gave it as his opinion that appendicitis occurred oftener in men than in women — another premise since discarded. It would be fourteen years before Murphy would return to the Chicago Medical Society with two thousand cases to back up his thesis for immediate operation and no voice would be left to oppose him. Dr. Dan might shake his head ruefully over this paper in later years, but he was in excellent company at the time.

What best characterized Dr. Dan's contribution was his minute and inclusive observation before diagnosis. After he sat down, Fenger remarked that "Dr. Williams has noted facts of utmost importance." His conservatism did not come from failure to be informed about the new; his brief paper revealed a broad knowledge

of both prevailing schools of thought. It came rather from a tem-
peramental thoroughness and attention to detail. It was not an im-
proper characteristic for a young surgeon. Innovation would
come, and soon, and be just as thoroughly grounded on observation.

During the first six months of '93, Dr. Dan had to work hard to
keep Provident Hospital on its feet. There was the inevitable
slump in enthusiasm that attends every new venture. It was magnified by the national economic situation. The country was going
through another of its recurring depressions, this time more severe
than ever. At one point it seemed the World's Fair itself must go
on the rocks. But new money was poured in and the magnificent
spectacle stretching along the lake front opened in May, only adding to Dr. Dan's burdens. He was on the Sanitary Board for the
Fair, which meant extra duties. And his sisters, Alice and Florence,
with young Zellie Ridgley came on from Annapolis to see the pag-
eantry. He had to find rooms for the girls and spend time taking
them around.

Dr. Dan spent some time, too, with the aging Frederick Douglass. The great Negro leader, a hunted slave in his twenties, an internationally famous editor and orator in middle life, had now for
years been a trusted government representative. Back from service
as United States Minister to Haiti, Douglass was in Chicago as
Haitian Commissioner to the Fair. Dr. Dan's mother called Douglass "cousin" and there were family traditions linking Dr. Dan's
grandmother, his mother's mother, with the same plantation and
the same white inheritance that produced the great race leader.
Dr. Dan was glad of the opportunity to see more of his famous
kinsman than had been possible in the past.

Douglass, after delivering an oration at the Fair denouncing the
ever-increasing lynching of Negroes in the South — an oration,
the *Tribune* said, that "burned itself into memory" — came to the
South Side and lectured in Bethel Church. Then, shaking back his
long white mane and striding along with the Indian erectness that
was his heritage — an erectness that belied his seventy-six years —

Douglass brought the lecture proceeds of $50.25 in his own hands and presented them to Dr. Dan's little hospital which so badly needed them. On one side he was escorted by Fannie Barrier Williams and on the other by the militant race journalist Ida B. Wells. Dr. Dan came out in his white coat to lead the honored guest up the high stoop and into the country's first and only interracial hospital while "every Negro in Chicago" stood on the curb. If there was anyone who did not know before where Provident Hospital was, he knew now.

Dr. Dan had other worries than money in those first years of operating Provident Hospital. He found it difficult to find the right young women to train as nurses. The first year 175 applied for training, but few were of the right sort. A people straining every nerve to pull themselves up by their own bootstraps, to escape from the servant class, saw no difference at first between the bedside work of the past and this new "trained" nursing. A girl who had gone to high school, and those were the girls Dr. Dan wanted, felt she was taking a step backward if she entered nursing.

Dr. Dan had to write letters all over the country, urging friends, relatives and acquaintances to send him recruits. Isabella Garnett came from Minnesota; Mabel Williams, his cousin's daughter, came from Rockford. Others came in strange and devious ways, hearing of the new opportunity from preachers, teachers or the few colored doctors. For many it was an upheaval of major magnitude involving a trip from a distance and a break with old ties and old ways. Dr. Dan's nursing course precipitated a sort of revolution in many a colored home. One of his first and most successful graduates was a young Canadian, Jessie Sleet, who, after her venturesome training, went on to New York City to become the first colored woman to do district nursing for the Charity Organization Society, and trained many other young Negroes in her field.

They went so far, these first brave pioneers, because Dr. Dan coached them well. Not only were they drilled to soldierly obedience and precision in their work and made to feel that anything less than perfection was not enough. They were carefully instructed as well in how to maintain the dignity of their person and their profession. Their superintendent must always be addressed as "Miss," no matter how small and modest the hospital in which they served. And they themselves must insist upon being called "Miss"; a practical measure to this end was never to tell their first names to patient or patient's family. Thoroughgoing Dr. Dan overlooked nothing.

Times grew worse. Wages were slashed, unemployment increased, and then came bank failures and a currency famine. Homeless transients crowded the saloons and the indomitable Frances Willard from Janesville, now a nationally famous temperance advocate, went around trying to mop up the grogshops. More sick people needed charity and fewer people were ready to give to charity. It was a trying time for Dr. Dan. One of his young student nurses, Isabella Garnett, later remembered how old and worn he looked at this time, though he was only thirty-seven. More than once she saw him reach into his own pocket and give the superintendent money for the day's food. Dr. Dan himself usually ate with the young interne Austin Curtis, whose little sister Hattie brought him a basket lunch each day from home. While they ate, they talked, and during those sessions young Curtis learned much from his chief.

In these hard times contributions from less wealthy persons had fallen off. True, Armour and Kohlsaat and Miss Pullman continued to give liberally, but Dr. Dan had to have more money. Judge Barnes in the Hamilton Club was his good friend. The judge spoke to his law partner, George H. Webster, about Dr. Dan's hospital and Webster, with his Puritanism and almost belligerent sense of racial justice, was easily persuaded to increase his original small contribution.

So Provident was able to hang on, even in years of financial panic. But Dr. Dan had to abandon for the time being all thought of a new building. That must wait for better times.

CHAPTER VII

"Sewed Up His Heart!"

EARLY July '93 was desperately hot in Chicago. People sought relief at the lake shore or rode about on the cable cars. Often the horses drawing the cars fell in their tracks and had to be replaced. Men were warned to place a cabbage leaf inside their hats before venturing on the streets. Despite precautions, many suffered heat prostrations and doctors were kept busy.

Tempers rose and on July 9 in a saloon not far from Provident Hospital irascibility flared into a brawl. A man was stabbed. The victim was a sturdy young Negro expressman, James Cornish. He was rushed to Provident. He could not say what kind of knife his assailant had wielded or how long the blade was. Dr. Dan examined the wound. It appeared to be only about an inch long, situated about three-quarters of an inch to the left of the breastbone, between the fourth and fifth ribs. The wound seemed superficial. The absence of external bleeding or evidence of internal hemorrhage gave no hint of deeper injury.

But after a while Cornish began to suffer persistent pain over the region of the heart and to show pronounced symptoms of shock. Dr. Dan concluded that one or more of the important blood vessels must have been injured, perhaps the heart itself. As he finished his examination and straightened up, he silently reviewed the situation. What should he do?

The X ray had not yet been invented, so he could not know

what condition lay within. Most writers on cardiac or thoracic matters gave warning to leave heart wound cases strictly alone. Keep the patient as quiet and as cool as possible. Some doctors said to pack the patient in ice or, if you had no ice, to put him in a cool cellar. The rest must be left to Providence. But surely, Dr. Dan thought, a surgeon could do something.

He knew that the heart had been revered by the ancients as the seat of life — "the chief mansion of the Soul, the organ of the vitall faculty" — and any wound in it was regarded as inevitably fatal. To interfere with destiny would be blasphemous. This attitude had persisted until the middle of the seventeenth century when someone noticed that not all cases of heart injury were fatal. After that records were kept and it was seen that in fact a good many recovered — without, of course, any medical or surgical aid.

To wonder as Dr. Dan was doing whether a surgeon might not assist recovery in such cases was a much bigger step forward. In some desperate cases of pericardial effusion, doctors had successfully used the aspirating needle to evacuate the fluid in the outer sac of the heart where it might interfere with heart action and cause the patient's death. But blood vessels and nerves, so abundant in this vulnerable area, were often injured by these blind attacks. Some patients died and the method was already in disrepute.

Not long before Dr. Dan's graduation from Chicago Medical, a Dr. Block in Danzig had conducted vivisectional experiments on rabbits and dogs and from them concluded that death could often be prevented if there were not so much dread of opening the thoracic cavity. A simple incision of the pericardium and suture would take only a few minutes, he said.

Block's experiments led John B. Roberts of Philadelphia to go further. Roberts argued that if cardiac distension and pulmonary engorgement could be relieved successfully by aspiration, then cutting through a portion of the intercostal cartilege and incising the pericardium should be a reasonably safe procedure. He ventured to add that "the time may possibly come when wounds of the heart itself will be treated by pericardial incision to allow extraction of clots and perhaps to suture the heart muscle."

Dr. Dan had read Roberts's article in the *Chicago Medical Journal and Examiner* when he was a senior student and he remembered it now, remembering too that Roberts had not fulfilled his own prophecy, nor had anyone else so far as he had ever read.

The eminent surgeons of the world had not looked favorably on Block's or Roberts's suggestions. The German, Theodor Billroth, a man of standing and by no means a timid surgeon – Dr. Dan used his text in college – utterly condemned the idea. "Any surgeon," Billroth charged, "who would attempt to suture a wound of the heart is not worthy of the serious consideration of his colleagues." That made a man stop and think.

Only two years before, in 1891, C. W. Mansell Mollin's book on *Surgery* had reached America. Many regarded it as the "best in the English language," and yet all that Mollin, Fellow of the Royal College of Surgeons, could say was that the only treatment "likely to be of any avail is absolute rest, cold, and opium; venesection has been recommended to relieve the heart, but it can very rarely be necessary. The external wound may be closed in the hope of arresting hemorrhage; but it must not be forgotten that accumulation of blood in the pericardium is one of the common causes of death. On one occasion I attempted to close the wound with sutures."

It was aggravating that Mollin had broken off abruptly at this point without saying why he had abandoned his attempt or what the outcome to his patient had been. And Nicholas Senn – who had just moved from Milwaukee to Chicago – daring and astute as he was, had concluded that "surgical interference with the heart is impracticable."

There was certainly not much to guide or encourage Dr. Dan. He would run no professional risks if he gave the man an opiate and let it go at that. Most doctors would approve. Of course the man would then probably die. But if he attempted surgical interference, if he took up Roberts's long-neglected challenge, he would have to venture into uncharted territory, with unforeseeable results. If he failed, he could expect nothing but condemnation from most of the profession.

He watched the dark face on the white pillow for a moment as he held the man's wrist. Cornish was coughing now — short, sharp, shrill barks. Slowly Dr. Dan laid the man's hand down and turned to the interne, Elmer Barr.

"I'll operate," he said.

While patient and operating quarters were being prepared, Dr. Dan sent a hasty word to a few medical friends inviting them to watch the operation if they wished. Six doctors, four white and two colored, crowded the small operating room, the converted bedroom. William E. Morgan came — tall, thin, angular, almost frail-looking, rejoicing over his appointment at last as assistant to Christian Fenger in the Dane's new clinic at Mercy Hospital. Morgan brought with him a student, Coleman Buford, who was living in his home while completing his last year at medical college. Buford had already come under Dr. Dan's spell in the dispensary classes and was delighted to be in on this exciting event. Two other white doctors were present: William Fuller, a young general practitioner with ambitions toward surgery, who came at every opportunity to watch Dr. Dan operate; and Howard Roy Chislett, another rising young doctor whom Dr. Dan had taken into his office as assistant. From the staff of Provident came George Hall and the interne, Elmer Barr. Among the surgical nurses, was Mabel Williams, Dr. Dan's cousin. All these crowded the small room to suffocation. The heat was intense. Buford, exasperated — and he still was fifty-odd years later — was pushed back into the corner where he stood on tiptoe, craning his neck to see.

Dr. Dan's first great problem of course was what might happen when air was admitted to the internal thoracic region. He had none of the modern adjuncts to fortify his entry into this dangerous territory. No X ray, and ony the crudest anesthesia. No trained anesthetist with his anesthetic machine and its tanks of gases from which to choose—oxygen, cyclopropane, ethylene, nitrous oxide, carbon dioxide. Not even a rebreathing bag and face mask for closed administration of ether under positive pressure, which would have kept Cornish's lung inflated. He had no artificial airway to keep the windpipe open. None of the new

intravenous anesthetics, such as sodium pentothal. No blood trans-
fusions to keep his patient alive and to relieve himself from the
terrific compulsion to make haste. No penicillin or sulfonamide to
correct any infection that might ensue if his aseptic technique
should be the least imperfect. He did not even have intercostal re-
tractors to widen transversely the opening he intended to make.

Thus, without even the minimum equipment that is a matter
of course today, and unaided by his own or anyone else's experience, Dr. Dan set to work.

Even if Cornish's lung did not collapse, the inrush of air would
certainly cause a shift of the chest organs to the right. Some shift
would be good; it would give him more working space. But too
much would cause shock and death. Well, those chances he had
to take.

What worried his watchers were the difficulties Dr. Dan must
face in gaining access to the heart. He would have to thread his
way through an uncertain, highly dangerous network of blood
vessels and nerves. At the same time, he must do nothing to interfere with the continuous beating of the life mechanism. Not a
man there but must have shuddered as Dr. Dan put the point of
his knife to Cornish's inert body.

Swiftly Dr. Dan lengthened the stab wound until he had an
incision between the ribs about six inches in length. This exposed
the breastbone, cartilage and about an inch of the fifth rib. Next
he chose a point two and a half inches from the breastbone and a
quarter inch from its attachment to the rib and quickly severed
the cartilage of the rib from its junction with the sternum, making
a neat little trapdoor two inches long and one and a half inches
wide. He now had an entrance into Cornish's chest, but a very
circumscribed entrance, no bigger than a small knothole. He was
being as conservative as possible and his caution was making his
operation even more difficult.

While everyone stood with bated breath, Dr. Dan lifted his
tiny trap door and, bending down, peered within. He could see
the large internal blood vessels. As he had surmised, one of them,
the important left internal mammary artery, was damaged. If

there had been continuous bleeding from this vessel, Cornish would have died before he arrived at the operating table, but the nature of the wound had contributed to the gradual cessation of hemorrhage. Even so, such recurrences as had been stimulated by the respiratory motion of the lungs and chest had been sufficient to throw the husky expressman into severe shock.

Rapidly Dr. Dan tied the injured vessel to prevent any further hemorrhage. Then with considerable difficulty, due to the shift of the lungs and heart and also to the fact the pericardium was rising and falling with each heartbeat 130 times every minute, he managed to inspect the quivering sac covering the vital organ. The assailant's knife had gone in much deeper than outside conditions indicated; there was a wound in the sac fully an inch and a quarter in length.

And now for the heart itself! Somehow Dr. Dan managed to hold the throbbing pericardial wound apart and examined the wildly beating, living dynamo. The weapon had penetrated the central organ also, but only to the extent of a tenth of an inch. The wound, Dr. Dan told the watchers, was about half an inch to the right of the right coronary artery and between two of its lateral branches. Half an inch either way and Cornish would not have reached Provident alive.

Dr. Dan found no active hemorrhage from either heart or pericardium now apparent. He considered the situation carefully and decided the heart muscle itself needed no suture. The pericardium was a different matter. If he did not suture it, infection might enter the pericardial sac from the pleural cavity, or, in healing, the pericardium might adhere to the pleural sac and cause Cornish constant pain in the future, if nothing worse. The pericardium, he concluded, must be sutured.

First he irrigated the wound with normal salt solution of 100 degrees Fahrenheit, which by that time was about room temperature. Then he grasped the edges of the pulsating wound with long smooth forceps. With not a little difficulty, he held the fluttering edges together and, using a continuous suture of fine catgut, he managed to close the wound. Next he closed the intercostal and subcartilaginous wounds, again using catgut. For the cartilages and the skin, he changed to silkworm gut and left a few long sutures in the external stitches. They would permit easy removal in case infection or hemorrhage should develop, though he prayed it would not. Then he applied a dry dressing, straightened his aching back, and mopped his brow. The silent intent circle around him stirred; someone spoke. The historic operation was over.

No one had thought to keep a record of the time. To young Buford, who reflected he had never seen an operator proceed with such speed and self-confidence, it seemed short. But neither Buford nor many of the others knew how many hours Dr. Dan had spent acquainting himself with human anatomy.

With no prolonged discussion the little group of busy men broke up, each hastening off about his own particular business. Results to the patient were yet to be seen.

During the first twenty-four hours Cornish's pulse was high, thin and weak, and his temperature rose to 103 degrees. He suffered some pain in the region of the wound, but he did sleep six hours without drugs. The second day the expressman's temperature fell a degree; however his pulse increased to 134 and was still weak. He slept only four hours and suffered paroxysms of coughing, followed by three dreadful hours of hiccoughing. Dr. Dan scarcely left his side. But the third day, while Cornish's fever remained high, his pulse went down to 118; on the fourth day it was 96, with temperature almost normal.

Seven days after the operation, the patient again had some pain. Gradually the spaces between his lower ribs began to bulge while at the same time his heartbeats sounded muffled and distant.

"There's fluid in the pleural cavity," Dr. Dan said to the interne Elmer Barr who stood watchfully beside him. That was not too serious, Dr. Dan added, unless there was also an accumulation within the pericardial sac. That he could not determine until he had emptied the pleural sac. But since Cornish's temperature continued to stay normal, Dr. Dan gave his patient as much time as he could to recover his strength before he operated a second time.

On August 2, a little more than three weeks after the first

operation, Cornish was trundled into the operating room again. This time Dr. Dan made a two-inch incision between and parallel to the seventh and eighth ribs and removed five pints of bloody serum. There was no pus whatever; his asepsis had been perfect! The accumulation of bloody serum was the natural result of irritation of the pleural tissues by an extensive operation and, perhaps, by the original stab wound. Gravity drainage in the direction of least resistance had carried the fluid to the base of the left pleural sac, where it did the least harm. This had kept the wound dry and provided a favorable condition for primary healing. There were no further complications, and on August 30, just fifty-one days after he had entered the hospital an apparently dying man, Cornish was dismissed and his case was checked off: "Termination: Cured." Twenty years later the man was still alive and well.

The doctors who had watched Dr. Dan make history were not slow in telling other doctors about the daring venture and its great success. For weeks surgical conversation dwelt on little else. Dr. Dan soon found himself a respected man in Chicago's topmost medical circles. The hospital staff, the Board, and friends of Provident, passed the exciting news around. Kohlsaat sent a reporter from the *Inter Ocean*, of which he was part owner, to interview the thirty-seven-year-old surgeon, ten years out of medical college, who had won this laurel.

Dr. Dan grasped the opportunity to publicize race accomplishments. He filled the report so full of information about the colored hospital, the colored nurses (a second class was about to graduate) and the capable colored doctors on the staff that it was only halfway through his column-long story that the reporter remembered he was sent to write about an operation on a man's heart. But Dr. Dan would not let him go until he added one more sentence at the end about the nurses. "Their presence," he said, diffuses an indescribable sense of security and gentleness throughout the operating room."

The caption writer, however, put on a headline strong enough to startle any breakfast reader dallying over his coffee before starting off for a Saturday at the Fair. "SEWED UP HIS HEART!"

cried the first line and went on for a five-bank heading: "REMARK-
ABLE SURGICAL OPERATION . . . DR. WILLIAMS PERFORMS AN ASTON-
ISHING FEAT . . ." Undoubtedly every household on the lists of
the ladies' auxiliaries west and south bought a copy.

Dr. Dan issued no official report of his pioneer undertaking,
because of the pressure of many events, until three and a half
years after he operated on Cornish. He had always meant to study
over the case in detail. He wanted to know why the extent of the
wound was not immediately ascertainable. At work one day
with a group of medical students, his old case occurred to him
and he proceeded to re-enact wound and operation on a cadaver.
He found that the intercostal tissues were so elastic that they
reclosed tightly enough after an incision to prevent the insertion
even of a piece of paper. That was why he had not seen at once
how extensive the wound had been. Also he determined to his
satisfaction that a stab wound in that particular position must
always sever not only the internal mammary artery, but would also
always pierce both layers of the pleura.

His students grew so excited over the review and study of this
dramatic affair that they urged Dr. Dan to publish the case,
and one in particular, J. W. McDowell, assisted in abstracting Dr.
Dan's notes. The report appeared in the *Medical Record* of New
York on March 27, 1897, a month after that publication had reported a similar but unsuccessful venture made in Norway in
1895 by Cappelen, and a month before it was to report a successful suture of the heart muscle made in Germany in 1896 by
Rehn. Dr. Dan's article contained the statement that neither the
Index Catalogue of the National Medical Library nor the International *Index Medicus* "give a single title descriptive of suture
of the pericardium or heart in the human subject. This being the
fact, this case is the first successful or unsuccessful case of suture
of the pericardium that has ever been recorded."

Immediately Dr. Dan was acclaimed, and has been ever since,
as the first man in the world to "sew up the heart." Occasionally
a writer, especially one Southerner, rejected the "Negro
Williams's" case because he said Dr. Dan had dealt with the en-

velope of the heart and not with the heart muscle itself. However most writers have said the great feat was the successful entrance of the dangerous area of the thorax and the performance of a surgical exploration of the heart, whether or not sutures were taken in the heart muscle or only in the pericardial sac which, after all, jumps about under the operator's fingers almost as violently as the "seat of the soule" itself. And today the *Cyclopedia of Medicine, Surgery and Specialties* says "it is good practice to think of the heart and pericardium together when considering trauma."

A month after publication of Dr. Dan's report a correspondent of the *Medical Record* called attention to a previous successful pericardial operation performed in St. Louis, September 6, 1891, by a Dr. H. C. Dalton. Though Dalton's patient remained in the hospital three months and twelve days, he was discharged apparently well. What caused his long stay in the hospital, twice as long as Dr. Dan's patient remained in Provident, or how long he lived thereafter is not known. Benjamin Ricketts, M. D., F. A. C. S., an authority on heart surgery, who began vivisectional experiments on dogs in 1874 and published his *Surgery of the Thorax and its Viscera* in 1918, knew about both Dalton's and Dr. Dan's cases and at one time included both in his early writing. Later he dropped Dalton's case, perhaps because the patient did not live, and he continued to call Dr. Dan the first, both in writing and from the lecture platform.

Like Dr. Dan, Dalton did not publish his official report for some three years. He read an account of his operation ten months after Dr. Dan operated on Cornish and officially published it in *The Annals of Surgery* a year and a half after the unofficial publication of Dr. Dan's operation in the *Inter Ocean*. Dr. Dan did not know about Dalton's operation when he performed his own; in fact he did not know about it when he wrote up his report. The *Index Medicus* was changing editors; issues were delayed and garbled when they did come out. Dr. Dan was as much a pioneer and innovator as if a precedent did not exist. It takes away nothing from his courage, originality and skill, even though first place may remain in doubt.

More important than official priority is an evaluation of the technique Dr. Dan displayed in what was to him, at any rate, an operation without antecedent or authority. In the first place he worked swiftly. This saved his patient from prolonged hemorrhage and exhaustion. In the second place he made no missteps, as did Cappelen (1895) and Parrozzani (1897); his surgery was correct and he did not add, as they did, to his patient's injuries. In the third place, his asepsis was perfect and there was no infection as in the German Rehn's case (1896). And finally, his procedure is the routine recommended today by Sauerbruch and others — namely, to close the wound in the pericardium and leave no drainage tubes, only reopening if necessary, as Dr. Dan did, to relieve any pericardial effusion that may develop.

Dr. Dan's success in operating on Cornish was no chance affair. He performed at least two later successful operations on stab wounds of the heart. One patient, George Albert Cotton, wounded in the early 1900's, lived for fifty years after the operation.

Dr. Dan's leadership gave authority to other innovators and his success encouraged surgeons both locally and far from Chicago. William Fuller, who watched Dr. Dan operate on Cornish, reported to the Chicago Surgical Society twenty-three years later that he too had sutured a pericardium. He used Dr. Dan's procedures almost step for step.

Today heart operations are not uncommon. But they are still hazardous — whether of the heart or the pericardium — and they are always dramatic. They still take courage and utmost skill and the mortality is still more than fifty per cent. The profession continues to bow to the accomplishment of Dr. Dan three quarters of a century ago.

Cornish had left the hospital on the 30th of August, completely sound and well. How sound and well was demonstrated unexpectedly a few months later when he reappeared at Provident Hospital late one night, bawling vociferously, his head covered with blood, a gory sight. Cornish, a young man of animal exuberance, had once more got into a fight, and once more had come off the worse for it.

"Where's Dr. Dan?" he yelled. "I got to see Dr. Dan!"

Attendants tried to silence him, but he had already roused Dr. Dan asleep in a nearby room. He came out tying his dressing gown around him.

"So it's you, Cornish," the sleepy doctor said. "How many policemen are after you this time?"

Cornish could only blubber and beg to be taken care of. "Oh, Dr. Dan," he moaned, "you can save me. For the Lord's sake, save me!"

Dr. Dan refused to smile. He said he doubted if Cornish was worth saving. When the man's howls redoubled and were about to waken the entire hospital Dr. Dan appeared to relent. "Well," he said, "you have got some nice fancy work in you, Cornish. I guess I can't afford to lose you. You're an important specimen."

A week or so later when he was removing stitches from Cornish's scalp, Dr. Dan told the young fellow he could be dismissed the next day. Then he added: "Look here. You've had enough free care in this hospital. I want you to go out of here and get yourself a job and stick to it and send Provident some money."

The next morning, Cornish's bed was empty, both of him and his blanket. But Cornish was not without gratitude. A few days later a grimy bundle was found at the back door of Provident Hospital. Upon examination it was found to contain one hospital bed blanket and a scrap of paper on which was scrawled in pencil: "Thanks Doc."

CHAPTER VIII

A National Task

WHEN in 1893 Cleveland triumphantly returned to the White House for his second term after the Republican interlude of four years, events were set in motion that were to have significance for Dr. Dan. Cleveland called to his cabinet as Secretary of State Judge Walter Q. Gresham, who had long been a friend of Dr. Dan's and a supporter of Provident Hospital. Gresham was now old and ill, and he did not want to be Secretary of State, but his sense of duty was strong, and back he went to Washington where he had previously served. When the judge and his wife returned to their home in Chicago for a brief stay, Dan made a friendly call. Gresham talked earnestly about Dan's work. He said he had long felt Dan should be working in a larger field. He said the new administration planned to make changes at Freedman's Hospital, the government hospital in Washington for Negroes, and he urged Dan to apply for the job of chief surgeon there. The judge would be happy to recommend Dr. Dan for the position.

"But what about Provident?" Dan asked.

"If it's service to your race you're thinking of," the Secretary rejoined, "Freedmen's needs you more than Provident, from all I hear."

That night Dr. Dan turned the matter over and over in his mind. Was he really needed in Chicago? Provident had many loyal supporters. The hospital was ending its third year in the black, with a small surplus. Charles Bentley, 'Viata's husband and Dan's longtime friend, would carry on as secretary with both devotion and efficiency. The consulting staff was strong and Allen Wesley was a good man in gynecology. Dr. Dan must have thought eagerly of the larger opportunities at Freedmen's, of the 200-bed hospital as compared with Provident's twelve beds.

He took up one of his letterheads with the small neat imprint in the corner and wrote Gresham his answer, still to be seen in Freedmen's files at the National Archives. Dr. Dan's large irregular script first sprawls, then contorts, seems to tumble forward with eager decision and then to draw quickly back. But Dr. Dan had made his choice.

Dr. Dan was not the only applicant. The news that an opening of so much prestige was imminent brought in a flock of applications from over the country, many urging that votes were in tow. Practically every colored doctor in Washington applied. Freedmen's Hospital and the affiliated Howard University medical faculty had been a closed corporation to them all for so long that they leaped at the chance of breaking in. Various applications illuminated the situation. Said one: "The large death rate of this hospital for many years has been so extraordinary that a radical change looking to better therapeutic methods should have been instituted therein long ago." Said another, a white applicant: ". . . no colored physician can fill the place properly because they have less respect for their own race than a good Christian white man feels."

Dr. Charles B. Purvis had been surgeon in charge of Freedmen's for a dozen years and had made of it a comfortable berth. Trained in the pre-Civil War, pre-bacteriological era, whatever contribution he could make he had completed long ago. Son though he was of the great Abolitionist, the wealthy, light-skinned, polished Robert Purvis who had helped nine-thousand slaves escape to the North and freedom, Charles Purvis was no idol of his people. His marriage to a white woman had been considered an act of disloyalty and his overbearing manner — he was a big, ferocious man with harsh, barking voice — made him none too popular in Washington or at Freedmen's. Attempts had been made before to oust him, but without success.

Now Purvis marshaled his forces again to resist this attack upon his position. He loudly proclaimed his status as a Civil War veteran, claimed to have been among the doctors who had attended the wounded President Garfield, called on Frederick Douglass, called on the local clergy, and secured a flood of letters from Howard graduates protesting any change. Finally he persuaded the Howard trustees to present a lengthy series of "considerations" to the Secretary of the Interior. These considerations said that the clinical advantages which University medical students enjoyed at Freedmen's Hospital, because Purvis also served on the faculty, would be endangered if a "complete stranger" were appointed.

Dr. Dan's endorsers were all medical men, white men, from the topmost rank in Chicago. It was a rank they accorded him too. His old teacher Isham was quick to write how "earnestly and actively" his one-time student had been at work in his profession. Professor Joseph B. Bacon, of the Post Graduate Medical School, testified to the "skill and energy" that had won a reputation, he said, for Daniel Hale Williams throughout the state of Illinois as well as in the city of Chicago. His sponsors spoke of the quality of the man in the same breath with which they spoke of the surgeon. Byron Robinson noted that he had had an intimate association with Dr. Dan in practical surgical procedure for several years and he recommended him "as an honorable man and a skilled surgeon . . . of wide experience and good judgment." Wyllys Andrews sent a lengthy communication in answer to a query put by the Interior Department.

> I am personally acquainted with this physician [he wrote], and esteem him highly. . . . I knew him as a student, and have kept up my acquaintance since his graduation some ten years ago. His professional standing is excellent. . . . I have often seen him in connection with accident cases. . . . He makes a good expert witness, being well in-

formed and ready. His practice among the colored people
here has been very large. It is not confined to the colored
people by any means, however. . . . I am informed that Dr.
Williams has accumulated considerable property since he
began practicing medicine. He is a man of good address, and
has great influence among the colored people here I am told.
He belongs to various medical societies here and certainly
has many business and social acquaintances outside the colored race. . . . You are correctly informed that he belongs
to the colored people. He has a very small strain of colored
blood about him, but to all appearances is a white man. I
was well acquainted with him for two years before I knew
that he was 'colored' so little does it show in his appearance.

The judgment of Dr. Dan's white associates was summed up by
Franklin Martin, now secretary of the Post Graduate Medical
School and Hospital.

I have known intimately Dr. Daniel H. Williams for more
than ten years [he wrote]. I know him to be a man of honor
and as a member of society a superior gentleman. Professionally he stands at the top of the medical profession of Chicago. He is a surgeon of great scientific ability, and his
executive ability, as demonstrated in the organization and
equipment of Provident Hospital of Chicago, is beyond
question.

Dr. Dan won the appointment, but he came into a difficult
situation. Local resentment of "foreign intrusion" seethed. Howard
University faculty and trustees smarted from being overridden.
Purvis was still there, still secretary of Howard medical faculty.
A man of bulldog tenacity, he was ready to fight for a comeback
at the first opportunity.

Dr. Dan was appointed toward the end of February. He took
the oath of office under President Cleveland and returned to Chicago to wind up his affairs. On the week end he went, as he often
did, for a round of quail shooting in southern Illinois. Somehow
he was shot through the right foot. Whether because the initial

care of the wound was not what it should have been, or because his general health was depleted, inflammation in the veins of his leg set in. For three weeks he was confined to bed in the hospital he had founded. Then, fuming with impatience, he refused to stay quiet any longer and left the hospital, cleared up his concerns and shipped off his belongings to Washington. As a consequence he suffered a relapse, so serious that amputation of his leg was suggested. Dr. Dan called for Fenger. The Dane, expert in endoscopy of gunshot wounds from his experience in the Prussian wars, took charge of his old student and saved his leg.

It was the middle of May before Dr. Dan got to Washington and still his leg was not completely healed. He had another relapse and had to return to Chicago. The infection that had started in the foot and spread to the veins of the leg now involved lymph vessels and glands as well. Fenger decided on the radical procedure of removing them. It meant long slow healing by granulation. Dr. Dan had little reserve strength. All summer he lay in the Emergency Hospital on the North Side to be near enough for Fenger's personal attention.

This long delay, so exasperating to the patient, was made good use of by some who were jealous of his success. George Hall, whose appointment several years before on the Provident Hospital staff had not been favored by Dr. Dan, took the opportunity to try to make matters difficult for him. He wrote the *Colored American* in Washington that Freedmen's new chief would never take his place at the hospital. The newspaper gave the letter no notice. Hall's friend James Blackever then wrote the Secretary of the Interior who was responsible for the administration of Freedmen's. Blackever called the Secretary's attention to Hall's letter, written, he said, by "an associate of Dr. Williams," and he added that he himself had been in Chicago "where I left Dr. Williams following his everyday profession." "Everyone knows," Blackever asserted, "that he is only baffling with the Department . . . at the expense of those he was sent to serve."

A small Negro sheet in Chicago took up the attack by saying

that "Freedmen's Hospital is in charge of an invalid who has drawn eight months' salary without performing a single week of service. . . . He is a fitter subject for a hospital than the management of one . . . and ought not to be a ward of the Government." The Washington *Star* joined the fray and brought up again the issue of local sovereignty:

> Believers in the equitable doctrine of home rule are properly disturbed because the Chicago doctor whom Secretary Gresham had appointed . . . is still an absentee. . . . Washington seems fated to suffer from the appointment of incompetent or careless or extremely obnoxious non-residents. . . . If Dr. Williams is unable or unwilling to assume charge of affairs at the hospital, it would be quite the proper thing for the authorities to require his resignation. Then a local physician should be appointed.

Meanwhile, to add to Dr. Dan's dejection, Traviata lay slowly dying of tuberculosis. Deprived of the distraction of work, he must have been tortured with memories of 'Viata, of their evenings together at the piano in the old home in Janesville, and later on, in Chicago. Now death would take her. Death had taken too many of those he had cherished. His father . . . Tessie . . . Ellen . . . Kittie May . . . and now 'Viata.

August dragged slowly by and the healing moved no faster. He tried riding out some each day in a carriage, but the heat oppressed him. A new abscess developed within the wound. A neglected silk suture had remained imbedded in the tissues. Completely disheartened, Dr. Dan pinned the offending knot to a letterhead and wrote his friend Gresham.

"From my sister I learn that some one has intimated to Mr. Sec'y Smith or other officials," he said, "that I have been drawing salary from the Government and have made no effort to get to Washington. I have never drawn one dollar from the Government," he declared and recounted some of the difficulties of his convalescence. "Secretary Smith," he added, "has been very, very kind to me. He fully appretiates the struggle I made for my life.

. . . I think he feels my heart is in the work, though he does not know as you do the sacrifice I made to leave everything here. I shall be deeply obligated if you will speak to him. I do not wish to be misrepresented to him in any way."

He sent another indirect answer to his detractors by issuing a somewhat premature announcement to the Chicago colored papers:

CARD OF ACKNOWLEDGMENT

To My Many Friends: After a siege of nearly six months illness, during a great part of which time I was unable to be seen even by most intimate friends and was forbidden the letters of sympathy contained in every day's mail, I am glad to be able to announce that I am rapidly recovering.

With the sincerest appreciation and thanks I desire to acknowledge the kind offers of the countless friends who by personal call, letters of considerate inquiry and other tokens of high regard, have done much to reconcile me to what at one time seemed an almost hopeless affliction. Unable to acknowledge the many favors at the time they were extended, prompts this general acknowledgment and assurance that not one word or token has failed of my most sincere appreciation and regard.

Daniel H. Williams

In mid-September, Dr. Dan was finally able to leave Chicago. He planned to rest when he got to Washington at the house in Kingman Place he had already bought for his mother and younger sisters. Just as he was leaving for Washington, he learned that a "Board of Incorporators" of Freedmen's Hospital — a paper body set up by Howard University trustees — were seeking to gain control of the hospital. Also, Purvis had filed a request with the local District government to recognize himself as surgeon-in-chief. His resignation, he said, had only been given because the federal government had demanded it. Purvis claimed that an act of Congress in March 1893 actually gave supervision and control of the hospital to the District Commissioners and removed it altogether from the jurisdiction of the Department of the Interior. But thanks to the ruling of the Attorney General, Dr. Dan's position as head of Freedmen's was confirmed.

The Howard medical faculty gathered in the college building to meet, if not to welcome, the new surgeon-in-chief. They were all white men with the exception of Purvis and his assistant, Dr. Furman L. Shadd. Dr. Dan stood to receive them with the short, thickset, white-haired Jeremiah Eames Rankin, president of Howard University, on one side of him, and on the other, broad-shouldered Thomas B. Hood, dean of the medical school.

Both Hood and Rankin were worthy men and men of good will. Rankin, author of the popular hymn, "God Be With You 'Til We Meet Again," had been for years pastor of the First Congregational Church in Washington and had welcomed there both colored and white. He was beloved by colored people. His very anxiety to give the Negro his due had led him to listen sympathetically to the grievances of Purvis when he was dismissed from Freedmen's. Both Rankin and Hood were extremely polite but noncommittal, to Dr. Dan, who looked more like a member of their race than of the race Freedmen's was supposed to serve.

On such occasions as this one, Dr. Dan's quality stood out. Husbands and wives, once they had shaken his long thin hand, retreated to the far corners of the room to peer over each other's shoulders and scrutinize the slim erect figure, so faultlessly groomed, so quietly poised. It was evident to all of them that he had been seriously ill. Dr. Dan no longer wore a beard and his thin face, clean shaven except for a heavy burnished mustache that hung well over his lower lip, was revealed in all its pallor and bony leanness. A handsome, finely chiseled face, but a little tired-looking. His hair had darkened until the reddish tinge of his youth had all but disappeared. The volatility of countenance that went with that lively color had been replaced by a quieter, more waiting attitude. Only his dark eyes were as lively, as penetrating as ever. When he looked at you he gave you his full attention.

Dan Williams,
apprentice to Dr. Palmer

Young Doctor Dan
with two companions

Dr. Daniel Hale Williams, Chief Surgeon,
Freedman's Hospital, 1894-1898

Neither of the colored doctors welcomed Dr. Dan, Purvis for obvious reasons and Shadd because of the disruption to his personal life. Purvis and his white wife lived in the city. Shadd had served as house physician and he and his family had occupied an apartment on the second floor of the medical building. Now he had to move out of these quarters to make way for Dr. Dan. He was obliged to find another home just as his wife and small son and daughter were returning from a year abroad.

When Shadd had cleaned out his belongings, Dr. Dan unpacked his books, filled the shelves and piled the overflow wherever he could. He hooked up the long green gas tube of his reading lamp, stood a demonstration skeleton in the corner, plunked down a gruesome skull on the brocaded cover of his study table beside inkwell, daily calendar, and a bowl of late zinnias from the grounds. The beflowered Brussels carpet was cheerful, there was a rocking chair in the corner if he would ever use it, and under the table he threw a pair of knitted slippers. Then he sat down to study the records.

Freedmen's Hospital and Asylum was more asylum than hospital when Dr. Dan took it over. Its Civil War past still overshadowed it, and all but the indigent of both races shunned it. Its name revealed its origin. The government had had no choice but to care for the ill and aged, the helpless and destitute "contrabands" who had flocked into the capital before the advancing armies. Various temporary expedients had been tried and finally the hospital had become one unit and adjoining Howard University another in a settled government program of relief and of guidance for both whites and blacks in what was hoped would be a planned transition from feudal agrarianism to modern farming and industry.

That magnificent program, however, had soon been abandoned to selfish interests North and South. The Freedmen's Bureau was closed in June 1872 with its work barely begun. Within two years fifty-six hospitals and forty-eight dispensaries had to be turned back to varying forms of local administration. Richmond and Washington complained with some justice that the large numbers of sick, lame, insane and blind left on their doorsteps were too great a burden. Richmond's patients were accordingly shipped to Freedmen's Hospital in Washington and the federal government continued to be responsible for the institution.

For a brief time the hospital was under the War Department, but soon was transferred to the Department of the Interior. The custom of having the head of the hospital also serve on the medical faculty of Howard University ensured the availability of hospital facilities for the use of medical faculty and students. There were also other interlocking arrangements.

The four two-story frame pavilions built a quarter century before were still in use. They sprawled over three acres and comprised four wards for men and four for women. Temporary barracklike structures to start with and since deteriorated through age, constant use, and insufficient repair, everything about the pavilions suggested the makeshift arrangements of an emergency period. Each ward, 25 feet wide and 115 feet long, was heated by a single stove. Patients near the stove baked and those far away froze. There was constant danger of fire. You could get ventilation only by opening the windows; temperature regulation was impossible. Water closet arrangements were primitive and unsanitary. Furnishings were poor and depressing.

The operating room was in the "Brick," the one solidly constructed building which housed classrooms of the medical department of Howard University, the administrative offices of the hospital, and the apartment of the surgeon-in-chief. A sixth building contained a chapel, dining room, kitchen, provision room, icehouse, washroom and engine rooms. Surgical patients had to be carried on stretchers from the wards into the open, regardless of weather or their condition, and carried back to the wards again after operation. Convalescent patients had likewise to expose themselves to the weather in going to their meals. Bed patients received trays which had been carried across the yard from the kitchen, and the food was cold.

Purvis's reports showed his long tenure had dulled his perception of inadequacies in the institution he served. Without modern hospital experience, he had accepted things as they had long been and had not sought to change them.

Dr. Dan picked up one of Purvis's last reports and no doubt a smile quivered under his long mustache as he read: "Considering that the patients are admitted from every phase of society, the order and decorum has been all that could be expected. . . . Mrs. Ada Spurgeon continues her missionary labors among the sick. . . . The rule requiring from the patients who are able some service has been continued. The following articles have been made by the women: bedsacks 16, pillow cases 140, sheets 162, towels 103, drawers 12, chemises 50, dresses 60, aprons 165, handkerchiefs 6, shirts 25, nightgowns 60."

Purvis seemed to feel no chagrin that out of 2605 patients 270 had died—a death rate of over 10 per cent. Dr. Dan must have wondered why it had not been even higher. There was no departmental organization within the hospital aside from the fact that men were separated from women and Ward 4 was set aside for "confinement" cases. Nursing was in the hands of old bandannaed mammies, untrained, many of them illiterate, unable even to tell time. That morning Dr. Dan had seen a ward mammy receive word from the office that the hour had struck, whereupon the old woman had waddled to a commanding position between the long rows of beds, clapped her hands and shouted:

"All you 'leven-o'clockers, take yo' medicine!"

What they took, or how much, or whether they took any at all, was known only to the patient and his guardian angel.

After some hours with reports and statutes Dr. Dan found that besides an almost hopelessly inadequate plant, he had inherited an historical mélange of government regulations and divided authority. He was responsible to the Interior Department for administration of the institution, to the District Board of Commissioners for the finances. He had no power over the admission or dismissal of patients and inmates. These came in on order from the Interior Department where no medical examination was made. Some were recommended to the Interior Department by the Physicians of the Poor, others by the Associated Charities, and by far the largest number by the police. Reports showed that as many as eighty to ninety inebriates could be found in the asylum at a time. In addition, the Commissioner of Pensions and the Board of Managers of the National Soldiers' Home were accustomed to ask that ex-soldiers be cared for if they were desirous of recuperating while waiting for their pensions, often a matter of three or four weeks. That year, Dr. Dan saw, 129 such "patients" had been received and supported for varying lengths of time.

Hospital grounds and buildings were situated near 6th and Bryant Streets, beyond the boundary and regulations of the District of Columbia. To the east, over the hospital's neat white picket fence, lay Cow Town, a miserable aggregation of squatters' shacks, cows, pigs, chickens and hapless humanity. Occupied by whites before the Civil War, after Emancipation these mean abodes had fallen to homeless black refugees from the South. Left to sink or swim as best they might, here they still were thirty years later. If Cow Town was an unsanitary neighbor for a hospital, LeDroit Park to the southeast was an unfriendly one. Apparently fearful of defilement by both Cow Town and Freedmen's, that fashionable area had withdrawn behind its high board fence and posted a watchman at its locked gate.

The hospital yard itself was neatly kept. There was plenty of help, of course, from the ambulatory male patients. They were free wards of the government and required to give their services. There were grass and trees, some flowers even.

The shambling plant was the worst. Somehow it must be transformed into a modern hospital.

Within three weeks after his arrival, Dr. Dan was able to report to the Secretary of the Interior that Freedmen's Hospital had been systemized into seven departments: medical, surgical, gynecological, obstetrical, dermatological, genito-urinary, and throat and chest. He had also set up those two modern adjuncts, a pathological department and a bacteriological department, though his equipment scarcely justified the terms.

Coincident with this departmental organization Dr. Dan established a nonsalaried medical staff of twenty "gentlemen who have achieved eminent success as practitioners in their respective lines of professional work." This was the system he had used at Provident. It was the system of the modern hospitals. Some of the men were doctors on the Howard medical faculty, but others were prominent in Washington medical circles. No longer should Freedmen's remain a secret festering place unknown to the medical profession of the capital city. If it had evils they must now know about them, and to know was to share the responsibility and help bring about a change.

And while he was opening Freedmen's doors to white doctors, he opened them also to colored doctors. He made his staff interracial and gave the few struggling Negro doctors of Washington an unprecedented enlargement of opportunity. He kept on Dr. Shadd as one of the attending gynecologists and Dr. John R. Francis as one of the obstetricians. Dr. Francis was an able local colored doctor who had been called in to manage Freedmen's during Dr. Dan's long illness. With it all, Freedmen's patients were no longer at the mercy of a few entrenched appointees of uncertain ability.

Immediately, too, Dr. Dan set up a system of internships to supplement the staff of twenty doctors. He was prompted, he explained to his superior Hoke Smith, Secretary of the Interior, by the economy of such a move — it did away with the need for two former paid assistants — and also because it was the best possible way to place within the reach of young colored medical graduates an opportunity for advancement which, so far as he knew, he said, was unfortunately not accorded them in any other hospital in the United States, except in the Provident Hospital in Chicago.

Over the world hospitals were becoming the real educators of medical men, whether medical schools grew out of hospitals as in France and England, or hospitals were established as laboratories to medical schools in university settings, as in Germany. Though Freedmen's had had a connection with Howard University from the beginning, it had offered students but little. As Dr. Dan saw it, Freedmen's ought to have a vital relationship to the colored race and its higher development. Waxing eloquent in his proposals to Hoke Smith, he declared that Freedmen's could be the national public training school for the colored physician; it could send him out into communities all over the country "richly endowed with practical experience and fully prepared to meet the intricate requirements of his profession."

The Secretary of the Interior was more interested in purging the pension list of fraud and in conserving the natural resources of the West than he was in conserving or aiding the colored race. As a Georgian he was committed to maintaining white supremacy in the South. He did, however, give Dr. Dan permission to accomplish what he could as long as he stayed within his budget and the legal network thrown over Freedmen's.

To meet the immediate situation, Dr. Dan chose four colored internes. At Freedmen's as in other hospitals, internes were given room and board at the hospital in return for their services. The living, plus the experience then gained, was generally considered a fair recompense for the work they did in the various departments. But Dr. Dan thought otherwise. "These men are poor," he pointed out to the Secretary of the Interior. "I feel they should be encouraged." He suggested they be given ten dollars a month compensation, but Smith said seven would have to do.

Dr. Dan had to pay his internes and finance his projected nurses' training program out of an ironclad budget. Since the two paid assistants to the chief surgeon were mainly interested in the clinical advantages they received at the hospital and since both had outside practices, he proposed to Hoke Smith that their salaries and working hours be reduced to a minimum. He would have preferred to dispense with them altogether, since under the new system of internships they were not needed. But the Secretary feared more upheaval in an already tumultuous situation; he urged "the retention of united interests." However, in the end, in order to save the nurses' training program so important to the whole project, Smith agreed that $900 might be taken out of the $3000 stipulated for the two assistants. Some money had been saved already out of Dr. Dan's salary while he was ill. Thus the funds for the new nursing program were assured.

So thoroughly had Dr. Dan worked out the course for student nurses at Provident that he could lift that plan intact and put it into operation at Freedmen's without a change. But he had another problem. His big difficulty lay in the prior existence of a so-called Training School for Nurses — a project undertaken by Howard University at the suggestion of Purvis less than a year and a half before. The Howard plan offered nothing but out-moded didactic instruction two evenings a week, with a promise of "some" practical experience in Freedmen's Hospital, and it admitted both girls and older women of varying or no back-ground to the same classes.

If he was to do anything to reduce the high mortality rate at Freedmen's, Dr. Dan knew he must first of all get rid of unfit attendants. Even if properly trained nurses were available, he had no money to pay their salaries. But carefully selected student nurses could, when supervised by a qualified superintendent and her assistants, give the bulk of the service in the hospital at the same time they were learning. Other hospitals in the country were finding this possible and it was Dr. Dan's plan for Freedmen's as it had been his plan at Provident. He advised Howard University of his views and a working compromise was arrived at. Both schools would be carried on side by side, one administered by Purvis, the ousted surgeon-in-chief, the other by Dr. Dan, the new surgeon-in-chief.

After this dubious solution, Dr. Dan appointed his superintendent of nurses, Sarah C. Ebersole. He had known Miss Ebersole in Chicago where she had been night superintendent of the Presbyterian Hospital. She was of course white, since the only colored nurses in the country were Provident's few graduates and none as yet had had sufficient experience to handle a 200-bed hospital.

His next step was to send a circular letter to all Negro centers — churches, schools and newspapers — inviting qualified young women to come to the capital and enroll at Freedmen's Hospital for training as nurses. Young women were more willing now to

undertake nursing than when he started Provident. From the
five-hundred applications which came in from all over the
country, he accepted fifty-nine. He asked these applicants to come
to Washington, bringing with them certificates of health as well
as of moral character. For a month they were on probation, and
during that time they had to pass examinations in reading, pen-
manship, simple arithmetic and English dictation. At the end of
the month forty-six had met Dr. Dan's standards. These forty-six
were now fully accepted as student nurses for the eighteen-months
training course.

In addition to board and lodging they would be provided with
caps, textbooks and notebooks, and five dollars a month.

The schedule of lectures, recitations and examinations for the
student nurses was a stiff one. Miss Ebersole supervised their practical work in the wards, teaching them both observation and re-
cording of the patient's condition. She fitted up a diet kitchen
and taught the girls invalid cookery. She taught them ventilation,
disinfection and antisepsis, and brought in a professional masseur
for demonstrations of massage. The program was on a par with
the best training anywhere; it was revolutionary for Freedmen's.

The student nurses were on duty for twelve hours each day,
but this included an hour off for dinner and additional time off
for exercise and rest. A free afternoon a week and a half day
on Sunday, with a two-weeks vacation each year, made a program
comparable to standards fifty years later. No one went on night
duty until she had been in the school three months.

Dr. Dan was a severe taskmaster. He insisted that everything
should be done in an orderly and proper manner. No nurse should
appear on the grounds without her cap. One day he stopped Kate
Gibson and said, "Daughter, you'd look better with your cap
on." Kate never left it off again. And she remembered the incident
all her life.

He called them all "Daughter" and treated them with a father's
confidence and trust. "Daughter," he said to Elizabeth Tyler as
she stood by a very sick patient waiting for his instructions,
"Daughter, this woman's *got* to live." Miss Tyler was full of the

sense of responsibility he put upon her and never forgot his words or the compelling tone of his voice, and was as thrilled as he was when the patient did live.

There was a passion in all Dr. Dan said and did — the passion of faith, the invincibility of boundless courage, the conviction of perfectibility. In his lectures to the medical students he hammered away — as well he might after his own experience — on the necessity for saving arms and legs, of always avoiding amputations except as a very last resort. "Amputation," he told them with vehemence, "is too often the easy course of laziness, impatience and incompetence." If they practiced modern asepsis intelligently, they could save limbs that in the old days had to be abandoned. "We must have continuity of the parts," he would repeat, "better a crippled leg than no leg."

He talked the subject so much that the students fell to calling him "Mr. Continuity-of-the-Parts." But they never forgot that legs and arms were precious possessions, not to be lightly dispensed with.

Dr. Dan was as rigorous with the internes as with the nurses. He said many times that an anesthetist must never take his eyes off the patient, no matter what was going on in the operating room. One day a scatterbrained young doctor allowed his eyes to roam and Dr. Dan called another to take his place and sent the offender packing from the room.

Dr. Dan was forgiven because he was as relentless with himself as with others. Not one but could testify out of his or her own observation that Dr. Dan had earned the awesome reputation he held. One or two sulked, but almost everyone recognized that he demanded perfection because he was determined to break down the prevailing belief that Negroes could not learn as well as whites. He loved his race, he wanted them to have their rightful place in life, and he demanded a performance from them that could not be criticized.

But he did not bear down on subordinates just because they were subordinates, they told each other. There was the time Elizabeth Tyler passed Dr. Dan out on the grounds as he was talking to

Old Boston. Old Boston had been a slave and he could not get over his slave ways. Though a drizzling rain was coming down, Old Boston held his hat in his hand while he bowed and scraped to the doctor. "Put on your hat, Boston," Elizabeth Tyler heard Dr. Dan say, "put on your hat, man, or you'll catch cold."

And he was as lavish with praise as blame, whenever it was earned.

All that first year Dr. Dan had trouble with the Howard University medical faculty about the two nursing programs. When Purvis saw people being won over to Dr. Dan's progressive program, he cried out that if the university abandoned "its nursing school" as he euphemistically styled his twice-a-week evening class, it would prove the initial step toward inevitable curtailment and eventual abandonment of the remaining departments of medicine, dentistry, and pharmacy. This was nonsense, but Purvis made the most of it.

At one point Dr. Dan agreed to let the university take over the course if Miss Ebersole remained in charge, but by fall he decided this was untenable and gave notice that he was going to keep jurisdiction himself. One by one members of the medical faculty came to realize the change was inevitable and, with Purvis still dissenting, they agreed to drop their competing class.

There were difficulties, too, over division of space in the one brick building occupied jointly by hospital and university. When Dr. Dan asked for a reallotment of rooms between the Dental College and the hospital, his proposal brought forth cries that the change would mean the "destruction" of the student division! However, after some months, the Dental College accepted rooms on the first and third floors and turned over the second floor to the hospital.

Funds or no funds, Dr. Dan somehow managed to get an inclosed passage built between the operating room in the Brick and the nearest ward, which he then made the surgical ward.

By January, Dr. Dan felt no further delay must prevent installation of an ambulance system. The vehicle he was able to get was not up to his standards. It looked much like a covered delivery wagon. But a lantern was hung at the back step and a horse held in readiness for the ambulance's use at any hour of the day or night. Its value was apparent when calls averaged thirty a month that first winter and spring. Smartly painted, with FREEDMEN'S HOSPITAL and the square cross of succor plain to be seen on either side, and attended by uniformed internes with the same cross on their arm brassards, it was a distinctive equipage as it sped through Washington streets.

A profound change had taken place. Freedmen's was transformed. Dr. Daniel Hale Williams might have been a long time getting to Washington, but the electric effect of his coming was manifest. A new order was everywhere apparent, and with the installation of system had come efficiency. No more loose ways. The dawdlers found him stern, but everyone thanked him for the improved meals and the nurses were grateful for new blankets and decent linens in their dormitory. Out in the Yard he had rosebushes set out. No one was allowed to touch them, but great bowls full were picked, by his orders, daily and placed in the barren wards and in the dining room and in the nurses' quarters.

Everybody had to admit that the new boss who walked so fast was businesslike. All saw it, including the hospital barber, a medical student working his way. Dr. Dan had little time to linger and chat after a haircut or shave, but he had not forgotten that he had been a barber once himself. When Duvall Colley ventured to ask him for his photograph one day after cutting his hair, Dr. Dan gave it readily enough and added that anyone who could cut *his* stubborn hair satisfactorily was an excellent barber and no mistake about it.

By the end of the year, the disgraceful mortality rate had tumbled to an unprecedented low. It was all due, Dr. Dan assured the Secretary of the Interior, to the quick intelligence, eager ambition and faithfulness to duty of the student nurses who flitted busily about the wards in their long voluminous starched skirts, big aprons, and bigger leg o'mutton sleeves.

Dr. Dan took opportunity at this point to remind Hoke Smith

that only a few of the many capable young colored women being graduated each year from the public schools could find jobs. Teaching and civil service did not offer enough opportunities, and prejudice kept them from entering the new field of stenography and typewriting, or from being clerks in stores or offices. So nurses' training, he said, was broadening the area of usefulness for a large number of hitherto unemployed girls.

At the risk of boring his superior, Dr. Dan tried to give Smith his own enthusiastic view of the new trained nurse. Just as the modern medicoscientist has advanced beyond the rural quack, he said, the modern nurse has advanced beyond the old mammy whose ministrations have done quite as much as disease to populate the other world. The physician, he insisted, must depend almost as much upon the nurse as upon his prescriptions, and the nurse best fitted for the work is one who knows about the human system, its friends and its foes, its dangers and its blessings. Dr. Dan warmed up to a great pitch when he undertook to show how an informed, comprehensive knowledge must be combined with a woman's tender sympathy to give a physician the indispensable aide he must have.

By the end of Dr. Dan's first year he might have crowed his victory from the housetops and no one would have contradicted him. But he continued to manifest a painstaking regard for the feelings of all individuals concerned. More particularly he sought to maintain an unbroken racial front before the whites. In his first annual report, while he set forth the changes and improvements in Freedmen's Hospital, he generously insisted that no account of the new condition would be true which did not properly emphasize the valuable services contributed through the professional skill and executive ability of his predecessors, one and all. He called especial attention to the efficiency and fidelity with which Dr. Francis had managed the hospital during his illness. He pointed out that the president of Howard University had taken a deep interest in the welfare of the hospital and added that the location of the medical department of Howard University within the hospital grounds had been of benefit.

In short he attempted to draw all into a position to receive credit while he played down his own role. "I can speak all the more freely," he said, "since my own management has been of such short duration as to render it unlikely that any one will be disposed to account for the improvements in the hospital service by attaching any undue credit to the present management." His purpose, he stated with charity and cheerful inaccuracy, was only that of carrying out and extending "the policy of progress and improvement pursued by my predecessor."

With endless patience and persistent demonstration, Dr. Dan had won Howard medical faculty away from the self-focused Purvis. The white president Jeremiah Rankin asked Dr. Dan to give medical service to his family, and colored Dr. Shadd found he could be a delightful dinner guest.

CHAPTER IX

"Snatched from the Womb"

FREEDMEN'S new ambulance filled an important and immediate need. Late one afternoon a call came in from Garfield Hospital to pick up an unconscious colored woman, a dwarf. Garfield said they had no room for her. When the interne arrived with the ambulance he found a note accompanying the woman saying she had been having convulsions for twelve hours and that she had been treated for "dropsy." She had another convulsion in the ambulance on the way back to Freedmen's. The frightened interne was glad to get her into the receiving room and turn her over to the assistant surgeon.

"You know they had room," he said to the surgeon. "They just didn't take her because she was colored."

"Just as well," replied the surgeon. "Now Dr. Dan can take care of her. But get him quick," he cried. "This isn't dropsy, it's childbirth!"

Dr. Dan came running. He saw on the bed before him, breathing stertorously, still comatose, the distorted, disproportionate figure of a young woman only three feet nine inches tall. Her arms were fourteen inches long; her legs seventeen and bowed. She weighed, even in pregnancy, only seventy-two pounds. Blood was drooling from the side of her mouth; she had bitten her tongue during the convulsions. Her face was puffy, the muscles twitched. While her temperature was normal, her pulse was down to 60.

Swiftly Dr. Dan took measurements. They indicated that a normal delivery could not be expected.

Convulsions at childbirth, the editor of *Obstetrics* wrote not long after Dr. Dan was confronted with this case, are a "supreme test in concentrated crisis form of obstetrical judgment as well as resource . . . we see death threatening from three directions: toxemia, convulsions and shock. We are so anxious in the short time available ere death may come, to advance our entire rescuing force — anesthesia, toxic elimination, and delivery — all at once, the result is often, in the struggle to apply each first, a therapeutic and surgical cross fire. Eclampsia is not an opponent for a novice."

Fortunately Dr. Dan was no novice. However, he had here not only convulsions which had been going on for twelve hours, but a woman who could not by her very structure give birth. His assistant had already taken a catheterized specimen of urine and sent it for analysis; that was Dr. Dan's rule. Now, with the report before him, Dr. Dan unfolded the situation to his assistants and internes rapidly but methodically.

"The specimen shows numerous pus cells," he said and explained that this meant inflammation in the kidneys and for that reason he could not undertake a Caesarean section at once as he would prefer to do. At the word Caesarean several started with surprise, but he calmly assured them that he always preferred the abdominal route to the vaginal one if surgery had to be resorted to. It saves valuable time, he explained, and consequently lessens shock. Moreover the operator has direct control of the seat of hemorrhage and infection and also, Dr. Dan pointed out, he avoids the possibility of rupture of the uterus, perforations, lacerating wounds or other serious lesions.

Dr. Dan's hearers were startled, with reason. He was voicing not the usual view of the day, but the advanced, progressive view. A dozen years before, when he was finishing medical school, the Caesarean operation as practiced in the United States was almost always fatal. When he attended the International Medical Congress in 1887, the conservatives were still against its use. Since that time, however, proper uterine sutures and wound closure had been developed. These, together with asepsis and more courage about tackling the operations earlier, before the mother became exhausted in prolonged and ineffective labor, were slowly turning the tide. Howard Kelly of Johns Hopkins was one of the earliest to achieve success and Dr. Dan had taken every opportunity since his arrival in Washington to go over to Johns Hopkins and watch Kelly operate.

So he was prepared to meet this desperate case by performing a Caesarean section, in spite of the kidney condition, because, as he pointed out, the poor condition of the pelvic tissues, the size of the child, and the almost hopeless condition of the mother allowed no hope that she could be safely delivered without surgery.

"I'll have to do a Caesarean," he said, "despite the infection." While he scrubbed his hands with laundry soap, he continued to discuss the case.

"But why not enlarge the birth canal?" an interne asked.

Dr. Dan lifted his hands from the soapsuds and immersed them in a hot strong solution of potassium permanganate. "I wouldn't even consider it," he said. He described how he had once assisted the late Dr. W. W. Jaggard in such an operation. Jaggard had separated the pubic bones by knife and chain saw. "I never have forgotten it," Dr. Dan said. "Women never recover from such an operation. They're invalids the rest of their lives."

Another interne wanted to know if it would not be justifiable to crush the baby's skull or otherwise reduce the child's bulk by surgery in order to save the mother. "No, no," Dr. Dan replied, lifting his now purpled hands and turning to the pan of saturated solution of oxalic acid which would remove the exotic stain. "The child is in a bad position for that sort of thing," he said, "and besides I think it is morally and surgically wrong to kill a living child in a living mother. We must save both."

Of course, he added, putting his now thoroughly punished hands into the waiting basin of bichloride of mercury solution, it was true Michaelis had managed to extract a child from a dwarf with a pelvis in the conjugate diameter of but an inch and a half. Barnes had done likewise. And Osborne performed the miracle through a pelvis but three quarters of an inch in the narrowest portion. But the babies were sacrificed. Those were desperate cases, performed before aseptic surgery was known. They would be universally condemned now, and should be. No, he said, the Caesarean in anything like a fair condition has taken the place of those mutilating and forced deliveries through the vagina. You could not call this a fair condition. Still he had no choice.

Quickly he dipped his almost raw hands into a basin of sterile water and slipped them into his new Halsted rubber gloves. The patient was going into another convulsion. "We can't wait to finish," Dr. Dan said to the assistant who was shaving and sterilizing the patient's skin at the site of operation. "We'd better risk infection," he said, "than let her die before we start."

As night closed in, the comatose woman was wheeled into the amphitheater before a few hastily assembled doctors, students and nurses, all agog with an excitement that was half fear and half awe. With lightning quickness Dr. Dan made an incision along the center of the patient's abdomen, beginning two inches above the pubis and ending two inches below the breastbone cartilage. As he worked, he talked in a quiet voice, master of the situation, steadying everyone around him.

"I'm not putting clamps on the bleeding points in the abdominal wall," he explained. "I want to encourage hemorrhage; it will lessen her blood pressure."

He lifted the uterus containing the baby through the incision he had made and set it down on the abdomen, quickly surrounding it with hot towels. Then he took three hasty stitches through the abdominal wall, closing it up snugly about the uterine neck. "These are only temporary silk sutures," he explained. Then he threw a rubber ligature around the uterus just above the abdominal incision, leaving it ready to be tightened, he said, if emergency should arise. Now he could turn his attention to the baby.

Swiftly he made an incision in the uterus. There was a sudden spurt. Dr. Dan's hands moved like darts of lightning. The hemorrhage ceased. He grasped the baby by the feet and lifted out into the world an infant of full normal size and perfect anatomical proportions. It weighed seven pounds twelve ounces and its head measured from $3\frac{1}{4}$ to $4\frac{1}{2}$ inches in its various diameters. A delighted murmur ran through the room and was quickly stilled.

The emergency rubber ligature was never used. An assistant controlled the uterine arteries on either side with thumb and index finger while Dr. Dan took the precaution of running a large glass tube through the cervix into the vagina and irrigated through the uterus from above downward with salt solution. He explained to the students that he was doing this to protect the patient from infection from below since there had not been time for proper antiseptic preparation. He then closed the uterine incision with three layers of sutures, the technique he had learned from Kelly. In forty minutes Freedmen's first Caesarean operation was over.

The patient suffered no more convulsions after the operation. In sixteen hours she opened her eyes and began to talk and from that time her recovery was, in the words of the record, "uneventful." But not to the small dwarf mother. Proudly she tossed her baby over her shoulder and walked the wards showing it to everyone — an offspring almost as large as herself.

Dr. Dan was constantly demonstrating now his ability to tackle a variety of complex cases. A young German farmer came from Maryland. He was encumbered by a $12\frac{1}{2}$-pound tumorous mass attached to the small of his back. It hung down a full fifteen inches — a soft, pendulous, branching affair that caused its unhappy owner to suffer constant tension and fatigue. For eighteen years the hateful thing had been growing, starting as a small flat mole when the farmer had been a boy of seven. Dr. Dan kept the farmer in the hospital ten days, observing the tumor. Finally he operated, and the farmer walked out of the hospital a free man.

About this time Dr. Dan removed a growth from the wrist of a young colored violinist, Daniel Murray, whose parents were prominent in Washington colored circles. The sixteen-year-old youth was afraid an operation might damage his bow arm, but Dr. Dan removed the growth and left the wrist unimpaired. The operation made Dr. Dan a lifelong friend of the Murrays and added to his ever-growing reputation.

Physicians in Washington began to bring Dr. Dan their complicated cases. Even members of the Howard medical faculty swallowed their pride and asked for the master hand. Drs. Robert Reyburn and J. R. Wilder brought in a woman of thirty-seven who was to have a child. They had correctly diagnosed that a tumor was complicating her pregnancy. The woman had noticed a nodular swelling in the lower right abdomen some two years before she became pregnant, but she had done nothing about it. With pregnancy and its subsequent displacement from the pelvis by the enlarged uterus, the tumor had increased steadily in size. By the time she was admitted to Freedmen's, her abdomen was so enormously distended and painful she was unable to stand on her feet. Her every breath was drawn with difficulty and her face looked pitifully anemic and haggard.

Dr. Dan examined her and found there was no free fluid in the abdominal cavity. The tumor, huge and solid, filled the entire upper half of the cavity, pushed up her diaphragm, and was responsible for her labored breathing. A urine test showed no untoward kidney condition. The patient had already borne several children without complications and the pelvic measurements were adequate. All this was to the good and Dr. Dan concluded to operate and remove the tumor and then to allow the pregnancy to continue its full term. About six weeks remained before birth was due.

The morning that Dr. Dan had set for the operation, Edith Carter, a student nurse, was coming off night duty. She recalled the occasion vividly, and years later told how she watched the crowd filing into the amphitheater. Tired and hungry as she was, she decided to go in and watch with the rest. She was glad ever after that she did, for it turned out to be an operation historic not only in Freedmen's and in Washington but in the medical annals of the country.

Edith Carter said she had never seen so many white doctors in Freedmen's before. She recognized James Tabor Johnson and swelled with pride that Washington's first white gynecologist had come to watch her race's hero. Dr. Dan, looking almost boyish in his short-sleeved white jacket and white trousers, was as cool and collected as ever, not turning a hair. She did not see how he did it.

First he tried a conservative incision from the lower end of the breastbone to the umbilicus, but the tumor was too large for that opening. He extended his incision down to the pubis. Still he could not move the growth. The tumor, he told his watchers, was still connected by a muscular pedicle with the uterus where it had originated, but it was also now attached firmly and extensively both to the abdominal viscera and to the abdominal membranes. Large arteries and veins, he explained, were radiating over the surface of the growth, throughout its pedicle, and throughout all its attachments.

It was a challenge such as Dr. Dan loved. Speedily, methodically, he tied off one artery, one vein, after another, close to the greater curvature of the stomach and along the adhesions to the intestines. When all were tied off, he incised them at the expense of the growth. Finally he made the crucial incision into the thin-walled uterus that called for the nicest blade imaginable. Perspiration poured from every pore in his body so taut did he hold himself, but his hand was steady. As he lifted his knife and everyone saw that the womb was still intact and the baby safe, a long releasing sigh filled the amphitheater. Dr. Dan placed both hands on the freed tumor, lifted the eighteen-pound mass and plopped it into the waiting basin. It filled the basin to the brim.

But he was not finished. With the huge overlying growth out of the way, Dr. Dan discovered two more tumors of considerable size embedded in the lateral walls of the uterus. These growths wedged the uterus in tightly between the bony walls of the pelvis and extended through the uterine body into the cavity. With such obstructions in the lower uterine segment and the segment flattened by seven months' constant pressure, Dr. Dan saw at once that he would have to abandon his plan to allow the pregnancy to proceed to its full-term conclusion. Normal delivery was out of the question.

"Gentlemen," he said, "I've no alternative, I'll have to do a Caesarean."

Already drenched with sweat, he raced on, made an interior median incision and "snatched the child from the womb." He handed it to the waiting nurse without lifting his eyes from the mother.

And again he had to change his procedures. The uterine walls now exposed were, he saw, infiltrated with several additional growths. He informed his audience, who felt they would never see anything like this again, that he was going on to complete removal of the uterus. With no letup, he finally finished the triple operation and proceeded with the lengthy suturing of layer after layer of tissues, taking the last stitch as carefully as the first.

As luck would have it, Edith Carter had to continue on duty again that night, but she did not complain for Miss Ebersole put her on with the new patient. All night Dr. Dan kept coming in, feeling the woman's pulse, watching over her, trusting nothing to the internes. "I never saw the patient again," Edith Carter said later, "but she made a wonderful recovery and the baby was fine. Everybody talked about it."

Other cases came to Freedmen's of pregnant women with tumors. One day an interne examined an incoming patient and said he felt the foetal heart. A staff doctor then examined her and exclaimed, "Nonsense, it's only a tumor." But when Dr. Dan's judgment was appealed to, he said at once, "It's both, a baby and a tumor." And he was right.

He seemed to have a miraculous ability to diagnose these cases of hidden complexity — complex still today when the press reports a suit brought against a surgeon who in operating to remove a supposed tumor made a mistake and inadvertently destroyed both the foetus and any future opportunity for the woman to have a child. But Dr. Dan told his students there was nothing uncanny about his diagnostic powers. You learn the human body, he said, and all will be plain to you. It just takes work.

Dr. T. C. Smith, a white physician of Washington, who had witnessed both of Dr. Dan's complicated Caesarean operations, brought them to the attention of the Medical Society of the District of Columbia. Dr. Smith said he felt very fortunate to have witnessed these operations and pointed out the unusual feature in both cases, that mother and child too were saved. Just two years previously, this same group had discussed the possibility of saving the mother as late as the third month of pregnancy, but without any hope of doing as much for the child. Dr. James Tabor Johnson had said on that occasion that Dr. Murphy of Chicago had done it at the fifth month. "It's too bad," Dr. Johnson said, "we cannot always go on to viability of the child." Now Dr. Dan had done just that, saved the child as well as the mother — in one case at the end of the full term of pregnancy and, in the other, within a month and a half of the end.

Freedmen's Hospital enjoyed an almost 200 per cent increase in operative cases the first full year of Dr. Dan's incumbency. He performed all sorts of operations known only to the specialist today — abdominal, brain and thoracic operations. Howard students had never seen the like. "Now," old Dr. Reyburn exclaimed with joy, and some ambiguity, "now, we can enter the abdomen without fear!" It was the joke of the campus, repeated on every hand.

Out of 533 operations, only eight cases died — an amazingly low mortality rate. Only one case failed to improve. Dr. Dan made no secret of what happened to cases brought to his care. It had been Purvis's habit to excuse his high death rates. He always pointed out just how many deaths occurred within ten days after patients entered, as though to say these were so poor, so ill-cared for, and so near death when they arrived that, of course, many died; they were not his responsibility. Dr. Dan scorned such tactics. He published a plain balance sheet — first, a classified alphabetized list, then the exact result obtained with each case: cured, improved, unimproved, not treated, or died. Everybody now knew exactly what was going on. And they saw not only the numbers of difficult cases being handled, but the astounding drop in mortality figures.

While Dr. Dan's great surgical victories were discussed by the District Medical Society, he himself was not invited to be present

and join in the discussion. That exclusive body never entertained
a doctor of any Negro blood, no matter how white his appearance or how high his attainments. At various times in the past,
capable colored doctors, Shadd and Francis among them, had attempted for principle's sake to breach the wall; they had always
failed.

Dr. Dan missed the professional give and take he had enjoyed
in the medical societies of Chicago. He felt, too, that the colored
physicians of the District of Columbia needed mutual conference,
interchange of thought, and the presentation of the results of experience. He well knew how important it was for the health and
preservation of lives of the community that no doctors be ex-
cluded from the consideration of public health matters. He reacted
to the problem the same way he reacted to the need for a hospital
that would train colored nurses and internes.

"Why don't we start a medical society of our own?" he asked
Dean Hood one day. "I mean a society that will open its membership to any doctor who wants to come in."

Hood explained that actually some of them had tried to start
such a society, about a dozen years before, but Purvis had held off
and the whole thing had died. "But I'll go along with you, if you
want to start up again," the dean said. "It's a good idea."

So in January 1895 the Medico-Chirurgical Society of the District of Columbia was revived by eight incorporators, three white
and five colored. The colored doctors included Dr. Dan, Samuel R. Watts, Arthur W. Tancil, Robert W. Brown and James R.
Wilder. The white men, all members of Howard medical faculty,
were Dr. Robert Reyburn, Dr. Neil F. Graham and Dean
Thomas B. Hood. If some of the lily-white doctors of the District
would rather maintain their isolation than exchange ideas with a
Negro, there were others who leaped at the opportunity to learn
from one of the greatest surgeons the country had ever known.
But Purvis still held aloof, as he had in 1884.

In December of that same year, Dr. Dan helped with the formation of a national organization of colored doctors. Like its
predecessor in the District of Columbia, the National Medical As-

sociation — which is still the only medical association in this country open to many Negro physicians — was made necessary by race prejudice.

The organization took form in Atlanta. Dr. Dan declined the presidency, but agreed to be vice-president. He gave what time, thought and energy he could to the new society. Also he talked it up among white doctors and won the support of some of them for the infant body, including his old preceptor, Henry Palmer. But Freedmen's kept him so busy that he had time for little else.

More than improved training and medical societies was needed for the success of the colored doctor. There were still few colored physicians in the country. The Negro surgeon was almost never heard of. Howard Medical School was only an evening school attempting to train men who had to work all day long at any sort of job they could get to support themselves and pay for their education. Little wonder that Negroes themselves lacked confidence in medical men of their own color.

If the Negro physician was to earn a livelihood after he had gained his hard-won training, if he was not to remain just a sundown doctor, working at a manual job by day, practicing medicine in the evening, he must, Dr. Dan knew, have more patients. And he must get them by and large from among the colored people. Dr. Dan pondered how the darker-skinned population of Washington might come to know they had doctors of their own color and that they could trust them.

Taking a leaf out of medical history, he did a daring thing. Like Andreas Vesalius, Belgian anatomist of the sixteenth century, he opened his Sunday surgical clinics to the public. Only the few seats in the last two or three rows were thus made available, too far away for the spectator to have much of a view. But it was possible for a person to sit in the scientific atmosphere and prove to himself that a colored man could operate. They could see colored assistants and colored nurses in attendance.

Dr. Dan was unprepared for the flood of abuse poured upon his open clinics. They were un-Christian, it was claimed, they were held on Sundays. They were unprofessional, they admitted the public. They were indecent, men saw women operated on. With the distance and the enveloping sheets no one really saw much of anything, but these were the arguments of trouble-makers. The press took up the affair and shouted back and forth, pro and con. Some busybodies went to Howard's President Rankin, but he refused to interfere.

Dr. Dan continued the clinics; the students had to have them — and on Sunday, the one day they were not working. However he did put the student barber Colley at the door of the clinic and instructed him to turn visitors away. But the public was now well aware that at Freedmen's there was surgical service equal to any in the country and that a colored person could go there and be treated both skillfully and considerately. White people, too, heard of the daring deeds successfully carried out in Freedmen's amphitheater. Some of them swallowed their prejudices and brought their difficulties to the famed Negro surgeon.

As the months went by, Dr. Dan was able to report to the Secretary of the Interior that changes in method seemed to have wiped out the distinction existing in people's minds between Freedmen's Hospital and others in the District. The idea of being cared for at Freedmen's Hospital, he said, had lost some of its repulsiveness with the better class of people. In fact, he told Hoke Smith, there had been a large demand for admission from those willing and able to pay. As much as $8000 could have been collected had not an antiquated law prevented the admission of anyone not penniless. Could they have been admitted, the expenses of conducting the hospital would not have been increased, while the added income would have been a great help, either toward his budget, which was only $54,000, or to form the nucleus of a building fund. Very soon after his arrival he had put plans and estimates before the Secretary of the Interior for a new building. He pleaded that since the institution was the only one of its kind under control of the government, managed by colored physicians, where colored people were received without restriction and without embarrassment, it was in a distinct sense a national institution, located in the national capital, and should, therefore, "be made typical of all that is best and highest in the public mind toward this particular class of our fellow citizens."

It was only fair, Dr. Dan continued, that Freedmen's should offer the three thousand people who came there annually, many of them from homes that afforded no comfort, no opposition to disease, the best means for recovery. Freedmen's should be up to date in every feature of its construction, have the most approved appliances, the best facilities for treating disease. The hospital ought to have a real pathological laboratory and a second operating room. It was much hampered for lack of telephone communications between wards, office, ambulance and police. It badly needed a sterilizer; he was using a wash boiler to sterilize his instruments, placing them on a tin tray perforated with holes and held above the steam by piles of bricks. Yet without these facilities they were obtaining results, he said, that were bringing bright young graduates from some of the foremost medical colleges of the country, both white and black, to enter Freedmen's as internes.

Dr. Dan told Hoke Smith that it was his belief the government could build, equip and maintain substantial brick structures at a cost but little in excess of the amount being expended to maintain the old, ill-adapted frame buildings in use. And when thus equipped with a proper plant, he wound up, Freedmen's should make no apologies nor offer any excuses for any defects or shortcomings in its management. The government and the people, he said, had a right to expect practical results. There should be no exception to the general rule because the institution was managed by colored people.

The Georgian must have wondered where this man got all his faith and enthusiasm for Negroes. Aloud he merely said to Dr. Dan that such matters could not be rushed; he would see what he could do. But he never did. Other things pressed the Secretary more.

CHAPTER X

Dr. Dan's Job in Jeopardy

WHATEVER Dr. Dan accomplished at Freedmen's Hospital was achieved despite the crosscurrents of intrigue and the uncertainties of government action, not because things quieted down. He was beset constantly by a million plagues. One day he went out to Cedar Hill and told his troubles to Frederick Douglass.

"My boy," the venerable Negro leader said when he had finished his recital of frustration and discouragement, "you say you see what ought to be done. Well, hoping will do no good, now or any time." Douglass flung back his long white locks and looked quizzically into the downcast face of his young kinsman. "There is only one way you can succeed, Dan," he said, "and that is to override the obstacles in your way. By the power that is within you, my boy," he said, "do what you hope to do."

Within a matter of months Douglass went to his grave. All too shortly the good Judge Gresham, long ill, succumbed to pneumonia. Dr. Dan had lost two good friends and strong supporters.

It seemed a time of death and change, with more and more responsibility for Dr. Dan. His older brother Price died suddenly. Now Dan was head of the family. He brought Price back from New York to be buried beside their father in the family lot in St. Anne's Churchyard in Annapolis — two Williamses among many Prices. As Dr. Dan stood beside the new-made grave with his mother on his arm and looked at the tombstones on that plot, he could not but think of the proud heritage that was his and determine to show no less courage than his forebears had shown.

His new determination was soon called upon. Another struggle lay ahead of him. In June 1896 a joint Congressional committee was authorized to investigate the management of all charitable and reformatory institutions in the District, Freedmen's Hospital among them. The committee was not organized, however, until the following February and before that date came one of the most vituperative presidential campaigns the country had ever known. Cleveland split with his party over the free silver issue and Hoke Smith split with Cleveland. Smith resigned from the cabinet in August. This meant a new appointment to the Interior Department, but Dr. Dan had barely begun to feel out a new working relationship with Smith's successor when the November elections with their defeat of the Democrats made it clear that he could only look forward to still another change in March.

The Republican victory encouraged the still smarting Purvis to undertake an energetic campaign for reinstatement — more energetic than consistent. In one breath he claimed the recent placement of Freedmen's staff under civil service was a device of the outgoing Cleveland to protect his appointees. In the next he invoked civil service status himself through the "old soldier" clause and applied to Cornelius Bliss, the new Republican Secretary of the Interior, for reappointment to the position from which, he said, he had been removed because of his well-known Republican principles.

Purvis's Republicanism was sounder than his ethics. Late in February 1897 the Washington *Bee* reported that a medical student had been discovered going round to the class due to be graduated in March requesting them to "sign a paper against Dr. Williams" and saying that if they did not they would not get their diplomas.

No sooner was Purvis's plot nipped than another difficulty arose. Dr. Dan was anxious to ensure the permanency of his reforms. So far he had had only Hoke Smith's verbal say-so and, with Hoke Smith gone, he asked for legislative confirmation of his reorganization of Freedmen's and his substitution of a non-salaried attending staff and internes for the former paid assistants. In this connection he asked that his own title be changed from the outmoded military appellation of surgeon-in-chief to the modern one of superintendent; he assumed that the position would remain a civil service one and that a satisfactory incumbent would not be removed except for cause. But the colored press, both Democrat and Republican, feared that civil service competition might eventually lead to appointment of a white man. They attacked Dr. Dan for trying to "abolish" his own job when, they said, there were few enough desirable offices open to colored men and this was one of the best.

Many a mouth was watering for the plum at Freedmen's; Purvis's was not the only one. Dr. Dan's first interne at Provident, Austin M. Curtis, who had often helped Dr. Dan scrub the operating room and with whom he had shared those basket lunches delivered by his young sister — Curtis let it be known he would accept the appointment if it were offered him. Inspired press comment said Dr. Curtis was "one of the most popular colored physicians in Chicago" and should not be kept from the job just because his wife had made herself useful to Mark Hanna, Republican chairman. Curtis may have excused his grab for his old chief's job by telling himself Dr. Dan was bound to be let out anyhow, but he did not wait for the event — or his wife did not let him wait.

Bliss may have felt that for a Republican Dr. Dan had been keeping bad company and should be punished, or, being a conservative party man, he may have resented Gresham's apostasy in leaving the Republicans to support Cleveland, and passed the resentment on to Gresham's protégé. At any rate he ordered a civil service examination held for the position of surgeon-in-chief of Freedmen's Hospital.

The announcement was a bolt out of the blue to Dr. Dan for Bliss had assured him he was not going to ask for the resignation of any of the chiefs of units under his control. Dr. Dan went around to Bliss's office immediately, but was unable to see the

Secretary. Instead he was told that Bliss understood he had resigned and had accordingly ordered the examination to fill the
vacancy. Dr. Dan hastened to see Senator James McMillan of
Michigan, Republican chairman of the joint Congressional committee appointed to investigate the District institutions. McMillan, nearing seventy, was not only wealthy and a respected force
in the party, but he was a man of integrity and sound judgment.
He listened carefully to Dr. Dan's predicament. Already he had
been looking into matters at Freedmen's, preparatory to his committee hearings, and had been impressed with the wonders recently accomplished there. When Dr. Dan had finished, he said,
"Let *me* drop Bliss a note. No one will dare tamper with a letter
from me."

In a few days Senator McMillan reported to Dr. Dan that he
had had an acknowledgment from Bliss, and the Secretary of the
Interior had assured him he would make no change in Freedmen's
management without consulting him. "There is no vacancy there
now," Bliss had added, "Dr. Williams not having resigned." The
civil service examinations, however, were held as ordered. Bliss
had asked for an examination only in Chicago where Curtis lived,
but the Civil Service Commission had added Newark and Washington. Results were not immediately forthcoming and the gossip
and innuendo, attack and counterattack went on in the colored
press. Dr. Dan proceeded with his work as best he could on the
meager assurance McMillan had secured for him.

Dr. Dan's medical and surgical schedule was heavy, and he had
to allot time for his many administrative duties. Nevertheless he
did find time for some recreation.

Once a week he ate dinner with his mother and sisters in Kingman Place. Florence, so much like himself in looks and temperament, was studying to be a kindergarten teacher on funds he supplied. He could not do much for Alice. She had outgrown the
emotional disturbances that bothered her youth and was now well
and strong, but she was not interested in books or studying. He
got her a small job in the sewing room at the hospital and there
she was content enough.

Dr. Dan liked a tennis game, when he could get it, with Henry Furniss, his Uncle Peter Williams's step-grandson who had entered Freedmen's as an interne. Young Furniss was a personable, intelligent young fellow. One day during an unaccountable lull they managed several sets running, to the delight of their audience, Charles Smiley, the prosperous caterer, and his wife, who had come on from Chicago for a visit to the capital. Mr. Smiley said he thought Dr. Dan looked thin, and urged him to come back to Provident Hospital and take life a little easier. "Sometimes I wish I could," Dr. Dan answered.

There were many persons in colored circles in the District who invited Dr. Dan to parties. They sought him out as much for his father's sake as for his own. These were men who had fought with the other Daniel Williams that bitter losing fight for civil rights after the war. Among these was well-to-do, consequential John F. Cooke on 16th Street. Dr. Dan went to the Cookes as often as he could, and sometimes to the Masons. C. M. C. Mason had long since forgiven his ex-apprentice for running away from shoemaking. In fact he had himself thrown over the family business for the church and was making a reputation as a preacher of the Gospel. Dr. Dan would tease pretty young Edith Mason and tell her he went for the doctor the night she was born, and Edith would toss her fair curls and blush. If he had had the time for it, and the inclination, Dr. Dan probably could have dined out every night in the week. His would-be hosts were from all walks of life and from both races, and many were of mixed blood like his own. A good many evenings he spent with out-of-town visitors; his acquaintanceship was nationwide and everyone seemed to visit the capital at one time or another.

Sometimes Dr. Dan's program was interrupted by the reappearance in the alcoholic ward of Paul Lawrence Dunbar. Ever since young Dunbar had come to the World's Fair to read his poem, "The Colored American," Dr. Dan had taken a warm interest in the shy, troubled youth who hid so much bitterness under his courtliness. Dunbar came frequently to wander through Cow Town, until, his heart breaking with the misery he found there, he would take to drinking and end up once more under Dr. Dan's care.

Very occasionally Dr. Dan got clear away to New York City to see his boyhood chum, the Reverend Hutchins Bishop, and his namesake, young Shelton Hale Bishop. Reverend Bishop was making St. Philip's Church his life work, but had removed his wife and children to the purer country air at Armonk.

Dr. Dan missed his week-end hunting. About the most strenuous exercise he got now was when he put on the natty cycling outfit that set his nurses chattering and went off on his high wheel with William Warfield of the first class of internes. Warfield was another blue-eyed "Negro," more Caucasian than African in appearance. He was publicly credited with being a scion of the socially and politically prominent Maryland white family of that name. At the end of his year of interneship Dr. Dan had promoted him to a staff position as second assistant surgeon and later made him first assistant surgeon. In this position he was next in authority to Dr. Dan himself, and in Dr. Dan's absence from the city Warfield served as executive. Dr. Dan was giving him every opportunity for training and experience, took him to clinics at Johns Hopkins Hospital, and used him as assistant in operations performed outside as well as within Freedmen's. Many people criticized Warfield — some of the student nurses were wary of him, called him a "heartbreaker" and a "backbiter," said he had a bad tongue, and some of the doctors thought him a pretty fool and mediocre medical man. Certainly he had twice failed to pass the Maryland licensing examination. But for once Dr. Dan seemed to have relaxed his rigid standards, for he continued to give Warfield every chance to get ahead.

Sometimes the two men would take Dr. Dan's surrey and invite Caroline Parke and Alice Johnson to go on a camera expedition to the country. Henry Baker of the Patent Office had introduced Dr. Dan to the two schoolteachers. Miss Parke had merry blue eyes and Miss Johnson had handsome aloof brown ones. Both were light-complexioned like himself and Warfield. The quartet could go anywhere and pass unremarked as far as skin color went,

and since they were all congenial their parties would probably
have been more frequent had Dr. Dan's schedule permitted.

Sometimes Dr. Dan would get to a social gathering only as it
was breaking up. He would escort Miss Parke and Miss Johnson,
who were neighbors, home under Washington's whispering elms,
cool black tunnels on a spring evening and doubtless wished as he
listened to the women's quiet, well-bred voices and their soft
laughter, that he had more time for feminine company.

Finally McMillan's committee began its long-belated hearings.
Freedmen's Hospital was not called until near the end of the sessions, after most of the charitable and reformatory institutions of
the District had been heard.

It was a sharply contrasted, sharply opposed group of men who
gathered in the stale hearing chamber late in April, and from the
Senate documents we can reconstruct the scene that took place.
Outdoors Washington was abloom with spring; inside the bright
sun ferreted out the dust and cobwebs of forgotten corners.
Of the committee of six, constituted equally from both houses and
both parties, all were present except Congressman Alexander M.
Dockery, Democrat from Missouri. With the exception of the Republican Congressman Mahlon Pitney, who was Dan's age and not
to sit on the Supreme Court bench until years later, all were considerably older than Freedmen's forty-one-year-old surgeon. Most
of the men were full-bearded and imposing in their stiff collars
and frock coats. The elderly chairman McMillan reduced the tension considerably by his quiet, unassuming manner. Senator
Thomas S. Martin was a Virginia Democrat and Confederate veteran, about fifty. Senator Charles J. Faulkner, of the same age and
party, was a West Virginian. Congressman Stephen Northway of
Ohio was almost as old as McMillan and like him a Republican,
but without McMillan's cool, intelligent objectivity.

To the group Dr. Dan might seem like a young man, a young
man called up on the carpet. But Dr. Dan was used to such proceedings. His poise as a trial witness for the City Railway of Chicago had been notable and his personal contacts for a dozen years

had included men of caliber equal to or greater than any of these. Besides, he welcomed this hearing. He had definite ideas about the position Freedmen's should occupy in the country at large and for the benefit of the colored people. He had laid them before the Secretary of the Interior more than once, but without securing the action he desired. The hearing would give him an opportunity to reach other ears.

While the hearing was not directly related to his incumbency in office, practically speaking his job was at stake. But Dr. Dan was confident of his record. He had nothing to fear but conspiracy. However conspiracy, he saw as he entered the hearing chamber, was there to be contended with. Purvis was present, and with him his close friend John R. Lynch, a trustee of Howard University. Also present were the editor of the friendly *Bee*, Calvin B. Chase, and the ministerial, white-bearded President Rankin.

The air was vibrant, but the hearing began routinely. Senator McMillan turned the chair over to Senator Martin and contented himself with listening. The older man's intelligent eyes darted from one to another as he pulled occasionally at his long gray mustache. Dr. Dan took the stand and started to read a prepared statement answering the questions set forth in the agenda: Should Freedmen's remain under the Interior Department or be supervised by the District? Should it continue its training school for nurses? Should there be a salaried hospital staff?

He had scarcely started before he was interrupted by Northway. Like a gadfly the Ohio Democrat flew from accusing Dr. Dan of turning away a colored infant whose working mother could not care for the ill child to implying next that he was somehow personally at fault because Freedmen's cared for numbers of unmarried mothers from outside Washington and illegitimate babies were abandoned in the District to become a burden on District charity. Northway charged Dr. Dan with carelessness in allowing those foreign cases to come to a hospital which he, Northway, said was set up to serve the indigent ill of the District.

Dr. Dan flung back his head. "I don't know about that, sir," he said. "Freedmen's was originated to care for the poor that came from any place in the United States and it has cared for them for years. It was not a hospital originally, it was a camp."

His voice grew deep and vibrant as he gave Northway a little history: "The poor refugee slaves were not asked where they came from. They came from all over the country and I think patients should continue to do so. There are so few hospitals that will care for the colored. It will work a great hardship on poor people dying for want of competent medical and surgical care if they are compelled to pay on the outside for services equivalent to those given in this hospital."

Dr. Dan went on and detailed the views he had so often set forth to the Secretary of the Interior. He minced no words and his straightforward presentation soon lifted the discussion out of the petty bickering of Northway to a level of human justice and compassion. When he had ceased there was a moment of silence, then Senator Faulkner leaned forward. The West Virginia Democrat's six-inch white beard and walrus whiskers jutted forward, too, his thumb and forefinger grasped the heavy gold watch chain that festooned his vest and escaped into view, thanks to his habit of buttoning only the top button of his coat. Faulkner was a friend of the Negro — he had filibustered to prevent a vote aimed at abolishing legislation which protected the Negro voter in the South — and he was impressed with this quiet, steady, white-skinned man who spoke up thus ably for "his people."

"I think the training of colored nurses should certainly go on," Faulkner said, and asked, "Are you training colored doctors, too?"

"Yes," Dr. Dan answered, "I am," and explained how with no increase in appropriation he now trained nurses and doctors, maintained an ambulance service, and conducted clinics open to both Howard University students and physicians of the city. The system, he explained, was the system used by Johns Hopkins, the Roosevelt, and all modern institutions. It was a system he was familiar with before coming to Freedmen's. "I knew it would work," he said, "and it has. We pay no salaries for assistant doctors. It is not necessary."

He wound up by saying, "I would especially like to ask the

committee to examine into my methods and the work of the hospital and then from their examination to judge of the possibilities of the future."

"But why," Faulkner wanted to know, "do you think the institution could not be run the same way if it were placed under District authority?"

Here was the moment to speak frankly, and Dr. Dan did. "Because," he answered, "I am afraid District control would result in the hospital's being thought of as a District institution and the care limited to District residents. Because I am afraid there would be a change in the national character of the educational services offered to nurses and internes."

This was a service, he told them and he did not mince matters, that colored young people were deprived of elsewhere by cruel prejudice. Moreover, he added, there were already indications that under District control Freedmen's would become the object of interminable political scrambles. Already there had been an attempt to place the hospital under District control in order to put it into the hands of a local group who called themselves a Board of Incorporators. "I would be very glad, gentlemen," he said, "if you would see fit to look into this scheme."

Purvis was almost apoplectic with restraint. Twice he had interrupted Dr. Dan and had been silenced. When he was finally called to the stand, his frustration and resentment burst their dam. "That staff Williams has is an imitation," he blustered, "just an imitation of other hospitals." There was no reason under the sun, he shouted, why the government should not pay the doctors at Freedmen's the same as it paid those at the Insane Asylum and he promised that if a Board of Incorporators was given power they would not take young men and put them in attendance upon patients without an hour's experience.

"If there is anybody on God's earth," Purvis cried, lachrymose with his own argument, "that should be experienced, it is a physician who has to attend upon poor unfortunate sick people!"

Purvis said he believed in training nurses, indeed he had been training them since 1876. The only difference he saw between his old mammies and this young upstart's nurses was that he had not hired a superintendent of nurses because the law allowed no money for that purpose and so he had drilled them himself personally.

Purvis was scarcely his own best witness. Finally he ceased shouting and sat down and Jeremiah Rankin was called to the stand. As the venerable old man took his seat, the committee looked with interest at the white president of the colored university. What would he say, to which of Freedmen's chiefs, past or present, would he cast his support? They sat there waiting and every one present knew that Jeremiah Rankin's word would have powerful weight upon the issue. His integrity as a churchman, his long incumbency of the pastorate of a distinguished congregation that had included many public men and government officials, his two decades as a trustee of Howard University before he became its president and the decade that had ensued since — all insured that whatever his judgment upon these two doctors, both, after all, on his faculty, it was very likely apt to be the final judgment of this committee. The four colored men were taut; the white men gave close attention.

Dr. Rankin began by explaining the fears the university trustees had had when it was rumored that Hoke Smith would make a change at Freedmen's. They had begged the Secretary of the Interior, he said, not to appoint a man just because he was a Democrat. The old man stopped, embarrassed. "Excuse me, gentlemen," he said, "I should perhaps not use that word. But anyhow Mr. Smith assured us he would appoint a man who would never be removed for political reasons. I think he kept his promise."

He had been very anxious, Dr. Rankin said, about his medical department and he had consequently been very observant of the changes made there. "Gentlemen," he said, "I heartily approve of them all." The room buzzed. The chairman pounded his gavel. Dr. Rankin continued steadily.

"I am a minister, gentlemen," he said, "and I speak right out." And he told them that as he now saw it the idea for a Board of Incorporators had originated with the previous surgeon-in-chief who wanted to retain his place, understandably so, he had been there some fifteen to twenty years. And he, Rankin, had agreed to be one of the Incorporators because he felt kindly toward Purvis then, as he still did. The Incorporators had met once or twice and agreed that if they got control they would retain Purvis. But so far as Dr. Rankin knew, he said, no meeting of the Incorporators had been called for some three years and he did not know by what authority Purvis was present to represent the Incorporators.

He knew the change had been very trying to Dr. Purvis, very legitimately so. And it had been trying to himself too. And he could also see now that it had been trying to the new man coming to Freedmen's. Dr. Williams had had uphill work there at first, attempting to get along without friction. But Mr. Smith had put a choice man in the job, a first-class surgeon, and he, Rankin, believed that every change Dr. Williams had made had been justified.

"And it no longer seems wise to me," the old president ended, "that the University should have any official control over the hospital."

The questioning continued. Did the students of the university have the benefit of the hospital? They did. Suddenly Faulkner turned to Dr. Dan. "Have you any politics?" he asked.

Dr. Dan was not to be caught. "No more," he answered, "than any other American. I have my own ideas about things."

"Do you take part in politics?" Faulkner persisted. Dr. Dan replied that he had never been a pronounced politician, whereupon the Senator demanded to know how he had got to Washington.

"Well," answered Dr. Dan, "I'll tell you. I was connected with a hospital in Chicago, the Provident Hospital, and on the board of trustees was that good man, Judge Gresham . . ." And he told them of the judge's suggestion that he apply for the job at Freedmen's and his subsequent follow-up of it. No sooner had Dr. Dan ceased speaking than Lynch was on his feet.

John R. Lynch had long been a Republican wheel horse. He had lost his job as Fourth Auditor of the Treasury when Cleveland came in. His private fortunes had suffered too; his wife, a beautiful New Orleans creole, had left him for a white man. In both misfortunes, Purvis had been Lynch's sympathetic friend and now Lynch was present to return the service. He was a formidable opponent and appeared with the more aplomb on the present occasion because he still had hopes that his recent "pleasant talk," as the press had put it, with McKinley would bear some tangible fruit.

"As one of the trustees of Howard University," Lynch said, "I should like to make one remark. I favor any plan that will take this hospital out of politics. It is in politics now, that is how Dr. Williams got it."

"Is Dr. Williams a Democrat?" asked Faulkner.

"The fact is," Lynch replied with relish, "there has been a good deal of doubt during the last four years as to just what constitutes a Democrat." But Faulkner would not be twitted by a doubly black Republican. "I have not known of any doubt," he declared. "Do you know of this young man's ever having voted the Democratic ticket?"

"I only know what I was told," Lynch said.

"Who told you?" asked the Senator.

"Judge Gresham," was the reply.

"What did he tell you?" persisted Faulkner.

Lynch got to his point in his own way. "As Dr. Purvis's personal friend," he said, "I did not want him turned out. So I approached Judge Gresham myself and Judge Gresham told me that he did not know Dr. Purvis, had no interest in him and had not recommended that a change be made, but that the Secretary of the Interior had informed him he was going to make a change because Dr. Purvis had made a political speech the Secretary did not like and since a change is going to be made, said Judge Gresham, 'I took the liberty of recommending Dr. Williams not only because he is competent and qualified' — all of which may be true — 'but because he is in harmony with the Administration. He followed me in voting for Cleveland.'" With this thrust, Lynch again declared that Freedmen's was a continual source of political contention. "We ought to remove that temptation," he said with great righteousness, "and place the appointing power either with the Incorporators or the District Commissioners."

As soon as Lynch finished, Dr. Rankin asked for the stand again. He deprecated the turn the discussion had taken. "This is a kind of confessional, Mr. Chairman," he said. "Now Brother Lynch will excuse me for talking frankly here. This Brother who is so adverse to having things go into politics waited on me and spent the evening going over the matter. When I told him my conclusions, that I did not think it would be wise to reappoint Dr. Purvis, or to appoint Incorporators, he then threatened to bring this charge of politics and said, moreover, that he himself was a politician and he would have a change made on political grounds. That's what he said."

"Now Dr. Rankin," cried Lynch, "let me interrupt you — " Before the Negro politican could go any further, the chairman brought his gavel down.

"Gentlemen," Martin said, "our time is up. We have nothing to do with your misunderstandings. We want to get at the facts and I think we have done so. . . . The committee is adjourned."

Perhaps in the end Dr. Dan would win out with the committee. Certainly President Rankin had stood by him magnificently. But it would be months before the issue would be settled. He needed a rest and he wanted to get as far away as possible. His good friend Charles Bentley, Traviata's husband, four years a widower, came on from Chicago and the two men went off for a quick trip to Europe. By June they were back.

Dr. Dan was soon filling as heavy an operating schedule as ever. The matter of his tenure seemed no longer a matter of conjecture, at least between himself and Bliss. Bliss assured McMillan he would await the report of his committee, expected in December, and when the Civil Service Commission reported a list of eligibles was now ready, he informed them there was no vacancy to be filled. Dr. Dan had won out against the attacks of both Purvis and Curtis and could now continue his work in peace.

Then suddenly on the first of February, a year after the Republican administration began and with it the sniping for his job, Dr.

Dan resigned. McMillan's report was still not ready and there
seemed no reason, with his victory won, why he should do so.
But he wrote Bliss that the work he had come to do — "my ardent
desire to give the patients the benefit of modern methods . . .
young colored men and women the opportunity to become
trained in medicine, surgery and nursing . . . to conduct Freedmen's on strictly business principles" — these things were finished
as far as they could be finished in the ill-adapted, dangerous buildings in use. Until Freedmen's had a modern plant, wholly satisfactory results could never be accomplished, he said. And so he
was resigning to resume his professional and business interests in
Chicago. He thanked the Interior Department for its "generous,
valuable and prompt assistance in the transaction of public business" and now stood ready, he said, to give his successor all the
information he could in regard to the work.

Bliss was taken by surprise. It was six weeks before he appointed a successor and two months before Dr. Dan was released.
Bliss asked the Civil Service Commission to certify their eligibles.
The Commission submitted its list: Dr. Charles I. West, Washington, with a grade of 91.50; Dr. Austin M. Curtis, Chicago, 79.10;
and Dr. James A. Wormley, Newark, 76.05. All were colored
men. Bliss appointed, not West of the remarkably high standing,
but Curtis whose wife had made herself useful to Mark Hanna,
chairman of the Republican National Committee. In accepting his
appointment, Curtis acknowledged the political character of his
appointment. "I assure you," he wrote Bliss, "I appreciate this recognition; it is a compliment paid the Colored people of Chicago
who are always identified with that party which champions and
administers a noble patriotism . . ."

Now Freedmen's was indeed a political football.

Alice Johnson

FOR months the Washington colored newspapers had covered the Freedmen's Hospital controversy in detail. Dr. Dan's name appeared in almost every issue. Whatever he did was news — whether he went off for a week end, performed a spectacular operation, or appeared before a Congressional committee.

On April 2, 1898, two days after Dr. Dan left Freedmen's Hospital, the *Colored American* reported that the redoubtable race protagonist, Ida B. Wells-Barnett, would address the mothers of the 19th Street Baptist Church on the moral training of the young. . . . Daniel Murray, of the Library of Congress staff, had entertained a distinguished delegation of Scottish Rite Masons at his home on S Street where salads, oysters, creams, jellies, wines, etc., were bountifully served. . . . Professor Booker T. Washington of Tuskegee Institute had spent a few hours in the city en route elsewhere. . . . But the item that made every reader gasp was the laconic three-word heading:

DR. WILLIAMS WEDS

And when startled readers saw the picture of the proud, reserved beauty, Alice Johnson, their astonishment was magnified. So those carriage rides and camera expeditions and those walks home from social gatherings with the two schoolteachers had meant something! But not many people had guessed it.

If looks were everything, few could question the forty-two-year-old surgeon's choice of the exquisite Miss Johnson, though it had long been common consent that her seclusion from society and her immersion in her school teaching meant she had decided never to marry. At thirty-nine, her beauty had become a tradition. As much as fifteen years before, children had stood entranced when Miss Alice descended from the horse cars at the corner of $4\frac{1}{2}$ and E Streets, S. W., and mutely watched her walk to the home she shared with her mother on the canal-surrounded Island at the foot of the Capitol. Even now, on the few occasions when she still appeared at gatherings, people saw no dulling of her beauty.

Alice Johnson was small and dainty, only five feet three, but, Caroline Parke said, "matchlessly formed." The Victorian mode seemed calculated to demonstrate her charms and her old friend remembered just how she looked. Her close-fitting red princess coat disclosed to consummate advantage her perfectly proportioned figure. Her long slim neck carried her large black velvet hat proudly and her modish willow plumes waved graciously to and fro as she daintily picked her way over the uneven mossy brick sidewalks, lifting sweeping skirts to reveal the smallest foot and the prettiest ankle in the District. Her photographs show an oval face, its rather high brow softened by loosely curling dark bangs over beautifully arched long eyebrows. Her eyes were dark, too, large and slightly somber; her nose was daintily pointed; while a long upper lip tried to hold firm a tremulous, tenderly bowed mouth. But this delightful face, in which the high color came and went in delicate olive cheeks, was always heavily veiled, according to Sally Fisher who had the story from her mother Cora Fisher. Only so protected could she escape unwelcome comment as she passed through the unsavory neighborhood of Mott School where she taught.

When Dr. Dan married Alice Johnson people had almost ceased to talk of her past. But her mother's death six months before and now this surprising marriage set every tongue wagging. Alice Johnson did not bear the distinguished name of her white father and to very few even of her most intimate friends did she ever mention his name. When words of the scandalmongers reached her ears — the charge that she did not even know the name of her father — she pulled her long upper lip down hard and remained proudly silent. If she wore his gifts, a gold French locket, an Italian brooch, or long dangling earrings from London, she always said she had bought them herself. The world-famous sculptor, Chevalier Moses Jacob Ezekiel, however, was neither knighted nor otherwise distinguished when his daughter was born.

Son of a wealthy Richmond merchant, young Ezekiel had grown up in an orthodox Jewish household. His father let no occasion pass by when he might protect or advance Jewish interests. Once when President Tyler referred to the American nation as a "Christian people," Jacob Ezekiel upbraided the country's chief executive for the impropriety of naming the whole by a part, and John Tyler in a lengthy letter apologized as best he could. When Virginia passed Sunday closing laws, Jacob protested the infringement of his freedom so vigorously that the law was amended. He was a stern father for a sensitive boy.

Perhaps Jacob Ezekiel's passion for justice to one minority group did not extend to another. More probably he never knew his young son had fathered a baby by the beautiful mulatto housemaid. Isabella Johnson's Spanish-like beauty and her sweet docility won the boy's heart. But what could he do — a youth writing poetry, trying to paint, rebelling against the dull trade of his father and uncles? He had no money of his own, no way to support a family even if the law would permit a marriage between white and mulatto, which it would not. He went off to his military training in turbulent '61 no doubt with a heavy heart.

When the Civil War was over, Moses Ezekiel's daughter Alice was already six years old. With her child, Isabella probably was swept on the great tide of hapless refugees out of burning Richmond and into the national capital. At any rate she was living in Washington by the time Alice entered grade school, earning a living for the two of them with her fine needlework. The Ezekiel fortune had fallen with Richmond. Young Moses returned with the defeated Greys to try again to be a merchant, but he hated

Alice D. Johnson as a young girl
about 1875

Dr. Daniel Hale Williams, 1883

Alice Johnson as a teacher at Mott School about 1890

trade as much as ever, and soon he turned, willy-nilly, to painting, and a little later to sculpture. Robert E. Lee and his wife encouraged him, as did others. Shortly he was off for Europe. For
several years he studied and lived on next to nothing. Finally he
won a prize that gave him two years in Rome.

In '74, when Alice was fifteen, Ezekiel returned to America and
secured his first big commission. It was an order from the Jewish
organization, Sons of the Covenant, for a marble group to depict
Religious Liberty and was to be ready for the Centennial Exposition in two years. He returned to his studio in Europe to execute
his sketch and that same autumn Alice entered the normal school
department of Howard University.

Two years later the Sons of the Covenant had their marble
group and Ezekiel had his money. Almost immediately these
words appeared on Alice Johnson's record at Howard University:
"Excused three weeks before close of term to go to England."

At last Ezekiel's feet were on the path to success. He could afford a home now with the woman he loved and their child, and
in Europe nothing would stand in the way of his marriage.

According to Caroline Parke, Isabella took Alice and went to
Europe, expecting never to come back. But somehow things were
not right. For seventeen years she had made her own life in Washington's unfashionable southwest quarter, unfashionable even for
colored people. Moses Ezekiel, despite his letters and occasional
visits, was a stranger now. The sophisticated circle in which the
artist moved, the alien race, the alien country — all left her insupportably lonely. She took her daughter and returned to America.

Ezekiel persisted with his sculpture and won innumerable
prizes, gold medals, ribbons of merit, and titles. His art followed
the choicest classical lines and an age that cared greatly about finish and smooth surface delighted in his skill. His works were welcomed in the Sans Souci palace, Berlin, in Westminster Abbey, in
Rome and Tivoli, and in a dozen schools and cities in his native
country. Among the portrait busts for which he became famous
was one of his friend, Franz Liszt. He spent summers with Liszt
and the Cardinal Gustave von Hohenlohe in the Villa d'Este at

Tivoli. Winters, in Rome, the Queen Mother, the royal household and all the rest of the *haut monde* were his frequent guests in the unusual studio he made for himself in the gigantic walls of Diocletian's Bath. Here he lived on after Victor Emmanuel knighted him Chevalier and Humbert made him Officer of the Crown of Italy.

His Friday open house drew artists, literary men and women, and eminent strangers from all parts of the world. His guests found him a rare personality. They called him a gifted, noble-hearted gentleman. They spoke of his simplicity and greatness, a man who welcomed all alike, famed and lowly, young students, people unknown but valued for some gift of character and heart. They talked of his helpfulness and generosity to the poor. Strange, they said, that a man of such depth of feeling should never marry.

Back in their Washington home, then at 313 F Street, S. W., the mother and daughter resumed their quiet life together. Isabella Johnson seldom went out. Her position was anomalous and she preferred to devote herself to her daughter. With almost animal fierceness she warded away harm from this beautiful, adored girl, so much like herself as to figure, so much like her father as to face and feature and soft dark locks. Alice Darling she had called her. The girl wrote Alice D. Johnson on her school papers and reddened when she was asked her middle name.

From the time she was small, Alice had to bear the taunt of being nameless. Her only retort was to hold her back straight, her chin up, and to look scornfully at her tormentors.

Silence was her weapon. She answered no questions, offered no explanations. She went off to Europe and came back and never discussed that glamorous trip, even to so good a friend as Anna Evans.

Alice was not a particularly good student. Her highest marks were in history, moral philosophy, geography and Latin. But she earned sadly low grades in arithmetic, geometry and algebra. In astronomy, botany and rhetoricals she did somewhat better. In June of '77 she was graduated. The next fall she began to teach in the first grade of Mott School, out beyond the District boundary, on Trumbull and 6th Streets, only a few squares from Freedmen's Hospital. Mott School was fairly new then, and well equipped. Its teachers were all normal school or college graduates. Alice's beauty, her taste in clothes and books, in music and art, won her good friends among intellectual young women of her own sort, mostly young women of mixed blood like her own — Nettie Langston, daughter of the Reconstruction Congressman, John M. Langston, of Virginia; Betty Cox, who soon married Dr. John R. Francis; Anna Evans, who married the scholar Daniel Murray; and blue-eyed Caroline Parke — Caddie, Alice called her — whose white blood had come from the Parke Custis manor house, but who, like Alice, preferred not to speak of painful subjects.

Even when Alice was grown up and earning her living, her mother supervised her carefully. When Alice had to come home after dark from her night school classes, her mother insisted she must have an escort. Alice was devoted to her mother and passionately resented any slight directed at her. Once when she was invited to a fashionable wedding and her mother was not, Alice refused to go. Loyal, silent, proud, she held her head high and brooked no action that might reflect on the only person in the world she had to love. When suitors flocked to her door, as they did, she expected the same loyalty from them.

Many sought Alice Johnson's hand. She had her pick of the Howard University campus, the Freedmen's staff, and the many ambitious young Negroes who poured into the capital eager for opportunities in government civil service. Rejected by Alice, her suitors married other girls, and the girls found they had no alternative but to forgive a first love so fabulously beautiful.

Finally, however, Alice made her choice. She settled upon Garnett Baltimore, a young engineer, son of one of the old mulatto families of Albany. He was handsome, well off, and altogether just right for the reigning beauty. But shortly after their engagement had been announced, Mr. Baltimore accepted an invitation to a party where Alice was not invited. He may have been softened up for this defection by the gibes of the hostess. Alice Parke's tongue was sharper and her heart harder than those of her cousin, Caddie. Alice Parke gloried that her white blood had come to her legitimately, if somewhat circuitously. "It's a shame," she cried, "that so distinguished a man as Garnett Baltimore should bestow his fine old name on that nameless Alice Johnson."

The day after the party, Caddie went to see Alice Johnson. Caddie found her friend with set face packing up Mr. Baltimore's gifts. No matter who came courting after that, she turned a deaf ear. She had gone to dancing class with Caddie at Marini's Hall. But now she was no longer seen at the winter assemblies and the germans nor on the summer boat trips down the Potomac nor at the euchre parties she had loved. Her pleasures became the Chautauqua Circle, the Ingersoll lectures, the appearance in the city of Sarah Bernhardt, Ellen Terry, Sir Henry Irving. At home she did needlework with her mother and took lessons from Sheraton in china painting. She had excellent taste and not a little talent, as the daughter of Chevalier Ezekiel should have had. Vacations she went to Annapolis to visit the Bishop girls, sisters of Dr. Dan's boyhood friend Hutchins Bishop. Occasionally she took a trip to Atlantic City with Mary Robinson Meriwether, an Oberlin graduate who had interests congenial to Alice's. In time most of Alice's friends married. When Christmas came around, she sent them some prettily bound volume, like *Pastels in Prose*, and inscribed it in her restrained, perfect Spencerian hand.

Twenty years after her graduation from Howard University, Alice Johnson was still teaching at Mott School. But Mott had grown old and shabby and out of date; the Commissioner's reports admitted the ventilation was not proper, the water closets only fair, and the light poor. Two decades in the slowly deteriorating structure, located in an unsavory district, would have discouraged anyone with less force of character than Alice. She was now teaching the seventh grade and serving as assistant to the principal. When any of the other teachers fell ill, she was quick to offer her help in catching up with grading of papers. She tried to inspire her pupils to better things. One morning after she had heard a concert by Edward Remenyi, she took occasion to try to recreate for a twelve-year-old boy the spell of the evening before.

"I was skeptical of the musicianship of any white man," Clarence Cameron White recalled years later when he had become a noted composer and violinist in his own right. "I asked Miss Alice if Remenyi could play as well as Will Marion Cook and I can still hear her laughing." Miss Alice finally was able to persuade Clarence White to go hear the famous Hungarian artist and the boy had an unforgettable experience, one from which he later dated the beginning of his own serious study of music.

By the middle '90s the young internes at Freedmen's Hospital, a stone's throw from Mott School, regarded Miss Johnson as a confirmed man-hater. They never approached her, though they admired her beauty.

One interne, more bookish than the rest, the same Henry Furniss who played tennis with Dr. Dan, discovered that Miss Johnson was a good companion with whom to read and discuss the latest books. She might be a little prim, he admitted, tied up in herself, serious — but he was serious too. His interneship was just beginning, and it would be years before he could think of marrying. Harry Furniss left romance out of his plans for the time being and found in the older Alice Johnson a safe comrade. He approved of the way she hated people who gossiped. He approved of the strait-laced life she led with her mother.

Isabella Johnson was aging now; her hair was growing white where it lay in soft waves on her brow. She would bring in the cake and wine when she thought the evening was getting on and that young men callers should soon be going home. Harry Furniss knew the signal.

Alice Johnson seldom went out now, but when she did Dr. Dan always seemed to turn up in time to escort her and Caddie Parke home. She asked Harry Furniss about him. He seemed dignified and reserved, but could he be trusted? Harry Furniss persuaded her that Dr. Dan, his kinsman, was entirely honorable. So Alice went riding in Dr. Dan's surrey, with Caddie and the assistant surgeon, William Warfield.

When Alice's mother fell ill, she consulted Dr. Dan. It was cancer. He would operate, he told her, and do his very best. Alice could not bear the thought of the hospital, and he reassured her on that point. Alice and her mother were living then in the new home she had bought at 1944 9th Street, just a block from Caddie. It was to the 9th Street house that Dr. Dan came with his young assistants, Mitchell and Warfield, and operated. He did not tell Alice it was hopeless, and at least it was temporary relief.

Soon after the operation, in May of '97, Dr. Dan had gone to Europe. After his marriage people wondered if that quick, hurried trip had not been to see Alice's father, but neither Dr. Dan nor Alice ever told. By late summer Isabella's condition worsened rapidly. On her deathbed, said Caroline Parke, she begged Dr. Dan to care faithfully for her daughter always, and Dr. Dan gave his ready promise.

The day of Isabella Johnson's funeral, a letter came to the 9th Street home. As Caddie Parke carried it upstairs to Alice's room, she saw it bore foreign postage. She handed it to her friend and considerately turned away. Alice read the letter, then threw herself in Caddie's arms. Broken with grief, her defenses down, for the first time in her life she mentioned her father to her friend.

"Oh, Caddie," she wept, "he says he hopes Mother will recover."

Life had taken one parent from her. Now death had taken the other. She went into deepest mourning and would not consider marriage under six months. Meantime Dr. Dan's sister Sally came to stay with her.

The house on 9th Street was sold. When Alice Johnson walked out of it a bride, she would be leaving it forever. The wedding was to be a quiet affair. Because of her mother's recent death, Alice wanted to wear black. But her dressmaker, a fashionable modiste from Boston, put her foot down and would not hear of gowning a bride in black. The two women compromised on a navy blue suit, with figure-fitting three-quarter-length coat, a navy blue hat, and white gloves for the ceremony, dark ones to change to for traveling.

Caddie played Mendelssohn's Wedding March for her friend. Mrs. Fannie Middleton was matron of honor. Milton M. Holland, member of the school board and uncle of Betty Cox Francis, stood in her absent father's place and gave her away. Dr. Rankin read the marriage service, assisted by Bishop W. B. Derrick of the African Methodist Church.

There were not more than a dozen guests. "Please tell them not to throw rice at us," Alice pleaded. But little Sarah Meriwether remembered that they did, and it seemed the only gay note in a solemn affair. Sarah stood goggle-eyed on the curb watching the ex-chief of Freedmen's hand his bride into the carriage and then step briskly up after her. Dr. and Mrs. Daniel Hale Williams were off for Chicago.

The new Mrs. Williams, said the *Colored American* that evening, is a lady of sterling worth, well equipped for the responsible duties she has now assumed. But privately, here and there over Washington, others said the former schoolteacher would never make a doctor's wife. Her freezing manner, they said, will drive all his patients clean away. Others, perhaps the disappointed, were sure Alice was not in love. Some even said Dr. Dan was not in love either; he really loved Edith Mason, they said. That fair-skinned disdainful butterfly tossed her head and cried, "She can have him and his money too."

Dr. Dan's friend Paul Lawrence Dunbar heard the news. He himself had recently married. Taking up his pen, the poet wrote:

TO DAN

Step me now a bridal measure,
Work give way to love and leisure,
Hearts be free and hearts be gay —
Doctor Dan doth wed today.

Diagnosis, cease your squalling —
Check that scalpel's senseless bawling,
Put that ugly knife away —
Doctor Dan doth wed today.

'Tis no time for things unsightly,
Life's the day and life goes lightly;
Science lays aside her sway —
Love rules Dr. Dan today.

Gather, gentlemen and ladies,
For the nuptial feast now made is,
Swing your garlands, chant your lay
For the pair who wed today.

Wish them happy days and many,
Troubles few and griefs not any.
Lift your brimming cups and say
God bless them who wed today.

Then a cup to Cupid daring
Who for conquest ever faring,
With his arrows dares assail
E'en a doctor's coat of mail.

So with blithe and happy hymning
And with harmless goblets brimming,
Dance a step — musicians play —
Doctor Dan doth wed today.

Whatever reservations and doubts a few Washington acquaintances might have about the marriage, everything started off well in Chicago. Old friends were overjoyed to welcome back their beloved Dr. Dan. That he brought with him a beautiful bride only added a happy thrill to the occasion. The disappointed mothers with marriageable daughters swallowed their chagrin and joined with the rest in paying tribute to their hero who had, said the press, "achieved national political and medical distinction." Charles Smiley, delighted to have his old friend back, turned his expert catering hand to the homecoming reception. The 9th Battalion Armory at 37th Street and Wabash Avenue was chosen for the event. In but a very few days war with Spain would be declared. Almost every night the Armory resounded to marching feet. But for the occasion of Dr. Dan's welcome home it was transformed by fragrant flowers, said a newspaper, "into a temple of peace."

> The reception [according to the reporter] was one of the most successful functions of the season. Music, dancing and refreshments contributed to the enjoyment of the evening. . . . Melodies from sweet-voiced mandolins emanated from behind a row of palms. Conventional attire was imperative for the men. The gowns worn by the women were elaborate. Many were Parisian creations. It was easily one of the most exclusive events ever given by the leading colored people of Chicago. The welcome extended to Dr. and Mrs. Williams was one which both appreciated. They received congratulations from 8:30 to 10:30 when a collation was served. Mrs. Williams wore a rich white brocade trimmed with pearls and liberty silk. She had diamond ornaments and carried a bouquet of bridal roses. Mrs. C. H. Smiley, the hostess, wore a novelty silk with tulle bodice and diamonds. Mrs. Lewis Warren, who assisted Mrs. Smiley in receiving the guests, wore black silk with red silk bodice.

On the reception committee was James Madden, who had so faithfully aided in the founding of Provident Hospital; the chairman was that long-time social arbiter of Chicago colored society, Julius N. Avendorph. Harry Anderson did not come. Perhaps he was feeling too old for parties. But young Bertie, a tall, broad-shouldered youth, planning to enter Northwestern University Medical School in the fall, was there to honor the man whose name he bore.

The list of the fifty favored guests who participated in the pleasures of the evening was duly set forth so that the envious might read and the program of the twenty-piece mandolin orchestra was given, number by number. Not a detail escaped mention. When the society reporter ran out of adjectives he wound up with the information that Dr. Williams and his accomplished bride would reside at 3301 Forest Avenue.

Forest Avenue, later renamed Giles Avenue, was a half century ago a pleasant, tree-shaded street, though a modest one. The joined frame houses with their high stoops were small, narrow and only two stories high. But Alice Williams made a pleasant, tasteful home there and settled down to being called upon and going calling.

Her husband plunged into his old activities — Provident Hospital, his private practice, community affairs.

CHAPTER XII

Betrayal

SCARCELY had Dr. Dan and Alice settled into their Chicago home when their busy, happy days were interrupted by reverberations from Washington. Senator McMillan's investigating committee had published an interim report stating that the Interior Department was giving Freedmen's Hospital no real management. They recommended that the hospital be turned over to a District board of charities.

If the Department of the Interior was not to lose a large institution from its purview, it must justify its right to continue its former prerogatives. Secretary Bliss appointed three employees of his own department members of a long inactive Board of Visitors to the hospital. On Tuesday, June 28, their report was ready and he gave it to the press at once. That same evening the *Washington Star* devoted two columns to the more sensational aspects of the document.

"The Secretary of the Interior," said the *Star*, "has ordered a complete reorganization of the Freedmen's Hospital. . . . Report of the Board of Visitors . . . shows a condition of affairs not only loose in method but in execution . . . strong intimations of looseness that are characterized as criminal. . . . When Congress appointed a special committee to investigate the subject of charities and correction in the District of Columbia, Secretary Bliss decided to have an investigation on his own account . . ."

The next morning the *Post* repeated the story under the heading: "GREAT ABUSES FOUND, UGLY CONDITION OF AFFAIRS AT FREEDMEN'S HOSPITAL." Immediately the Senate requested the Secretary of the Interior to transmit to it any information he had concerning abuses at Freedmen's as well as his suggestions for more effective management of the hospital. Bliss transmitted his Visitors' report in toto. Proposals for legislative action he begged to defer until the next session of Congress.

The report was voluminous. It rehearsed, though without credit, matters that Dr. Dan had sent the Secretary year after year and which only now were transmitted to the Senate. The report also recommended that payment to internes be stopped, that drastic cuts be made in the amount allowed student nurses; that both internes and nurses, as well as all other employees except five top-ranking persons, be removed from civil service classification. Worst of all, Secretary Bliss recommended a return to the old closed system of a small paid staff, with Warfield as executive officer under Curtis. There were to be no cuts in pay for Curtis, Warfield, Miss Ebersole and the clerk, but the matron was cut from fifty dollars a month to thirty, and the engineer was cut.

As if to silence forever the Lynch-Purvis crowd who had been by-passed in the appointment of Curtis, the report criticized the constant encroachment, so called, of Howard University upon Freedmen's Hospital. Dr. Dan's efforts to compromise and keep peace with the university — to have each benefit by co-operation with the other — were derogated. Instead Secretary Bliss recommended that Howard be completely dissociated from the hospital and that its medical students be admitted only at stated times and upon presentation of credentials.

The report was suspect on several counts. It largely avoided crediting Dr. Dan with its most important recommendations. And it attacked him for anything that was wrong or could be made to seem so. While necessarily admitting that "Dr. Williams enjoyed a considerable distinction in the field of operative surgery," this achievement was spoken of slightingly as his "hobby." Dr.

Williams, it was blandly stated, "evidently lacked . . . administrative ability . . . no adequate records were kept and no sufficient guard existed to insure a capable and economical administration of the hospital . . . formerly the hospital rendered quarterly reports of property to the Secretary of the Interior, but for several years now such a thing has been practically unheard of."

Before Dr. Curtis took over, the report continued, the hospital was without any written code or definite rules. Custom and tradition appeared to have been the chief if not the only sources, said Bliss's Visitors, from which the staff acquired any understanding of their duties, responsibilities and limitations. Wherewith the Secretary presented a list of rules and regulations in whose preparation he had been, he said, assisted by the "extensive experience" of Dr. Curtis.

Finally, said the Secretary, "no inventory of hospital property could be found. . . . The clerk, who appears to be a capable and bright gentleman, frankly admitted to us his own surprise at the loose methods employed. . . . The auditor's office . . . shows that large sums of money, amounting to hundreds of dollars, have been expended for surgical instruments and medical literature of which very few if any . . . are now in the possession of the hospital. . . . we will later submit a supplemental report covering the matter."

The Senate referred this astounding document to the Senate Committee on the District of Columbia, of which McMillan was a member as he was of the joint investigating committee. This was on Saturday, July 2, the first day that the colored newspapers, being weeklies, could mention the matter. The dignified, conservative *Colored American* ignored the insinuations of the report, in fact ignored the report altogether. Instead the newspaper carried a prominent story commending the state of Illinois for appointing Dr. Dan with rank of colonel to a board of notable surgeons to examine those applying to be medical officers in the regiments forming for service in the war with Spain. The *Colored American* added that Dr. Williams, who had so ably demonstrated his talent at Freedmen's Hospital and won favor among all classes by his "winning presence, becoming modesty and perfect freedom from self-assertion," would give *again* an "eminently satisfactory account of his stewardship."

The volatile *Bee*, however, was not satisfied to show its faith in such indirect fashion. The *Bee* pulled out an editorial already set on the Negro's role in the war — in its haste leaving two lines standing — and published an impassioned defense of the colored world's idol: The "smelling committee, otherwise known as the Board of Visitors," said the *Bee*, might have saved time and space in the *Evening Star* had it devoted itself to a decent investigation rather than a personal and cowardly attack on Dr. Daniel H. Williams. In the opinion of the *Bee* there had never been anyone appointed to Freedmen's who demonstrated his ability better as a surgeon or as an executive, and his honesty could not be questioned. "The *Bee* often warned Dr. Williams," that newspaper said, "of the treachery and infidelity of certain associates he had around him . . . he has been treacherously betrayed in the home of his pretended friends."

The *Bee* was only too correct. William Warfield, who had been Dr. Dan's companion on those happy excursions with Caddie Parke and Alice, who had received his special tutelage, and who had been promoted by Dr. Dan to the position of first assistant surgeon, now attacked his former chief. When Dr. Dan had left for Chicago he had invited Warfield to come on later and act as his assistant. The younger man had been glad enough to be offered a job in Chicago, should the new regime at Freedmen's bring in their favorites and sweep him out. But he knew Dr. Dan for a hard taskmaster and when he saw an opportunity to ingratiate himself with the new powers and thus entrench himself in his job, he did not hesitate. He made a lengthy sworn statement to the Board of Visitors charging his former chief with theft of medical books and instruments.

Warfield stated that instruments left by Purvis in February 1894 were in May 1898, four years later, no longer in the hospital; that others purchased on government accounts during Dr. Dan's incumbency never had got into the hospital stores, or were no longer there; and that vouchers had been paid for which no official requisition could be found.

Most of the items Warfield enumerated were picayune, of the sort that are bought in quantity and damaged rather quickly — artery forceps, Halsted forceps, curettes, scissors. Out of the twenty-seven scissors purchased, straight and curved, said Warfield, only fifteen were found in the hospital after Dr. Dan left. That a dozen pairs of scissors should have disappeared in three and a half years was taken with great seriousness by the Visitors.

A list of medical books was itemized. "None of these," said Warfield, "are in the hospital, nor ever had been as property of the hospital." He named five books and said he had seen them in Dr. Dan's room, had been lent them to read and been told by Dr. Dan they were his private property.

And so on, through twenty-six pages of testimony. Cameras, a lens, shutters, plateholders, were mentioned. Such items appeared on vouchers, Warfield stated, but there were no official requisitions. The requisition book for the period in question had mysteriously disappeared.

It also seemed Dr. Dan had sold to Warfield for fifty dollars a camera, tripod, diaphragm shutter, six plateholders, and one rectilinear lens, and that he had made a gift of another camera to Dr. Curtis. The implication was that these were government property.

Warfield's testimony was an indictment of himself, if of anybody. Of the three storerooms at the hospital, one small one had been used by Dr. Dan personally and no one had keys to it but the matron and Dr. Dan himself. Once in the chief surgeon's absence, said Warfield, he had asked the matron for the keys. His purpose, he explained, was to get a pair of trousers for a patient, though why such an article should be in Dr. Dan's personal closet was not clear. The matron had refused the key, and Warfield had had the engineer make him one. This key he had kept unknown to the chief surgeon and on several future occasions, when Dr. Dan himself had refused him access, Warfield had entered with his secret key. Thus he had convinced himself, he told the

Board of Visitors, that large stores of red flannel and white duck had been kept there which "looked like" hospital stores. These had disappeared, Warfield said, coincident with Dr. Dan's departure. Warfield's clandestine methods of obtaining his testimony seemed not to have damaged that testimony in the slightest in the eyes of Bliss's committee.

Warfield went still further and claimed that Dr. Dan had suggested he sell the unclaimed bodies of paupers who died in the hospital to Dr. Walter A. Reed of the Medical Museum and keep the money. This illegal suggestion, Warfield said, he had indignantly refused to consider. Eager as the Visitors were to hear evidence that could be used to blacken the former administration, they could not forbear asking their informer if he had reason to believe his chief would prostitute his position for private gain. "Yes," said Warfield piously, he had reluctantly come to just that conclusion. Why? Well, once when the Interior Department had asked for back reports on old soldiers staying at the hospital, Dr. Dan had said no reports had been kept previous to his own administration, but Warfield had found some old reports, and while they did not definitely classify patients they did have indications like "P. O." or "Int." after names and these, Warfield thought, meant Police Officer or Interior, and so names without such indications were probably old soldiers.

It seemed curious evidence on which to base a charge of lawbreaking, and evidently the Visitors or Warfield himself feared this choice bit had better be withdrawn. At any rate all the testimony about the cadavers was scored out before Warfield put his name to the twenty-six pages of testimony. But he allowed the charge of stealing instruments, stores and books to stand. And he also recounted Dr. Dan's offer to take him to Chicago with him, thereby implying that Dr. Dan was trying to undermine the new Curtis administration.

The day after the Board of Visitors had heard Warfield, they called in Miss Ebersole. The superintendent of nurses stated she was in charge of the operating room where the hospital instruments were kept and had made a list of the instruments. However, she said, Warfield and the internes, as well as Dr. Dan, had access to the instrument case at will. This was not backing Warfield's testimony very well. The Visitors pressed her for details as to quantities and kinds of instruments bought, but Miss Ebersole was not able to remember with the unusual definiteness Warfield had exhibited. She did have a *feeling* that there was never as large a supply of small items like thermometers, artery forceps, scissors, curettes, or tongue depressors on hand as vouchers indicated had been bought. With this vague support the Visitors had to be satisfied.

Miss Ebersole did say she felt material for shirts, gowns, towels and table linen disappeared out of the general storeroom and *must* have be 1 put in Dr. Dan's small private storeroom because "there was no other place to put it." No one sought to check up on what had been sewed up into garments, nor to take testimony from the matron who had a key to Dr. Dan's storeroom and who had refused it to Warfield. The matron was dismissed for insubordination; no one wanted to hear what she had to say.

Further questioning of Miss Ebersole attempted to show Dr. Dan had a sharp tongue. She said she had once threatened to resign because of it, but she had received a handsome apology and so she had stayed. She said that Dr. Dan had offered her a job in Chicago, too. She said she resented his assuming she would accept it. She added she had had one letter from him — "the nurses had given him a present the night before he went away, and he was telling me how he felt about it. . . . I never answered the letter." There was more than a hint that Miss Ebersole had suffered a reversal of hopes in Dr. Dan's marriage and was now reacting in classic fashion with the fury of a woman who felt herself spurned.

Harry Cordoza, the clerk, was not a very good witness. He admitted he did not know the names of instruments very well, so he could not recall ordering a calibrator, a cystoscope or a Reverdin needle. He said the requisition book that should have covered these items was lost. He had seen it in the storeroom the day after Dr. Dan left, but later it disappeared. With some prodding he was led to change his statement and say that it was "maybe earlier" that he last saw it. Warfield had claimed the book had gone "three or four months" before Dr. Dan left.

Asked who had access to the storeroom, Cordoza first said he didn't know, but added, embarrassingly enough, "I found out afterwards some people went in there I didn't know of." He was pointedly not asked who these were. It took nine pages of questioning to tie Cordoza into the implications of Warfield and Miss Ebersole that because Dr. Dan had assured them all he would give them jobs if they were dismissed in the political turnover, he was therefore seeking to embarrass the Curtis regime. Again and again Cordoza would fail to rise to the baited questions, or, led into implicating Dr. Dan, would quickly turn around and absolve him.

The Visitors protected the witnesses. Their testimony was not included in the published report. To get to the bottom of the matter, Dr. Dan hastened back to Washington and went to see Secretary Bliss. He was referred to the Board of Visitors. Fortunately he took with him an attorney, his friend Judge Jerry Wilson.

As the charges the witnesses had made were unfolded, Dr. Dan sat as if turned to concrete. When the last word was read, Judge Wilson snapped, "So my client is charged with felonious theft?"

At that moment Dr. Dan crumpled to the floor in a dead faint. Someone grabbed a newspaper and fanned him, Judge Wilson forced some whiskey between his teeth, and he was soon revived. The blow must have been almost too great for him to bear. Curtis and Warfield, his students and his friends, both men he had trained to serve their race, had betrayed him. Dr. Dan had forgiven Curtis for reaching out for his job before he left it, but now this was too much. And Warfield — with whom he had bicycled and picnicked, whom he had instructed and encouraged and even invited into his Chicago office — Warfield, a Negro and a man of his own blood, had invented this calumny and taken it to *whites* to use against him!

Judge Wilson repeated his question. Was Dr. Williams being charged with a felony? The chairman answered cautiously. The printed report, he said, stated that a comparison of the list of instruments and books bought for the hospital with the inventory taken by Dr. Curtis upon assuming control showed very few of either were in the possession of the hospital. "We have not learned," said the chairman, "what disposition has been made of this property."

Dr. Dan began to speak. With regard to the books, he said, 90 per cent of purchases were for the nurses, elementary works on nursing and physiology, Hampton's *Nursing*, Kimber's *Anatomy* and *Physiology*. "No medical man has any use for them in the least," he said. There were perhaps a hundred of such books bought in three and a half years and they were used up, lost, or stolen. "As they always are in such places," he pointed out. He mentioned that on two separate occasions the bookcases had been broken into. As for books of medical character he supposed that not more than fifteen had been bought during his incumbency, perhaps twenty at the outside. "When I was leaving," Dr. Dan stated, "I left twelve or fifteen medical books, I cannot tell how many, upstairs in my room and in the storeroom."

The Board of Visitors made no comment and he went on to explain to them what any medical man would have known. Every hospital, he said, of more than a hundred beds uses up in the wear and tear and loss of instruments from one hundred to three hundred every year. "We can't help it," he explained, "they are lost, or they are worn out. Very often, instruments break. I have destroyed twenty-five instruments in one day."

Dr. Dan explained that certain operations required valuable needles costing from eight to twenty dollars. If the eye of the needle was broken, he said, the instrument was useless. There were instruments for reaching into the pelvis; if they were broken on the ends they could not be repaired and they were unfit for further use. A pair of forceps for instance was often broken. Forceps cost five to eight dollars, more often ten. What was plainer, Dr. Dan said, than that several hundred dollars' worth of instruments, a thousand dollars' worth, should be used up and disappear in three and a half years, especially when a man was performing three hundred to five hundred major surgical operations annually? "I think you will find it amounted to more than five hundred," Dr. Dan said wearily, "if you look over the reports."

When he came to Freedmen's, he explained, the hospital owned practically no instruments. His predecessor Dr. Purvis had done no surgery. So Dr. Dan had used his own instruments. He had had $2500 worth of instruments. "I remember," he said, "I bought $70 worth at the World's Fair." And all the time he was at Freedmen's he had continued to use his own instruments, and when he went away he went away short, with only $2000 or $2100 worth. Any surgeon who had a full complement of instruments found, he explained, that he had a shrinkage of from $200 to $300 a year in his instruments — from loss, wearing out, or from theft. At Freedmen's a great many instruments were lost.

"I lost some of my most valuable instruments," Dr. Dan stated. There would be an emergency case brought in, staff and students would gather to watch, he would be engrossed with the patient, and when the excitement was over he would be short several more instruments. "No one could help it," he said, "but since I was using my own instruments in the service of the hospital I had permission from the District Property Clerk, Mr. Beckett, to replace such losses and breakage from hospital purchases. Even so, I went away $300 to $400 short."

The chairman was set back. Beckett would undoubtedly verify Dr. Dan's statement. He tried another tack. "Why didn't you make an inventory report to the Interior office?" he demanded.

"Because my instructions were to make my quarterly reports to Mr. Lewis," rejoined Dr. Dan.

"Who was Mr. Lewis?" peppered the chairman.

"Mr. Lewis," patiently replied Dr. Dan, "is Superintendent of Charities for the District of Columbia." The Visitors could not have remained ignorant of this fact, but they had chosen to ignore the yawning gaps of divided jurisdiction when they complained in the public press and to the Senate that "for several years such a thing as a quarterly report to the Secretary of the Interior has been practically unheard of."

Warfield's charges were shot full of holes, but the examiner angrily kept on, trying to find at least one item he could pin on Dr. Dan. He pulled out random vouchers, some two and three years old, and barked his questions. Did Dr. Williams ever purchase such and such and on what date? Dr. Dan answered with but partial attention. He seemed almost not to care whether he made a proper defense or not. "I really don't know," he answered, "I think so. . . . No, I don't remember."

The chairman picked up another voucher. "I see that on April 2, 1897," he read, "one Kelly's cystoscope, one calibrator and one Reverdin needle were purchased. Do you remember anything about them?"

Dr. Dan apparently tried to collect himself. "I remember the Reverdin needle," he said. "Don't remember the cystoscope. I have so many in my own stock."

"Did you ever see any cystoscopes in the hospital?" was the next question.

"I left several in the hospital," Dr. Dan answered.

The examiner wanted to know whether any cystoscopes had ever been bought by the government for the hospital and Dr. Dan said he could not tell him. "Then," argued the questioner, "the cystoscopes left in the hospital were *your* property?" Dr. Dan replied dully that he could not tell, they might be, but he did not think so.

"Please try to reflect, doctor," prodded the chairman. "Do you know whether any calibrators were bought for the hospital?" But Dr. Dan could not remember. "I know I had one or two calibrators," he said, "I brought them with me when I came."

"And did you buy any of these instruments for your private use while you were in charge of Freedmen's?" the chairman persisted.

"Yes," Dr. Dan finally said, "yes, I remember now, I bought Kelly's cystoscope — from Truax in Chicago."

"But did you ever buy one from Gilman here?" the chairman

wanted to know. Dr. Dan did not remember. "Or a calibrator?" Still he did not remember.

"Well, you do remember a Reverdin needle," the chairman said. "Was it bought for the hospital?"

Here was something in all this tangle that he could hold on to. "When I bought my collection at the World's Fair," said Dr. Dan, "I bought a very valuable Reverdin needle. I broke it in Freedmen's Hospital and when I reported the matter to Mr. Beckett, he told me to replace it."

The chairman wanted to know if he bought it from Gilman and Dr. Dan answered that he didn't remember. Then the chairman asked whether he took a Reverdin needle from the hospital when he left and again he said he didn't remember.

Warfield had sworn that he had never seen a cystoscope or a calibrator in the hospital at any time and that he first saw a Reverdin needle in the hospital after Dr. Dan's return from Europe in June 1897. But Dr. Dan remembered he had brought both cystoscopes and calibrators with him and had bought a Reverdin needle at the Fair, broken it in Freedmen's, and replaced it. The voucher was dated April 2, 1897, he had appeared before the joint investigating committee on April 22, and had not gone to Europe until afterward. Despite his state of shock, his memory agreed with the records; Warfield's statement did not.

And so on, and on. Did Dr. Williams remember that six tongue depressors had been bought on July 19, 1897? No, he did not. The procedure was absurd to the point of being nonsensical.

Warfield had made much of a voucher showing that a Zeiss lens and a diaphragm shutter worth $72 were ordered from a local dealer, later returned as unsatisfactory and other items taken in exchange — including a 5 x 7 Montauk camera worth $23 and a 5 x 8 rapid Universal lens worth $36 and a diaphragm shutter costing $15, plateholders and miscellaneous items to total $72. Warfield's implication was that Dr. Dan had kept these items and sold them to him, while at the same time he had made a gift to Curtis of another camera purchased by government money.

Dr. Dan admitted freely enough that he had sold a camera

and accessories to Warfield, but insisted it was his own private property he had sold, though he could not remember exactly when he had bought it. He denied he had ever given a camera to Curtis; he had left one in his room because it was hospital property, but he had not made a gift of it to anyone.

At this point Judge Wilson evidently sought to cut short the nonsense. He asked to insert a statement in the record and was granted the request. He turned to Dr. Dan and asked: "Dr. Williams, did you ever purchase any property of any kind whatever and pay for it out of government money and then convert the property to your own use?"

"No," Dr. Dan answered, "I did not. I went away $300 to $500 short on my own property."

And with that flat statement the two men left. The matter of the bolts of material was not brought up and the cadavers were not even mentioned.

Fortunately Dr. Dan was able to find in his papers receipts from Bausch & Lomb showing payment by his personal check in May 1895 for the lens and shutter sold to Warfield. The next day these were identified to the Visitors by their serial numbers. He could not find his receipt for the camera, which was about five years old, but the Visitors did not press the subject further. Bliss never forwarded their report to McMillan. McMillan was only confirmed in his conviction that Freedmen's Hospital should be taken away from the Secretary of the Interior and placed under a District board of charities and he so recommended to the Senate.

On Saturday, July 23, three days after Dr. Dan had his interview with the Visitors, the irrepressible *Bee* devoted its entire front page to the surgeon. His picture appeared heavily garlanded with ornate borders and underneath was this paragraph:

COL. DANIEL H. WILLIAMS

This distinguished surgeon, formerly surgeon-in-chief of the Freedmen's Hospital, arrived in this city this week. He received a great ovation. He called upon Commissioner

J. W. Ross, Secretary Bliss and others who assured him that he had their confidence and respect. Several receptions and dinners were tendered him by admiring surgeons, physicians and friends. Col. Williams is the first colored man in the United States to be appointed surgeon for the army.

Dr. Dan had successfully defended his honor, but when he boarded the train for Chicago, he must have felt bewildered and disgusted. What had happened to the colored people? he might well ask himself as he was carried westward across the state where the Williams clan had fought so valiantly for the common dignity. Where was the mutual concern and loyalty he had been taught from boyhood? To be sure, this was a new generation, a generation not refined by the fires of common suffering, but rather corroded and poisoned by repression. If whites continued to prevent colored people from making the most of themselves, what recourse had they but to turn and rend somebody — each other, if not their oppressors? So he might try to excuse Curtis and Warfield, but again this had been the kind of blow he apparently had little power to withstand — a blow from his own people.

In Chicago he told his wife he would not take any assistant into his office. He would not even have a girl to answer his telephone or keep track of his appointments. Some thought he was frugal to the point of penuriousness. More likely the truth was that he dared permit no one in close proximity to his affairs again.

CHAPTER XIII

Destroying Myths

THOUGH he had been away four years in Washington, Dr. Dan had kept in close touch with Chicago so it was easy to pick up the reins again. He had left young Howard Chislett, his white assistant, in charge of his old office at 31st Street and Michigan Avenue. Now Chislett relinquished the two small rooms and went elsewhere — to become a surgeon of standing and a credit to his colored teacher.

Dr. Dan must have moved back into the familiar quarters with a sigh of satisfaction. Here he could be his own man again, a surgeon and nothing else, free of sordid politics, ready for work and professional give and take among his peers — and color lines seldom drawn.

"Dr. Dan's back" — quick as lightning the word went around. He had never been absent from their thoughts. When he had performed a spectacular operation at Freedmen's, the news was on the wires and in Chicago's Negro press the next day, down to the smallest detail. Now patients, both black and white, crammed his reception room and even swarmed on the stairs. Soon he had cases, his wife wrote a friend, in five hospitals at once.

He had remained on the board of trustees of Provident and had been active in Provident affairs all during his stay in Washington. On the spot, Dr. Dan's close friends Lloyd Wheeler, James Madden and Charles Bentley had never slackened their work for the institution they had all built together. Bentley, as secretary, took over all correspondence. Clarence Darrow, who had been Dr. Dan's patient, came on the board and he and Wheeler divided their attention between the beauties of nature and the problems of Provident as they cycled through the countryside on Sundays. Julius Avendorph arranged baseball games and the gate receipts swelled hospital funds. Jenkin Lloyd Jones continued to lend his encouragement. Despite all these, it was necessarily Dr. Dan, the physician and surgeon, who was the guiding mind in the affairs of the institution.

Herman H. Kohlsaat and George Webster, two of the hospital's wealthiest white supporters, also trustees, several times had called him to come to Chicago when they felt his advice was needed. The new building had at last materialized in late 1896. Kohlsaat had given the land on the corner of 36th and Dearborn Streets. It was seven blocks farther south, but the cable cars now ran to 39th Street and only below that point were horse cars still in use. The location was excellent. Armour paid for the new 65-bed building with its "complete and superior operating room." There was an enlarged dispensary; it could serve six thousand patients a year. George M. Pullman, Marshall Field and Otto Young purchased two adjoining properties; a nurses' home would eventually be erected on them.

Early in the fall Webster had taken satisfaction in writing Dr. Dan that "the interior work of the Hosp'l is progressing & it looks as if by Nov'r 1st the whole building will be ready for occupancy. In the meantime the col'd people have arranged a 'house warming' the latter part of this mo. & I am at work in regard to the Furnishing." A few weeks more and the momentous move had been made to the new quarters — "material realization of *your* dream," Webster wrote Dr. Dan. Armour had made a speech. "He talked all about Dr. Dan," later recalled James Gordon of the original committee; "he said, 'You be proud of him.'"

Despite the fine new building, all had not gone smoothly. A man of really big caliber was lacking. Very soon Webster had written Dr. Dan that there was dissatisfaction over the recent medical appointments. A month later Kohlsaat had urged Dr. Dan to come to Chicago for the holidays and look into the matter. The men who had given so much did not want the usefulness of their gift dissipated.

So all were delighted when Dr. Dan came back to stay. "We need men of your stamp here," Kohlsaat said. Dr. Dan was again Provident's chief surgeon. How much Dr. Dan was needed at Provident was known to no one at the time. It would have taken a prognosticator of unusual powers to foresee what was ahead, and Dr. Dan was far too busy to look for trouble.

But trouble was present in the person of George Hall.

At that time George Hall's motives were not plain. No one knew of his letters to the Washington newspapers attacking Dr. Dan during his long illness. But those letters were the opening guns in a battle to which Hall gave continuing pursuit — imperceptible at first as he was feeling his way, but increasing in momentum as events played into his hands.

George Hall was a big man, dark-skinned and heavy-featured. He was ambitious, fearless and full of boundless energy, quick to enter a fight, to defend what he felt were his rights. He seemed to feel that the original reluctance to accept him on the staff of Provident Hospital was a personal affront rather than a professional rejection of his Eclectic diploma.

He did, however, attend evening classes at Harvey Medical School and brought back an allopathic diploma. The most tangible stumbling block to his progress was thus removed. When Dr. Jaggard died and Daniel N. Eisendrath was brought in to head the obstetrical department, there was no longer any concrete reason why Hall should not be advanced from the children's department to assist him. A year later, he was allowed to move still further up, into gynecology.

But advancement through professional attainment was slow and Hall, though intelligent, was not brilliant. He had other means. Ingratiation was an art with him — a compliment here, an innuendo there. He made himself *persona grata* with Nina Price, the superintendent of nurses. That young white woman, daughter of wealthy parents, had chosen in missionary spirit to work among the darker race. In her fervor for good works she was perhaps indiscriminating about the wronged folk she sought to serve. Hall delighted her with his affable ways and his eagerness to co-operate with her. She saw no reason not to believe in him and spoke well of him when occasion arose, as a superintendent of nurses is in such excellent situation to do.

With white lay members of the board of trustees, Hall got on well too. Agreeable, full of good cheer, never openly obstructive to anyone, he seemed to them a fine young fellow, somewhat flashy in dress and careless in grooming, perhaps, but creditably ambitious. They were glad to help him get ahead. They knew nothing of what was apparent to some of the colored professional men — that Hall was tricky. He seemed always to have something on people. He made a point of watching a man's movements, attempting to discover his secrets, if he had any, something to hold over a person he might want to influence. But the white men knew nothing of this and the colored men who did see it kept silent out of race loyalty.

While Dr. Dan was away a vacancy had occurred on the board of trustees and Hall had secured the seat. He managed, too, to get on the executive committee of the staff which ran the institution in Dr. Dan's absence. Later this staff committee was replaced by a house committee, appointed by the board and responsible directly to it. This house committee was the center of power and policy for many years and Hall was never off it after that moment.

Dr. Dan upon his return made no move to go on the house committee. Instead he went on the finance committee, the fund-raising committee where he was particularly needed but where he was not involved in the actual operation of the institution. Under pressure of many other commitments, still prone anyhow to want younger men to have their chance, Dr. Dan did not push himself into the daily routine of the hospital. It was a serious omission, but he more than had his hands full.

One of Dr. Dan's first jobs after his return to Chicago was to examine recruits for the 8th Illinois Regiment — the old 9th Battalion now expanded for service in the Spanish-American War. This was the first colored regiment to be entirely officered by colored men. He might have been major of the medical department on active duty, but went on the examining board instead and Governor Tanner commissioned Allen A. Wesley in his place. Dr. Dan with two young colored doctors — Wilberforce Williams and James R. White — examined 1500 men in a few days.

Wilberforce Williams had finished his interneship at Provident Hospital three years before; James White was but just through. The young men knew themselves to be green and inexperienced, but they soon lost their self-consciousness with Dr. Dan. Under his quiet courtesy toward them, they relaxed despite themselves. "He never made me feel inferior," White said years later.

Young White appreciated Dr. Dan's encouragement all the more because, from another quarter, his self-confidence had been shaken. White was engaged to be married and George Hall had taken the occasion to remark to his fiancée that if she were interested in that young interne White she better get him to go back to Tennessee where he came from. "He'll never succeed here in Chicago," said Hall, shaking his head knowingly.

Hall's words had been cold water to the youth's aspirations until Dr. Dan came along. But with the great surgeon evincing faith in him, White decided to take a chance and stay on in the big city. Only years later, when he was well established, did White realize that Hall's motive had been to safeguard himself from possible encroaching competition. Hall made a point of advising Provident's internes to start up anywhere else but Chicago. Fortunately Dr. Dan had come back and was soon encouraging the young colored doctors to gather regularly for reading and discussing their own papers, as he had in Washington. It was true enough, he said to James White, that in Chicago colored men had entree to the Chicago Medical Society, the A. M. A., and so on, but they had special problems of their own and they needed to discuss them together.

Soon Dr. Dan was as much at the service of the colored community as in the old days. He rendered free medical service to the newly founded Old Folks Home on West Garfield Avenue. He made speeches and urged a more generous support by colored people. "We are well able to take care of this home," he pleaded, and reiterated his constant proud thesis: "We need not be dependent on white people."

With half a dozen other prominent colored Chicagoans — S. Laing Williams, E. H. Morris, Commissioner Edward H. Wright — he threw himself into the organization of the ill-fated United Brotherhood Fraternal Insurance Company. It was to be a liberal interracial institution built on a national scale. Dr. Dan wrote a friend that it was the most comprehensive and promising business proposition colored men had ever entered into. He was so enthusiastic about it that when the first executive pulled out after a year, he allowed his own name to be used in an effort to bolster the organization. The time was ripe for such a venture and within a year or two other such companies succeeded, but one of the founders of the United Brotherhood absconded with the funds and this project failed.

One of Dr. Dan's biggest services to the colored community lay in the position he maintained in white medical circles. With everything else he did he still managed to attend professional society meetings and join in the discussions. Indeed, after the circumscriptions of segregation in the national capital, he must have thoroughly enjoyed these contacts with his fellows.

After his report on his heart operation, which he had finally published four years after the event, in the spring of 1897, Dr. Dan had no opportunity to do any medical writing. But away from the turmoil of Washington and ensconced in a restful home with a book-loving wife who wanted no more social life than an occasional lecture or evening at the opera, Dr. Dan settled down to evaluate his now extensive surgical experience.

In December after his return to the Middle West, he presented at a clinical meeting of the Chicago Medical Society the case of the unusual *molluscum fibrosum* he had removed at Freedmen's from the German farmer's back. Dr. Lamb, who had prepared the specimen and had shown it to the Medical Society of the District of Columbia soon after its removal, forwarded it to Chicago. Dr. J. M. Beffel in the Northwestern Pathological Laboratory made several microscopic slides and Dr. J. Nevins Hyde presented a photograph of the gross specimen to the American Dermatological Society. Altogether the 12½-pound tumor, thought to be the largest of its kind operated upon in the United States, had widespread notice. Dr. Dan's paper was published first in the *Chicago Medical Recorder*, journal of the Chicago Medical Society, and later was reprinted in the *Philadelphia Medical Journal*.

The same evening Dr. Dan presented this matter, he also presented two others of interest. The first was a repair of hernia of the bladder through the groin. The case was rare and had led him to search the literature on the subject. These findings, together with his own, he presented to the society. The other affair was a specimen of a large branching uterine tumor that consisted of a half dozen masses the size of an adult's fist and larger, with many nodules varying in size from a bean to a hen's egg. Some of the tumors were imbedded in the walls of the uterus; others were attached to the outer surface. This multinodular growth had complicated a five-months pregnancy. The situation had been referred to Dr. Dan when the patient was already in an extremely unpromising condition and the diagnosis had been difficult to make. He had been able to determine the fact of the pregnancy, but, in the end, he had found it necessary to remove both uterus and tumors. His case drew much interest and the journal *Obstetrics* reprinted the paper.

Dr. Dan's vast experience with uterine tumors at Freedmen's had led Stillman Bailey, his office neighbor, to ask him to prepare a statement on surgical treatment of such cases. This Bailey had read, while Dr. Dan was still in Washington, before the Clinical Society of Chicago along with his own paper on medical treatment of uterine fibroids. In that statement Dr. Dan had emphatically contradicted the prevailing opinion that colored women harbor fibroid tumors more frequently than white women, or that fibroid tumors were the prevailing disease in black women.

Now he spent some time working up another paper which he presented to the Chicago Medical Society on December 26, 1900, and in it he proceeded to dispel yet another medical myth. Colored women, he declared, definitely do develop cystic tumors of the ovaries, the same as white women. The contrary statement had been made by professors in the best medical schools of the country since the time of MacDowell. So strong was the belief that even when a tumor presented all the features of an ovarian cyst, a surgeon would say that, since the patient is a Negro, this cannot be a cyst, it must be a tumor of some other origin. Dr. Dan, however, had seen 1301 cases of tumor sent to Freedmen's in his three and a half years there, and had operated on 210 of them. None of his hearers could doubt that he had not only developed a skill worthy of the better-known names of DeLee and Kelly, but that he had gained an over-all picture that gave him authority for his thesis.

Dr. Dan was pleading for the scientific, laboratory approach. The myth, he said, would undoubtedly have gone on unchecked had not methods of study and diagnosis changed. "He is an indifferent surgeon," declared Dr. Dan, "who would *today* extirpate a tumor and base his diagnosis on the naked-eye appearance of the specimen." Fifty years earlier a distinguished operator might express an opinion on a pathologic specimen and never be questioned. But now, said Dr. Dan, the opinion of the most learned operator in the world would not be accepted until the specimen had been worked through a pathologic laboratory and a written report submitted on it. Dr. Dan was putting the case boldly, more ideally than was yet true; he was pushing for progress.

It was a fine paper, illustrative of the true detached scientific spirit. It showed extensive experience and intensive research and was not without humor. He assured his hearers that not only fair-skinned Negro women, but dark-skinned ones too had now evoluted to the cyst-bearing stage. And, anyhow, he took occasion to say, of twelve million Negroes listed by the Census Bureau not one fourth were full-blooded. It was a well-known fact, he said, that in the same family were often found brothers and sisters — black, mulatto, and white — born of the same parents. "The color of the skin in this country," Dr. Dan blandly pointed out with forgivable relish, "furnishes no correct index of the purity of the blood of a colored person any more than it does the purity of the blood of a white person." So, he said, it might be pertinent to inquire if this interesting question was to be confined to Negroes of black skins, brown skins, olive skins or to any shade of color. "Who is to determine," he asked, "where the line is to be drawn?" He then referred them for a further study of the relative shades of color in native Africans themselves to a colored plate in Meyer's *Konversations-Lexikon,* published in Leipzig, giving types of all the principal tribes of Africa. "That plate," said Dr. Dan, "shows complexions varying from a clear mulatto to those of ebony black."

While some of his hearers were doubtless smiling sympathetically and others were frowning with annoyance, he proceeded to work in some pertinent observations as to why so few ovarian tumors had been found in Negro women in the past. "Before the war and for years afterward," he said, "little attention, if any, was paid to the surgical diseases of the Negro. Very few had been operated upon, and very small was the number of hospitals in the South for either white or colored people . . . a ruptured cyst, a twisted pedicle, or a hemorrhage would cause death and only by an autopsy would we be acquainted with the real cause." Or if a colored woman did go to a doctor for examination, he pointed out, too often her case was given faulty diagnosis. Many cases of ovarian cyst were wrongly treated as dropsy, as Dr. Lamb's autopsies showed.

Dr. Dan went on to speak of the appalling mortality in cases of removal of ovaries in the early days of operation. At that time, when septic infection was almost a certainty, even white women preferred to carry their tumors, have them tapped, and worry along until death relieved them of their burden. It is no wonder, he said, that the poor colored woman, unable to receive the advantages of proper diagnosis and treatment, died without operation. There was no place where she could present her case for a full hearing, and little or no attention was ever paid to her condition. Doubtless hundreds of them, he said, have had their cysts and died a natural death rather than an operative one. Fortunately the situation was changing. With the advent of hospitals for the colored and the training of colored physicians and surgeons, Dr. Dan said in conclusion, with a bow to his confreres, the investigation and study of diseases in the colored race inaugurated by the white profession was now being continued by colored scientists.

To some doctors present, Dr. Dan's paper was an unwelcome declaration of colored independence. Albert J. Ochsner, known for a sly unctuous manner, tried first to demolish Dr. Dan with insincere compliments, and then to undermine him by attacking the studies made by Howard Kelly at Johns Hopkins, studies which Dr. Dan had just been quoting. Wrapping his barbs neatly in false humility, he presented them in his best mortician manner.

The points the doctor had made, said Ochsner, are undoubtedly of great practical value; they are based upon an unusually large experience, Dr. Williams must be looked upon as an authority. "My own ignorance," said Ochsner, "is founded on the lectures I have heard and the books I have read and also every Negress I have ever examined has had fibroids, consequently I thought the various authors must be correct."

Ochsner was powerful. To cross swords with him meant retaliation or frustration somewhere along the line. But Dr. Dan did not hesitate. Sarcasm was a game two could play at. He delivered his own thrust neatly, then followed it with a barrage of evidence that won him the battle of the evening, whatever it might do for his future opportunities at the hands of so powerful an adversary.

First Dr. Dan disposed of Ochsner's false humility. He did not doubt at all, he said, that only women who had fibroids presented themselves at the Postgraduate School for treatment. But he had perhaps had as large a gynecological experience as anyone in the Postgraduate School. For four years he had had charge of a hospital of two hundred beds and had made over one thousand pelvic examinations each year and had had reports from as many more. "Not five per cent of the colored women who presented themselves," said Dr. Dan flatly, "had fibroids."

While Ochsner blinked helplessly, Dr. Dan continued without mercy. Dr. Ochsner might be correct about Dr. Kelly's enthusiasm, he said, nevertheless there was no denying that Dr. Kelly was in a position to study these cases more accurately than any other man in this country. Also Kelly did not go into the pathological laboratory himself and examine these cases. "I have had some experience in Johns Hopkins," said Dr. Dan, "and I know these specimens are removed from the operating room and examined in the laboratory by entirely different men." With due deference to Dr. Ochsner's opinion about Dr. Kelly's methods, Dr. Dan said, his own personal knowledge of the man and familiarity with his surroundings inclined him to give Kelly's opinion some weight. And therefore he would continue to cling to the ideas he had already expressed and would not question the methods employed at Johns Hopkins.

Dr. Dan's paper was reprinted and commented upon in various Eastern journals. But he was not invited to join the Society of Clinical Surgery which Ochsner, with Will Mayo and Harvey Cushing, founded three years later.

In March 1900, not many weeks after his tilt with Ochsner, Dr. Dan was guest at a meeting of the Chicago Gynecological Society when Albert Goldspohn read a long and controversial paper on the Alexander method, which he favored, for surgical repair of certain displacements of the uterus. Lengthy, heated discussion followed. Dr. Dan presented some experience that indicated caution would be appropriate. Then Reuben Peterson remarked that he could only wonder at the greatness of Dr. Goldspohn's diagnostic ability if he could always tell by bimanual examination what there was within a pelvis. He always told his students, he said, that what was found by bimanual examination and what was found after the abdomen was opened were very apt to be entirely different. Dr. Dan seized the opportunity to support Peterson. It was refreshing to him, he said, to hear a man say he did not know what pathology there was in the abdomen before he opened it. "It is seldom," said Dr. Dan, "that.such a frank expression is made before a medical society." Dr. Dan was always in the vanguard now, always pushing the old fogies to the wall, and apparently thoroughly at ease among his associates as he did so.

A few months later Dr. Dan was again a guest of the Gynecological Society. This time he presented a report of the two complicated Caesarean sections he had performed in Washington three and a half years before. Most of the discussion at the meeting swung upon the question of whether or not such operations were justifiable. One critic thought Dr. Dan should have attempted, in the case of the dwarf, to enlarge the pubis surgically and extract the child by the normal route. Another critic admitted that special conditions had made the operation necessary, but he argued that otherwise it would be a doubtful procedure with convulsions present.

The noted Joseph B. DeLee had engaged in the discussion throughout. Now he arose and backed Dr. Dan on both counts. Only yesterday, DeLee said, he had not done a Caesarean section on a mother with convulsions and now he wished he had. He had considered it, he said, for she was attempting to give birth to twins. The foetal heartbeats of both were strong in the morning when he had examined her. But he had dismissed the idea. Her labor had lasted until seven in the evening, and, while she had survived it, both babies had died.

"Had we done a Caesarean section in the morning," the honest man confessed, "both children and mother might have been saved."

Courage is better than conformity when it is coupled with skill and directed by a passion for saving lives. Dr. Dan was showing them the way and DeLee was great enough to recognize it.

Dr. Dan sometimes discussed his papers with his office neighbor Charles Kahlke before he presented them. He liked Kahlke's quick and darting mind, so in accord with his own, and he could not but respond to the man's evident friendliness. When Kahlke asked his advice concerning a contemplated real estate investment, Dr. Dan gave it readily. "It was canny advice, too," said Kahlke years later.

Soon the two doctors were off shooting quail and partridge together out of Michigan City. Once or twice they went with Dr. H. B. Woodward and Dr. C. Gurnee Fellows on a fishing trip to Rice Lake. His white companions liked Dr. Dan's strong face, strong jaw and yet reticent, soft-spoken manner; and they liked the way he quietly ignored any discrimination that came his way. Dr. Dan's friendships were based on congeniality, not race. Among his colored friends, Julius Avendorph and Robert L. Taylor were his frequent week-end companions.

Dr. Dan resumed his hunting and fishing with immense satisfaction. The elemental joys of forest and stream were in his blood, the blood of his Indian forebears. Away from the city and pressure of people, he was at peace. He would light the last of the three Little Tom cigars he allowed himself in a day and enjoy its fragrance while the others talked.

Bringing his trophies back to town he persuaded Alice to hang their dining room walls, not with pictures, but with four particularly brilliant specimens of pheasants he had first shot, then stuffed with his own hands. Guests never failed to exclaim over the splendidly marked birds, the sole decoration in the room.

Dr. Dan needed these week ends all the more after his schedule was further burdened by his appointment to the attending staff of Cook County Hospital. His old classmate, Dr. Charles Davison, was on the staff, as were Drs. William E. Schroeder, Thomas A. Davis, and the colorful Weller Van Hook, pioneer in surgery of the genito-urinary tract and ardent theosophist as well. However, the big showman dominating everything was John B. Murphy. In contrast Dr. Dan, on the same service with Murphy, stood out for his opposite qualities. Kindness is not a characteristic always exhibited by the older staff toward the younger men, and the internes, among them James M. Phalen, years later editor of the U. S. Army surgeons' organ, *The Military Surgeon*, were grateful for Dr. Dan's gentle courtesy.

At St. Luke's Hospital where Dr. Dan had many white patients, he had opportunities too, and used them, to be kind to another young interne, Dr. Frank W. Van Kirk. Van Kirk's father had been Dan's friend in the old days in Janesville and he was glad to be useful to the son.

Dr. Dan went back to Janesville occasionally now and took his beautiful wife to spend week ends with his old classmate, James Mills. Frank Pember was not there; he had failed in health and gone South. Mills, the Scot, was dividing his time between medicine and the temperance cause. Occasionally Mills came up to Chicago and he and Dr. Dan attended a class reunion. Sometimes Dr. Dan served on the committee. Returning to Janesville, Mills would drop into the *Gazette* office and insert an item:

QUARTETTE OF LOCAL DOCTORS
GRADUATED A SCORE OF YEARS AGO

Dr. D. H. Williams, the prominent Chicago surgeon, Dr. Frank Pember, Dr. James Mills and the late Dr. Hugh Menzies, all of this city . . .

What Dr. Mills's small sons could never understand was why their father's white-skinned visitors were Negroes. Even today they remember how quick were Dr. Dan's every move, his conversation, his darting bright eyes. And how very fond their father was of his old associate.

These were pleasant interludes in Dr. Dan's heavy schedule. Relaxed among these old friends, perhaps he occasionally strummed a guitar once more and sang Carrie Jacobs Bond's new song, "I Love You Truly." Carrie was Ida Williams's stepsister, and the song was written right in Janesville, on East Milwaukee Street.

Alice Williams enjoyed greatly her first experience of living in the North. It seemed marvelously unrestricted to one who had suffered the color line all her life. "What I like about Chicago," she wrote back to Washington, "is its *Freedom*" — and she underscored the word. Later she found race prejudice was not lacking in the North too. She returned home one day in great indignation. Some white woman on the trolley car had refused to sit by a colored woman.

"So I went right up to the poor thing and sat by her," she reported. Since Alice Williams showed not the slightest trace of her African blood in her appearance, her act could only be taken as the reproof it was meant to be.

All agreed that Dr. Dan had chosen a most beautiful woman for his wife. Her taste in dress was strikingly simple and set off her loveliness to every advantage. Years later women remembered exactly what she had worn and the date when she wore it. "The first time she came to call on me," said one, "she was all in white, with a big white hat, a little black velvet bow at her neck with long streamers, and a black velvet bow on her hat . . . it was the summer of 1899, after she lost her baby."

The baby that might have made so much difference in the lives of Alice and Daniel Williams did not reach this world alive. Everything that could be done was done. Dr. Dan's friend DeLee, who saved so many babies, could not save this longed-for little creature; only his great skill saved Alice. Dr. Dan could not hide his grief. He wept unashamedly in Otto Schmidt's car one day when in the company of Schmidt, Frank Billings and DeLee. John Mallet, Schmidt's chauffeur, came home and told his wife.

Alice Williams was ill a long time. "I went to the very brink of the grave," she wrote Caddie. But in the Victorian manner, out of consideration for the circumstances, people did not call or talk of the disappointment. Afterwards Alice never mentioned the subject to Chicago acquaintances though she wrote an intimate Washington friend that she was still hoping for a child. Dr. Dan never told her how drastic DeLee's operation had been and that she would never have another baby.

Her ordeal over, Alice regained excellent health though she had to admit that she had grown stouter. Whenever she wrote to Washington she could not help but remember that there were those back East who had doubted her capacity to be a good wife to a busy and popular doctor. One day she sat down and filled sheet after sheet of her engraved notepaper in a long letter to her first schoolteacher, Sarah Fleetwood.

"When I came," Alice wrote in her even copperplate hand, "I determined that I would help my husband keep his friends and that I would aim to have them take me into their hearts. They were quite ready to do so. They were anxious to see what manner of woman 'Dr. Dan's' wife was. Much to the surprise of my Washington friends — " she put a question mark after the word — "who predicted that I would not make a physician a good wife, I have made," she ended triumphantly, "a pretty good one. I miss my associations in Washington very much and often find myself thinking wistfully of them. But there are so many compensations," she finished, "I have made hosts of friends."

If the local press was any evidence, Alice Williams had little time to herself. "Mrs. B. K. Bruce will be guest of Mrs. D. H. Williams," said one issue. A few days after she had entertained the widow of the famous colored Senator, the newspaper reported that "Mrs. Dr. Daniel H. Williams gave a very instructive talk at the Phillis Wheatley Club on how to teach the children of the sewing school in a more systematic and methodical way, and showed the ladies samples of work done in the sewing schools of Washington, D. C."

And then in another few days, Mrs. Williams had turned over her home to the King's Daughters for an Evening of Shakespeare. The entertainment was to raise funds for charity and so twenty-five cents was collected from each one present. Violin solos and numbers by the Crest Trio opened and closed the evening and were interpolated throughout the program. Alice Williams had worked conscientiously over her paper on "Some Women of Shakespeare" and doubtless it did show, as the society reporter said, "evidence of the highest mark of intelligence," but people perhaps enjoyed more the production of the courtroom scene from *The Merchant of Venice*. Richard B. Harrison, a clerk in the post office, put enough passion into his Shylock that evening in Dr. Dan's parlor to explain his later Broadway success as De Lawd in *Green Pastures*. Antonio was portrayed by Albert George, somewhat later Chicago's first colored judge, and Portia was played by Mrs. George C. Hall — towering, red-haired, effervescent.

After the program everyone flocked into the dining room and was served refreshments by maids and pages costumed in pink and white. The whole first floor of the house was decked out with pink and white "cut flowers," the reporter called them, and scintillating candelabra. Altogether it was an occasion long to be remembered and the newswriter carefully recorded all names. Julius N. Avendorph of course was master of ceremonies, as he was for every major event in the colored social scene. On the committee were the wives of Dr. Dan's old friends and associates at Provident Hospital, including the new Mrs. Bentley, formerly Florence Lewis, another booklover like Alice Williams, and Harry Anderson's new wife, the former Julia Settles. Harry Anderson had found life lonely with all his children gone from home and had married for the third time.

These women did not ordinarily welcome the aspiring Mrs. George Hall, whose laughter and clothes were both apt to be a little loud. But the King's Daughters was a church group, open to everyone, and Theodocia Brewer Hall was a King's Daughter. Besides this was an entertainment for charity and all bars were down. However, when Dr. Hall called for his wife, unfortunately the housemaid left him standing in the hall holding his hat and failed to invite him into the parlor, while she fetched his wife. George Hall was sure it was an intentional slight and told one of the doctors Dr. Dan should pay for it some day.

It was not the same Dr. Dan who had come back to Chicago from the pain and disillusionment of Washington. To old friends and adoring patients he was unchanged, still their tireless friend and advisor, the one to whom they inevitably turned in trouble. Newcomers, however, found themselves somewhat diffident in Dr. Dan's presence. As he walked along the street in his eternal black suit and black derby, black topcoat added in colder weather, his long, narrow black shoes with the toes a little turned up, looking as though they had been polished, as they doubtless were, by himself — he was a somber figure. And he was forever lost in thought, with his shoulders bent forward, his head down and his gait compulsive to some inner drive. He saw no one, so absorbed in study would he be. To get his attention, he must be spoken to. Then if it was an old friend, he responded warmly and cordially, and even occasionally indulged in a mild sort of witticism. To someone less known to him, while he was always polite, there was something remote, cool even, in his courtesy. His manner sometimes repelled sensitive persons, already awed by the fame that now attended his name, while to envious persons this man was arrogant, a snob.

In contrast George Hall seemed a fine man, jolly, full of anecdotes. He was popular. He got on committees easily, went into politics, was a wonder on the platform. He understood crowd psychology, knew how to sway large groups, became a public figure. You perhaps had the key to all his activity when you heard him orate to a younger man: "These doctors who stick so hard to their doctoring, it wouldn't hurt their business a bit if they mixed around more, got on some committees."

Negroes who did not see what harm he was doing — and few did — came to look upon George Hall as a great fighter for the race.

Moses to Negro Medicine

WITHIN a few months after Dr. Dan's return to Chicago, on three separate occasions, colored women traveled up from Alabama and Georgia to be operated on by him. Southern Negroes desperately needed medical care. Forbidden entrance to white hospitals, or treated offensively when they were admitted, or worse still treated as guinea pigs, they died by the thousands annually. Dr. Dan's soul revolted against this cruelty and human waste. To change white prejudice was hopelessly slow. Negroes themselves, he felt, must exert greater effort to advance medicine and nursing within the race.

He decided to urge again upon Booker T. Washington the need for a medical and surgical center for the colored in the South. It was a matter he had already suggested, but without success, to the Tuskegee Institute principal, now turned national Negro political leader.

These two Negro pioneers, exactly of an age, both educators and organizers, yet so different in background and temperament, had met in 1895. Even before that Dr. Dan, Lloyd Wheeler and other prominent Chicagoans had given support to Booker T. Washington and his struggling industrial school. They had sent money, magazines and clothing. At the Cotton States Exposition in Atlanta, where Dr. Dan helped organize the National Medical

Association and where Booker Washington made his famous con-
ciliatory speech to the Southern whites and won leadership of the
race, the two men met, if they had not met before.

A couple of years later Booker Washington, already a candidate for the political mantle of the late Frederick Douglass, visited Freedmen's Hospital and afterwards wrote Dr. Dan that he
had never seen anything done under the supervision of a man of
their race that had given him so much encouragement. "I was not
in your hospital two minutes before I saw as I had never seen
before, what you are," he declared and then asked Dr. Dan if he
could spend two or three days at Tuskegee showing them how to
get their "medical and nurse training departments" on a proper
footing.

Tuskegee's medical facilities consisted of a two-story frame
cottage set aside as an infirmary for sick students. There was no
training of nurses in the modern sense. Dr. Dan leaped at the
chance to turn this infirmary into a real hospital and training
school to serve not only Tuskegee but all the area round. To his
mind the need was so clear, the means for meeting it so ready to
his hand, that he never stopped to guess Booker Washington might
not have the desire to go so far.

Dr. Dan wrote the Tuskegee principal that he had a scheme
that would be almost self-supporting. "You could draw work
from all over the South," he said, "and build a Monument there
and care for thousands of those poor people who die for the want
of surgical attention." And then, probably as a gesture of generous reassurance, he added, "I would stand for the success or failure of the work."

It now looks as if this last remark proved disturbing to Washington, who was just beginning to taste the delights of leadership.
Tuskegee Industrial Institute was still small. Booker Washington
wanted his own project to grow up before adding a tail that
might outwag it. If there were to be any Monuments, Tuskegee
itself must become one first. To get Dr. Dan down there for three
days of advice was a different matter from having so forceful an
organizer about too long. So he asked Dr. Dan to train an interne

to run his little infirmary and evaded any idea of expanding it into a community hospital.

But Dr. Dan could not forget the vision he had caught of another hospital for his race, a hospital needed even more than had been Provident or Freedmen's. Again he wrote Booker Washington. Patients had come to him, he said, all the way from Alabama. They had talked of colored people back home, dying for lack of care. Would it not be a good idea, Dr. Dan asked Booker Washington, "to develop at Tuskegee under *your* direction a *self-paying* institution? Many who would come for treatment could pay for it. And the progressive colored physicians of the South would flock to Tuskegee to take advantage of the opportunities *you* would offer them for their development."

All that colored men want, Dr. Dan pleaded, is the opportunity. They made the best soldiers in the world, he reminded Booker Washington — it was but a few weeks past that colored infantry had rushed in to save Theodore Roosevelt's Rough Riders and to take San Juan Hill — and they would make the best surgeons too, given the proper chance to learn. He offered to come at stated intervals to assist. "I think it is a great field," he ended, "and one that would pay its own way. Give me your idea of it." And then he added cordially, "When you come to Chicago, come to see us."

Booker Washington came to Chicago in October and Dr. Dan wrote him again, addressing a note to his hotel. Again he assured Washington he was interested in *his*, Washington's, plan. He said he had talked it over with some wealthy Chicago people and they thought highly of it. He hoped to discuss the matter with Washington while he was in the city. "Could you spare time," Dr. Dan wrote, "to take dinner with us at 5:30 any day but Wednesday?"

Even with this self-effacement on Dr. Dan's part, even with all the eloquence he could bring to bear, Booker Washington was not to be won. He left the city without seeing Dr. Dan or expressing any interest that funds might be available for a healing and teaching center for his neglected people. He wrote only that his time was more than taken.

Fortunately others were not so indifferent as the politically ambi-

tious Booker Washington to what Dr. Dan had to offer. Within
a few months he was approached by George W. Hubbard, aging
white dean of colored Meharry Medical College in Nashville.
Dean Hubbard came, at the urging of two colored doctors on
his staff, R. F. Boyd and F. A. Stewart, to lay claim to Dr. Dan's
services.

Meharry Medical College, "dedicated to the worship of God
through service to man," had begun educating Negro doctors ten
years after Emancipation. Nashville, like the national capital, had
become a center for Negro education as a result of the influx of
colored refugees there during the Civil War. The religious con-
science of the country had sent a throng of missionaries South in
the wake of the Union armies. At Nashville efforts to feed and
clothe the hungry and naked were followed by the setting up of
schools in churches and other buildings hastily prepared for the
purpose. Three denominations vied with each other in the good
work and out of it grew as many universities: Baptist Roger Williams University; Methodist Central Tennessee College; and Congregational Fisk University.

All birth is wonderful but none more so than the travail out of
which was brought forth these war-begot Negro universities. First
the hungry and frightened refugees, naked or in tatters. Then, no
sooner fed and clothed, these eager men and women begging the
long-denied privilege of learning to read and write. The first year
there could be only a first grade, and all ages sat on the rude
benches together. Next year there were both first and second
grades. Each year a new grade was added. Finally a normal department could be set up for those who were now ready to turn
around and impart the cherished knowledge to others. A theological department would come next, thanks to the churches.

Some colored men began to inquire whether they could not
learn to be doctors. Central Tennessee College organized a medical department ten short years after its primary school had been
opened, safeguarding the venture by requiring all students to take
an oath not to drink, swear or divulge the secrets of the dissecting
room. In time the theological and literary departments of the col-

lege, rejuvenated briefly as Walden University, faded away. The medical department survived, thanks to aid from the five Meharry brothers, and in their honor the school was renamed Meharry Medical College. By the turn of the century, Meharry had graduated 410 persons, fully half the doctors who attempted to serve the colored South.

Dean Hubbard was anxious that with numbers there should be no flagging in quality. Though Flexner's exposé would not come for a decade, the reform wave was on in American medical education. Meharry Medical College had always given an honest training. Meharry was founded to meet a definite need. Its teachers had been earnest and enthusiastic. Now problems of standards, staffs and curricula were agitating the medical educational scene the country over and there were to be many fatalities among medical schools, white and colored.

Dr. Dan agreed readily enough to go down to Meharry as visiting professor of clinical surgery for a week or ten days each year without recompense. Ever since he left college he had been teaching as well as leading an active life as doctor and surgeon. He loved to teach and he was a master before whom clinical students, and older men too, sat spellbound. His techniques were unerringly at his command, his judgments came unhesitatingly, his explanations were clear and fluent. Above all he passed on to those who sat before him his own passion for knowledge. At Howard University he had touched one of the two main nerve centers of surgical education of the Negro. Now, fortunately, at Meharry he would touch the other.

He threw himself into the work with zeal. The situation, however, demanded more than a yearly visit from him. That visit could not be effective without hospital facilities. A temporary operating room could always be rigged up, but patients must have postoperative care, and no colored doctor or interne was allowed in the hospitals of Nashville. Meharry had struggled along without bedside instruction, either medical or surgical, as long as it could; its continued existence as a proper medical school demanded practice facilities and continuing care of patients.

The faculty recognized the problem. Dr. R. F. Boyd, a courageous, self-made man, first president of the National Medical Association, had done what he could. Some years previously he had opened up two "hospital" rooms in the basement under his offices. Here a few obstetrical cases could be attended by Meharry seniors before they went out to attempt professional work. The last Meharry *Announcement* had pointed with pride to these "excellent" clinical privileges. It was a great advance over nothing at all. In one of these dark basement rooms, by lamp and candlelight, Dr. Dan performed four successful operations on his first visit to Nashville. But these were scarcely the quarters for a clinic and they would scarcely impress the Committee of Standards of the American Medical Association.

Before he left Nashville, Dr. Dan had a frank talk with Dean Hubbard in the presence of Boyd and Stewart. There was no use, he told the dean, educating colored men to be doctors if they could not give them interne training. A young man who has had the advantage of the hard practical drill received in a hospital, he said, is ten years ahead of the man who is deprived of that advantage. If the white hospitals of the South would not accept colored internes nor permit colored physicians to practice in the hospitals, then there was only one thing to do. "We can't sit any longer idly and inanely deploring existing conditions," he said. "*We must start our own hospitals and training schools!*"

Hubbard was doubtful but Stewart and Boyd listened attentively as Dr. Dan recounted how Provident was started.

At the end Boyd asked, "Will you come down here and tell that story to our people here?" Boyd had worked for years as a bricklayer and a janitor to get his own education; he knew what could be accomplished when the will was there.

"We'll gather them in, if you'll just talk to them as you've talked to us here today," Stewart cried, and added slyly that he would arrange some quail shooting on his brother-in-law's farm.

Soon after New Year's Day 1900, Dr. Dan went back to Nashville. All day after his arrival — his talk was not scheduled until evening — a half dozen Meharry instructors tramped with him over the brown fields and in and out of the copses on the W. H. Compton farm, attended by the faithful soft-eyed bird dogs. Dr. Dan enjoyed his hunt and won the lasting admiration of his host. Years later Mr. Compton recalled what a "splendid shot" the great surgeon was.

That evening, before a capacity audience of his people gathered at the Phillis Wheatley Club, Dr. Dan began to speak. Every city in the South, he said, with a population of 10,000 colored people should have a hospital and training school. There was no education, he pointed out, which would yield such permanent and practical results as training young colored women to be nurses. Aside from the fact that a young woman was personally benefited, given an opportunity for lucrative employment, she was made a useful and valuable member of any community where she might live. She taught people cleanliness, thrift, habits of industry, sanitary housekeeping, the proper care of themselves and of their children. She taught them how to prepare food, the selection of proper clothing for the sick and the well, and how to meet emergencies. "In short," said Dr. Dan, no doubt stirring the imagination of more than one woman in his audience, "I consider the trained nurse the most desirable addition to a community, not excepting the school teacher."

He told them how highly the colored trained nurse was regarded both by some of the best families in the land and by the most distinguished surgeons. There had been doubts, he frankly said, as to whether young colored women had the ability to stand the test of emergency, to preserve composure at the operating table, to learn the techniques of surgical preparation and the details of the operating room. But, said Dr. Dan beaming upon them, it has been amply demonstrated that colored women make excellent nurses. Only seven years ago, he told them, Provident had sent out its first class of three graduate nurses. Now there were two hundred, and as many more in training. What better way was there, he asked them, to escape the prejudice that kept down an educated, refined colored woman than to enter nurses' training?

The way was open wherever a colored community started a hospital.

"You can and you should," said Dr. Dan, "establish such an institution in Nashville at once." He did not let them think things would be too easy. "You will have many discouragements to contend with at the start," he warned them. "Lack of confidence," he said, "has always been a deterrent in our relations with each other." The ignorant and naturally suspicious would have to be induced gradually to relinquish their unquestioning faith in the infallible skill and judgment of the white man. "On the other hand," he cautioned, "we must demonstrate our right to confidence."

He mentioned other things they had not thought of. The first requisite to the successful formation of any undertaking, he told them, was that those who entered into it should be unselfish and firmly of the opinion it was the right thing to do. They must examine themselves, he said, and determine to their own satisfaction that they had the qualities within them, or among them, for organization, industry, perseverance and self-sacrifice. After that they might select a leader — someone with influence and enthusiasm. "Bring to that leader," said Dr. Dan, "all the support possible."

After they had elected officers and assigned to each the work for which he was best fitted, then they could start to raise their first money. Go about it systematically, he said, cover the field. Few people would refuse to contribute something towards the support of a hospital. And by all means, he said, make an early start, however small. "It is better to start in a small way and grow," said Dr. Dan, "than to commence with a flourish and dwindle down to a failure."

He explained that a hospital of twenty-five beds, properly managed, was almost self-supporting. He advised them not to attempt to build a hospital right away. "Rent a house," he said, "of ten or twelve rooms, preferably one with a basement, furnish it modestly, so that it can be easily cleaned and kept clean. Select a level-headed graduate nurse for superintendent. . . . Appoint upon your staff the best physicians obtainable. . . . Have your head nurse appoint as student nurses as many well educated, well-mannered young women as can be accommodated." As always he set a high standard for personnel. It was the cheapest in the long run, he said. "Then, when you have completed your preparatory work," he said, "open your doors and your success will be assured!"

"Before the founding of Provident Hospital," Dr. Dan told them, "there was not in this country a single hospital or training school for nurses owned and managed by colored people . . . that was nine years ago . . . now there are twelve! And without a single failure!" These were facts to stir an oppressed people.

As Dr. Dan looked down into the rows of black faces, he may have thought back to his early days in Janesville. He may have seen in memory Harry Anderson's Tonsorial Parlor and Bathing Rooms on Main Street, himself snipping away at Orrin Guernsey's whiskers, listening to Guernsey and Anderson and the local Congressman talk. "Pity won't help us," Anderson had so often said. Dr. Dan went on:

"Our white friends cannot do for us what we can do for ourselves. Dependency on the part of the Negro has always proved a detriment. When we have learned to do well *what we have the ability to do,* we will have accomplished much towards changing sentiments now against us."

He believed this, he made them believe it, but he was also a realist. He did not leave them without saying one more word. "Do not be deterred," warned Dr. Dan, "by the thought you may encounter antagonism. Few enterprises, even those for the betterment of mankind, have smooth sailing from the start. The Provident Hospital project," he told them, "met with fierce opposition in some quarters . . . and when I entered upon my duties at Washington, I was very much discouraged by the condition of affairs." He mentioned then the name sure to stir them, Frederick Douglass, and he repeated the words Douglass had spoken to him a half dozen years before:

"The only way you can succeed is to *override* the obstacles in your path. Hope will be of no avail. . . . By the power *that is within you* do what you hope to do!"

By September colored Nashville had opened its own hospital, a large residence on Cherry Street in which were placed twelve beds at first, later twenty-three, and then thirty-five as the work grew and prospered. Here Dr. Dan held his clinics, the great event of the Meharry medical year, attended not only by students but by alumni and doctors from the country around. After a while even the white doctors in Nashville began coming, as white doctors had come in Washington. "They never saw such a clean, swift operator," said John Hamilton Holman later when he himself had served many years as Meharry's professor of pathology and bacteriology. "Why, Dr. Dan could sew up a man faster than any sewing machine ever made!"

Dr. Dan opened the whole field of modern surgery to Meharry students, and faculty too, as he had opened it to Howard University students and faculty. The annual school catalogue enumerated the "rare and difficult" list: removal of fibroid tumors, diseased ovaries and tubes, ovarian cysts, appendectomies. . . . After the home tonsil removals of F. A. Stewart and the hernia repairs of W. J. Snead, Meharry's previous professors of surgery, these were exciting adventures. Enrolments climbed sixty per cent in no time. Meharry's immediate future was secure.

Young men did any sort of menial work to finance themselves at Meharry while Dr. Dan was there. "We knew he had worked hard himself, on lake boats, in barber shops," said Dr. W. A. Reed of these days. "I thought about that sometimes more than I thought about his techniques when I watched him operating." Dr. Dan's example gave his students the courage to go on waiting on tables, cleaning out laboratories, working on Pullman cars during vacation. Some of them would never become surgeons just because they would not be able to "afford the setup," but they were stimulated to be better doctors.

Everything had to be shipshape when Dr. Dan arrived to conduct his clinics, Dr. G. Hamilton-Francis recalls, for he would tolerate no less. But he was always encouraging, always willing to lend an ear to the problems of the inexperienced. He made a special effort to temper his explanations to a fellow's comprehension and ability to understand. After he left, his operations and lectures were subjects of conversation and discussion for weeks and his influence was felt throughout the year. Some of the young men he trained were graduated with honors and joined the Meharry faculty — W. A. Reed, J. A. McMillan, J. H. Hale — and in their turn handed down the Williams tradition to others who came later.

The same autumn Dr. Dan started his clinics at Meharry, he went to St. Louis to participate in the National Medical Association's annual meeting. Dr. J. Edward Perry remembers how colored doctors of the West and South surged in at the promise of seeing operations performed by the great Daniel Williams. The Municipal Hospital grudgingly agreed to allow the colored group to hold its clinics in its amphitheater and promised to provide the patients.

Dr. Dan was advised that an accident case needing brain surgery was being furnished him. A hospital cart was rolled in, on it a baby of nine or ten months who had fallen from a window. The baby was dying, Dr. Dan saw as soon as he looked at it. He turned to the waiting colored men and described the moribund condition of the little creature.

"This is what they think we will operate upon," he said, "but we will kindly return it to the ward and not add insult to injury."

He then sought to make up to the disappointed men by lecturing at length on head injuries and various types of fractures of the skull. It was a classic discourse. When it was completed, Dr. Dan engaged his audience in a heart-to-heart talk on the surgical and medical situation confronting the Negro.

"Men," he said, "you must bestir yourselves." If they sat idly by and waited for Providence and luck, he told them, they'd be there a thousand years. When they left that amphitheater, they must go out with the determination to have more hospitals, better medical men and more scientific surgeons, he declared, and they must build the hospitals themselves. "I'll come and help you," he said, "whenever I possibly can." Booker Washington's indifference had made him redouble his own efforts.

Out in Missouri a few months later, young Perry remembered Dr. Dan's words. He had as patient an elderly woman who showed the beginnings of cancer of the breast. He knew an immediate operation might prolong her life as much as five years. He felt all the more concern about the case because he felt he owed his own life to the care with which this woman had nursed him, a worn-out young practitioner, through pneumonia. When the local hospital at the state university refused to admit her because of her color and despite the fact her husband was well able to pay the fees, Perry was in despair until he remembered Dr. Dan's words. Immediately he posted a letter to Chicago and to his joy received a quick response. Dr. Dan would come. First he sent certain advance orders and Perry and the woman's husband proceeded to carry them out, strange though they seemed. Perry remembered every detail years later.

The two men took all movable furnishings out of the big kitchen-dining room and painted the ceiling, walls and floor. By the time the paint was dry, Dr. Dan's nurse had arrived, a brisk, starched woman who kept them busy for two days. Under her direction, they baked sheets and towels in the oven of the stove out in the summer kitchen. On top of the stove they set the five-gallon wash boiler, after careful cleaning, to sterilize water. They kept the water bubbling a full half hour, then the nurse spread over it one of the baked sheets. With others she covered the stove and dish cupboards in the proposed operating room. At her bidding the men went over the freshly painted walls again, with a solution of permanganate of potash. They stretched out the dining table to capacity and added all its extra leaves, then scrubbed and covered it with a clean quilt, next with a sheet. A sterilized sheet would be added at the last minute. When all was ready, they closed doors and windows, stuffed the crevices with cotton, and set formaldehyde crystals to fumigate the immaculate room.

There were only two other colored doctors in that part of Missouri. Perry sent them word and they came, by buggy, getting up at dawn and driving, one twenty-five miles and the other thirty-five, to watch the operation. To these three men Dr. Dan gave a full classroom lecture. He described minutely the anatomy of the breast. He told how the cells of the milk ducts change when attacked by cancer, and why there is retraction of the nipple. Lost in his subject, his voice rose and took on an excitement that communicated itself to Perry and the other two doctors. He described the various types of operation in vogue for removal of the breast, and what method he would use, and why. He went to as much pains to make everything clear as if a full amphitheater were before him. Then under their watchful eyes, greedy of every move he made, he set swiftly to work, continuing to talk as he operated — explaining, describing, answering questions.

Never had they had such an opportunity before. More than probably, they never would again. When Dr. Dan was through, they knew they had been in the presence of a great man, a modest man who put them at ease. They felt a new sense of their own worth, and responsibility, as colored doctors. They would never completely lose courage after that.

As for the patient, Dr. Dan's nurse stayed with her for a week and her recovery was "uneventful." She lived for six years.

This was the beginning. Soon Dr. Dan, despite his marriage, despite his heavy private practice and all the demands upon him in Chicago, was traveling everywhere, from the Great Lakes to the Gulf, at the call of colored doctors who needed him. He might have gone back to teaching at his alma mater and added to his stature among white men, but he was a Williams and he devoted himself to black men as his clan had always done.

Sometimes the call came from a former student or interne, lonely practitioners struggling to find their way in a difficult white-dominated profession that gave them little welcome. Sometimes several colored doctors would group their serious surgical cases, collect a fund to cover travel expenses, and invite Dr. Dan to spend several days with them, operating, demonstrating and lecturing.

When he was not traveling, he was writing letters, answering questions. "I have a case of enlarged cervical glands. What shall I do?" came a plea from Arkansas, and Dr. Dan's prompt advice gave confidence and assured success to an isolated young professional.

"He never failed to respond to our requests," said Edward Perry later after he himself had built up two hospitals. The more difficult the situation, the more Dr. Dan's pioneer blood raced to conquer it. He operated and lectured in kitchens, dining rooms and parlors. Once the only light was a kerosene lamp and it had to be held at some distance lest the ether fumes ignite. Once, in the Deep South, the crowd of knowledge-thirsty doctors was so much greater than the available small bedroom could accommodate that the patient was carried out under the boughs of a tree and there Dr. Dan, pressed round by eager black faces, poured out the gospel according to Æsculapius. To an unknown number of these informal schools Dr. Dan carried the light of his skill and understanding and left with countless ardent young doctors the inspiration and courage that enabled them to live out lives of desperately needed usefulness.

Despite the satisfactions of his work in the South and West, Dr. Dan grieved over the setback in the East to his magnificent achievements at Freedmen's Hospital. His successor Curtis was a good surgeon, but Curtis had not retained the direction of Freedmen's very long. In 1901 Warfield, despite his failure to pin dishonesty on Dr. Dan, was emboldened to make similar charges against Curtis. This time he succeeded and Curtis was forced out. Warfield, who had taken pains to make the proper connections, was appointed surgeon-in-chief. Shortly he again for the third time brought charges against a colleague — this time against Charles West of the remarkably high civil service rating. West, when he failed of appointment as surgeon-in-chief, had been compelled for lack of other opportunity to accept an assistant surgeonship in the institution where he should have been head. But Warfield did not want him around. So West was accused of dishonesty and ousted. Thereafter Warfield had held undisputed sway. A man with pitiful lack of professional ability, clever only in self-seeking, he allowed the hospital to sink back into conditions almost as bad as when Purvis was chief.

As he traveled, Dr. Dan bucked the color line — sometimes, as in Dallas, by refusing to operate in lily-white hospitals; other times, as in St. Louis, by rebuking the cynicism of white doctors. Always he had to be on guard against those who sought to trip up a colored surgeon at whatever cost to the patient. But Dr. Dan was more than a match for unprincipled provincials.

In Indianapolis, he put a white staff to shame. Dr. J. H. Ward, president of the newly founded Indiana state organization of colored doctors, invited Dr. Dan to their annual meeting. Rather grudging permission had been obtained from the City Hospital to hold a surgical clinic there "if a qualified colored surgeon could be found." The men assembled happily; they were secure in the knowledge they indeed had a qualified man, and they were eager to see even one operation and learn from it.

A white attendant wheeled in a patient, announced it was an "abdominal" case, and stood aside with a scarce suppressed sneer on his face, as if to say, What can a Negro do?

"Where is the patient's record?" asked Dr. Dan. Surprised into action, the interne brought it. Dr. Dan gave the record a glance and laid it down.

"Please wheel the patient out," he said.

Like automata set in motion against their will, the attendants obeyed. When the patient was out of earshot, Dr. Dan picked up the record and turned to the little group of colored doctors, now augmented by several white men who had slipped in.

"Gentlemen," he said, "this case is diabetic and therefore inoperable. The urinalysis shows . . ." and he proceeded to give a thoroughgoing lecture on the whys and wherefores of the situation. It was a masterly dissertation, but there was no operation, and that was the end of the first attempted surgical clinic of colored men in Indianapolis. "We didn't get what we came for," said Dr. Lawrence A. Lewis, "but we went away with reinforced faith in ourselves."

Dr. Dan never talked much about the frustrations he encountered from racial prejudice. Hard work and worthy accomplishment would eventually win the Negro his rightful place, not talk. However, he did enjoy the opportunity presented one day for a little mild retaliation. Returning from a trip, he found on his desk a letter from the editor of a medical journal published in North Carolina. The Southern editor had been reading some fine articles, he said, by Daniel Hale Williams in the national medical papers and he would deem it a favor if Dr. Williams would allow his next article to appear in the North Carolina journal. Dr. Dan knew this journal had been running pseudoscientific articles declaring the Negro physician could never gain efficiency in his profession because of the formation of the Negro skull. He took some pleasure in sitting down and answering that he was a Negro and too busy just now to send an article.

Dr. Dan's Nashville speech of 1900 was reprinted and broadcast far and wide. Soon colored hospitals were springing up everywhere — Knoxville, Kansas City, St. Louis, Louisville, Memphis, Birmingham, Atlanta, Dallas. In a very few years his moving appeal and his practical advice had fostered forty hospitals in twenty different states. Today there are a hundred. One little North Carolina hospital spoke for them all:

> The hospital has had a wonderful effect on the death rate among our people. The deaths used to be three to one when compared with the whites, though the colored population was only half as large as the white population. But since we have had the trained nurse, there is a marked change.

At one time, seven different Negro schools in the country were training colored doctors. Five have failed. The only ones to survive are Howard University Medical School and Meharry Medical College — the two schools which, when newer techniques and more stringent standards entered all American medical education, were fortunate enough to be injected with the fervor, the unremitting labor, and the uncompromising perfectionism of Dr. Dan, Moses to Negro medicine and nursing.

CHAPTER XV

History-Making Operations

SELDOM has history produced a doctor as versatile as Dr. Dan.
His ability to organize and administer was a high quality in itself.
His talent to inspire and instruct has left an unending influence
upon doctors both black and white in this country. And with all
this went his masterful, ever-developing gifts in several areas of
surgery.

On a sultry July night in 1902, just such a night as the one when
Cornish was stabbed, Dr. Dan encountered another patient injured in a brawl. This time the assailant's instrument was a gun,
not a knife, and the victim was white, not colored. The man had
been shot in his left side while stooping over and the ball had
passed through the space between the eighth and the ninth ribs.

Though nine years had ensued since Dr. Dan had successfully
operated on Cornish, surgeons were still reluctant to open up the
thorax. Abdominal operations had become common, but not so
with the chest. Throughout the Spanish-American War, men
wounded in the upper part of the body by gunshot, if they did
not die at once, were abandoned with a sterile dressing, a strapped
chest, and a dose of morphine. The possibility of surgical investigation and repair was not even considered. Textbooks still expressed a timid conservatism on the subject.

When Dr. Dan was told the position the man had been in when
shot, he remarked that there was probably no abdominal injury.

"Balls don't turn corners," he said to the staff men who stood watching while he examined the young Irishman, "not unless they come into contact with some hard substance." As far as he could tell from outer examination there was no injury either to the diaphragm or to the abdominal viscera. However, as he always did with emergency patients, he ordered an examination of the urine, while the man was still on the table. Blood was present and Dr. Dan said probably the kidney was involved after all.

Again he examined the abdomen and found muscular rigidity on the left side, with absolute flatness from the twelfth rib into the flank. He pointed out to the internes that abdominal respiration was completely absent — an important sign in men, he said, of a peritoneal injury. He washed out the bladder, made a second catheterization, and again blood was present.

"Well," said Dr. Dan, straightening up, "only one ball entered the body. It must have turned the corner after all." He said he was sure now that the abdominal viscera had been injured and he would operate at once.

He made a five-inch incision following the angle of the eighth rib, raised and retracted the tissues, and cut through about three inches of the seventh and eighth ribs. He was much bolder than when he operated on Cornish and gave himself ample space to reach the diaphragm. As he worked away quickly, but calmly, confident he could master any problem that arose, he explained each step to the men standing by. Surgeons worry too much, he said, about the invasion of air into the body through an incision; he himself had found aspirating the air from the cavity and strapping the chest firmly with plaster was all that was needed.

His opening made, Dr. Dan found the diaphragm actually had been penetrated, but that tissue had plugged the wound so that temporarily the abdominal and pleural spaces had been separated as usual. Quickly he repaired the wound in the diaphragm, irrigated the pleural cavity with salt solution, aspirated the air with a syringe and closed the outer incision. His hands, nimble as a pianist's, moved with lightning speed, without a false motion, almost rhythmically, it appeared to those who watched.

He still had to discover where the bullet had gone after passing through the diaphragm. And he must stop the man's loss of blood before it proved fatal. Swiftly he made a seven-inch incision to the left of the median abdominal line. With fingers that seemed to carry in their sensitive tips the faculties both of seeing and of thinking, he examined the intestines and the organs one by one. In the inner upper surface of the kidney, he found a wound. His opening did not give him good access, and before proceeding with the bleeding kidney he hastily closed the incision he had just made and made a third one, an oblique incision in the left loin, the standard procedure for approaching the kidney.

When he reached the deep tissue of the lower back, he found it bulging into the wound and the space dark with escaped blood. As he cut in, dark clots appeared, followed almost immediately by profuse arterial hemorrhage. He ceased speaking, his movements lost their rhythm, became jerky, took on blinding speed. Grabbing a tampon from the assistant he controlled the hemorrhage. Then under his direction the assistant continued the deep pressure while he separated the damaged kidney from its surrounding fat and removed it. As he dissected down to the ureter he found both that duct and the large branch of the renal artery had been cut by the ball.

Thanks to Dr. Dan's independent judgment, his intelligent deductions, and his courageous assumption of responsibility for whatever procedure, orthodox or not, which each step indicated, the Irishman's life was saved. His recovery was slow, but steady, and a year later he was in excellent health.

The very next day after this challenging operation, Dr. Dan was called to Provident Hospital by another chest injury — a stab wound. It proved to be the most interesting and instructive case, he said later, he had ever met. Like his heart operation, it was another history-making case.

At first examination there were no indications for immediate operation. It was the sort of thing usually treated on the expectant plan and usually resulting in death. The temperature of the patient, a man of twenty-seven, was 98, his pulse 92, and good quality. He complained naturally enough of pain in and about his chest wound, but there was no hemorrhage from the wound, which had closed valve-like, and his heart was normal. But he breathed with difficulty and soon he developed a short, shrill, hacking cough and complained of pain in the left abdomen. Dr. Dan found dullness there and some muscular rigidity, but no positive signs of hemorrhage into the abdomen.

As he continued to watch the case, the symptoms became progressively urgent. The man could not lie down, his pulse increased from 92 to 140, the dullness in the left abdomen increased and the muscular rigidity became extreme. All this, with an increase in white corpuscle count, pointed to active internal hemorrhage and Dr. Dan decided to wait no longer but operate.

Following the angle of the eighth rib, he cut a trap door as in the gunshot case of the day before. Again he found the diaphragm had been penetrated and plugged with tissue. Proceeding into the abdomen and finding it full of free blood and clots, he discovered the spleen had been damaged. It was hemorrhaging profusely. Slight traction on the surrounding tissue enabled him to deliver the organ onto the abdominal wall for examination. Hastily he threw a turn of gauze with a drawn loop about the pedicle and controlled the hemorrhage. The wound, he saw, extended the length of the spleen.

Dr. Dan stood and looked at the injured organ. What should he do? The soft, pulpy, fist-sized mass, so highly vascular, held together only by a delicate network of tissues, seemed to defy any attempt at repair. Six years earlier Lamarchia had tried to suture a spleen; he had failed and his patient had died of secondary hemorrhage.

Despite history, despite uncertainty, Dr. Dan was willing to try. He began suturing, but every stitch tore out of the cheese-like tissues as he attempted to draw his loop down. He saw he would have to give up or change his tactics.

Although the properties of catgut had not been extensively investigated and were not well known, Dr. Dan was aware that wetting catgut caused it to swell. If it swelled, it should engage the tissues and hold more firmly to them. Immediately he took up a full curved round Mayo needle, threaded with No. 2 catgut, and introduced it a half inch back from the margin of the wound. Without exerting the least force, he allowed the needle to follow its full curve and emerge on the opposite side of the wound the same distance from the edge as it had entered. Then he made a triple loop, without a reinforcing knot. As the edges of the wound came together he applied hot gauze compresses to each loop. The catgut swelled, and the stitches held firm! Not one pulled out. For twenty minutes he waited to make sure the stitches would hold. Satisfied then that the hemorrhage would not start up again, he returned the spleen to the abdomen, surrounded it with the abdominal tissues, explaining as he did so that the omentum had a protective quality important to the healing, and then he closed the outer incision. The patient made a rapid and permanent recovery and was discharged from Provident thirty-one days later.

A little over a year later, Nicholas Senn published a review of surgical experience with the spleen on both sides of the Atlantic. In America there had been only one successful suture for traumatic hemorrhage previous to Dr. Dan's, an operation performed by Tiffany in Baltimore in 1894, which Dr. Dan had not known. Abroad, out of fourteen cases sutured, two had died; out of ten treated with tampon, one had died. While these ventures were few in number, the percentage of recovery was high and Dr. Dan was stimulated to urge that more men at least attempt repair of injured spleens. He sat down and wrote a paper on his own case and presented it before the Chicago Medical Society one evening in mid-June 1904.

Not the suture itself but the method of applying the suture was the crucial thing, Dr. Dan said. You could not apply suture to a bleeding spleen as you would to almost any other tissue in the body. "It requires method, technique and a proper adjustment of the omentum in the completion of the operation to have a successful result," he said. Previous failures were due to ignorance of these points. Now, there was every reason not to be discouraged, not to reject the challenge. But despite Dr. Dan's urging, men still today shrink from tackling a damaged spleen and the encyclopedias still say there is only one thing to do — remove the injured organ.

Dr. Dan included in his paper the gunshot affair and added still another case to show how greatly penetrating wounds of the chest can vary.

This third patient showed no symptoms relevant to any organ or viscera within stabbing distance of the walls of the thorax, and, without operation to discover the extent of his injuries, the man would have died. The fellow had been stabbed, Dr. Dan explained, below the sixth rib, one inch from the nipple of the breast. When Dr. Dan examined him, his temperature was 97, his pulse 110, fairly full and regular, and his respiration was 40, but his skin was cold and clammy. The heart and lungs were negative, except below the sixth rib; from there dullness extended downward to the tenth rib. The abdomen was negative too. Arterial blood was escaping from the intercostal vessels.

Dr. Dan made an incision, he told the medical society, four inches long, following the curve of the sixth rib, forming a trap door as in his other cases. When he opened the pleural cavity, he had considerably more trouble than in his previous cases. The lung collapsed and the right heart was unable to accommodate itself to the emergency. Circulation was interfered with dangerously and the patient turned blue. Great haste was required. Dr. Dan found two wounds perforating the diaphragm, one on the outer or pleural side near the dome, and one in a direct line on the inner or pericardial side. He sutured these rapidly and then found an irregular wound in the pericardium. Fortunately the heart was not injured.

Ten years previous almost to the day Dr. Dan had sewed up his first pericardial case. Then he used very fine catgut. This time he chose fine silk. Suturing the fluttering pericardium was like repairing the wing of a bird in full flight. But he had done it before and he managed to do it again. Then he irrigated the pleural cavity, closed the chest wound, and continued his incision below the diaphragm to explore the abdomen. There he found a punctured wound of the transverse colon.

So with no outward indications whatever, his patient had actually suffered four internal injuries. Only Dr. Dan's prompt and dexterous surgery had saved the man's life.

From this experience he felt it proper, Dr. Dan said, to urge the surgical exploration of the great majority of penetrating wounds of the chest below the sixth rib. Not otherwise, he pointed out, could one decide the important question of whether or not the diaphragm had been perforated. In every case he himself had found the "omnipresent omentum" had temporarily plugged the wound openings and masked the symptoms. And since the dome of the diaphragm varies in height, it was equally impossible to be accurate in estimating the extent of the injury done to the viscera. Neither probe nor finger were proper instruments of exploration. It was far safer, he declared, to open the chest and make actual observation, positive diagnosis and direct treatment. The imminent risk of lung collapse that always attends operative treatment of wounds of the heart and lungs he considered less of a danger than blind waiting.

Dr. Dan's paper had wide circulation. It was printed in its entirety in *The Annals of Surgery* and in more abridged forms in the *Chicago Medical Recorder* and the *Illinois Medical Journal*. First-rate surgeons still find it good reading today.

Dr. Dan did not confine his surgery to any one area of the body. His interest carried him into several fields where he developed a skill that would now earn him the title of specialist. Throughout his career he was opposed to amputations. His early railroad cases, his own threatened loss of a leg, had fixed his attention upon the possibilities of saving injured extremities, while his love of people and concern for their welfare made of every case a warm, living actuality.

One day in 1904 a little six-year-old Irish boy was brought into the emergency ward at Provident. He had fallen off a wagon and suffered a bad laceration of both skin and tissue from knee to ankle, plus a fracture of the ankle. The torn tissue was badly infected. Tomietta Stokes Beckham, one-time assistant superintendent of nurses, remembers how every doctor in Provident who passed through the ward and saw the case said nothing could be done but amputate. But Dr. Dan tenaciously clung to his treatments. This was a poor boy, he said, who must some day make his living. "I'm going to wait," he declared, "until I feel there is no chance at all to save that leg." After all Fenger had worked half a year to save *his* leg.

So Dr. Dan waited, and worked, a week, a month, six months, and the boy was finally discharged with just a slight limp, a limp that would eventually be outgrown.

Another time a Rhode Island railroad brakeman was brought in with a crushed foot and ankle. Current practice indicated amputation. But Dr. Dan refused. He trimmed off evident nonviable tissue, including the toes, which were hopelessly crushed, and made no attempt at the primary operation to cover all the raw surfaces. After the wound was granulating clearly, some four weeks later, he fashioned skin flaps and applied razor-cut skin grafts. The result was a foot upon which the patient could walk. It was a question who was the prouder – Dr. Dan or the brakeman.

For all the extraordinary operations, the history-making surgery, Dr. Dan was still the family physician too. Old friends could not do without him. When Julius Avendorph's sons were born, it had to be Dr. Dan who ushered them into the world. When the children in the household of Louis B. Anderson, once Price Williams's newspaper partner and now a rising Chicago lawyer, had to have their tonsils out, their ordeal was made easier by riding to the hospital in Dr. Dan's shiny new Red Devil of Mitchell make. No other colored doctor had such a car. Jessica, six, and her young Uncle Archibald, nine, screamed with delight from the rear seat as Dr. Dan turned the handlebar this way and that and the corners whizzed by.

The Williamses had moved to a larger house at 3149 Forest Avenue, next door to Bishop Archibald Carey. Madison Davis Carey, aged four, tried to walk the fence between Dr. Dan's back yard and his own. Davis fell and tore the palm of his hand on a projecting nail. On Eloise, seven, fell the responsibility of the situation; her mother and her father, the bishop, were away at a church conference, and the maid, in a dead faint, was useless. Eloise ran for Dr. Dan. It was a nasty wound and it hurt, but Dr. Dan talked to the children as to contemporaries, to contemporaries whom he respected. Davis stopped sobbing while Dr. Dan showed them what had to be done and called upon them to help him do it. Another time when Dorothy Carey developed a carbuncle on her ankle and Eloise accompanied her to Dr. Dan's office, the great surgeon carefully explained all about gangrenous tissue and why it had to be cut out like a rotten spot out of an apple. Dorothy was fascinated and submitted to the necessities of the situation with good grace.

Mrs. Carey sent a note saying "Money could not pay for what you have done," and then forgot to enclose the check — which gave everybody a good laugh. Mrs. Williams might be jealous of Mrs. Carey, and Bishop Carey and Dr. Dan might not always see eye to eye in race matters. Still Dr. Dan was always the family physician as well as neighbor and the Carey children loved him.

Dr. Dan never totally escaped from obstetrical work. He administered "twilight sleep" to Mrs. Richard Rainey and asked her to name the baby Daniel. He laughed at the frilly bassinet. "I was put in a cracker box," he said, "and I got along all right." Dan Rainey, when he was grown and married, still carried the newspaper clipping about Dr. Dan and his twilight sleep birth and still worshiped the great man for whom he was named. "But you wouldn't know he was great," Dan Rainey said, "he was so simple and he had simple offices with old-fashioned furniture."

Dr. Dan never grew so great but that his patients felt free to come to him about all sorts of things. One woman consulted him about her first-aid lessons and he suggested she get a sheep's heart at the stockyards to help her understand things. Another woman telephoned and said "Dr. Dan, there's no money in it for you, but I want you to come and tell my neighbor how to care for her ailing daughter." The next day he went and saw the neighbor;

he stayed an hour and told the family to move to the country and how to diet the daughter to build her up. His instructions were followed and the girl got well.

There never was a squarer man, people said. He would not doctor a man if he did not need it and he tempered his fees to a person's pocket. "I can't charge my people much," he told a friend. Even at his prime, after he was nationally famous, his income was only $10,000 a year and he still lived in a modest frame house on a side street.

When a case was hopeless and there was nothing he could do, Dr. Dan stayed on anyway through hours of waiting, helping a wife keep watch until her man's last, struggling breath was drawn. A woman never forgot that.

It was as though in the sickroom, and only in the sickroom, could Dr. Dan be a whole man, a man of feeling as well as a man of science and intellect. Here emotions, buried deep by pride and circumstance, were set free. Here he need put up no guard and could pour out sympathy and affection as well as knowledge and skill, without fear of rebuff or betrayal. In return his patients gave him a devotion that amounted to adulation and brought to him the recital of all sorts of troubles beyond the medical.

In the early 1900's more than one colored youth, reading of his race's great doctor, was stirred to follow in his steps. Some could not be satisfied until they came to Chicago to study, where he was. They came from far and near, Ulysses Grant Dailey from Texas, Reginald Smith from Florida, and they came despite poverty and every drawback. They searched him out, at first on the street, later drawn to his office as by an irresistible magnet, swallowing their timidity, to seek his encouragement and advice. Dr. Dan was never too busy to see them.

Each one he received with grave courtesy and to each he gave his fullest attention. Sometimes a stripling with preconceived ideas of how great men look and act was a little disappointed when he met his hero face to face. Dr. Dan's slight build, quiet ways and modest, almost diffident, demeanor were not what had been expected.

Though he had little time to mingle socially with the medical students, Dr. Dan saw to it that they enjoyed at least one party in his home every winter. For several years Arthur J. Booker from El Paso was commissioned by Dr. Dan to invite thirty to forty medical students for a big feed and evening of hilarity in his home, but Dr. Dan himself was often called away.

To young doctors starting up in practice, Dr. Dan was more than generous. He invited them to call upon him for advice and he gave them consultation service without fee. It was the day when the woman physician had everyone against her, but he encouraged both sexes alike. It was a big help to Dr. Marie Fellowes when Dr. Dan got her a job in a life insurance company as examining physician for woman applicants.

He urged the young practitioners to read up on their cases, just as a lawyer did, and to know all about the problems they tackled. A. Wilberforce Williams was one who followed his advice to such good effect that he became a specialist in the treatment of tuberculosis, worked with the Chicago Health Commissioner, and was sent to Europe to lecture to colored American soldiers. Andrew McKissick, another bright student, also profited by Dr. Dan's teaching and became a notable surgeon in Mexico.

At meetings of the National Medical Association where Dr. Dan went almost yearly to operate and read papers, he kept his eye open for promising young men. When he found them, he encouraged them and advised them as to their individual progress; he invited them to Chicago, sometimes to stay in his own home, and opened doors for them so they might visit the important hospitals and surgeons of that important medical center.

The late Dr. John A. Kenney, for years resident physician at Tuskegee and donor of a $93,000 hospital to the people of Newark, New Jersey, was one of Dr. Dan's finds. In 1903 Dr. Dan tried Kenney out as his anesthetist and after that used him each year at his Meharry clinics. His encouragement and instruction impelled Kenney to go back to Alabama and emulate his mentor. Like Dr. Dan, Kenney improvised operating quarters in a small room with wooden floor and whitewashed ceiling. Like Dr. Dan, he scrubbed and sprayed before he operated. Like Dr. Dan, he met emergencies bravely. Kenney operated in Negro cabins by oil lamp, tallow candle, and once even did a forceps delivery with one old midwife for assistant, by the light of a pine torch on the open hearth.

In 1907 Dr. Dan invited Kenney to Chicago. Kenney spent three weeks as his guest, and, thanks to Dr. Dan, visited eight hospitals, heard many lectures, met leading surgeons and witnessed nearly a hundred operations. It was an experience of unbelievable good fortune to the young Southern Negro. When George Hall inserted an item in the newspaper stating Kenney was *his* house guest Kenney wanted to make it clear to everyone that Dr. Dan, and no one else, was his benefactor. When he reached home he published a lengthy article of appreciation in the Tuskegee paper, *The Student*, recounting Dr. Dan's good offices and eulogizing his attainments.

He was proud of the fact, Kenney said, that the race had such an eminent physician and surgeon as Dr. Dan. There were prominent *white* men in medicine and surgery in Chicago who had been his pupils and others who had been his internes. "He is at perfect ease with the best surgeons in the city," wrote the segregated Southern Negro, "they all recognize him and accord him a high place."

Kenney exulted that Dr. Dan had the privilege of operating at St. Luke's. He had watched Dr. Dan perform two abdominal operations there one morning. "The nurses and internes, all white, paid him the same deference that I later saw them giving the white surgeons in the same operating room." There was absolutely no difference. It made Kenney feel glad, he said, to see it and to feel that here, at least, was a place where merit was being recognized for merit's own sake.

Dr. Dan's student ways and his study well stocked with medical works impressed young Kenney. "He follows closely the best authors on medical and surgical subjects," Kenney wrote. Dr. Dan's books were not on the shelves just for ornament. Kenney looked into them and found them interlined and appended with the penciled notes of the reader.

Dr. Dan did not, however, take another assistant into his own office for some years after his unhappy experience with Curtis and Warfield. Some had asked for the privilege and had been refused. Their complaints swelled the murmurs that he was selfish and carried weight with those who had no comprehension of what a great surgeon's requirements might be. It was not until 1908 that Dr. Dan ventured upon the uncertainties of a close professional relationship.

On a raw day late in February when it seemed the lake wind was everyone's foe, Dr. Dan encountered young Grant Dailey near 33rd and State Streets. The late Dr. Dailey remembered almost a half century afterward every detail of that meeting. He had recently won his M.D. at Northwestern with a record high enough to be teaching anatomy there as Dr. Dan had done. Already he had assisted Dr. Dan in operations at Provident Hospital.

The men greeted each other. "How are you getting on?" Dr. Dan asked. "Well enough," answered the younger man and explained that he was now located nearby in rooms with another doctor and a dentist.

"Oh," said Dr. Dan, "why have you left Hall?"

Dailey had had office space with George Hall during the past year and a half since graduation. He explained to Dr. Dan that Hall had once promised Spencer Dickerson an assistantship if he came out to Chicago. Dickerson had come on from Massachusetts and Dailey had had to find another berth. Dr. Dan stood silent a moment, turning his penetrating look on the young face before him.

"So you're no longer working at all with Hall? Your disattachment has been orderly, then, and complete?"

"Yes, sir," replied the puzzled Dailey. Another moment of silence ensued and then Dr. Dan spoke, slowly.

"Well," he said, "it's some years since I've had an apprentice with me. I thought I wouldn't again, but how would you like to come in with me and act as my surgical assistant at Provident?"

If he had been offered a heap of jewels on a golden platter, Dailey would not have been more astounded. Since that day years before when a Negro newspaper had fallen into his hands on the Texas frontier with a photograph of Daniel Hale Williams in it, Grant Dailey had vowed to be a surgeon. By hard, often menial, work and exacting self-denial he had won his education. But his wildest dreams had not included such a moment as this. To work at close hand with his idol, to see all his techniques and to learn them! Somehow he gasped his acceptance.

Later Dailey realized that his news had been no surprise to Dr. Dan. This proposition had certainly been duly weighed before Dr. Dan broached it.

A few weeks later Dailey brought his few possessions and moved into the front room of Dr. Dan's suite at 3129 Indiana Avenue; Dr. Dan had moved to the new address a few years back.

The two men shared a small waiting room. There was no office girl or office attendant of any kind. Dr. Dan was opposed, Dailey found, to office attendants. He felt his patients would be discussed and he knew how sensitive some of his women patients were to privacy. Negrodom was a circumscribed community and many colored women in those days preferred to consult white physicians rather than risk gossip about their affairs. Dr. Dan respected their feelings and ran an office that, in comparison with those of other practitioners, was severely sanctumlike.

Dailey was inexperienced, but Dr. Dan was infinitely patient. He was also fussy, Dailey found, about many little things — cleanliness, neatness and order, and especially about never accepting even the smallest thing, a pencil or a nickel to make change, from anyone. His honesty, or independence, whichever it was, was trying at times. But Dailey did not know how Warfield had accused Dr. Dan of thievery ten years back. Apparently ever since, Dr. Dan had been on the watch lest some careless action be used by someone with evil intent.

Dailey gave the anesthetics in home cases, of which Dr. Dan still had many, assisted at the hospital operations, and gave the aftercare on obstetrical cases. Like Dr. Dan himself years before in Dr. Palmer's office, Dailey was ever alert to learn. Dr. Dan's surgical judgment and bedside diagnostic skill continually amazed the younger man. "It was uncanny," he said.

Dr. Dan was getting to the age, the middle fifties, when many men lose their enthusiasms. But fortunately for Grant Dailey, Dr. Dan was as buoyant and keen in his interests as ever. Whenever the opportunity arose to do an anatomic review on a cadaver, Dr. Dan's whole being vibrated with joy.

One day as the two men walked up Dearborn from Provident after an operation for hernia through the groin, Dailey brought up some questions regarding the surgical anatomy of the lesion. He had seen E. Wyllys Andrews demonstrate his overlapping method of repairing a hernia in the classes at Northwestern, but from the amphitheater benches, Dailey said, the view had been too poor to get a clear conception of the process.

"Your answers," replied Dr. Dan, "can only be found in the dissecting room."

Arrived at his office, Dr. Dan went straight to the telephone and made arrangements. The two men, dropping everything else, hastened off to the anatomical laboratory. "Wyllys Andrews was my classmate," said Dr. Dan on the way, "and his father was my professor of surgery."

For the next three hours the two were alone in the laboratory. Carefully, patiently, Dr. Dan went through the entire operation and would not stop until Dailey thoroughly understood every step.

Another day Dailey asked about the techniques for providing a substitute passage from the stomach to the intestines when the normal route was damaged. The same thing happened. Dr. Dan took Dailey to the dissecting room. Dailey never forgot that operative surgery must be built upon sound anatomical foundations and even after he had reached surgical eminence himself and had carried his skills beyond the United States to India, to Pakistan, and to Africa, Dailey looked back with awe upon the uncanny accuracy of Dr. Dan's knowledge of the human body and the perfection of his surgical technique. For his part, Dr. Dan never stinted with his knowledge nor spared himself in teaching Dailey, for this time, he knew, he had found the right man to train.

Not every genius is able to train other men. Dr. Dan's contemporary, the brilliant Murphy, according to his biographer, wore out his assistants, but did not make great surgeons out of them. Fortunately for posterity, Dr. Dan could, and did.

Dailey proved to be as eager for knowledge and as painstaking in his labors as Dr. Dan himself. He would go on to make his own individual contribution to this great work for the race, for humanity.

Dailey did more. His quiet ways and high standards were happily congenial to the great surgeon at his zenith. Dailey must have accomplished something toward healing the wounds inflicted by Curtis and Warfield.

CHAPTER XVI

Alice Tries to Be a Good Wife

WHILE Dr. Dan was operating, training Dailey, traveling and lecturing in the South, his wife was active in colored society. Dr. Dan's friends became her friends. With Florence Bentley, Charles Bentley's new wife, she joined a white literary club downtown. She devoted herself to the South Side colored people, helping ambitious young women secure suitable positions, making talks here and there.

When the Reverend Reverdy Ransom asked her to take charge of the kindergarten work at the Institutional Church and Social Settlement two blocks from Provident Hospital, Alice responded willingly. First she must raise funds. She decided to put on a good lecture course and accomplish two ends in one — intellectual stimulation for the neighborhood and money for the kindergarten. She tried to get Booker Washington to open the course but, failing that, secured Mary Church Terrell, the distinguished colored suffragette and now one of the first two women on the Board of Education in Washington, D. C. Mrs. Terrell proved an excellent choice. She was followed by other good lecturers — Dr. Gunsaulus and Rabbi Hirsch who had helped Provident Hospital, Professor Shailer Matthews, Dr. Carlos Montezuma. Thanks to Alice's efforts enough money was raised to make it possible to increase the number of children cared for from sixty-five to eighty-two, and to pay the kindergarten principal a salary. Five girls were accepted as students in training for kindergarten work. So well did the whole scheme work out that the next fall a kindergarten school "equal to the best" was opened. Alice Williams could be well satisfied.

Hard as she worked for the kindergarten, she found time for other activities as well at the Institutional Church and Settlement. She helped raise funds for the day nursery which cared for seventy-five babies a week while their mothers were out working, and she served on the committee for the kitchen garden. Both Dr. Dan and Alice had a special interest in the Reverend Mr. Ransom's venture, the first attempt by Negroes anywhere in the country to do social settlement work. Twenty years before, Reverdy Ransom had been minister of a church in Hollidaysburg, where Dr. Dan was born and spent his early childhood. Dr. Dan was doubly glad to support the Reverend Mr. Ransom.

The Institutional Church did not bother about denominational lines. That pleased Dr. Dan. This was a kind of religion, practical religion, he could subscribe to — a church with a reading room and library, music, an employment bureau, clubs for all ages, classes in manual training, stenography, cooking, plain sewing and dressmaking.

Dr. Dan liked the way Ransom entered fearlessly into all that affected the neighborhood. The Armour men struck for better conditions and the management retaliated by manning the trucks with Negroes, whereupon the strikers threw rocks at the scabs and knocked them from the seats. Ransom, to Dr. Dan's delight when he heard about it, strode into the middle of the fray and did some plain talking. "Our colored men," he told the strikers, "are not trying to take the bread out of your mouths. It's not *our* fault we aren't in organized labor!" Then Ransom invited everyone involved to come to his Sunday Forum and talk things out, with Clarence Darrow on the platform leading the discussion.

Dr. Dan had always been optimistic that race relations would improve. But Darrow was pessimistic:

"When I see how anxious the white race is to go to war over nothing and to shoot down men in cold blood for the benefit of trade, when I see the injustice everywhere present, the rich people uniting and crowding the poor into inferior positions, I fear the dreams we have indulged in of perfect equality and unlimited opportunity are a long way from realization."

Darrow said more:

"The colored race should learn this: if the white race insults you on account of your inferior position, they also degrade themselves when they do it. Every time a superior person invades the rights and liberties and dignity of an inferior person he retards and debases his own manhood."

Dr. Dan attended Ransom's Sunday Forum whenever he possibly could. He met many friends there — Louis B. Anderson, soon to be alderman; Ed Wright, already County Commissioner; Oscar DePriest, who had married one of Dr. Dan's many cousins. DePriest was a house painter and had not yet thought of sitting in Congress.

A number of theatrical people attended, who were not welcome in most churches — Dick Harrison, Burt Williams, Sam Lucas who wrote songs. There were many singers, too, and Mrs. Potter Palmer was enchanted when Ransom brought them to sing for her guest, Mascagni. Once a month there was a big orchestral concert of thirty to forty pieces. Dr. Dan was reminded of the days when he played bass viol in All Souls in Janesville. As he listened, he doubtless wished he could get up there himself and pull a stumpy bow once more back and forth across the deep-throated strings.

In late July 1900, Dr. Dan was called back East by the death of his mother. At seventy-two, Sarah Price Williams was still lively and vital when a sudden stroke ended her life. Dr. Dan attended the funeral but was unable to go to Annapolis for the burial. A seriously ill patient demanded his attention in Chicago.

Alice told Hale (she called Dr. Dan "Hale") that with his mother gone he should charge his sisters rent for the house in Kingman Place. They were both working and should support themselves; he had done enough for them already. His family were always draining him, she said. The sisters replied that if they were to pay rent they would pay it for something that suited them better, and they moved to Pierce Place.

Dr. Dan's friends felt Alice Williams had an unfortunate effect on him. Her exclusiveness, the standards she set, cut him off from people, one after another — he who had been so close to many, who had a passion for friendship, and who required a great deal of affection. They felt she encouraged him to harbor grievances and to resent slights. She was forever defending him where no defense was called for, and would point out flaws where he had seen none. If a student wrote him to say, "Thanks to your tutelage I was able to do that operation and go home and relax with a novel," Alice was sure to remark that novel-reading was shallow and Dr. Dan would forget the gratitude his student had expressed.

When young Dr. J. W. McDowell, once Dr. Dan's student at Howard University, moved to Chicago and came rushing to see his former teacher, he was met at the door by a Swedish maid, replete with uniform and card tray. McDowell was upset. He had no card, but he was eager to see Dr. Dan. He brushed by the maid and went right in. Alice welcomed him pleasantly enough, but McDowell was added to the group who were shaking their heads and saying, "She's not the wife for a doctor."

Certainly Alice Williams tried to be a good wife to Dr. Dan. She entertained constantly. In the summer of 1904 when the Republicans assembled in Chicago to nominate Theodore Roosevelt, many prominent colored Republicans from all over the country attended the convention. Many were friends of Dr. Dan and of his wife, and they took this opportunity to entertain them. They gave a party in their home to honor the Honorable Judson W. Lyons, Register of the Treasury, and James Carroll Napier, the Nashville banker. Mrs. Napier was the former Nettie Langston who had taught at Mott School with Alice Johnson. She helped her hostess receive, and the society reporter, already bedazzled by the new electric lights, went into ecstasies over two such beautiful women, so handsomely gowned and gracious in deportment.

To say that the scene was one of splendor, yet simple and elegant, is but to put it mildly. The gentlemen were all in full dress. Burnished silver, fine china, and cut glass glistened in the soft flood of electric light like a sparkling array of huge gems. But why attempt to polish the lily or burnish the rose? The affair was all it possibly could have been.

Alice Williams was a society reporter's dream come true. The newswriters followed her social calendar with meticulous attention, describing her parties and her costumes in every detail, until no superlatives were left and comparisons ran out. "She appeared never to better advantage," the reporter would sigh, and her readers presumably sighed with the reporter, "a very beautiful and graceful lady in a lovely creation of white crepe meteor and taupe and pink, trimmed in real lace." Whether entertaining sixty-five of her husband's prominent friends or a dozen of her own intimates at luncheon, simple elegance and correctness were always the keynote Alice Williams sounded.

The Forest Avenue neighborhood deteriorated, and first the Careys left, then Dr. Dan and Alice. By the fall of 1905, they were living at 270 East 42nd Street and a year later they moved to 470 on the same street. This was largely a white neighborhood. Some Southern white people on the adjoining property put up a twelve-foot "hate" fence. People flocked to see the monstrosity which shut off the daylight from the Williams's windows. Dr. Dan had to seek an injunction and the judge ordered the fence down. Times were changing in Chicago.

In these years, the name of Alice Williams's father was frequently in the news. In 1903 Moses Ezekiel presented his school, Virginia Military Institute, with the sculptured group "Virginia Mourning Her Dead." In 1907 his heroic bronze of Homer went to the University of Virginia, and Thomas Nelson Page spoke on the occasion. The next year he was executing his Napoleon for President Theodore Roosevelt's sister. All this was never spoken of outside the Williams household. Alice kept his framed photograph hidden in a drawer, but once was moved to show it to her friend Christine Shoecraft Smith. Tongues wagged in

Chicago, as previously in Washington, and the malicious said, "She does not even know who her father was."

Alice tried hard to be as friendly with people as her husband was. Every season she gave a luncheon for a club of the younger girls; but they did not enjoy it very much, nor did she. People stood in awe of her and she could not reassure them, for she did not know how to unbend. When she was growing up some people had drawn lines against her mother, against herself, and it had become her defense to draw lines of her own — lines of manners, decorum, good breeding. She herself was ill at ease; she had been a recluse too many years, had grown didactic through too much schoolteaching. She was always formal according to code, never casual.

Unfortunately for one of Alice's inflexibility, times were changing and she could not change with them. She was forever cutting from her list someone who could not cling, as she clung, to the Victorian pattern by which she had been reared.

One day as she was about to enter Jennie Avendorph's parlor for a meeting of the Ladies' Whist Club, she saw triumphantly seated in that exclusive circle the breezy Mrs. George Hall, who had come uninvited. The other women, taken aback by her boldness, sat uncomfortable but unresisting. Alice Williams, however, caught a glimpse of the intruder's towering red coiffure from the hall and turned on her heel and left, never to return.

To be steadfast to her early principles was part of her loyalty to her mother. From her women friends she tried to get that same absorbing, all-enveloping affection that Isabella Johnson had given her. She adored Mary Lizzie Tibbs, wife of her husband's protégé, Wilberforce Williams, and was jealous because Mary Lizzie had other friends besides herself.

For some reason she was also jealous of Mrs. Carey. Her feeling made for difficulties in Dr. Dan's circle of friends. When Mrs. Jerry Stewart, wife of one of his earliest associates on the Provident board, gave a luncheon and invited Mrs. Carey, she could not invite Alice Williams.

Alice Williams knew more about books than she did about

life. "I'd rather stay home and read a good book," she wrote Caddie Parke, "than mingle with ill-bred people."

One hot day Mary Lizzie gave a party, a boat trip to Benton Harbor, and Alice consented to go. She sat by the rail, tapping kid-gloved fingers on the polished wood, as she discussed religion with Louise Mingo, the elocutionist. Mrs. Mingo found Alice's ideas a little startling. She could not believe in God, Alice said, certainly not in a God who was good or omnipotent. She had had a wonderful mother, who had worked hard to bring her up. Yet just when she had married and could do things for her, her mother had died. "How can God be good?" Alice asked Mrs. Mingo.

Retaining her child's outlook on life, with her immature emotions, her feeling that God — like her father, perhaps — had been unjust, Alice Williams could not care for anyone in an adult fashion. She demanded, but she could not give, love. Her dilemma was Dr. Dan's dilemma too, for Alice had married a man who required a large measure of love, who found himself frequently insecure without the reassurance that approbation gave him. It was not surprising then that Dr. Dan, who had sought and won affection from a number of women before he met her, in time was seeking emotional fulfillment elsewhere than with the unmoved, and, for all her beauty, unmoving woman he had married.

A Frenchwoman came to his office one day as a patient. She was not so much beautiful as she was engaging. She came back for further consultations and it was not long before it was apparent these calls could not be purely for medical advice. Then she stopped coming altogether, but coincidentally Dr. Dan's medical calls to the North Side seemed both more frequent and more lengthy.

Dr. Dan was discreet, he planned that no one should ever know, for he had no desire to hurt Alice's sense of dignity and right decorum. He probably knew that nothing more deep in her would be touched, even if she found him out, for he knew now that nothing deep in her ever had been touched. He had made a promise to her mother and he intended to keep that promise. He would always take care of Alice. But someone must care for him. He poured himself out constantly to his many patients. Somehow he must be replenished, even if it were an unworthy sort of replenishment, not the fulfilment he had once dreamed of, caught sight of for a moment, and had snatched from him.

The affair went on for some years. Alice might never have heard of it had not the janitor in the Frenchwoman's apartment building on the far North Side been both colored and a medical student. He talked.

When Alice heard of Dr. Dan's defection she fled to Washington to give herself time to think. She tried to get up the courage to talk things over with her old friend Mary Robinson Meriwether.

"Mary," she began hesitatingly, "I have something to tell you."

Mary saved her the embarrassment of going further. "I know, Alice," she said.

"What shall I do?" Alice asked.

In the end, Alice decided to do nothing. She returned to Chicago; and Dr. Dan, in the immemorial fashion of erring husbands, welcomed her with a Woods electric coupé of midnight blue. Alice was nervous about running the autocar with its unpredictable steering device. Finally she ran it up on a sidewalk, knocked down a fence, and would have overturned it if someone had not reached in and cut the switch. The coupé was finally sold. But it had been a magnificent gift and many said, "How good he is to her," and the undiscerning continued to remark, "What a perfect couple they make."

After that Alice Williams went frequently on long visits to her friends, several times to Christine Shoecraft Smith in Detroit. Coming home from one such visit, she walked into a surprise party of all her close friends. Dr. Dan had asked Mary Lizzie to invite them and had sent in a caterer to do the supper. "Alice is such a good woman," he said to Mary Lizzie when he asked her help.

But it was a cold home. The fire had died out of it.

Break with Booker T. Washington

IN the half dozen years immediately following Dr. Dan's return to Chicago, Booker Washington reached the height of his power. In those years, too, severe critics arose to confront him, younger Negroes better schooled than he, men who felt the Tuskegee principal was overemphasizing industrial training and thereby stifling the cultural education of a potential Negro leadership — the Talented Tenth, they called it. They were all vocal and their views were circulated in several Negro journals. In Boston, Monroe Trotter, Harvard '95, and George Forbes, Amherst '95, published the bitterly satirical *Guardian*. In New York City, the able T. Thomas Fortune edited the more restrained weekly, *The Age*. In the South, J. Max Barber managed *The Voice*, a flourishing monthly. From the scholarly pens of W. E. B. DuBois and Charles Waddell Chesnutt came essays and novels that were winning national attention from both colored and white.

Disturbed by growing disfranchisement, these men felt Booker Washington should push harder for their political rights. When he in his own person became political referee for the whole race during the Theodore Roosevelt administration, they were outraged. They felt he bowed too easily to the spread of Jim Crowism, that he even put the chief blame for the situation upon the black man. They wanted to organize in defense of their civil rights, to fight back, and they bitterly resented what they claimed

Washington's muffling of all ideas but his own. They
more clearly than he did what the acceptance of
by Tuskegee did in this respect. Barber published a
e Voice showing Washington with a padlock on his

In the winter of 1907, young Barber was in Chicago, stopping
with the Bentleys. One night Alice and Dr. Dan invited the Bentleys to bring Barber and come help eat the last of Dr. Dan's prairie chickens frozen away from his autumn hunting.

Dr. Dan received the fiery youth with quiet but warm cordial-
ity. Inevitably the conversation turned upon race interests. Dr.
Dan let Bentley and young Barber do most of the talking while,
with his usual deep reserve, he measured and weighed. Barber recalls his dignity, his refusal to be argumentative or quarrelsome.
"He must have thought me sophomoric indeed," Barber says in
retrospect. But Dr. Dan had given Booker Washington his interest, his effort and his belief over the years and he was not inclined to change now despite the best reasoning of the other two.
Bentley grew exasperated. He settled his pince-nez more firmly.

"Don't you see," he cried, "Booker Washington hasn't the *capacity* to conceive a comprehensive race policy!"

"Nor the ability to carry it out," Barber added.

But at the end of the evening they had to go away without either their host's sympathy or his money.

These divisions within the race disturbed Dr. Dan. They were
occurring all over the country. His oldest friends on the Provident Board were divided now. Madden had gone over with Bentley to the opposition, the so-called Niagara Movement. Wheeler,
like himself, refused to abandon Booker Washington. Dr. Dan
thought colored people should stick together, keep a united front;
that had always been his feeling. There was enough for all of them
to do without fighting each other.

Yet almost before he knew it, Dr. Dan was drawn into the fray.
Perhaps nothing else could have won him but his passion to save
Freedmen's Hospital for the greatest usefulness of the colored
people.

During the years since Dr. Dan had come back to Chicago, the struggle had continued in Congress and committees whether to build a new municipal hospital and send Freedmen's patients to it, or to give Freedmen's the new plant so long overdue and maintain its special character as Dr. Dan had pleaded. Controversy continued too because the jurisdiction of the hospital was still divided among the Department of the Interior, Howard University and the District of Columbia. One by one these matters were settled. An appropriation was finally made for a new Freedmen's Hospital of two hundred beds, on land owned by Howard but leased to the federal government *in perpetuum* at a dollar a year. The support of District of Columbia funds was discontinued and with it the District's partial authority over the hospital, leaving complete jurisdiction to the Department of the Interior.

As the new building neared completion, Dr. Dan could bear the betrayal of Freedmen's no longer. Somehow Warfield must be got out and a capable man appointed who would make the very best of the new facilities for the benefit of the race.

And now Dr. Dan was up against the very situation Bentley and Barber had complained of. The job at Freedmen's was now a political job, and all Negro patronage came from Booker Washington. If S. Laing Williams wanted an appointment in the Department of Justice in Chicago, he must address himself to Tuskegee, Alabama. If he got little attention at first, fortunately his wife guessed how to bring into play her battery of wiles, blandishments and useful journalistic articles glowing with praise for the Wizard of Tuskegee. Fannie Barrier Williams helped put across the first little Provident Hospital and she put across her husband with Booker Washington; the arbiter of Negro destiny wielded his influence and S. Laing Williams got his job.

Dr. Dan was no fool. To get the attention of the dictator, busy manipulating his far-flung empire, he must somehow offer Booker Washington useful service. Already Dr. Dan knew to his sorrow how little vision Washington had when it came to Negro medicine and nursing. He could not approach the Tuskegee principal directly about Freedmen's Hospital. He must begin somewhere off at a tangent.

Booker Washington was concerned about his failure to get the support he wanted from the Negro press. Eulogistic articles emanating from his own secretary, the very able Emmett Scott, whom some thought the brains of the Tuskegee machine, were too often turned down and critical comment published instead. In Chicago, the *Conservator* was one such derelict.

Like most colored newspapers, the *Conservator* had financial difficulties and like the rest kept alive on contributions from the more well-to-do citizenry. The next time Dr. Dan was approached it was a simple matter for him to say he was not inclined to support a paper that was attacking Booker Washington. In short order, Dr. Dan was quietly blue-penciling everything that went into the *Conservator* and was lining up the *Broadax* as well. Booker Washington was grateful.

Now Dr. Dan could broach the matter of Freedmen's and rest assured he would be listened to. He lost no time. The new hospital offered a prize for which many were aspiring, including a mediocre white sundown doctor in the Interior Secretary's own office.

Dr. Dan put the matter before Booker Washington in strong terms. If an inefficient man were appointed, he wrote — letting his spelling get out of hand as always when he was deeply moved — "it would be a *calamaty* to the whole aspiring race." It would turn the clock back years. In no other position, he said, could such harm be done. "It is too important to our men of science," he pleaded, "to be dealt out through favoritism. You are unbiased; only you can put the true situation to Secretary Garfield." Dr. Dan ended with an appeal perhaps more in keeping with his own character than Washington's. "I am appealing to you," he wrote, "for the interest of deserving men who will never know anything of this unselfish move on your part."

Booker Washington replied that he would do whatever seemed wise to prevent the appointment of an inefficient man. But to Dr. Dan's horror, both Washington and Scott assumed he himself

wanted the job, else why had he bothered? Tuskegee's mail was
heavy every day with the letters of job seekers. They saw no real
difference between his plea and the rest.

Dr. Dan tried again. He wrote Scott, "I want you and the Dr.
[Washington had been given an honorary degree and Dr. Dan
carefully used it] to understand me. My interest is sincere, it is
not for preferment." What he wanted, Dr. Dan said, was to ensure the retention of this splendid new plant for the perfection of
their young men and women in nursing, scientific medicine and
surgery. They needed postgraduate work and they could get it
no other place. "As the hospital stands now," he said, "it is simply running itself, just existing." It could be a grand place for
work, he urged, "a credit to us all," if only the proper person
were named surgeon-in-chief.

Dr. Dan wanted the brilliant, much abused Charles West appointed to the job. Then if he himself could be placed on the
Board of Visitors, he would work with West and between them
they would put Freedmen's in the front rank and keep it there.
This Board position, he explained, was a purely advisory one, no
pay, nothing but work. He wanted Booker Washington's assistance, he said, in what he knew was a good project, one that would
show results in the future. "Now is the time," he urged, "when
we can do much for our young men and women who are grop-
ing in the dark for leadership. They can do little for themselves
without opportunity and guidance."

So Dr. Dan pleaded with Booker Washington the case of the
Talented Tenth — the education of Negro leadership — though he
refused to join with the Niagara Movement.

The summer went by and Booker Washington failed to see Secretary Garfield, though he assured Dr. Dan he had tried. He was
working for an October appointment, he said, and suggested Dr.
Dan himself go talk to the Interior Secretary. Dr. Dan replied he
was willing to do so only if the Secretary invited him; otherwise,
he said, his visit would just stir up the Wolves who would assume
he was an applicant. He pointed out that Garfield's private secretary, James Parker, was a member of the Board of Visitors. If

ould sit in on the interview, he would repeat what was
he other Visitors, all of whom were working for the ap-
nt of the third-rate white doctor in Garfield's office.

e Booker Washington could answer Dr. Dan's letter, Dr.
Dan followed it hard with another. He had received a letter, he
told Washington, from a friend in the Interior Department, a
white man who kept him posted on the affairs of Freedmen's.
This friend had written:

"Do you know Mr. Washington very well? I am informed on
what I regard as good authority that he is endorsing strongly a
Chicago physician for the position of Surgeon-in-chief of Fr.
Hospital."

Dr. Dan said he could not harmonize this statement with his
present understanding, relations and confidences with Booker
Washington. He felt the proper thing was to communicate directly and ask if he had been misinformed. His own feeble efforts,
he said, would come to naught without Washington's all-powerful
assistance. That was why he had appealed to Washington to save
all they had in sight for the general good. "So-called society, outside show, sham, humbug of any kind," Dr. Dan said, "I have
nothing to do with."

The unnamed Chicago physician was George Hall. While Hall
was steadily entrenching himself in Provident Hospital and creat-
ing a flourish in colored society, he was also busy bringing himself to the attention of the Tuskegee principal. Mrs. Hall helped
him. She wrote to thank Booker Washington for a copy of his
newest book — ghostwritten, the Niagara men thought, by Scott:

"When the Dr. returns [from his trip], he will find your delightful gift awaiting him. To say he will be pleased is putting it
very mildly. The Dr. indulges in a sort of hero worship for the
'Wizard of Tuskegee,' you know, a condition to which the rest
of the family must also plead guilty. His books therefore occupy
a unique place in our affections and the autograph renders them
altogether priceless."

A few glances through *Tuskegee and Its People*, she said, had
increased her already great longing to see his "big wonderful

Tuskegee." Immediately Booker Washington wrote back: "I wish very much you will decide to come here to spend a portion of the winter. I think you would enjoy it here very much."

There was no question but that Theodocia Hall enjoyed her stay at Tuskegee or that George Hall enjoyed the prospect of closer and closer contact with the Tuskegee machine. He seized every occasion to let Chicago Negroes know he was a loyal — Barber called him a "raucous" — supporter of Booker Washington. But if Hall was now asking Washington for a plum, Washington denied it. His answer to Dr. Dan was categorical: "I not only have endorsed no Chicago party for this place," he said, "but I have not been asked to do so."

Dr. Dan was easily convinced, especially when Washington kept his promise to mention Freedmen's to Garfield. At the same time Booker Washington mentioned Dr. Dan. "I had not finished telling him about you," the politician reported, "before he, himself, suggested he would like to see you and wondered whether you would come to see him on his invitation."

Before an appointment could be made, however, Booker Washington's faithful secretary, Emmett Scott, who had had chronic appendicitis for some time and who was worn out with overwork, became worse. Washington was away in the North. Kenney wired Dr. Dan to come down and operate on Scott. Washington, informed of the situation, plied Dr. Dan with telegrams and urged him to give Scott his best attention. Dr. Dan dropped everything and went down to Tuskegee, performed the operation, and watched the patient for two days before returning to his work in Chicago.

That the private secretary to the principal of Tuskegee Normal and Industrial Institute had been ill, had been operated upon by Dr. Daniel H. Williams of Chicago, and was now recovering, was duly noted in the *Tuskegee Student*. As Washington's mouthpiece, the *Student* enjoyed a wide circulation all over the United States. It was no ordinary school newspaper. Negroes everywhere read it before they did their local white newspaper. It must have been hard enough for Hall to swallow the long "Appreciation" of

Dr. Dan which Kenney had published in the *Student* some months previously. The publicity about the operation on Scott was more than he could stand.

Hall had at last reached a long-coveted position on the surgical staff of Provident Hospital. By confining his efforts to pelvic surgery he had become a fair operator of the rough and ready sort in that part of the body. He had arrived where he wanted to be, where, so he himself put it, the money was. Not that he would chance too much. Several remembered how Hall had cautioned Austin Curtis not to risk his reputation by operating on a rich white patient. "Suppose he died," he had said to Curtis, "where would you be?" Hall, says a former associate, kept his mortality record low by prudently not operating unless he could see certain success; if a patient died through his omission to operate, Providence could be blamed, but not George Hall.

Hall was scarcely appointed to the surgical staff before he felt himself altogether on the same footing as Dr. Dan. He sought to emulate Dr. Dan's surgical tours by offering his own services in the Negro hinterland, and to offset Dr. Dan's campaign for hospitals he proposed to set up infirmaries. Such was the need, Hall was frequently invited, but frequently, too, he was not invited back. In Birmingham a local surgeon had to take the knife out of Hall's hand in the middle of an operation to save the patient's life. But in Hall's own eyes he was now an actual rival of Dr. Dan and as such he demanded equal rights, including equal appreciation in the *Student*. He sat down and poured out his indignation to Booker Washington. His six-page letter may still be read in the Washington files in the Library of Congress.

Hall told Washington he still prized and appreciated his friendship above all others, but certain things had occurred, he said, that led him to believe his enthusiastic support might be a source of embarrassment to Washington and of humiliation to himself. He was not complaining, he assured Washington, about the leader's personal treatment. Nor was it in his mind to expect Washington to interfere with any of his teachers or subordinates on his behalf. "It was not that I desired so much to do an operation on Mr.

Scott," Hall said, "as that I desire that through the *Student* he stop operating on me." Hall had an engaging, ready wit and he used it now. He also had a very tender ego.

"My grievance," he said, "is the use the *Student* is put to, exploiting a man whose professional rivalry with me is known to you and to every one around Tuskegee. A man who lets everybody know when he has just received an urgent telegram from Mr. Washington to come to Tuskegee. When my friends, on whom he has taken special pains to impress how important he is to you at Tuskegee, asked me about it, I said it was not true. So you can well imagine I was embarrassed beyond all measure when there appeared in the *Student* a column and a half of Appreciation of this great man!"

Hall complained he had received twenty marked copies of that issue from various parts of the country and many personal letters asking how this had happened, a number of them "I-told-you-so" style. Further to appreciate his chagrin, Hall asked Washington to remember that not long ago he himself had performed several operations at Tuskegee, lectured to the nurses and to the student body, and not a word of it had appeared in the *Student*. He had noticed the omission at the time, he said, but had dismissed it, thinking it must be the policy of the paper. But no, just let Dr. W. go to Tuskegee and perform one operation, grumbled Hall, and his name was boosted as high as printer's ink could go, including a quarter-page account of an old operation performed eighteen years ago.

Dr. Dan's famous heart operation rankled sorely with George Hall, who could not hope to produce anything like it. Partisanship was another matter; he was sure his record beat Dr. Dan's. "When I think of my unquestioned well-known stand for Tuskegee and all concerned, in Chicago and everywhere," he said, "as compared with one who has never opened his mouth in public to advocate the school or the policy of its principal, I think I have earned the right to seriously object to such a plain case of partiality."

Hall wound up his long diatribe with a neat bit of humor. He could always get people to laugh and while they were laughing he often got his way. "Like the old Negro in the bear fight who," he said to Washington, "called upon the Lord and prayed, 'If you don't help me, don't help the bear,' all I ask is that whatever little struggles we may have here, we be left alone and if any help is given, let it be along the lines of consistent loyalty and work for Tuskegee."

Booker Washington answered in his suavest fashion, thanking Hall for his kind letter and assuring him that no one at Tuskegee had intentionally meant to offend him. Everyone felt the highest appreciation for his interest in the school and his valuable services for it. "Sometime when I am in Chicago," the principal said, cannily putting nothing on paper, "I shall hope to have the privilege of talking to you and of telling you more in detail just how I feel toward you."

Hall's letter appeared to have no effect on the close relationship of Dr. Dan and Booker Washington. Unknown to the public and even to Dr. Dan, the Tuskegee boss had managed through an intermediary to buy out *The Age* and so had shut off Fortune's criticism in New York, but he still needed Dr. Dan's services in Chicago. Letters continued to flow between them weekly, often daily, if not about Freedmen's then about the newspapers. Washington would write Dr. Dan to let the treasurer of the *Conservator* have fifty dollars, letting him believe it was a contribution from Dr. Dan himself. Dr. Dan would send his receipt to Tuskegee and Scott would reimburse him.

In March Dr. Dan went East and saw the Secretary of the Interior. The men talked for two hours. Dr. Dan came away happy. He liked Garfield. He thought him a fine manly person, "not a politician," and found him very understanding about the bad conditions at Freedmen's. Garfield promised to clean things up and asked Dr. Dan to keep in close touch with him. Booker Washington was in the city and Dr. Dan spent an hour telling him everything, but he also took care to write Scott all the ins and outs of the matter. He knew as well as anyone who the real tactician was at Tuskegee:

"I so much want your interest and help in this important matter, this one grand opportunity of our time, to finally develop an exceptional institution. If it is lost or carelessly handled, it will put our doctors and nurses back 25 years."

Later Booker Washington himself saw Garfield and wrote Dr. Dan that the Secretary of the Interior wanted recommendations for a reorganization of Freedmen's. Washington asked Dr. Dan to send him by return mail the names of six or eight colored doctors who in his opinion represented the very highest and best in Negro medicine, men as far as possible who had specialized in some direction. It was the Secretary's idea, he wrote, to have a staff of visiting lecturers in the medical school and the nurses' training school. "Of course," he said, "we want to include your name." Having disposed of Freedmen's, Washington added that when he saw Dr. Dan there were "other and more important matters" he wanted to take up with him. So much of Booker Washington's negotiations could not be committed to paper.

Dr. Dan was elated. "It is very encouraging," he wrote, "to know you would take the time from your busy life for a matter so entirely foreign to your work and interest. This is the only opening in America for our men along this special line." With superlative selflessness, he thanked Washington for permitting him to *assist* in this important work. The entire race, he said, would be permanently advanced and benefited by the foresight of Secretary Garfield and by Booker Washington's wise counsel.

Dr. Dan's list of outstanding men in Negro Medicine included F. A. Stewart and C. V. Roman of Nashville; John E. Hunter of Lexington, Kentucky; John A. Kenney of Tuskegee; Harry McCard of Baltimore; Marcus F. Wheatland of Newport; Felix Antoine of Chicago; Charles I. West and John R. Francis of Washington; and Henry M. Minton of Philadelphia. The others, he said, were only "surface men."

Washington's next letter brought an ominous small cloud on the promising horizon. "Do you not think it a good idea," Washington wrote, "to put Dr. Hall's name down in some department? Of course," he said, "I understand the conditions surrounding him, but sometimes I find it pays to overcome littleness with bigness and to do our whole duty regardless of how people may feel toward us. What do you think of it?"

Booker Washington had asked Dan for a list of the "very highest and best" among Negro doctors. Hall had no claim to such distinction. Dr. Dan might conceivably have named Austin M. Curtis for surgery, but he chose West. Either was head and shoulders above Hall. Washington might not have known this, but now he was not asking for the best man, only that his touchy supporter in Chicago be included. It put Dr. Dan on the spot, but he replied forthrightly, and his life philosophy was in his words:

"In selecting the names sent you, I drew upon my knowledge of what each individual had actually done to merit recognition, and not upon newspaper notoriety. I believe the names seldom appear in the Negro Press, though they are powerful factors in race progress. They are doing something. You know I am a great admirer of the doctrine you advocate: 'The Man Who is doing Something,' quietly adding something to the sum total. That is the man who can get my endorsement.

"I cannot say that I consider the party you named in this class. There is so much that you do not know and have no way of knowing.

"All of the Gentlemen I named are not friends of mine. Some of them I never saw, but I do know of their ability and honor, and assure you that they are men of such standing that I would be perfectly willing to serve with them.

"And again, I want to impress most sincerely, Mr. Washington, that I am in this for the love of the work and the advancement of my people, to make conditions better for them, to prepare them for serious life work. I am serious in everything I undertake. If I go into this, it is not for social prestige or outside show; it means to me long days of patient hard work from home."

Dr. Dan added that he would be glad if Booker Washington would keep him informed of whatever action was taken, but he did not feel sanguine, he said, as to the success of Garfield's idea of visiting lecturers. However the Secretary was a grand man, with a humane heart and a noble spirit, and he was willing, Dr. Dan said, to work hard to support his plan.

He added that the Secretary had advanced the idea of making the hospital assist in supporting itself by arranging for paying patients. "This is quite feasible," Dr. Dan said and, without referring to his own plea for such a plan years before, he enclosed an estimate of income that might be expected from private and semi-private patients and remarked that it would raise the tone of the hospital and attract a good class of people to it.

The next day Dr. Dan wrote Booker Washington again. He said he had reread Washington's letter and thought perhaps he had not been frank enough in his reply. He said he did not want to embarrass Washington, but he was sure that to add George Hall would dismember the working harmony of the staff of lecturers in short order. "I have tried it," said Dr. Dan, "many times I have subserved for peace and harmony, but it never came." In a sentence this had been the history of Provident Hospital for the past ten years. It had been a weary time and he could not face entering upon a similar situation elsewhere. "I cannot see my way clear," he said to Washington, "to serve in association with him. I am sure it would only eventuate again in cliques and factions and accomplish nothing. That is what would happen by the inclusion. I think I know you well enough to say that I believe you want me to be frank."

No more to Dr. Dan than to George Hall did Booker Washington take a clean-cut stand. "For the present," was his answer, "let the whole matter concerning the party about whom I wrote pass out of your mind. Nothing has been said or done to obligate me or any one else in the matter, and there is no special reason why he should be taken up just now at least." He had recommended to Garfield, he said, that Dr. Dan be appointed a member of the Board of Visitors.

Dr. Dan referred no more to Hall. He thanked Booker Washington for his courtesy and confidence in recommending his appointment. Probably his friend in the Interior Office had been in touch with him, for he added: "I am of the opinion the Secretary has some plans of his own. I rather incline to the view those Washington City factions are working on the Sec'y to contravert your plans. You will know best."

Dr. Dan was altogether right in his fears. The faculty at Howard University had submitted their plan for reorganization, with their candidates for staff. Purvis had written his usual letter about his lifelong sacrifice for Howard and put up his own candidate for surgeon-in-chief. Warfield, taking a leaf out of Purvis's Bible, had stirred up his own supporters to write the Secretary urging no changes lest dire things result.

James Parker, Garfield's private secretary, was in a strategic position to influence the well-intentioned but overburdened Secretary of the Interior. He had seen Dr. Dan call on Garfield and remain closeted with him for two hours; he had read Booker Washington's letter recommending the appointment of Dr. Dan to the Board of Visitors, the Board on which he himself sat. When he prepared his memoranda for Garfield on the subject of Freedmen's, he inserted a paragraph where it was sure to be read:

> Dr. Williams of Chicago, who called here a few days ago, was formerly surgeon in chief of the hospital. Upon an investigation before the Board of Visitors of charges of alleged misconduct, where he was attended by his attorney, Hon. Jerry Wilson, now dead, he was unexpectedly confronted with charges that he was compelled to admit, and when told by his attorney that he had committed a felony, he was so startled and confused that he fainted and had to be resuscitated by the assistance of the committee. The details of this matter, I am advised, will be found in a report now on file in this Department.

Parker felt safe in so twisting the facts. He counted on Garfield's not asking to see the ten-year-old report, and Judge Wilson was dead. The easiest thing for Garfield, confronted with a confusing situation, was to leave the matter in abeyance. He went off for the summer without doing more than to acknowledge receipt of Booker Washington's suggestion, not indicating what action he would take.

In August the National Medical Association was to meet in New York City. A few weeks before the medical meeting, Booker Washington wrote George Hall a letter from his summer home on Long Island. It showed he had made up his mind as to his real answer to Hall's long letter of the previous March.

> MY DEAR DR. HALL:
> My son whom you saw at Tuskegee when you were there, is now in Denver, Col., and has been there since early in June. He is seemingly better, but we are not quite sure as to his exact condition. Mrs. Washington and I are both very anxious that you give him a thorough examination and prescribe for him. He will be returning East about August 1st. We have planned for him to stop in Chicago for as long a time as you think it necessary for him to stay in order for you to see him thoroughly.
> Are you coming to the National Medical Association? If so I wish very much that you and Mrs. Hall might make a visit to us at our summer home at Huntington. We are not far from New York and are right on the seashore, and would extend you both a hearty welcome here.

No matter now to Hall if the great leader's secretary were attended by the man he aspired to rival. *He* was commanded to serve the royal family itself, even to visit with them in their summer palace! As George Hall commuted back and forth between the North Shore and the medical meetings in the city, he must have been in top form, feeling his oats, and ready for mischief. Opportunity was not long in presenting itself.

Five hundred colored doctors, pharmacists and dentists from twenty-nine states gathered for the tenth annual meeting of the National Medical Association. While the doctors met in the Plaza Assembly Rooms on East 29th Street, fifty-nine colored nurses, representative of 450 in the country at large, congregated in St. Mark's Methodist Episcopal Church on West 53rd Street and formed the National Association of Colored Graduate Nurses. Kenney reported on the ever-growing number of hospitals now operated by and for colored people in the United States. The harvest of Dr. Dan's sowing was coming in.

At the surgical clinic held in Lincoln Hospital, Dr. Dan performed three major operations, one on the breast and two abdominal cases. He also read a scholarly paper on "Conservative Treatment of Crushing Injuries of the Extremities," the subject which had long interested him. He had expended a considerable sum on stereoptican slides and showed forty views — both drawings and photographs — all taken from his own cases and illustrating various apparently incurable injuries. As he showed them he explained in detail how he had treated each case and successfully maintained "the continuity of the parts." His explanations, said a reporter, were couched in such simple language that the humblest person readily grasped his thought. Every doctor present agreed it was a magnificent treat. When he had finished, the entire hall full of men and women rose and enthusiastically clapped their thanks.

Professionally Dr. Dan was the bright star of the conference. Politically it was another story. Dr. John E. Hunter, a rising young surgeon of Lexington, Kentucky, another who had received inspiration and friendly encouragement from Dr. Dan, placed the name of his hero in nomination for the presidency without consulting him. Immediately George Hall, fresh from his victory with Booker Washington, plunged into a campaign to defeat the man he hated.

Already Hall had won adherents in the National Medical Association among others like himself who were disgruntled at their lesser position, men whose pride had been hurt when, as in one instance, Dr. Dan had been forced to take the knife out of fumbling hands to save a patient on the clinic table. Such men were only too ready to respond to Hall's sniping tactics — the well-placed hint, the lifted eyebrow, above all the ridicule of which he was past master and with which he could make the most innocent and upright squirm. Dr. Dan with his old-fashioned loyalties and formalities, with his adoration of his Mistress Medicine, and all his underlying timidity and sensitivity, was only too easily victimized by Hall.

At the Association meeting in 1905, Hall had dared to bring his fire into the operating room, a precinct that to Dr. Dan was little short of sacred. Dr. Dan had been lecturing to the assembly preparatory to operating upon a fibroid tumor of the uterus. It was apparent the case would not be simple. As he lectured, he began to operate. He dwelt upon the possible complications that might be present, especially the possibility of a tubo-ovarian abscess. He described the changes in technical approach and the drainage that such a finding would demand. As he proceeded, such an abscess was in fact found; in addition, the uterus was firmly fixed in the pelvis. It was a difficult problem. Hall was sitting in the front row.

"If it's too much for you," he taunted, "why don't you come out and close up?"

Dr. Dan ceased lecturing instantly. He pushed his assistant aside, took over and handled all the instruments himself. In a few minutes the tumor was lying on the table. Then he drained the abscess and finished the operation, all in complete silence.

Eyewitnesses found it hard not to embellish their accounts of what happened. One Mississippi doctor told how he saw Dr. Dan pull off his gloves and gown with a curt "Thank you, gentlemen," stride from the room, "never to return again" to a meeting of the association he had helped found.

Actually Dr. Dan did return, though it was only to bear increasing humiliation. There was not only backstair electioneering against him in New York, but the emboldened Hall now thundered in resounding tones from the very convention platform against "those who come among us only when the honors are being dispensed." Dr. Dan was defeated. Afterward, when Dailey tried to draw him into an account of the meeting, he refused to discuss it. Dailey thought his humiliation had much to do with his never publishing the valuable paper he had read.

Dr. Dan could only regard this as another rejection of a deep and painful sort. He did not care to be president of the National Medical Association; he had had that opportunity if he had desired it. But he did not want to be voted down.

In these months Dr. Dan was pressed with patients, patients who came halfway across the country to seek his skill, patients he traveled miles to serve. In September he was in North Dakota, in October he spent a week operating in Dallas, Texas, and followed it by another week holding his annual clinic at Nashville. Returning to Chicago, he found Lewis M. Dunton, aged white president of Claflin University, South Carolina, bedfast in the Auditorium Hotel where he had been waiting a week for Dr. Dan to return and care for him.

Correspondence between Booker Washington and Dr. Dan had almost ceased. Dr. Dan had little opportunity for it, and Washington needed no more help with the Chicago press, the *Conservator* having been reorganized with his henchmen in control. Scott, however, kept up a flow of letters to the man he felt had saved his life and Dr. Dan scrawled an answer when he could between trips. In October he wrote Scott: "Just saw Dr. W. off for Washington in the best of spirits. He is fully alive to the matter you and Mrs. Washington discussed. He sees the point and has observed certain things himself that are very clear to others."

Matters had come to a pass where the potentate had to be protected from the wiles of the flamboyant Theodocia Hall, or so his wife thought. Mrs. Hall had arrived at Tuskegee too many times with her numerous trunks and set that simple rural community agog with the lavishness of her wardrobe and her cosmetics. At Huntington she doubtless outdid herself. While Booker Washington was an excellent politician and manipulator of people, fully aware of Hall's maneuvers and willing to accept them, or even to sympathize with them, he was apparently not so objective about Mrs. Hall's tactics. Evidently Dr. Dan had been enlisted as someone who could speak to Booker Washington on so delicate a matter and be listened to. Every appearance of scandal must be kept from the great man and tongues once set wagging are hard to stop.

Dr. Dan risked a good deal in approaching Washington on so ticklish a subject. Despite Washington's going off in apparent good spirits, this act may well have put the seal to the death sentence Washington had already written to their long-time relationship.

That sentence was inevitable, first, because of Hall's intractable demands and, second, because of Booker Washington's precarious position during the presidential election year. If he were to retain his political power, Taft must be elected. Dr. Dan was not in politics, Hall was on the executive committee of the Hyde Park Republican Club. So Washington dropped Dr. Dan to favor Hall and Hall gave his effective support to the Washington-Taft campaign. When it was all over, a lieutenant in the capital city wrote Booker Washington: "The election of Taft is a distinct triumph for Tuskegee Institute."

All this time nothing more had been said about Freedmen's Hospital. Late in November Dr. Dan asked Scott to remind Booker Washington of his promise to write him about a certain matter when he got back to Tuskegee. Scott answered that Washington found himself unable to recollect what the thing was. "He will be glad," Scott said, "if you will let him have a memorandum. The only thing he seems to remember is that he was to send you five dollars which he borrowed and which he thinks he has already returned."

This must have hurt Dr. Dan deeply. How could either Scott or Washington entertain the idea for a moment that he would ever refer in words or writing to the five dollars! To him it had been, he said, a mark of friendship, a mark of cordial relationship. What he wanted to hear about was how matters stood with relation to Freedmen's. As he had walked to the train with Mr. Washington in Chicago, Washington had said he would be looking over affairs in the capital city next day and when he got home would write Dr. Dan. "My interest," said Dan, "led me to inquire further knowing it must have slipped his mind."

Booker Washington still did not answer Dr. Dan for over three weeks. Then he explained he had not written because, as a matter of fact, he had nothing to report. "I find the Secretary has made no move in the direction of carrying out his promises," he wrote, "and when a man does not keep his promises I soon get cold feet on him." He said that until the Secretary did make some move in the direction mentioned, he would not feel encouraged to go further. Dr. Dan could plainly see there was nothing further to be expected from the dictator at Tuskegee on behalf of the national Negro hospital.

Warfield retained his hold and Freedmen's, despite the new building, continued in mediocrity for many years, at one time being threatened with loss of its license from the National Association of Trained Nurses. Dr. Dan had not exaggerated when he said the wrong man at Freedmen's would be a calamity to the entire aspiring race.

While correspondence between Booker Washington and Dr. Dan, from being a weekly and often a daily matter, ceased altogether, that between Washington and the two Halls mounted steadily. At the same time their letters grew warmer and warmer in tone and finally reached a freedom and intimacy of expression never set to paper by the dignified Dr. and Mrs. Williams. From making reservations for the Washingtons when they came to Chicago, the Halls began taking the royal couple into their own home. Regularly they went to Tuskegee to return the visit.

Mrs. Hall undertook to do little shopping errands for Mr. Washington. Into the correspondence this entailed crept coy phrases understandable only to the initiated: "Met Mrs. White just as I left you. The luck of some people!!!" Or when the "magnetic Teddy" (Roosevelt) came to Chicago, "How can you stay away? Whew! Mr. Banks!!!" Or, T. J. H. wrote that she found Major Moton a charming visitor and had enjoyed piloting him to Hull House. "You see," she said, "he was so much more tractable than some other visitors we've had. I didn't take him to Marshall Field's however."

"You will be glad to know," Washington wrote to Mrs. Hall, "I have settled my bill at Moffetts and you are therefore free to call upon them for your picture." Mrs. Hall answered by return mail that it was a positive relief to her to know she could look Moffett square in the face. "I haven't been going on Congress St. you know," she said, "I shall claim my picture tomorrow." There

were gifts, too, of Southern possum and Tuskegee swee
sent Mrs. Hall and disappointment expressed when ū.
failed to make their winter visit. On the occasion of their previou.
visit so many eyebrows had been raised that Mrs. Washington had
decided Mrs. Hall must be told she had overstayed her welcome.
This fact was either not known to Washington, or he pretended
not to know it.

It was George Hall now, and not Dr. Dan, who got press notices into the Chicago papers favorable to Washington and his affairs. It was Hall who manipulated this one and that one and enjoyed himself thoroughly. "If you will just leave that newspaper
reporter to me," he wrote Washington, "I think when I get
through he will be good. He is hugging me now to save himself
and I am sawing off his limb close to the tree." Things were quiet
in the Windy City now, Hall assured the Tuskegee principal.
Anyone who spoke out at all spoke for Washington. "You have
absolutely nothing to think about," Hall told his overlord, "as far
as the Chicago Negro is concerned."

In January 1908 Dr. Dan was chairman by common consent of
the three hundred men and women who worked industriously on
the various committees for the big charity ball held in the First
Regiment Armory for the benefit of Provident Hospital. In May
doctors and leading professional men gave him a complimentary
banquet at Bethel Methodist Episcopal Church to celebrate the
twenty-fifth anniversary of his work. Colored doctors from all
parts of the country sent tokens of their affection and esteem — a
cut-glass and silver inkstand from New York, a solid silver water
pitcher from Philadelphia, a "nice little sum of money" from
Texas to make the hall a "profusion of flowers." Chicago doctors
presented a silver loving cup. In the thirty-seven names inscribed
on it that of George Hall is conspicuous by its absence.

Dr. Dan was still the community's hero, but Hall, emboldened
by his success with Booker Washington and with the National
Medical Association, now began to speak out more and more dar-
ingly against Dr. Dan. The envious and the ne'er-do-wells re-

sponded willingly enough to his insinuation that this "fair com-
plexioned fellow doesn't quite seem to know what race he wants
to belong to." Mrs. Hall tossed her head at the women's parties
and declared she didn't know why they should be forced to accept as colored everyone who *said* he had colored blood. "And besides," she added, "the younger men should be given their chance."

Step by step, the Halls promoted their thesis that Dr. Dan and
his wife were not only snobs but disloyal as well. Whispers went
around that you never saw really dark people cross their threshold.
And since so many of the old settlers, their long-time friends, were
of free mixed lineage, there was a modicum of truth in this asser-
tion that gave it plausibility.

Where the dark-skinned George Hall could maintain an easy
approach to all and sundry, the fair-skinned Dr. Dan was at a dis-
advantage. In the ever-growing colored colony there were now
many who no longer knew him by sight, who threw hostile
glances in the street at one they assumed was alien. One day as
Dr. Dan strode up Dearborn Avenue, the fire bell rang out and he
spoke to an old colored woman in the friendly common vernacu-
lar. "Where's the fire, sister?" he asked. She gave one look at his
pale Caucasian features and drew back outraged. "I ain't no sister
of yourn," she retorted. The South Side had been Dr. Dan's home
for a quarter century, but it was less homelike now.

Neither Dr. Dan nor his wife possessed the qualities demanded
to wage the sort of warfare confronting them. Dr. Dan, ever ready
to discuss medicine and surgery and professional articles, would
not waste his time dallying in the Provident corridors over what
he considered chitchat. Besides he thought a hospital, and particularly a race hospital, ought to present the highest standards of
busy, quiet efficiency. George Hall on the other hand, says Dr.
Max Gethner, then one of the white internes, was always extremely sociable, ready with a smile and a story. New people
might admire Dr. Dan for his extraordinary abilities, but admiration is not liking, and they fell only too easily under the sway of
Hall's hearty cheerfulness. George Hall was human, people said.

More than one hospital has been the scene of a struggle for

power. Petty jealousy and dissension often crop up among doctors and surgeons. Perhaps something of the daring, the life-and-death aspects of the work, makes some enjoy their power and seek more. While George Hall was undermining Dr. Dan at Provident, John B. Murphy and Nicholas Senn, in another part of Chicago, were carrying on an ugly feud. The chief surgeon of a white hospital on the North Side remarked that he was retiring with pleasure from the petty politics and bickering of the active staff to the restful status of an emeritus. At Provident all such factors were overemphasized because it was the only hospital in Chicago where doctors of dark skin could function. Had there been no race barrier in the other institutions, envy and rivalry need not have been bottled up to explode in mortal fashion.

While Dr. Dan, immune to restrictions by virtue of his light skin and his long-established eminence achieved in a more tolerant, less competitive day, was free to operate in other hospitals and was very busy doing so, the ambitious George Hall had no other outlet for his energy than Provident. Dr. Dan's occupations elsewhere left Hall a clear arena and he made the most of it. He was always on hand, at every board meeting and on all the important committees. The staff came to feel their jobs depended on Hall's favor, and he was shown every possible attention. The superintendent of nurses, Jeanette Lyon, became his devoted lieutenant. Her obeisance to Hall led her to express criticism, even hatred, of Dr. Dan at every possible episode, says Gethner. If Dr. Dan gave the nurses a party, she said he was promoting insubordination. Her attitude was demoralizing to discipline among the nurses and internes, some of whom were only too prone anyhow to regard Dr. Dan's uncompromising standards and his severity toward laxness as needless fussiness.

Gradually his service was impaired at every turn. The operating room would not be ready for him. Nurses would not be detailed to him. His patients were shown little discourtesies. If internes did not actually countermand his orders, they indifferently forgot them.

Even Alf Anderson, a man now and forgetful of the times Dr.

Dan had fetched and fended and protected him in Janesville, allowed himself to be turned against Dr. Dan. Almost daily Mrs. Hall was seen hobnobbing with Alf at his clerk's desk in the Provident lobby and Alf did what he could to throw confusion into Dr. Dan's affairs. Dr. A. J. Booker remembers how he would turn some of Dr. Dan's patients over to other doctors or urge private patients to enter the free ward.

The Halls were a perfect team for their purpose. Hall pressured any younger doctors who manifested a show of independence by cutting them off from opportunities for advancement. At the same time he offered to "fix it up" for the meek who allowed him to dominate. Mrs. Hall dictated the social destinies of their wives, kept them out of clubs, off party lists, and otherwise assigned them to outer limbo if their husbands misbehaved. It took those who had lived in Chicago a long time and who knew Dr. Dan in the early days not to succumb to this kind of skirmishing.

In spite of their success with the newcomers, however, the Halls never penetrated into more select groups. Women nurtured in gentler ways shrank from the aggressively aspiring Theodocia Hall. Scrupulous men drew back from her husband's uncertain ethics. The Bentleys and the Joneses never invited the Halls into their homes. Hall met other defeats. He was never accepted into the exclusive Negro fraternity, Sigma Pi Phi. Dr. Dan grew sick of Hall's pressures to get in. He had been a charter member of the Chicago Boulé, but in 1909, tired of the constant drumfire kept up by Hall's faction, he resigned. Immediately Hall circulated the report that Dr. Dan had been kicked out. Despite everything, however, Hall failed to muster enough votes to get in.

Dr. Dan must have found it a relief to get away from the contentious scene in Chicago. His trips to assist struggling colored doctors in the South and West renewed his spirit. His annual week at Meharry Medical College came to seem like a vacation, though he performed five operations a day. Dean Hubbard always gave what amounted to a dinner of state, with all the medical faculty present. The F. A. Stewarts gave a dinner too.

Sometimes Dr. Dan stopped with Dr. C. O. Hadley, and sometimes with the James Carroll Napiers when Alice accompanied him. Usually, however, he stayed with the Stewarts. Little Annie Stewart looked forward to the annual coming of childless Dr. Dan. He tossed her on his shoulder and called her Mooks, a name of his own invention. Young Ferdinand Stewart looked upon this Northerner as a remarkably free person and resolved to get out of Jim Crow Nashville as soon as he grew up. Mrs. Stewart invariably found her stock of china increased by a few pieces of Haviland or Dresden after each visit. Invariably too Dr. Dan carried home a bag of game, for a little shooting was always squeezed in somehow.

In 1910 his Meharry visit was marked by the opening of a fine new hospital with facilities for forty patients, later extended for eighty, and an amphitheater that allowed 125 students to witness operations. Only ten short years before, his operations were performed by lamplight in a crowded basement room. Now Meharry graduates flocked in from all over the South, and patients were brought from a half dozen states for Dr. Dan's services. Grateful students unveiled a life-sized portrait of Dr. Dan in the lobby of the new hospital.

There was no question in Nashville as to where credit should be given or honor paid for a student body tripled in numbers in a decade. But in Chicago George Hall was now circulating the statement that Provident Hospital had been "kept alive" by him when Dr. Dan went off to seek, Hall claimed, greater honors elsewhere.

Soon he was attacking Dr. Dan's weekly clinic at Provident, a clinic to which young Negro doctors had come across the miles, the one clinic in Chicago where a black man could get an intimate view, ask questions and be answered. But Hall found reasons why Dr. Dan's clinic was not practicable and it was eliminated. The best a man could do was to watch the postings and try not to miss such operations as Dr. Dan still performed at Provident despite all hampering. Dr. Dan, on his part, did what he could to visit the operations of the younger men and give them his quiet, unobtrusive advice. Dr. Gethner never forgot how Dr. Dan stood by at his first abdominal operation, asking questions, making certain suggestions, praising his effort. This was now the only way the younger men could enjoy the kind of instruction that Dr. Dan gave so superbly.

Dr. Dan had staunch friends who were impregnable to Hall's maneuvers. Their numbers did not dwindle through any change of heart, but death took its toll of some and the influx of newcomers gradually outweighed the others. This was true of the Provident board of trustees. In the beginning there were colored men on the board who were not so susceptible to Hall as were the white members — Negroes who had begun the institution with Dr. Dan, given of their funds and their time, as they knew Hall had not — Lloyd Wheeler, James Madden, Charles Bentley, Charles Smiley, Jerry Stewart, Theodore W. Jones. As long as they were on the board, Hall's progress was slow.

Allen Wesley should have been another. He was among the founders too. He was scholarly and well prepared, but Wesley was vacillating. "He couldn't make up his mind where to cross the street." Wesley grew less and less interested in surgery and more and more interested in his job with a fraternal order. He never tried to oppose Hall. As head, figurehead, of the interne committee, he was influenced by Hall's idea that colored internes were too inclined to stay on in Chicago. More and more white men were appointed and colored graduates had little opportunity for a dozen years in the institution founded to train them. Had Wesley been different, this story might have been different, for he outlasted many of the colored board members who dropped from the scene through death or disgust.

Lloyd Wheeler would have helped counteract Hall, but he had business misfortunes and went off, a brokenhearted man, to take a job at Tuskegee. His loss at Provident, where for eleven years he had been president of the Provident Hospital Association of supporting members, was a great one. By 1907, aside from Wesley, there were only four others of the original fifteen on the board; by 1912, but two.

So as the early founders disappeared from the scene, Hall had worked his way up. Dr. Dan did what he could to make the situation tolerable. His hand may be seen in the appointment, too late, to the surgical staff of James F. Neff from the Mercy Hospital staff, and of J. Charles Hepburn of Northwestern. This was some support for Dr. Dan, but not enough, and Neff left at the end of a year and Hepburn shortly thereafter.

In 1911 Hall strengthened his position still further by the formation of another powerful committee — the committee on selection of staff. On it were Allen Wesley and the white Judge Robert McMurdy. Judge McMurdy was already interested in and later married Jeannette Lyon, the superintendent of nurses who by now was telling around that Dr. Dan drank too much and even that he used drugs.

Hall's campaign drew to a head in 1912. In that year he was on four of the six hospital committees, as well as on the board. His network was complete, he only awaited a test of his power. He found it in Dr. Dan's appointment as associate attending surgeon at St. Luke's Hospital. This was an unprecedented honor for the race, but it was bitter gall to George Hall.. He chose to interpret it as an act of disloyalty to Provident. By careful preparation he brought the board to feel that Dr. Dan ought to bring all his patients — rich and poor, black and white — to the 65-bed Provident Hospital.

As early as 1900 Dr. Dan had had patients in five hospitals at once. Many of his colored patients as well as white ones preferred St. Luke's or some other hospital to Provident as it was then run. For a half dozen years after his return to Chicago he had been attending surgeon at Cook County Hospital. Those things had not been considered disloyal to Provident, but now this appointment, with its honor and acclaim, the prestige it brought the race, was declared an act of faithlessness.

George Webster had become the first white president of the board when Lloyd Wheeler left Chicago. Fifteen years before, Webster had regarded Dr. Dan as the cornerstone of Provident Hospital, kept in the closest touch with him in the capital, and welcomed his return with admitted relief. But soon Webster, too, succumbed to criticism of Dr. Dan. He set his clean-shaven, tight-lipped mouth in a hard line, stuck out his belligerent chin beard, and put into his support of Provident the passion and hardness of a zealot. This was a man who could come to believe, when properly prodded, that Dr. Dan, child of a dark mother, son and grandson of men devoted to the race, did not love his own people. Webster could believe that he, a white man, loved them better.

Only Bentley and Madden of the old friends, if Allen Wesley is discounted, still sat on the board. They could not prevent the addressing of a letter to Dr. Dan ordering him to bring all his cases to Provident. From the professional point of view, it was absurd; from the race point of view, it was ridiculous. But there it was. What was Dr. Dan to do?

In Washington he had fought valiantly for Freedmen's against Purvis and had won out with Howard University faculty and Congressional committee alike. He had faced down Warfield's dastardly attack and preserved his honor, only to find himself hounded by Hall. For fourteen years he had endured an increasingly nasty situation. He had tried to show Booker Washington what Hall really was, but to no effect. How could he convince these white men?

The truth was, he couldn't. Grimly he wrote his resignation from the staff and the board of the hospital he had conceived twenty-one years before. He said no word in defense or explanation, but made it as brief as possible and signed his name.

He must have felt as though he had dismembered his own body, destroyed forever the continuity of the parts. He felt insupportably lonely.

The Record Made Straight

IN August 1926, Chicago was sweltering in a heat wave, but Dr. Dan, propped in a wheel chair on his big screened porch in the north Michigan woods, his feet up and a rug over his knees, was comfortably cool. Old blood runs cool anyway. At seventy, he would not have been too hot even in Chicago, but he would not have been so happy.

Every year he could hardly wait to get back to the pines and oaks of Idlewild, "back to the sticks," he called it, and he made a long six months of it when he got there. He had roamed the north woods in his old Ford, ferried delighted children over the lake in his speedboat, or, best of all, sat silent in the flat-bottomed rowboat and fished with Charles Chesnutt, the novelist. But now, facing eastward over the shimmering water at the foot of the slope before him and letting his gaze shift from the clump of silver birch north of his boathouse to the big pines southward, he could only reflect that his fishing days were probably over.

As dusk approached, Margaret Croker, his German housekeeper, widow of his friend Fred Croker, a colored doctor, could be seen tucking another rug about him, picking up William Fuller's letter from the porch floor and putting it back in his nerveless hand. It was a letter to bring back memories.

Young Fuller was forever at his elbow in the old days in the first little Provident Hospital, watching him operate, asking questions, demanding to be shown how. He was there in '93 when Dr. Dan operated on Cornish's heart. And then, twenty-three years later, Fuller repeated that operation himself and he hadn't forgotten a step; he followed Dr. Dan's technique almost to the letter. Dr. Dan may have smiled at the recollection, a twisted half smile, the best his paralyzed muscles could accomplish.

Fuller was a good student. When a hundred Chicago surgeons, Dr. Dan the only Negro, were formally installed as charter members of the newly founded American College of Surgeons back in 1913, Fuller was there too. Fuller was always filled with gratitude for what he said Dr. Dan had taught him. His letter said so again. As soon as he had heard Dr. Dan had suffered a stroke he had written. "I thought I would drop you a line," Fuller said, "to let you know your friends miss you and hope to see you back in harness very soon."

The bad news had come at a meeting of the credentials committee of the American College of Surgeons, and the business of the meeting had been forgotten and boiled shirts and collars wilted in the humidity while one after another told what he knew of the famous Dan Williams and his ability and reputation as a surgeon. Coleman Buford — Buford had been at the heart operation too — swore he had never seen a finer operator and Carey Culbertson chimed in there was no doubt about it. "When they got through," wrote Fuller, "I took a shot at what I knew of you when the rest of us were just embryo surgeons."

Ah yes, it had been a long time, Dr. Dan could have mused, his gaze on the purpling twilight. "Rest, eat, sleep, laugh and be of good cheer," urged Fuller, "you will soon be well and back at work." Fuller knew how a man hated to give up. "Business is not very rushing anyway," Fuller assured him, "you are missing but little or nothing. Even if you were, they will come flocking back when you are here." Fuller and Buford and Culbertson. Doubtless they didn't make up for Curtis and Warfield and Hall, but they must have helped greatly.

The fourteen years since Hall drove him out of Provident had been busy, fruitful years for Dr. Dan, though the harvest had ripened above a graveyard of buried hope and endeavor. His success at St. Luke's had been complete. His remarkable reputation had preceded him and he had fulfilled it in every way. The other staff men — Samuel C. Plummer, Arthur Elliott, Louis Schmidt — found him an outstanding person, well grounded, faithful, sincere, a gentleman and extremely satisfactory to his patients. They appreciated his discriminating surgical judgment and gave no one higher standing either as a man or as a doctor. He got his white patients, they pointed out, on merit, not notoriety. Younger men, like N. C. Gilbert, one day to be chairman of the department of medicine of Northwestern Medical School, Dr. Dan's own alma mater, were happy when they caught him in the smoking room and could draw him into talk of cases.

Everyone liked the way he did not fuss about his rights but quietly took them for granted. His poise was perfect. "You never saw him go off," said one. They called him by his first name and he called them by theirs. When Margaret E. Johnstone, director of the nursing school, died after years of service, Dr. Dan presented a marble bust to the hospital in her memory. He saw to it that his colored patients were given private rooms if they wished them and he refused to have a ward named for him. "I knew it might lead to segregation," he told a friend.

While white doctors stood beside Dr. Dan in St. Luke's operating rooms and watched and questioned and learned, colored doctors at Provident, deprived of their heritage, struggled unhappily under the Hall regime. "You let Hall do something for you," said Spencer Dickerson, "and you soon wished you hadn't." Anything short of complete vassalage was unacceptable to this man of unabashed ambition. He brooked neither rivalry nor rebellion. Any show of independence was swiftly punished. He left Dickerson off the staff for years, refused Carl Roberts's request for transfer from gynecology to surgery for eight years, forced Dailey to set up his own private sanitarium. J. W. McDowell resigned as staff president and took his patients to Dailey's.

Bentley resigned from the board and Frank Billings, now a noted member of white medical circles, refused curtly to have anything further to do with the hospital on whose original staff he had been. A whole group of young colored doctors — Wilberforce Williams, Roscoe Giles, Herbert Turner, Spencer Dickerson, Carl Roberts and others — lived on the hope another interracial hospital might materialize in the neighborhood.

Provident lost 250 patients the first year after Dr. Dan left and almost 300 the second. It was five years before the old figure was approached and many more before a normal rate of increase was again achieved. Provident outlived Hall's machinations, and Dailey, when Hall was gone, returned to help build the institution again to first rank, but meanwhile the struggle was long and needlessly difficult.

The legend grew that Dr. Dan came back in the dead of night and paced the Provident corridors. Certainly his heart never left there. Not infrequently during the years he had telephoned Dailey or Reginald Smith and asked them to drop over for a smoke, then half wistfully inquired how things were going. Meeting Roberts and Turner on summer vacation, he stopped and listened while the two men twanged guitars and sang. "I used to sing," he said, "tenor." Then abruptly he asked, "How are things at Provident?"

It was a bitter time all around. The South Side, once a friendly, neighborly place, bound in mutual interest for the race, divided into two warring factions. Doctors and laymen, sick and well, men, women and children took sides. Families split. It was civil war in all it ugliness. Harry Anderson stood by Dr. Dan as he had ever since the stripling won his heart, and so did his wife Julia, but Alf and Bertie too joined the hue and cry against him. Bert resented Dr. Dan's not taking him into his office and then later taking Dailey. Harry Anderson died in 1922. Dr. Dan begged to be allowed to erect a tombstone over the grave of the best friend, he said to Bert, that he had ever had, but Bert refused. Of Dr. Dan's Rockford cousins, now living in Chicago, some stood for and some against him: Jessie Williams DePriest and her sisters voiced hatred of him, Mabel Williams Parrish and her brother Hugo loved him dearly and visited with him weekly. Howard

Woodson, a young engineer, descendant of one of the Lewistown branches, came often too. This division of Dr. Dan's cousins was only too like the divisions that had rent the Williams clan a century earlier; old suspicions and resentments only inflamed the new dissension, and color of skin had more to do with it than any one cared to admit.

Dr. Dan himself did not enter the fight. His refusal to defend himself was incomprehensible to some and disgusting to those of tougher fiber. Hall, swaggering along in his flashy clothes, was ever ready to back up his views with his fists — in fact he put down his doctor's bag on more than one occasion and did so. This was easier for most people to understand than Dr. Dan's withdrawal. Dr. Annie Beatrice Schultz, graduate of the first nursing class and later become an M. D., could hardly bear the way things turned out. She adored Dr. Dan, but her make-up was simple, like Hall's own. Once when she had differed with Wilberforce Williams over a medical case, she had slapped his face. Now she offered to horsewhip any one who said a word against her hero. She could not understand Dr. Dan, but she would defend him with her life if need be.

Dr. Dan never had had the stomach for quarreling; he had given up law because it seemed a matter of listening all day to people's quarrels. But he could not help wanting his friends to take up the cudgels for him, as he had hoped for so long that Sarah Price Williams would do . . . fend off the world . . . love him.

White controversialists Dr. Dan seemed to meet with vigor and equanimity, perhaps because he met them on an intellectual basis, a mature basis. But colored people were different. All his dreams and illusions were woven about colored people, his people, and when any one of them acted less than ideally, he was cut to the quick. He always met colored people on an emotional basis and here he was never altogether mature. Here he had a way often, one devoted friend said, of suddenly throwing himself on you, expecting you to enter into his pain and trouble with him.

There was always somewhere deep inside Dr. Dan, never entirely recovered, a hurt little boy. So he could not help feeling warmly gratified and a little triumphant too when fifty-five of his old friends gave a fine banquet on his birthday, a full-dress affair with place cards, and toasts, and exhibition dancing. Or when the colored doctors of Missouri presented him with a silver loving cup in "appreciation of his work in advancing the medical profession in Missouri and in the nation." Or when Wilberforce University, and later Howard University, gave him honorary degrees. Or when he was asked to speak at the graduation exercises of nursing classes in some of the hospitals his inspiration had helped to found, or at some school or other organization.

In his sixties Dr. Dan made a good many addresses before both colored and white audiences. One of the best he had delivered in Rochester, Minnesota, before the Surgical Association of the Chicago & Northwestern Railway. Invited to speak on "The Malingerer" he attacked the subject with such mental vigor and probing for truth as to give his audience a considerably larger view of the matter than they had bargained for. His old eyes might well gleam at the recollection. He had told them plainly that the problem of the malingerer, linked as it was with the problem of the dishonest physician and the dishonest lawyer, was only one aspect of the whole moral problem of a selfish, materialistic age. "Those who toil," he said, "get too little of the benefits of their labor." If the power of the state were used to regulate economic conditions and raise the standard of living of humbler folk, then a wider diffusion of education might be expected and after that of ethics and religion. The way to solve malingering was to accelerate the evolution of a better society. Dr. Dan had come a long way from the simple theory with which he left college — that hard work and thrift are all that are needed. He had lost his admiration of Booker T. Washington's philosophy as "best for the masses" even before Washington died, as he did unexpectedly in 1915.

Washington's sudden death must have been a blow to George Hall. The Tuskegee dictator had commanded wide publicity in the Negro press, after he gained control of it, for the dictator of Provident. "Send me your best photograph and a sketch of your life," Washington had written his Chicago henchman, "put in the most prominent and successful operations you have performed. I can use this in a way to be of great service." Hall speedily complied. Within a few weeks Washington sent Hall a marked copy of the Baltimore *Afro-American* spreading forth the self-styled successes of the mediocre Hall; the article had appeared in thirty-five Negro newspapers. Within another few weeks, Washington requested his pay: he wanted the confidential list of colored subscribers to the recent big YMCA campaign in Chicago.

The game went on between the two who suited each other's purposes and temperaments so well, until Booker Washington died. Hall then tried to make capital for the last time of his relation to the big boss. The flowers were scarcely withered on Washington's grave before members of the Tuskegee board of trustees received a letter from a certain Robert White who said he was compiling a book to perpetuate the memory of Dr. Booker T. Washington. In this work he was being assisted and supported, he stated, by Dr. George C. Hall, "one of Dr. Washington's most intimate friends." "You," wrote Mr. White, "together with a number of the world's most prominent men and women, are called upon for a short reminiscence of Dr. Washington to be used in this work." The trustees, instead of complying, replied that they were referring this request to the secretary of the board, Emmett Scott. Whereupon White immediately wrote Scott that though he had neglected so to state in his previous letter, it was the intention of himself and Hall to donate twenty-five per cent of the profits of the book to Tuskegee Institute. Scott probably never had greater satisfaction in his life than he did in replying that the board was not in a position to take official cognizance of the proposed publication or to say or do anything that would place the seal of authority or approval on the effort. Moreover it would not be possible for the board to accept the offer of twenty-five per cent of the profits.

All suns set in time, and George Hall's proved no exception. But the event came too late to make much difference to Dr. Dan.

George Hall was never able to disrupt the relationship of Scott and Kenney to Booker Washington. Washington needed both his secretary and his staff doctor and both stayed on at Tuskegee despite their dissatisfaction with many things. But throughout the years Scott and Kenney remained deeply loyal to Dr. Dan, corresponding frequently and sometimes going up to Chicago for a visit in the Williams home.

When Kenney's first wife lay ill and dying he sent for Dr. Dan and Dr. Dan rushed South, taking with him Stewart from Nashville. He operated, but to no avail. Dr. Dan was brokenhearted and swore never again to operate on a close friend. His attempt however, drew the two men, if anything, closer together than ever. Kenney plunged into work and brought out a compilation of the achievements of Negroes in medicine, and Dr. Dan hastened to give him every praise. It was a fine, comprehensive job, he said, it would find its way into every library in the United States, "this pioneer collation and presentment of the work of a new people in an old field. It shows," he wrote, "the light and glory of opportunity — it shows the vanguard easing on to greater and fuller development — the men of work, serious work, patience and endurance going to the front, not as colored men, but as part of the world's best thought and work." It had inspired him, said Dr. Dan, and added, "I see so much in your little book to encourage us all."

When at first correspondence between Booker Washington and Dr. Dan had dropped off, Scott sought to make his own loyalty clear. "Somehow I am able," he wrote Dr. Dan, "to keep in touch with your movements through newspaper publications. Probably there is no special reason," he continued, "for my writing to you except to say I still have the keenest recollection of your great service to me several years ago." Scott assured Dr. Dan of his willingness to be of whatever aid he possibly could in any matter at any time that interested Dr. Dan. "I very much hope," Scott said, "there will be no doubt in your mind as to my eagerness to serve you and I hope you will not hesitate to write me when the spirit moves you."

Dr. Dan, always quick to be touched by sincere expressions of friendship, kept in closer touch with Scott after that. He inquired about Scott's physical condition, never of the best, sent him instructions for his diet, his exercise, and his hay fever, told him about the baseball games he still enjoyed. When Scott needed a stenographer, Dr. Dan found one for him. Scott on his side sent Alice Williams butter from the Tuskegee dairy and Dr. Dan crape myrtles, running roses, and wistaria for his garden. When he heard that Dr. Dan had been called to New York to attend the ailing Bishop Derrick, he hastened to congratulate Dr. Dan on this recognition, "not that you need it," said Scott, "but only because it makes your friends feel good that there is widespread appreciation everywhere of the high place you hold in the profession." To Dr. Dan, sore from many a betrayal, Scott's words must have been balm. "Your letters always have the ring of sincerity and good will," he answered. "We prize you as a friend, one to whom we can cling, always dependable, and true. . . . Come to us again this summer for a quiet visit."

It was not until Ocober 1917, two years after Washington's death, that Dr. Dan ever mentioned to Scott the rift between himself and the Tuskegee leader. The United States was at war; six hundred colored officers were to be commissioned at Camp Funston near Des Moines. Emmett Scott, now in the position of wider usefulness that Dr. Dan had thought his due, was serving in an advisory capacity on behalf of Negroes to the Secretary of War. He asked Dr. Dan to accompany him to Funston for the ceremonies. They rode all day across the state of Wisconsin amid the solemn splendors of the dying year, across the state where Dr. Dan had spent his youth. James Mills had just died and Dr. Dan must have been in a pensive mood. Suddenly he turned to Scott and without warning mentioned Washington's name.

"Why did he stop calling me up when he came to Chicago?" he asked. Scott told him of Hall's letters to Washington. "He just decided Hall could be more useful to him than you could," Scott said. Dr. Dan made no comment.

That night at the dinner given to celebrate the commissioning of these volunteer colored officers, Dr. Dan was not a scheduled speaker, but he was called on to make some extemporaneous remarks. He arose slowly, looked up at the ceiling, down at the table, and finally began to speak in a quiet, almost monotonous tone of voice, a tired voice: You are giving to your country . . . but they won't thank you for it — such was the gist of what he said.

The presiding officer jumped to his feet. He could not let those remarks pass unchallenged, he said. The next minute Scott took over, drawing upon all his resources of tact and suavity. "Dr. Williams's loyalty to his race is very great," Scott said, "that does not mean he is not also loyal to his country. In Chicago he has been putting in long hours as Medical Examiner for the Board of Appeals . . ." Jumpy nerves were soothed; there was no protest to the War Department afterward.

The story leaked back to families and home towns. Some said it was an example of Dr. Dan's tactlessness. Others quoted it as proof of his race loyalty. Still others were glad Dr. Dan had shown he could speak out and only wished he had sometimes done it in defense of himself.

Through changing times and passing years Dr. Dan cherished old friendships. He went back to Hollidaysburg to visit the sons of Moses Brown, his father's associate in the Equal Rights League. His onetime playmate and lifelong confidant, David Kennedy, long since married to a Williams cousin, came to visit him. He went on a vacation trip in Wisconsin with Hutchins Bishop's daughter and her husband. When his friend J. Carlos Davis was having some difficulty, he wrote a letter Davis folded away and treasured. If there was any assistance he could render, wrote Dr. Dan, Davis must call on him, or if Davis had any expense, let him know. "I feel deeply for you," wrote Dr. Dan, "always remember I feel very near to you and am at your command." When in 1923 his old fishing and hunting companion of so many seasons died, Dr. Dan wrote Jennie Avendorph a letter she too treasured and kept:

"Thinking of you in these saddest hours of your life, and knowing something of your ambition for your boy Julius, my heart goes out to you and with this I am impelled to assure you that if

Julius rings true in his professional attainment and development, and if I am alive and active, it will be my pleasure to assist him in paving the way to success in the Practice of Medicine and Surgery."

Dr. Dan did everything he could to keep active. He continued his office hours long after he was able, stoutly denying that his diabetes made any real difference. During winter months in the city he went down cellar and chopped cords of wood to keep up his muscle tone, and summers in Idlewild he gardened vigorously.

Idlewild was one thing Dr. Dan could thank George Hall for. Hall had not been satisfied with driving its founder out of Provident Hospital. In a rage one day at some deference shown the name of Dr. Dan, he cried to Carl Roberts, "Curse him! I'll punish him worse than God ever will. I'll see he's forgotten before he's dead!" Within a few years, while Dr. Dan was still very much alive, though rarely seen any more among the colored medical fraternity, a group of Southern colored doctors visited Provident Hospital and asked, "And whatever became of the famous Daniel Hale Williams?" Before Roberts could answer, another of the visitors spoke up: "Oh, didn't you know? He died years ago." Carl Roberts shivered.

Hall carried his campaign to Benton Harbor where H. O. Bailiff operated one of the first Negro summer resorts. The patronage was dignified and conservative and Dr. Dan and Alice had enjoyed several summers there before Hall came with his familiar tactics to spoil the place for them. He forced Dr. Dan to look elsewhere for a vacation retreat. In the end Dr. Dan found it at Idlewild.

Here in Lake County was a perfect site — high sandy soil, good water, a lake for fishing and swimming, endless forests for hunting. He and his friends, Ed Wright, Louis B. Anderson and some others, formed a company and developed a fine summer resort on the location. Many of his old patients, his nurses and internes, his friends who could not be budged from their faithfulness, came to build homes there. In the end he had peace. He saw no more of Hall.

Idlewild had a big clubhouse with great stone fireplaces where friends and neighbors might gather on rainy days and delightful verandas facing the lake for fine days, a boat dock and a diving pier. Forums and concerts soon made Idlewild a cultural mecca. Dr. Dan built a summer hotel, Oakmere, which drew a good clientele from Washington, Cleveland, Chicago, St. Louis and the South. He fitted up a little hospital for emergencies and hung a fire bell in a high tower. His old organizational faculties made him remember every detail.

Dr. Dan called his own home Oakmere too. He laid out a little park across the road. Both properties were enclosed by neat white picket fences, and white arches carrying the words Oakmere and Oakmere Park stood over the gates. He built a small hexagonal summer pavilion in the park, where one could sit and watch the sunset. Everything was left as natural as possible. Gravel walks wound under the trees, their edges kept neat by his own efforts. Early risers saw him out at dawn, down on his knees, clippers in his hand. He fussed endlessly over his prize tulips, his many varieties of fine roses, his burgeoning peonies, and gave them away right and left — to the colored postmistress in Idlewild and the wife of the white banker in the neighboring town of Baldwin. Wherever the sun filtered through he planted flowers. He grew a vegetable garden too and got Dailey up on a visit to show off his Swiss chard.

He located his house, a simple bungalow made luxurious with electricity and Oriental rugs, on a high knoll facing eastward over the lake and he had never tired of the site. He cut as few trees as possible. His bungalow, his small chickenhouse, his workshop where the tools were kept as precise and clean as a laboratory, his garage, all were nestled under the inviting shelter of whispering green branches. "Save your trees," he urged everyone and did a job of tree surgery on Ed Wright's place that proved his hand as clever with bough and trunk as with human leg and arm.

But now his hands had lost their cleverness. He doubtless sighed there on his quiet porch watching the long evening shadows creep across the grass. He might recover temporarily from this stroke, it looked as though he would, but this was the beginning of the end. He was a doctor and he knew.

Alice had already gone, and gone bravely. She had enjoyed Idlewild but four years and most of that time she had spent in a wheel chair, victim of Parkinson's disease. Dr. Dan had called in N. C. Gilbert from Northwestern to care for her, but Gilbert could do little. Even those who had not loved Alice admired her fortitude and the vigor with which she kept her intellectual and artistic interests to the end, going to hear Clarence Cameron White play a violin recital when she was far from able. "Of course I am going," she said, "he was my pupil."

As Alice lay dying someone timidly ventured to suggest a minister be sent for, "some one to pray." "A little late, don't you think?" the intrepid Alice remarked and turned her face to the wall. So at her memorial service a friend read "Crossing the Bar" from Alice's own marked copy of Tennyson and no pretense was made of getting in a clergy for whom Alice or Dr. Dan had little use.

Religion had to be lived before it could mean anything to Dr. Dan. Jenkin Lloyd Jones, Reverdy Ransom, those were the preachers Dr. Dan had liked, preachers who were not so much concerned with the hereafter as with here and now. "All that develops the bodies and minds of men . . . all that renders us more intellectual and more loving, nearer just . . ." Ingersoll had voiced Dr. Dan's creed for him there in Janesville so long ago.

These were the things his father had worked for, and his grandfather, all the Williamses. And now, Dr. Dan might have thought in the ever-deepening twilight, he would soon be gone and there would no longer be a Daniel Williams to carry on the fight. This hurt undoubtedly was the greatest hurt he had known, not to have a son . . . But perhaps he remembered the children of his tutelage.

"Daughter, this woman's got to live." Perhaps his own words rang again in his ears, perhaps he felt again the oppressive Washington heat, smelt the sweetish odor of chloroform that hung heavy in Freedmen's operating room, saw the white-capped, dark-eyed nurse standing obedient, concentrating on his words. "Daughter, this woman's got to live." "Yes, sir."

What fine young women those nurses were — Isabella Garnett, Jessie Sleet, Elizabeth Tyler, Edith Carter — wonderful daughters. Yes, to be sure, Dr. Dan could tell himself, he had daughters, sons too. Their faces may have passed before him — Kenney, Perry and West, McDowell, Hale and Reed, Holman, McMillan and Francis, McKissick, White and Wilberforce, Roberts, Gethner and Giles, Dickerson, Kendall and Stewart, Jackson, Chislett and Phalen, some dark and some lighter, Buford, Fuller and Dailey. These were his sons, his heirs. He would never know the full line of his progeny, stretching down the years, passing on their heritage, the skills he had taught them, saving lives, easing pain. "The men of work" — that was what he had said to Kenney — "the men of work, serious work, patience and endurance . . ."

When Mrs. Croker came out to wheel him into the house, probably he looked very peaceful there asleep in the dusk, the only sound the gentle lap, lap of the lake at the foot of the slope.

Dr. Dan rallied and lived five more years. He sent his medical books to Henry Minton in Philadelphia to start a library for Mercy Hospital. "It only takes a small room and some chairs and shelves," he wrote Minton, "but why not a pretty room, neatly furnished. It will add so much to your hospital." He could never stop dreaming and planning for Negro hospitals. He had dinner with Billings and after it Billings agreed to head the campaign for funds for a third and greater Provident Hospital. He gave Dailey some files and a chair.

He made his will — provision for his sisters and his brother's widow, his housekeeper, his secretary; he forgot no one, and even added $1000 for Ida Williams Lord, the sweetheart of his Academy days, now a widow. There was $2000 for the colored YWCA in Washington, a similar sum for the operating room of the proposed new interracial hospital on the South Side, and $5000 each to Meharry and Howard to assist indigent medical students. The largest bequest, $8000, went to the National Association for the Advancement of Colored People, spiritual heir of the Niagara Movement, and that organization was also his residuary legatee. In the end he had joined his old friends Bentley and Madden in their support of the DuBois program. His will provided plain evidence if any was needed of his loyalty and love for his race. It was not an immense fortune, not such as many a surgeon less skilled than himself had accumulated, but as he had said to Mrs. Rainey, "I cannot charge my people large fees." And a good deal he had already given away.

But his rally of strength was short-lived. Other strokes followed. Those last five years were a sad time for Dr. Dan and his friends — a time of slow death, with his mental powers going first.

Finally on Tuesday, August 4, 1931, in his beloved Oakmere at Idlewild, Daniel Hale Williams died. The race's great pioneer surgeon was dead. The wires flashed the news and white and colored newspapers noted his passing, recounted his great deeds, his service to both races. Nowhere was a finer tribute written than that published in the *Lake County Star* by his white neighbor and friend Herbert Davis. The editor gave front-page headlines to Dr. Dan and never once in two columns of type felt it necessary to mention that he had had Negro blood.

. . . an invalid for nearly five years . . . His departure from Idlewild was attended with honors and reverence of exceptional character. With the summer season at its height and several thousand residents and visitors at the resort, all activities were suspended for the day and in the evening a memorial service was held in which all joined in paying tribute to the splendid character of a beloved associate. . . .

It is remarkable that so famous a man should carry his honors so lightly. In 1920 he built his beautiful cottage in Idlewild and went there summers to rest. He did not practice, but he never turned a deaf ear to a call for help. One of our bankers owes his life to the skillful ministrations of "Dr. Dan," and many others found him willing and ready to serve without pay in the cause of humanity. Modest, retiring, unassuming, he found his little world here full of reverent,

loving friends. To the children he was "Dr. Dan" and a
friend, even though regarded awesomely as a miracle man.

Like many other truly great men he found peace, solace
and instruction in nature. He loved his flowers and his garden
was filled with lovely native and exotic plants. He loved
the woods and waters and the living things in them. . . .

To have known him was a pleasure — to know him intimately was a priceless privilege. He was at once an inspiration and an aid. To emulate his simplicity, his kindly spirit
and his great modesty is to pay tribute to the truly great.
The world has lost greatly. . . .

The owner of a local historical museum, a white man, began to
assemble what relics he could of the departed Negro surgeon.

In Chicago funeral services were held for Dr. Dan in St. Anselm's Roman Catholic Church. His housekeeper had called Father
Eckert to baptize him a few months before. Few of his Catholic
friends approved, since everyone knew that Dr. Dan was now
helpless; and those who felt such an act was necessary were satisfied that his mother, who had been converted to Catholicism
after her husband's death, had had him baptized as a child. St.
Anselm's was then a white church, and while hundreds of people
packed it to overflowing not many of them were colored.

Dr. Dan was buried in a corner of Graceland Cemetery, separate from his wife. No stone was erected over his grave. When
representatives of the Negro National Hospital Association came
some years later to put a wreath on his grave, there was nothing
to show where he lay, and the wreath had to be carried back. In
Provident Hospital his picture stood in a basement corridor, its
face to the wall, covered with dust. Five years later, when the
dream of the third and greater Provident Hospital was realized, a
portrait of George Hall, who had died in 1930, was hung in the
lobby. There was no memento anywhere of Daniel Hale Williams.

But the life of a lie, Ingersoll said, is simply a question of time.
Nothing but truth is immortal. One day James Gordon, last sur-
vivor of the original hospital committee of 1891, entered the new
Provident as a patient. When he saw the state of affairs, he sent

up a protest that had considerable repercussions. A new administration had its eyes opened. There was a scurry for souvenirs of Dr. Dan. A case filled with silver cups, certificates of honor and some of his own surgical instruments appeared in the lobby. On the wall was hung a portrait and under it a bronze plaque misquoting his birth date but setting the essential record straight: DANIEL H. WILLIAMS, 1858–1931, DISTINGUISHED SURGEON, FOUNDER OF PROVIDENT HOSPITAL.

Genealogical Chart of the

Joseph <u>Williams</u> •?
b. 1760? York Co. Penn.

(Joseph or his wife or his
daughters-in-law were
wholly or part German)

1.(son) 2.(son) 3.(son)
m....Kolklazier •
(Dutch)

4. **Samuel**
b. 1780?
(his son grew
up speaking
German)

5. **Daniel <u>Williams</u>**
1783 –1854?
m. Sarah.....•
b. 1789
(Scotch-Irish)

---

1. **Peter A.**
1813–1897
m. Caroline
F. Jackson
1829–1911

2. (dau.)
b. 1815?

4. (dau.)
b. 1825?

5. **Thomas**
b.1827

3. Daniel <u>Williams</u>, Jr.
1820–1867
married 1843

---

1. **Ann Effine**
1846–1933
m.(1)....Clay
(2) Samuel
Barbour

2. **Henry Price**
1847–1895
m.(1) Matilda M.
A. Maduro
(Mexican)

3. **Sarah C.**
1849–1915
m.(1) Bluford
Turner
(2).....Nesbit

4. **Ida**
1853–1902
m. William
Cornell

5. **Daniel Hale
Williams**
1856–1931
m. 1898
Alice D. Johnson
1859–1924

Williams and Price Families

NOTE ● = white
●● = went white

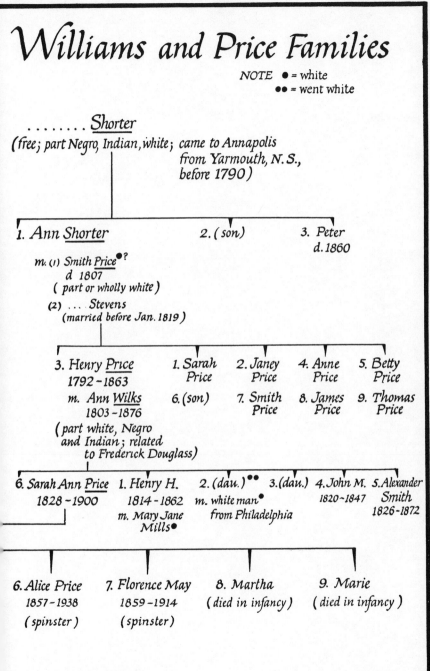

.... Shorter
(free; part Negro, Indian, white; came to Annapolis from Yarmouth, N.S., before 1790)

1. Ann Shorter 2. (son) 3. Peter d. 1860

m. (1) Smith Price ●?
d 1807
(part or wholly white)

(2) ... Stevens
(married before Jan. 1819)

3. Henry Price 1. Sarah Price 2. Janey Price 4. Anne Price 5. Betty Price
1792 – 1863 6. (son) 7. Smith Price 8. James Price 9. Thomas Price

m. Ann Wilks
1803 – 1876
(part white, Negro and Indian; related to Frederick Douglass)

6. Sarah Ann Price 1. Henry H. 2. (dau.) ●● 3. (dau.) 4. John M. 5. Alexander
1828 – 1900 1814 – 1862 m. white man ● 1820 – 1847 Smith
m. Mary Jane from Philadelphia 1826 – 1872
Mills ●

6. Alice Price 7. Florence May 8. Martha 9. Marie
1857 – 1938 1859 – 1914 (died in infancy) (died in infancy)
(spinster) (spinster)

Notes and Sources

Abbreviations used: BTW for Booker T. Washington Correspondence, Manuscript Division, Library of Congress, Washington, D.C. NA for National Archives, Records of the Secretary of the Interior, Washington, D.C. JNA for scrapbook of the late Julius N. Avendorph. NMA for the National Medical Association. NMA Jnl for *Journal* of the National Medical Association. Publications No. 1–14 for the articles by Daniel Hale Williams, which are listed in detail on page 366 together with the journals where they appeared.

I have mentioned in the Foreword something of my experience in securing the data for this book. Nothing extensive has heretofore been published on the life of Daniel Hale Williams — one or two magazine articles, entries in various biographical dictionaries. Much of the data had to be secured from persons who had known Dr. Dan or knew his story. A list of those consulted is found on p. 362.

The Williams Family

History of the Williams family was given by the following descendants: Harriette Kennedy Brown; Elizabeth McCard Clark; Berta Cornell Coleman; Alice Williams Cuffee; Virginia Powell Florence; Chester A. Franklin; Alamanda Williams Garnet; Josephine Williams Garnet; Helen Williams Ramsey Gray; Charles Kelly; John W. Kelly; Pearl Barbour Marchant; Blanche Williams Stubbs; Florence Prettyman Suydam; Ada Blanche W. Z. Williams; Hugo Williams; the late Raphael Dumas Williams; Sadie Fitzgerald Wilson; Howard D. Woodson.

Also by the following who are related by marriage: Henry W. Furniss, M.D.; the late Sumner A. Furniss, M.D.; the Reverend G.

Lake Imes; Harriet Layton McFadden; the late Howard D. Scott; Mr. and Mrs. James Scott; Lizzie Ramsey Still; the late Gardner Thomas; William B. Turner.

The genealogy of the Williams family is given on pp. 276–277.

U. S. Census records were examined for the years 1790–1880 for all localities where the Williamses lived. Tax lists and deed records were also examined. Marriage and birth records for the earliest years do not exist. Old city directories were often a useful source.

By the time York County was erected in 1749 the Williamses — Joseph, Thomas and Isaac, Abraham, Samuel and Daniel — were many among the thinly scattered population of that frontier. These names persist down through the generations. They are numerous in the 1790 U. S. Census of York County and are found in the rolls of the Revolutionary War as set forth in *The Pennsylvania-German in the Revolutionary War, 1775–1783*, Part XVIII of a *Narrative and Critical History*, prepared at the request of The Pennsylvania-German Society, published at Lancaster, Pennsylvania, 1908. Thomas Williams's oath of allegiance is in the hands of Dr. Francis Jamison, Wilmington, Delaware, who showed it to me.

The early settlement of York County is described in *The Beginnings of the German Element in York County*, Abdel Ross Wentz, B.D., Ph.D., Part XXVI of *Narrative and Critical History*, published by the Pennsylvania-German Society, Lancaster, Pennsylvania, 1916.

The notion that intermarriage was heinous was one to which people yielded slowly. Again and again the Pennsylvania Legislature refused to pass bills that would have voided mixed marriages. In the early nineteenth century, the tall, spare, fair-skinned Williams men married not only into other free mixed families of southeastern Pennsylvania like themselves — the Armstrongs, Underhills, Browns, the Scotts, Kellys and Vashons — but also frequently married white wives. Of the offspring of Joseph Williams — Grandpap Joseph, Dr. Dan's German-speaking great-grandfather — at least two sons and three grandsons are known to have married white women. But, as more and more black refugees flocked in by underground from Virginia and Maryland, bringing with them the problem of cheap labor and lowered wages to antagonize the working classes and the burden of pauperism to irritate the upper classes, prejudice grew.

Within the Williams clan the children of one set of parents might differ greatly from each other and among them show characteristics of all the racial strains that had entered their inheritance. Of eight children in one family, two sons were "as white as any one," one daughter had Indian features, hair and coloring and was tall and "walked very straight," while another daughter was short and plump and African in feature, "always laughing," and the remaining four children showed varying combinations of traits. In Dr. Dan's family, his oldest sister Annie was fair like their father, as was young Dan; Sally, the next daughter, and the son Price were dark like their mother; Ida, Alice and Florence, the three youngest girls, were "middling."

All that we know about Dr. Dan's Great-Grandpap Joseph is that he lived in Dauphin County in his old age among numerous grandchildren and kept busy selling Bibles. He and/or his wife were doubtless German-speaking since two of his grandsons are known to have grown up speaking German rather than English. Whether he was altogether white or of mixed blood we do not know. Joseph's descendants, as their opportunities and privileges grew more and more restricted (Pennsylvania disfranchised colored persons in 1838), moved farther and farther westward.

Dr. Dan's grandfather, Daniel Williams, followed the Juniata River beyond the Tuscarora Mountains to Lewistown, the route of the state-wide, state-owned canal system. He was settled there with his Scotch-Irish wife, his three sons and two daughters, by 1830. There were thirty-five colored families among the 1200 inhabitants, and two African churches. In one of them Daniel Williams, already approaching fifty, preached on Sundays. On weekdays he operated a barbershop. He looked "mostly white" and had some Indian and some African characteristics. He owned property on the canal. In 1846, according to the tax list, he went to Haiti. The press was constantly urging free Negroes to leave the country and go to Liberia or Haiti. Perhaps the sixty-three-year-old preacher went seeking a new home either for himself or his flock. But he returned to end his days in Lewistown and last appears in the Lewistown Census for 1850.

For the history of Lewistown, Pennsylvania, the following were consulted: *History and Topography of Northumberland, Huntington, Mifflin, Centre, Union, Columbia, Juniata and Clinton Counties, Pennsylvania*, etc., I. D. Rupp, Lancaster, 1847; *History of That Part of the Susquehanna and Juniata Valleys Embraced in the Counties of Mifflin, Juniata, Perry, Union and Snyder*, No author, Vol. I, 1886; *A History of the Juniata Valley and Its People*, John W. Jordan, Vol. I, New York, 1913; *The Pioneers of Mifflin County, Pennsylvania: Who's Who in the Early Records before 1790*, John Martin Stroup and Raymond Martin Bell, Lewistown, 1942.

Other Williams cousins lived in Lewistown. Thomas had a German wife and their daughter became one of the town's early schoolteachers.

Dr. Dan's uncle, Peter A. Williams, born in 1813, was a tall dashing magnetic fellow, full of initiative, much admired for his commanding figure and courtly manners. He went off to New York and, after operating a barbershop for a time, rose to be chief steward for a line of coastwise vessels. His position was lucrative and he set up his wife in a fine brownstone house in Brooklyn, gave her an Irish servant girl, and maintained a carriage and pair. Peter gave his name to a daughter of his wife by a previous marriage and that daughter's sons are the two physicians, Sumner (recently deceased) and Henry Furniss, the latter for a number of years U. S. Minister to Haiti.

Dr. Dan's father, Daniel Williams, Jr., was seven years younger than Peter. He too learned the barbering trade from his father and at seventeen undertook to buy a house and lot on the canal in Lewistown that had once belonged to his father. The purchase price was $55, twice what he could hope to earn in a year. It proved too large a burden for him to carry and the property was sold at sheriff's sale. But he had a stubborn persistence that was to appear later in his son. After a few years he bought back the desirable holding and kept it throughout most of his life, though he early left Lewistown. For a while he worked in Harrisburg and there met the girl he married. Sarah Ann Price had come from Annapolis to visit her brother, Harry Price, established in good property in Harrisburg by his father, Reverend Henry Price of Annapolis.

The Harrisburg Business Directory and Stranger's Guide, with a Sketch of Its First Early Settlement, H. Napey, published by the author, 1842, lists two uncles of Dr. Dan, brothers of his mother: John M. Price, Cake Baker, and Henry H. Price, Barber, Hair Dresser & Wig Maker. There is also a relative, Jacob Smith, Barber, Hair Cutter & Violinist. Dr. Dan's father seems to be the partner in Williams & Thomas, 3 Third Street.

The Free Negro

That there was a considerable body of free Negroes in this country, both North and South, before Emancipation is not generally known. The following are useful sources: Elihu S. Riley and Jeffrey R. Brackett, works cited below under *THE PRICE FAMILY*; *Sketches of the Higher Classes of Colored Society in Philadelphia*, by a Southerner, 1841; *The Negro in Pennsylvania: Slavery, Servitude, Freedom, 1639–1861*, Edward Raymond Turner, 1911; *The Free Negro in Maryland, 1634–1860*, James M. Wright, 1921; *The Free Negro Family*, E. Franklin Frazier, 1932; *The Negro, Too, in American History*, Merl R. Eppse, 1938; *Speech of Col. Curtis M. Jacobs on the Free Colored Population of Maryland*, delivered in the House of Delegates, 17 February 1860, Printed by Elihu S. Riley, Annapolis, 1860; *Proceedings*, Eastern Shore Slave Holders' Convention, 1859; and the following works by Carter G. Woodson: *Free Negro Heads of Families in the United States in 1830, together with a Brief Treatment of the Free Negro*, Washington, 1925; *A Century of Negro Migration*, 1918; *The Negro in Our History*, 1928; *Free Negro Owners of Slaves in the United States in 1830, together with Absentee Ownership of Slaves in the United States in 1830*, Washington, 1924; *The Education of the Negro Prior to 1861*, Washington, 1915. See also Notes for page 5.

The Price Family

The story of the Price family was given by the following descendants: Alice Thornton Butler, Pearl Barbour Marchant, Blanche Thornton Parnall, Ada Blanche W. Z. Williams, the late Raphael Dumas Williams. Also by descendants of Peter Shorter, "a kin": Sarah Jennings, Anna Pounder Sorrell, and Lola Brown Whipple. Also by two old residents of Annapolis: Mrs. Clifton Moss and Mrs. E. H. B. Parker. The Reverend L. L. Berry of the Asbury M. E. Church stated that the Reverend Henry Price, Dr. Dan's grandfather, donated the land for the church.

Additional sources were: *The Ancient City, A History of Anne Arundel County in Maryland, 1649–1887*, Elihu S. Riley, Annapolis, 1887; Article 19, Part I, of a series written for *The Maryland Gazette*, Elihu S. Riley (undated clipping in the scrapbook of Mrs. E. H. B. Parker); *The Negro in Maryland*, Jeffrey R. Brackett, Baltimore, 1899.

The Price family's wills, deeds, marriages, manumission records and travel papers are found in Anne Arundel County Courthouse, Maryland, and the Annapolis Hall of Records. I also consulted the U. S. Census records for Anne Arundel County for the years 1790, 1800, 1830, 1840, 1860. Harrisburg property records are found in Dauphin County, Pennsylvania, Courthouse.

I visited the old Price home on Main Street near Church Circle and the Price burial lot in St. Anne's Churchyard, Annapolis.

The genealogy of the Price and Shorter families is given on pages 276–277.

The Prices of Annapolis were, like their contemporaries and friends, other old free mixed families — the Shorters, Browns, Butlers, Ridgleys, Bishops — "of a marked and elevated standing," according to an early white chronicler, Elihu S. Riley. "There was no need of one's being told," wrote Riley, "that these were capable, intelligent, and high-minded people. They carried these virtues and qualities in their very bearing and associations with each other and with their white fellow townsmen." They filled places of credit and engaged in leading occupations. A young free woman of color kept a small school, and white children attended it. They voted in the city elections, along with other persons who owned a lot with a house on it or had an estate of the value of £20 sterling. Those who wished worshiped in St. Anne's and when they died were laid to rest in an unsegregated cemetery, unless, like Smith Price, they had a private family burial ground on their own land.

Dr. Dan's great-grandfather, Smith Price, may have been altogether white since his will does not state specifically, as does that of his son, that he was a "free colored citizen." His wife was of free mixed blood, Indian, African and Caucasian. When Smith Price died in 1807 he left a considerable inventory of property, farm, shop and household, with many amenities — walnut furniture, framed pictures, tea table with china cups and saucers, wine decanter and glasses, stores of tea, spices, tobacco. The executrix of his estate, his wife, was bound in the not small sum of £250 for faithful performance of her sad task. During his lifetime he had purchased slaves in order to liberate them. The manumission records of some he "forever set free" may be seen still in the Annapolis Hall of Records: ". . . Zack whom I bought of William Glover of Annapolis for $100 . . . Rachel, 35 years old, and her child. . . ." Pitiful little, when you thought of the tens of thousands of men in slavery. But each free man did what he could, reached back and pulled up out of the horror a few — one man set forever free, one woman and her child, each was a human soul in a human body.

Dr. Dan's grandmother, Ann Wilks Price, had Indian hair; her inheritance, like that of his great-grandmother, included the three racial mixtures. She was a slave until freed by her husband's purchase. (For her relationship to the famous Abolitionist, Frederick Douglass, see Notes for page 82.) She was an excellent cateress and a stickler for cleanliness. She would not allow her sons to put up the horses lest their clothes become redolent of the stable. She sent a grown granddaughter back upstairs to bathe properly "all over" while her beau cooled his heels in the parlor and horse and buggy waited at the curb.

Dr. Dan's grandfather, Henry Price, built well on his inheritance and like his father exhibited the same openhandedness. He manumitted slaves, gave his mother a house and land, loaned money to relatives, and acted as trustee for the minor children of his friends. Despite his shop and real estate interests, his main concern was religion. He gave the land for the Asbury M. E. Church where he preached. His sermons were awaited eagerly and quoted weekly; his eloquence became a tradition. When the Nat Turner slave insurrection flared up in Virginia in August 1831, and Maryland fearfully restricted movements of all colored, free or slave, the Reverend Henry Price went into action. He secured permission to hold a meeting in his church of the free colored of Annapolis. He sought to allay fears and suspicion on both sides and the *Maryland Gazette* published the memorial he then drew up. As the freedom of the free colored people was more and more curtailed, their movements restricted, Henry Price would walk up the hill behind his home and go into the white-pillared Capitol and say he wanted to see his sons up North and would the gentlemen be so kind as to issue travel papers. He did not always get what he wanted, but he never stopped trying. His religion sustained him until Emancipation came. Seven weeks later he died "in great peace and joy," said the *Baltimore Sun* of February 24, 1863, giving his obituary unusual space. Though snow was falling in Annapolis, the church was crowded with both white and colored mourners, and ministers of both races conducted his funeral.

The marriage of Sarah Ann Price and Daniel Williams, Jr., is recorded in the Anne Arundel County Courthouse, Annapolis; the date was October 31, 1843. A portion of their marriage certificate, the rest torn off and lost, is in the possession of Pearl Barbour Marchant, a granddaughter.

Publications Mentioning Dr. Daniel Hale Williams

The following is a list of the various published articles and biographical entries mentioning Dr. Daniel Hale Williams. The items differ and are often in flat contradiction; the inaccuracies are many.

Biographies of Eminent American Physicians and Surgeons, R. French Stone, Indianapolis, 1894.
Physicians and Surgeons of America, Irving A. Watson, Republican Press Association, Concord, New Hampshire, 1896.
An Era of Progress and Promise, 1863–1910, W. N. Hartshorn, Boston, 1910.
The Book of Chicagoans, A. N. Marquis, ed., Chicago, 1911.
Who's Who of the Colored Race, Franklin Lincoln Mather, ed., Vol. I, 1915.
The National Cyclopedia of the Colored Race, Clement Richardson, Montgomery, Alabama, Vol. I, 1919.
Who's Who in America, A. N. Marquis, ed., Chicago, Vol. XI, 1920–1921.

Who's Who in American Medicine, 1925, Lloyd Thompson and Winfield Scott Downs, eds., New York, 1925.

Who's Who in Chicago, A. N. Marquis, ed., Chicago, 1926.

Another Daniel Who Dared, Rebecca Caudill, included in *The Upward Climb: A Course in Negro Achievement,* Sara Estelle Haskin, New York, 1927.

In Spite of Handicaps, Ralph W. Bullock, New York, 1927.

Who's Who in Colored America, Vol. I, 1927.

Journal, American Medical Association, Vol. XCDII, No. 10, p. 721, September 5, 1931.

Dr. Dan Williams: I, His Life, Irene M. Gaines, *II, His Place in Medicine,* U. G. Dailey, M.D., in *The Crisis,* Vol. 41, No. 1, January 1932.

Negro Builders and Heroes, Benjamin G. Brawley, Chapel Hill, North Carolina, 1937.

Daniel Hale Williams: Pioneer Surgeon and Father of Negro Hospitals, reprint of address by Ulysses Grant Dailey, M.D., before the National Hospital Association, August 18, 1941.

Daniel Hale Williams, Juliana Willis Rhodes, in *Negro History Bulletin,* May 1942.

Dictionary of American Biography, article on Daniel Hale Williams by James M. Phalen, M.D., 1943.

Daniel Hale Williams, by Harold Farmer, in *The Annals of Medical History,* 3d series, Vol. I, No. 3, May, 1939, Whole No. 103. Farmer's article wrongly ascribes a medical article by David H. Williams to Daniel H. Williams.

Daniel Hale Williams, Mary E. Moxcey, in *Rising Above Color,* Philip H. Lotz, ed., New York, 1943.

Notes by Chapters

CHAPTER I

The Wandering Barber Finds a Home

3

I visited Janesville, walked its streets, saw the former Anderson home on Glen Street, and Jefferson Public School in its elm-shaded park.

Dr. Bert Anderson, the late Mara Franc Edwards, Minerva Guernsey King, Mary Louise Hall Walker (daughter of Eva Johnson Hall), the late Allan Burdick (son of the postmaster at Edgerton) and Effie Lord Williams furnished contemporary information concerning Dr. Dan's youth in Janesville. Further details were added by Richard Lloyd Jones, Etta E. Loomis, Angie T. Roethe, Mary Elizabeth Sutherland, Dr. Charles Sutherland, Grace S. Lord, Lillie Smith Alexander, Emma L. Warren-Mallet, the late Julia West Paul, and William B. Turner.

The files of the Janesville *Gazette* for the late '70s and early '80s, kindly sent me on microfilm by the publisher, Robert W. Bliss, were excellent sources for events, persons and weather.

Although a half dozen biographical dictionaries place Daniel Hale Williams's birth date in 1858, I use 1856, which is the date given in the U. S. Census records of Hollidaysburg, Pennsylvania, for 1860 and of Janesville, Wisconsin, for 1880; these agree on 1856, and the former was given by his parents. Also when Dr. Dan registered officially with the Illinois State Board of Health as a physician, on April 18, 1883, he gave his age as twenty-eight. This too points to 1856, making him at his registration twenty-seven years and three months old, or in his twenty-eighth year.

Dr. Dan's parents may have chosen his middle name Hale for the Abolitionist, John Parker Hale, nominee of the Free Soilers for the Presidency in 1852, or for a lawyer named Reuben Hale who seems to have acted as intermediary for members of the family in certain property transfers in Lewistown.

I visited Hollidaysburg, saw Dr. Dan's birthplace, the Diamond, and the location of the old canal and the Portage Railroad. Reminiscences of early Hollidaysburg were told by Charles Brown, Harriet Dennis Hollinger, and Harry A. Jacobs. Mr. Jacobs gave the location of Dr. Dan's father's barbershop on the Diamond, a fine situation to which he moved from the earlier location on the docks.

Dr. Dan's birthplace at 315 Blair Street still stands, though it has been added to and now almost touches the street. Originally a square frame structure, solidly built, it stood some distance back from the street on a plot 60 by 100 feet and cost, with its outbuildings, $600 in April 1849. There were two rooms and a hall downstairs, and two rooms upstairs. Before Dan was born, his father had sold off 26 feet of the lot. The remaining property sold for $800 in 1866. We know the children had a dog, because a dog tax was paid. They could watch the Conestoga wagons lumber in with farm produce and deliver it at the new market place which stood across Wayne Street to the east and watch the engrossing stream of strangers coming to the Exchange Hotel across Montgomery Street to the west. Two blocks to the south lay the canal and its teeming docks and above those towered gaunt, tawny Chimney Rocks. A runaway slave hid among Chimney Rocks before the Civil War and during it little Dan, aged seven, his mother and sisters, and other women and children, spent a cowering day there fearing the arrival of Southern troops, which fortunately did not come. Directly back of Dan's home was the Town Hall; Mr. and Mrs. Tom Thumb came every year. A traveling circus came twice a year. There were good swimming holes in the Juniata River and wonderful Emancipation Day celebrations on its banks.

The interesting history of Hollidaysburg, the canal and the Portage Railroad is told in: *A Pleasant Peregrination through the Prettiest Parts of Pennsylvania*, Peregrine Prolix, 1836; *History of the Early Settlement of the Juniata Valley*, Uriah James Jones, 1856, with Notes and Extension by Floyd G. Hoenstine, 1940, Telegraph Press, Harrisburg, Pennsylvania; *History of the City of Altoona and Blair County*, James H. Ewing and Harry Slep, 1880; *History of Huntingdon and Blair Counties, Pennsylvania*, J. Simpson Africa, Philadelphia, 1883; *American Notes*, Charles Dickens, Carleton's New Illustrated Edition, New York, 1885; *Biographical and Portrait Cyclopedia of Blair County, Pennsylvania*, Samuel T. Wiley and W. Scott Garner, 1892; *A History of Blair County, Pennsylvania*, Tarring S. Davis, ed., 1931; *A History of Blair County*, A Project of the Students and Teachers of the Social Science Department of the Altoona Senior High School, 1938; *The Juniata Canal and Old Portage Railroad*, Harry A. Jacobs, published in mimeographed form by the Blair County Historical Society, September 20, 1941.

DR. DAN'S FATHER

When Dr. Dan's father, Daniel Williams, Jr., moved to Hollidaysburg, the town, the canal and the Portage Railroad were internationally famous. Engineers and government officials and important people came from all over the world to exclaim at man's genius in conquering the Allegheny barrier by a series of inclined planes and cable cars. Charles Dickens found it "very pretty traveling" and Jenny Lind was so entranced with the view, so like her own Sweden, that she burst into rapturous song to the delight of the bystanders. Boatload after boatload of human beings, whole households, their belongings and their cattle, went westward through Hollidaysburg. Machinery was invented which swung the filled canal barges out of the water and directly onto railroad trucks for their trip over the wooden rails of the inclined planes surmounting the Alleghenies, and at Johnstown they were swung down again for the continued canal trip further westward. Travelers were many and Dr. Dan's father did a thriving barbering business. His sprightly advertisement appeared in the Hollidaysburg *Democratic Standard* for November 7, 1846:

MONEY WANTED
LEWISTOWN MONEY TAKEN AT PAR!
South-west corner of Juniata and Montgomery streets

The subscriber having neatly fitted up his establishment, is prepared to accommodate all who may give him a call, on the most reasonable terms. He has a superior preparation for effectively removing dandruff from the hair, which he applies to his customers, *gratis*.

D. Williams, Jr.

Wigs, Curls, Braids, &c, &c, always on hand.

D. Williams, Jr., was the acknowledged leader of the small colored group in the town's three thousand inhabitants. He lent money to the preacher without much hope of getting it back. (See the *Minutes of the Baltimore, Philadelphia, New York and New England Annual Conferences of the African Methodist Episcopal Zion Church in America*, published by Rev. T. Eato, Rev. Peter Ross, and Rev. Sampson Talbot, for the Conferences, Zuille and Leonard, Printers, New York, 1852.) He was the trustee in whose name was placed the deed for the site of the African Wesleyan Church. And when the free colored people met over the years in state and national conventions seeking freedom for their race and relief from their own burdens, and when Hollisdaysburg could send only one delegate, he was the one to go. At Syracuse in 1864 he helped frame the National Equal Rights League and returned to Pennsylvania to work valiantly organizing, trying to bring about harmony, urging work and more work, education and more education. (See the *Democratic Standard* of Hollidaysburg, Vol. III, No. 31, Whole No. 217, December 8, 1847; also issues for April 21, June 23, and November 17, 1847; August 8, 1855; July 8, 1863. Also the *Hollidaysburg Register*, Vol. XXIX, No. 32, June 7, 1865.)

He helped with the printing and distribution of a Preamble and Constitution, reassuring the faltering: "We have seen the giant Slavery melt away in an incredibly short time and may quite as reasonably hope to see the rights of man acknowledged . . . the true interests of the coun-

try demand our recognition . . . do not fear, eternal justice is on our side . . . we ask no special privileges . . .
only a fair chance in the race of life and recognition according to our personal merits. To ask less is not manly —
to ask more is foolishness." Schooling, schooling for old
and young — Daniel Williams, Jr., and the others urged
schooling constantly. "We must get education. Those who
have not had early advantages should form day schools
and night schools and try to learn each other . . . we utterly fail in our duty to our children if we neglect to give
them education. Far better it is for us to do with plainer
food and less finery and carefully cultivate the minds of
those who must take our places."

The League addressed an appeal to Congress: ". . . in
the name of God, we ask you not to allow us to be robbed
of the price of our blood, our sufferings, and that which is
ours by birth-right and taxation." Congress parried and
equivocated. League rallies were held up and down the
state, women joining with the men. Songs were written,
printed and fervently sung:

> *Are you a member of the League,*
> *Contending for the right?*
> *Have you already done your part,*
> *Or will you start tonight?*

Some songs rang with religious fervor; others saucily paro-
died popular tunes:

> *We've fought the Union's battles, yet*
> *They will not give us suffrage*
> *And as we think we've earned it quite,*
> *At this we've taken umbrage.*
>   . . . . . .
> *They've given us a "Bureau," and*
> *They think they're our promoters,*
> *I think they'd benefit us more*
> *By making us all voters.*

In August 1866 the Pennsylvania League held its second
state-wide meeting at Pittsburgh. Forty-one auxiliary
Leagues were reported in the state; membership in the
churches had doubled through the League efforts. Daniel
Williams, Jr., had less than a year to live, but he was there
and working as hard as ever. He sat on a half dozen com-

mittees and was chosen one of three delegates to represent the colored people of Pennsylvania at a national meeting to be held in Nashville in the fall. The national meeting was not held, however, and the following May Dr. Dan's father died of consumption.

5

The active work of Dr. Dan's father and other Williamses in both national and state conventions of free colored people before and after the Civil War is found in the Minutes and Proceedings, and other publications of those conventions: national, 1832, 1833, 1835, 1843, 1847, 1853, 1855, 1864; state, Pennsylvania, 1838, 1841, 1848, 1865, 1866, 1868; Ohio, 1849; Illinois, 1853, 1856, 1867. Titles are lengthy and space forbids listing them. A synopsis and evaluation of the conventions is given in *The Early Negro Convention Movement,* John W. Cromwell, The American Negro Academy, Occasional Papers, No. 9, 1904.

6

Just when Sarah and Daniel Williams moved their brood to the old Price home in Annapolis is not certain — or whether they went initially for a visit or as a permanent move, knowing Daniel Williams was fated to die soon. On October 9, 1865, the barber arranged with Attorney Essington Hammond in Hollidaysburg to "bargain and sell or lease" the home and what remained of the original lot on Blair Street. Six months later Lawyer Hammond made the sale. So they might have gone in October 1865, when Hammond was given power of attorney and when another hard winter was approaching, or they might have gone in April when the house was sold. The following August when the barber attended the State Equal Rights League meeting in Pittsburgh, he was listed as a delegate from Hollidaysburg. In September when his daughters were enrolled in St. Frances' Academy in Baltimore, their home was given as Hollidaysburg. Perhaps the family was still in Hollidaysburg, or perhaps they hoped to go back there eventually. If so, they never did, for the barber died in Annapolis.

The *Hollidaysburg Register & Blair County Weekly News* of May 15, 1867, tells of his death on Sunday, May 5, in Annapolis. His age is given as fifty years, one month and eighteen days, which would place his birth in 1817, an obvious error. Two U. S. Census reports, taken ten years apart, place his birth date in 1820. He was therefore only forty-seven when he died. A joint tombstone erected in Annapolis over the graves of Dr. Dan's father and his brother Price gives erroneous ages for both.

A number of photographs seem to date from this time. There was a photographer's shop upstairs over the Hollidaysburg barbershop. What more natural than a wish to record this epoch as it ended? Sarah Williams, her Indian tresses still raven black, unstreaked with gray, seems to turn her face away from the future. Her husband, his cheeks sunken, his eyes large and shining, faces you squarely, undaunted. Young Dan, every feature a replica of his father's, stands at his knee, his small hand on the paternal shoulder, his gaze turned away, perhaps to the window, to the Allegheny hills where he would like to escape.

The late Caroline Parke told of Price Williams's activities as a young man.

Dan's sisters, Ida just older than himself, Alice just younger, remained in St. Frances' Academy, Baltimore, four years, a famous school founded by the Oblate Sisters of Providence. Wealthy Southern planters sent their illegitimate mulatto daughters to genteel St. Frances' Academy for education. Sarah Price Williams sent her daughters there because, after her husband's death, she, along with other friends in Annapolis, was converted to Catholicism. Alice had poor health and her record was modest as to grades but ardent in religious aspects. Ida, who was lame from an improperly set broken leg and always wore a high orthopedic shoe, took a prominent part in activities. At her graduation she sang a solo, played the piano, and delivered the Farewell Address. Alice never married, but Ida married William Cornell and had two daughters. She became a dressmaker, as her mother had been before her, taught younger women in Annapolis, made costumes for a traveling *Mikado* company, and even sent some of her fine sewing into the White House. The Mother Superior of St. Frances' Academy kindly searched out old records, handwritten in French, to show me, and brought to my attention *The Oblates' Hundred and One Years*, Grace H. Sherwood, 1931.

Annie who returned East with her mother married a Mr. Clay and, after his death, Samuel Barbour, whom she divorced some time following the birth of a daughter.

The Rockford cousins were four, all men of considerable property and important in community life: David, John and James Williams, sons of Peter Williams of Columbia, Pennsylvania, and Reuben Armstrong, the wealthiest, who in 1870 owned property valued at $7000, a high figure for those days. David and John had wandered far, through the wilds of Michigan and Wisconsin, before settling in Rockford, and after some years they wandered still farther. David settled finally in Mexico City. John trekked to New Mexico in '53 with the army; his son Hugo Williams has a letter written him by Colonel John C. Tidball, April 27, 1886, affectionately recalling the rigors they endured together on that adventure. In Rockford after the Civil War, John organized war widows' relief and helped found Grand Army Post No. 1. Reuben finally went further west and settled in Arkansas.

The shoemaker to whom Dan was apprenticed was C. M. C. Mason, whose daughter Anna confirmed the fact. Sarah Jennings said William H. Butler, another Annapolis boy, went at the same time as Dan to "Mr. Mason's Training Schools for Boys." Both Anna Mason and Dr. Dan's niece, Ada Blanche Williams, say Dr. Dan "ran away." Gaines, *op. cit.*, says his mother sent for him and he proudly traveled alone. Caudill, *op. cit.*, tells the story of the railroad pass and that his mother did not scold him. And Ada Blanche Williams added the remark that he could take care of himself.

Neither the Andersons nor Dan were in Janesville in 1870 according to the U. S. Census, nor was Dan in Edgerton then, or in Rockford. Allan Burdick remembered Dan in Edgerton about 1873 and Dr. Bert Anderson said "Dan went for the doctor the night I was born," which was in 1876. The years 1868–1873 are unaccounted for in Dan's life, from the time he reached Rockford at about twelve until he appeared in Edgerton, running his own barbershop, at seventeen.

PAGE
7
(*Cont.*)

Dr. N. C. Gilbert, who attended Dr. Dan in his last illness, said Dr. Dan told him he was a pilot on the Sault Ste. Marie, also that he played baseball at the University of Wisconsin. I have been unable to verify either statement, and the University of Wisconsin has no record of Dan's attendance there, though I have a photograph of Dan bearing the name of a Madison photographer and apparently taken when he was about sixteen or seventeen. Dr. Charles L. Sutherland, a classmate at Chicago Medical College, stated Dan told him he had worked on the boats and assumed it was as a steward since he felt that would account for Dan's excellent table manners! A patient, Louise Rainey, remembered Dr. Dan once remarked: "Lots of the boys got their medical education working on the railroads; I used to work on the boats." Caudill, *op. cit.*, says he played in an orchestra on boats, but places the event during summer vacations at medical college. Those vacations are otherwise accounted for.

I can find no foundation for the legend Dan was abandoned in Janesville in rags by his mother. There is no evidence his mother ever went to Wisconsin. Mary Louise Hall Walker lived near the Andersons as a child, when Sally and Dan first came there, and remembered that Sally "had a way of earning her living; it was not sewing." The way, of course, was the hair goods trade.

Everyone from the late Allan Burdick, the earliest living acquaintance of Dr. Dan that I met, onward through his life, spoke of his meticulous grooming and polished manners. The same was said of his uncle, Peter Williams.

Accounts of barbering in the early days and the Negro's role in that occupation are found in *Early History of Negroes in Business in Philadelphia*, a paper read by Henry M. Minton, M.D., before the American Historical Society, March 1913, and in *The Tonsorial Art*, a pamphlet by M. J. Vieira, 1877.

A contemporary account of the hair goods work Sally Williams did may be found in *Self-Instructor in the Art of Hair Work, Dressing Hair, Making Curls, Switches, Braids, and Hair Jewelry of Every Description, Compiled from Original Designs and the Latest Parisian Patterns*, Mark Campbell, New York and Chicago, 1867.

Dan's sister Sally married a mulatto, Bluford Turner, whose family owned considerable property in the heart of Portage. A nephew, William B. Turner, remembers how the bride from the East taught him "gestures and diction" when he was a high school boy. Sally divorced Bluford Turner and years later, some time after 1898, married a Nesbit.

Who's Who, 1921 states Dan *attended* Janesville High School; other biographical dictionaries say he *was graduated*, one says in 1873. Rosemary Enright, Attendance Department, Janesville Public Schools, says he was not graduated; attendance records are not now in existence for those years.

"Red Iron Ore" is from *Ballads and Songs of the Shanty-Boy*, collected and edited by Franz Rickaby, Harvard University Press, Cambridge, 1926, 1954.

8

The Harrisburg uncle, Harry Price, besides being a good musician and a barber, was also a phrenologist. When barbering he would run his hands over a customer's head to feel the bumps and tell what sort of man he was. One day a customer no sooner sat down and Harry Price started work than the barber cried: "Why, you're a dishonest man. You've stolen something!" At that moment the police walked in and took their man, all lathered up as he was. Harry Price left a large family of ten children. One daughter married a white man. Another daughter, Victoria Adelaide Nicholson, was an accomplished pianist, the first woman of color to play the organ at the New England Conservatory of Music. A son died an army cook in Albuquerque, New Mexico, from which distant place his eight year old daughter returned East, saying her prayers in Spanish. After Harry Price's death, his white wife, Mary, continued for years in business at the house in Harrisburg purchased by her father-in-law, Reverend Price of Annapolis. M. J. Price & Son, Wigmakers, had customers from Seattle to New York.

Dan loved playing the bass viol. He urged Allan Burdick to learn. The famous Anderson band numbered twenty pieces — winds, strings and drums — all white men except the Andersons and Dan. Old-timers remember it as "the best I ever danced to."

The early history of Janesville is from the *History of Rock County and Transactions of the Rock County Agricultural Society and Mechanics Institute*, Orrin Guernsey and Josiah F. Willard, eds., 1856; *The History of Rock County, Wisconsin*, Western Historical Co., Chicago, 1879; *Picturesque Janesville*, brochure, 1892; *Janesville, Wisconsin, Illustrated*, brochure, Art Gravure & Etching Co., Milwaukee, 1892; and *Rock County, Wisconsin: A New History*, William Fiske Brown, Chicago, 1908, 2 vols. City directories of the period were useful too.

9   Minerva Guernsey King told of her father's lending books to Dan. Caudill, *op. cit.*, gives the subjects which were favorite with him.

The Janesville Classical Academy, run by the tall, spare Reverend John P. Haire and his short, plump wife, a graduate of the first class at Mount Holyoke, had none of the dignity of the red brick Jefferson Public School set in its elm-shaded square. The Academy was located downtown in rented quarters over a drugstore in the Mitchell Block. Only about fifty pupils attended, children of the "best" families; they were of all grades, some still in the lower branches of study.

10   The *History of Rock County, Wisconsin*, cited above (Notes for page 8) gives the oculist's name as J. F. Hullihin and says he was from West Virginia. I use data furnished me by the late Mara Franc Edwards, preferring it to the uncertain editing of the old volume.

12   The *Gazette*, in describing a ball at the end of January 1877, where "spacious Apollo Hall swarmed with beauty and fashion of the city" and where "Anderson's orchestra discoursed the music until 4:00 A.M.," said also that "Miss Ida Williams appeared handsomely in white Paris muslin." Her mother Mrs. J. P. Williams wore "pink silk en train."

14   Carrie Jacobs, in the years to come, when she was Mrs. Bond would set the whole country to singing her songs —

"I Love You Truly" and "The End of a Perfect Day." She and Ida Williams, her stepsister, were not very fond of each other, or of the fact their widowed parents had married. They chose separate schools.

Biographical notes on Dr. Simeon Lord may be found in: R. French Stone, *op. cit.; Portrait and Biographical Album of Rock County, Wisconsin,* published by Acme Publishing Co., Chicago, 1889; *Commemorative Biographical Record of the Counties of Rock, Green, Grant, Iowa, and LaFayette, Wisconsin,* published by Beers, 1901; *Portraits and Biographies, Including the Governor of Wisconsin and the President of the United States,* no author, copyrighted by Chapman Bros., 1885.

CHAPTER II

A Medical Apprentice in 1878

15
　　The biographical dictionaries differ as to the date of Dan's graduation from Haire's Classical Academy, also called the Janesville Classical Academy; some give 1877, others 1878. Both the late Mara Franc Edwards and Minerva Guernsey King told me that Dan was in attendance with them and that they were graduated in the spring of 1877. Minnie Guernsey left to study in Boston in September 1877, a date confirmed by an item in the *Gazette.* Presumably then Dan Williams also was graduated in the spring of 1877, studied law the winter of 1877–78, and went into Palmer's office the spring or summer of '78.

　　The Janesville *Gazette* for August 2, 1877, gave most of its front page to the Emancipation Day speech of the local Republican Congressman, the Honorable Charles G. Williams. Mr. Williams said in that speech, quite possibly quoting Harry Anderson: "I heard a better answer to this [the Negro] question in one of the barber shops of Janesville than I should expect to find in all the books of the philosophers. A colored man said: 'The white people pity us, but pity won't buy bread. We have a harder row to hoe than they, and what the colored men of this country need is to obtain property and hold it.' "

PAGE
15
(*Cont.*)

Caudill, *op. cit.*, states Dan studied law with a Janesville lawyer, and Ada Blanche Williams confirmed the fact, but neither gave the name of the lawyer. Dan's explanation of why he hated law is from Caudill, *op. cit.*

16

Mary Louise Hall Walker told of Dan's driving her mother, Eva Johnson Hall, to Mt. Zion with her carpet rags. The case of Hopkins's gunshot wound was described in the *Gazette*.

17

Mrs. John Siebert Taylor and the late Mrs. M. O. Mouat, daughters of Dr. Palmer, told of Dan's study with their father, as did Dr. Charles L. Sutherland, who told as well of Pember and Mills. City directories confirm all three. In September 1879 the *Gazette* said Will Palmer had gone to Chicago to "continue" his medical studies. This could mean he had been in Chicago the year before, 1878–1879, or it could mean that he was continuing after his apprenticeship with his father. His sister, Mrs. Taylor, thinks Will went in 1879. Hartshorn, *op. cit.*, says Dan studied with Palmer two years; R. French Stone, *op. cit.*, says four years. Two years seems correct by other data.

18

The old preceptor system is described in *The Life of Chevalier Jackson: An Autobiography*, 1938; in *The Doctors Mayo*, Helen Clapesattle, 1934, as well as in numerous other medical biographies.

Biographical notes on Dr. Henry Palmer are found in works cited for Dr. Simeon Lord, Notes for page 14.

20

I date Pember and Mills's coming to Palmer by the dates of their leaving Milton College and by Janesville city directories.

Dan Williams was devoted to his preceptor. When Henry Palmer died in 1895, he left an important post to come back to Janesville for the funeral, and called on each member of the family in turn to express his gratitude to the man who had started him off so well. "All I am, I owe to him," Dr. Dan said.

21

Dan's new clothes and his mustache are described from a photograph.

PAGE
21
(*Cont.*)

Julia LeBeau Thompson and Emma L. Warren-Mallet told of Harry Anderson's desire that Traviata and Dan should marry.

22

The *Illinois State Medical Register* for 1877–1878, D. W. Graham, A.M., M.D., ed., Chicago, 1877, lists the following medical sects: Botanic, Eclectic, Homeopathic, Physio-Medical, Regular, and Thompsonian.

The superiority of Chicago Medical over Rush is set forth in a statement of Nicholas Senn found in *Joy of Living*, 2 vols., Franklin Martin, Chicago, 1933. Description of the college is from this work and from personal recollections of Dr. Coleman Buford and a manuscript speech of the late Dr. William E. Morgan furnished me by Dr. Buford.

The early history of Chicago Medical College is taken from *Dedication of the Montgomery Ward Memorial Building*, by various authors, Chicago, 1927.

25

John Jones is briefly spoken of in *Black Metropolis*, St. Clair Drake and Horace Cayton, New York, 1945. Further details of the story of the Joneses are from the *Chicago Tribune*, May 22, 1879, reminiscences of the granddaughter, Theodora Lee Purnell, and data furnished by Franklyn A. Henderson from his personal files of historical material. The Jones home on Ray Avenue (now 29th Place) was identified for me by Mr. Henderson. The participation of John Jones in the early Negro conventions is established by the Proceedings of those conventions – national for 1848 and 1853, and Illinois for 1853, 1856 and 1867. John Jones was born in 1816 on a plantation in North Carolina, son of a free mulatto mother and a German father, John Bromfield. Though he was free, his mother feared he might be reduced to slavery, and apprenticed him at an early age to a man moving to Tennessee. This man in turn bound him out to a tailor who refused him his liberty at twenty-one. John (who now used his mother's name) prayed the court for a writ of habeas corpus, was allowed to return to North Carolina where he secured proof of his age and free status, and returning was allowed to go his own way. In 1845, protected by his freedom papers, he brought his bride Mary to Chicago, a slow seven-day trip by stage and canal. They had $3.50 with which to start life. They rented a one-room cottage and a shop 6½ by 20 feet on a spot now the Clark Street entrance to the Sherman House. By pawning his watch and laying out his money judiciously, and with $2 worth of groceries obtained from a colored grocer on credit, the Joneses started their tailoring business. Before the Great Fire of 1871 he was worth $80,000. The fire destroyed much of his property but he recovered enough to leave a good fortune to his family when he died. He had to learn to read and write after he came to Chicago; he managed to do this and became a leader for Negro rights. His house was a rendezvous for Abolitionists, black and white, and a station on the underground railroad, sheltering many fugitives on their way to Canada. His freedom papers repose in the Chicago Public Library.

26

For the story of Samuel F. Williams of Johnstown, see his *Four Years in Liberia, A Sketch of the Life of the Rev. Samuel Williams with remarks on the missions, manners and customs of the natives of Western Africa: Together with an answer to Nesbit's book*, Philadelphia, King & Baird, printers, 1857. Nesbit took a pessimistic view of colonization. His book is *Four Months in Liberia, or, African Colonization Exposed*, by William Nesbit of Hollidaysburg, Pennsylvania, June 1855.

CHAPTER III

Dan Goes to Medical School

28

The description of the opening of Chicago's medical colleges in the fall of 1880 is from the *Chicago Tribune*, Vol. XL, September 29, 1880.

Dan's timidity in meeting new white people was explained to me by W. E. B. DuBois, who was his friend.

The description of Dean Davis and his opening remarks are based on Martin, *op. cit.*

29

A packet of Dan's letters to Harry Anderson were found in Dr. Dan's effects after his death and were given to me

PAGE
29
(*Cont.*)

by his niece, A. Blanche Williams. Copies of excerpts of other letters from Dan to Anderson were given me by Dr. Bert Anderson.

30

Advertisements of Goodwin's Froliques and Josh Whitcomb are found in the *Chicago Daily Inter-Ocean*, Vol. IX, September 25–30, 1880.

It appears that $3.75 was a weekly rate, although Mrs. Jones may have finally made it $10 a month. Later he says he owes Mrs. Jones $8.75 and it will seem this covered a month's room and board, since he also says he needs $1.25 for incidentals and that $10 will see him through a month. The College catalogue stated: "The price of board and lodging will vary from $4 to $6 per week. Vacant rooms for those who desire to board and lodge themselves may be had at prices ranging from $6 to $10 per month."

33

The requirements, courses of study, faculty, lists of students and graduates, etc., of Chicago Medical College are taken from the *Announcements* of the school for the years in question, kindly lent to me by the Northwestern University Medical Library.

Additional material on Chicago Medical at this period, its faculty, etc., and on Mercy Hospital can be found in *Dedication of the Montgomery Ward Memorial Building*, by various authors, Chicago, 1927; Martin, *op. cit.; The Medicine Man*, Emilius C. Dudley, 1927; *History of Medicine and Surgery, and Physicians and Surgeons of Chicago*, Chicago Medical Society, 1922; *Sixty-second Annual Report of Mercy Hospital*, Chicago, January 1, 1912.

Chicago Medical College indeed required "hard work and much study." The schedule was heavy, the instructors demanding, and the student's preparation poor. If Dan had no bachelor's degree, neither did Frank Pember nor two other Janesville youths then enrolled, Charles Sutherland and Hugh Menzies. Only Will Palmer and James Mills of Dan's home-town contemporaries were so fortified. Actually only fifteen per cent of Dan's class was equipped with a preliminary degree. The usual prior education of a medico of the early '80s was eight years of grade school and no more.

34   Theodora Lee Purnell told how medical students continually dropped in to visit Dan in her grandmother's home.

36   Dan's despondency was added to by the poor health of his sister Sally, who had divorced Bluford Turner and returned East with her young daughter. When he failed to get further word from home, he was sure she was going to die. James Mills had been ill too, and, though now out of danger, Dan felt his beloved friend had come very near losing his life. Dan always expected the worst.

37   The smallpox epidemic is described in Martin, *op. cit.*

38   The failure of 20 per cent of Dan's first year class is stated in the *Chicago Medical Journal and Examiner* for May 1881. A partial record of Dan's grades, all that was available, was furnished me by the Registrar of Northwestern University Medical Department. Dr. Charles Sutherland stated Dan was rather below average as a medical student.

    I was disappointed not to discover more about Dan's Aunt Charlotte. He mentions her twice in letters to Anderson, and with respect. But living descendants could remember only that she lived to a great old age and frightened them almost to death when they were children by getting up in the night and creeping about like a ghost, tucking covers solicitously over them. No one knew whether she was a Price or a Wilks.

    Price and his wife had separated, despite their five children. That was the end of the whirlwind romance that had begun when Price had persuaded the red-haired, blue-eyed Matilda Maria Agnes Maduro to elope with him from her convent school near Poughkeepsie.

CHAPTER IV

The Barber Becomes a Doctor

41   Descriptions of prebacteriological medicine and surgery and the introduction of modern surgery are drawn from the following: *How We Treat Wounds Today*, Robert T.

PAGE
41
(*Cont.*)

Morris, 1886; *The Rules of Aseptic and Antiseptic Surgery*, Arpad Gerster, 1887; *Fifty Years a Surgeon*, Robert T. Morris, 1935; Martin, *op. cit.*; Dudley, *op. cit.*; *American Doctors of Destiny*, Frank J. Jirka, 1940; *A Surgeon's Life*, J. M. T. Finney, 1940; *Transactions*, Southern Surgical and Gynecological Association, Vol. 24, pp. 609–611, 1911; *The Chicago Medical Journal and Examiner*, 1880–1884.

42

I have drawn heavily on Martin, *op. cit.*, for description of Dan's first operation (Martin does not say whether or not the patient recovered). The two men were contemporaries. Martin was graduated the spring before Dan entered Chicago Medical and during Dan's first year was serving as interne at Mercy Hospital. The two began at this time a friendship that lasted for life.

46

There was no hospital in Janesville at this time. Births took place in the home; perhaps apprentices were not allowed to attend. Women were more prudish then. Dr. Palmer, though he did some surgery, undoubtedly took childbirth cases too. Specialization did not come in the Midwest until much later. There is no evidence that Dan's racial mixture had anything to do with his remark that he could not see childbirth cases in Janesville.

47

The following receipt was found in Dr. Dan's papers after his death:

"Chicago Aug 22nd 90

"Received from Dan'l H Williams one thousand dollars payment in full of all demands against him for money advanced to begin and complete his medical education and in consideration of the above sum I hereby release him from all obligations. [*signed*] C. H. Anderson."

The handwriting, except for the signature, is in Dr. Dan's hand. The sum seems much beyond anything that Dan was borrowing to pay for his room, board and the fees for his second and third years. The first year he borrowed money at the bank for his fees. The second year fees were $91 and the third year $111. He may have paid only $60, or as much as $97.50, a year for board, depending upon whether his rate was $3.75 a week or $10 a month. Even at the higher rate, it appears he borrowed only about $500 for the three years. The wording of the receipt sounds a little strange, as though some sort of demands were being made upon Dr. Dan at this date, if not by Harry Anderson, always so good a friend, then perhaps by George who was just now entering dental school belatedly at the age of thirty-five. The debt may have been paid some time before this date. Dr. Bert Anderson thinks his father also loaned Dr. Dan money while he was getting started in practice, but the receipt does not mention this, and Dr. Anderson was a young child when Dan went to college and was only fourteen in 1890.

48

DeWolf's work as health commissioner is told by Dudley, *op. cit.* An editorial in the *Chicago Medical Journal and Examiner* for August 1884 says: "No! Chicago will not have the cholera! She is protected by 'vaccination' from a great deal worse! She has her wash-pot, her chamber-pot, and her drinking cup in the great lake at her feet, and can look with a smile into the rheumy eyes of the 'Filth Plague!' "

Dudley always remembered Dan, and years later, finishing an operation at St. Luke's before a group of visiting Southern white doctors, he took occasion to say as he drew off his rubber gloves: "Gentlemen, I recommend you stay on for the next operation. It will be performed by the famous Negro surgeon, Daniel Hale Williams." But the visitors, loyal to their prejudices, all filed out. Dr. Dan told the story to Dr. U. G. Dailey, and Dailey told it to me.

Accounts of Fenger are from *Bulletin of the Society of Medical History of Chicago*, Vol. I, p. 99, March 1919, "Christian Fenger: A Biographical Sketch, 1840–1902," Coleman Buford, M.D.; Vol. 3, p. 55, January 1923, "Christian Fenger As I Knew Him," L. L. McArthur, M.D.; and *A History of Medicine and Surgery, and Physicians and Surgeons of Chicago*, Endorsed and Published under the Supervision of the Council of the Chicago Medical Society, Chicago, 1922. Also letters from Dr. Coleman Buford.

American College of Surgeons records indicate Dr. Dan served as interne or resident assistant to Mercy Hospital April 1 to October 1, 1883, but a letter dated March 14, 1947, written to me by Sister Mary Therese, R.N., Medi-

PAGE
48
(*Cont.*)

cal Director of Mercy Hospital, states that hospital records show the internes for the year 1883–1884 were J. F. Pember, P. Dougherty, W. M. Kelly, and D. Scudder, and that there is no record that Dan Williams served in this capacity at Mercy Hospital at any time. We know from his letters, however, that he did assist in Mercy wards in an unofficial capacity from April to October 1882.

Dan's beard is revealed in the class photograph sent me by Dr. Charles Sutherland.

The *Chicago Medical Journal and Examiner*, March 1883, gives the prize winners of the Class of '83 and describes Commencement. The program was found in Dr. James Mills's scrapbook kindly loaned me by his son, Dr. James Mills, Jr.

CHAPTER V

Operating in a Dining Room

50

A letter from F. V. Cargill, American Medical Association, states Dr. Dan secured a license to practice medicine in the District of Columbia, March 1883 (day not given).

The Official Register of Physicians and Midwives Now in Practice to Whom Certificates Have Been Issued by the State Board of Health of Illinois 1877–1886, H. W. Rokker, State Printer, Springfield, 1886, gives the following entry for Dr. Dan: "Registered April 18, 1883, Address 3034 Michigan Avenue, Age 28, Certificate issued April 16, 1883, on basis of Chicago Medical College diploma, dated March 27, 1883, Certificate filed for record April 18, 1883."

The experience of Morgan and Billings in starting practice is from Martin, *op. cit.*

Street addresses of the offices of Morgan, Billings and Dr. Dan are found in the *Medical Directory of Illinois* for 1883.

51

Description of the colored colony in 1885 is drawn from Drake and Cayton, *op. cit.*, and from *The Colored Men's*

PAGE
51
(*Cont.*) *Professional and Business Directory of Chicago, and Valuable Information of the Race in General,* I. C. Harris, July 1885.

Franklyn A. Henderson, who has done considerable research on the early history of the colored colony in Chicago, where his own family were among the first settlers, states that Henry Hutchinson and George Revels were two colored doctors in Chicago before the Civil War. I have found no official record of Revels. H. C. Hutchinson, age forty-seven, 406 South Clark Street, registered January 11, 1878, under the Act of May 25, 1877, which allowed physicians to continue to practice without certificate who had been practicing in Illinois ten years prior to July 1, 1877; Hutchinson had been practicing in Illinois nineteen years then, or from 1859.

The late Mrs. George Cleveland Hall told me that Dr. C. H. McAllister was the only colored doctor in Chicago when Dr. Dan began practicing there but there seem to have been three officially registered and one more not officially registered. The *Official Register of Physicians and Midwives,* etc., for 1877–1886, already mentioned, states that McAllister was graduated from Jefferson Medical College in 1879, and was issued a certificate April 22, 1879, at the age of thirty-nine. This same volume lists Woodson L. Simpson, who was graduated from Bennett College of Eclectic Medicine and Surgery, 1882, age twenty-eight, and Mary E. Green, also Bennett, 1883, age thirty-seven. It does not mention J. Milton Williams who is included with these other doctors in the 1885 *Colored Directory, op. cit.*

The fight between the "regulars" and the "irregulars" was bitter and continued for years. The Eclectics maintained a college in Chicago (Bennett Medical College) until 1915 and the Homeopaths held out until 1922 when Hahnemann Medical College closed its doors. The fight was perhaps all the more bitter because the regulars themselves were confused and changing. The recognition of disease as well as its treatment was not clear. Lavish overdosing with calomel brought rebellion of patients as well as false prophets, herb doctors, steam doctors, and so-called Indian doctors with secret cures presumably obtained from the aborigines. The Eclectics scorned all min-

PAGE
51
(*Cont.*)

erals and claimed that the green vegetable tinctures they extracted from roots and herbs would cure all ills; while they found no panaceas, they did add many valuable drugs to materia medica. And the Homeopaths with their infinitesimal small doses at least allowed a patient to recover sometimes when the fashionable huge doses of mercury did not. Out of all the controversy regular medicine emerged finally secure against the "isms" and the "pathies" because from time to time it pursued systematic introspection to eliminate its defects. See *History of Medical Practice in Illinois,* compiled and arranged by Lucius H. Zeuch, M.D., issued by the Illinois State Medical Society, Chicago, 1927, Vol. I, p. 647.

Dr. Dan's office hours are from Harris, *op. cit.*

According to James Gordon, Dr. Dan roomed in the home of Charles Poynter and Poynter, when the man was old, "had the run of Dr. Dan's place up at Idlewild [his summer home]."

52   Mrs. Jones's remarks about Dr. Dan were told by Theodora Lee Purnell.

Dr. Dan's operation of Mrs. LeBeau was recounted by her daughter, Julia LeBeau Thompson, who also told how people called the young physician Dr. Dan, a fact also reported by others.

53   Early operating in private homes, and the experiences of Billings and Martin, are told in Martin, *op. cit.*

Dr. U. G. Dailey told of the horseplay among medical students of those days.

The earliest biographical dictionary in which Dr. Dan's name has been found — R. French Stone, *op. cit.,* 1894 — states that Daniel Williams "has been Attending Physician to the Protestant Orphan Asylum nine years" and that he is "also Attending Surgeon to the South Side Dispensary," etc., Watson, *op. cit.,* 1896, made the dates of the latter position 1884–1892 and the former 1884–1893. Mather, *op. cit.,* stated nineteen years later that Dr. Dan took up the Dispensary job in 1884 and the Orphan Asylum position "on the retirement of Dr. H. P. Hatfield in 1885," and adds that Dr. Dan was "Demonstrator of Anatomy at Northwestern University Medical School four years." *Who's Who in America*, 1920–1921, gives the same information as Watson. *Who's Who in American Medicine*, 1925, omits the Dispensary and Orphan Asylum connections, but makes him demonstrator in anatomy at Northwestern, 1885–1888. *Who's Who in America*, 1926, agrees with the 1920–1921 volume of that publication. The obituary notice in *The Journal of the American Medical Association, op. cit.*, omits reference to the Dispensary and the Orphan Asylum and states he was "Demonstrator of Anatomy at his alma mater, 1885–88." A letter from the Reference Librarian of Northwestern University Medical School, under date of January 5, 1944, states "The records in our Dean's office show only the following information about Dr. Williams: 'Served in South Side Dispensary, 1887–1893?'" Northwestern University *Announcements* for these years do not list Dr. Dan as Demonstrator, but list Frank Billings for 1882 and William E. Morgan for 1883–1886. Another source, a memorial brochure on Billings, states that Billings was Demonstrator 1882–1886, which makes Billings overlap with Morgan several years. Probably there were several demonstrators of anatomy with one in charge of the others, and quite likely Dr. Dan did serve among them. "Trying to place a person's relation to and in a medical school is difficult after years have passed," Dr. Coleman Buford wrote me. "There are so many departments and such large numbers in each department and so many grades of teachers. . . . In the old days [there were] several persons of equal rank with none of them [actually] the head of the department."

54   Several doctors, medical students under Dr. Dan, have written me of their experience in his classes, among them: Drs. Isaac A. Abt; James Alderson; Paul C. Boomer, who instigated the sale of iodized table salt; Andy Hall, 1952 chairman of the Fifty Year Club of the Illinois State Medical Society; Frank C. Jones; Coleman Buford, who served on the surgical staffs of a half dozen Chicago hospitals and was Professor of Surgery at Chicago Polyclinic. Several remember Charlie Mayo '88, one of the famous Minnesota brothers, as being present.

The Chicago City Railway Company has no record of their medical staff in the early years. A newspaper article by Mrs. M. R. Rogers Webb, published in *The Colored American*, Washington, D.C., November 11, 1893, states that Dr. Dan "is on the staff of physicians employed by the Chicago City Railway Company." A letter from E. Wyllys Andrews to Hoke Smith, Secretary of the Interior (NA), confirms the fact and states his high respect for Dr. Dan's courtroom work.

The late Julia West Paul told of Dr. Dan's popularity, his singing and guitar playing.

Dr. Bert Anderson, the only surviving member of Harry Anderson's family, was only six when his mother died and has little knowledge of the circumstances of either her death or Tessie's. He remembered more about Traviata and Bentley.

55
Clarence Eddy, educated from the age of eleven for a musical career, was the director of the Hershey School of Musical Art in Chicago and for seventeen years organist and choirmaster of the First Presbyterian Church. He played at the Vienna Exposition 1873, the Paris Exposition 1889, at the Chicago World's Fair in '93, the Pan-American Exposition 1901, and at the St. Louis Exposition 1904. He was the author of many organ works. That he accepted Traviata Anderson as a pupil is an indication of her musical ability.

Jennie L. Avendorph and Emma L. Warren-Mallet quoted Traviata's remark about her feeling toward Dan.

The Reverend Shelton Hale Bishop and his sister Victoria Bishop Schuster gave the data on their father's life and Dr. Dan's friendship with their family.

Dan's attendance at Stanton School is stated in Mather, *op. cit.* The attacks of whites are recounted in *Report on Schools and Finances of Freedmen*, J. W. Alvord, Inspector, etc., for the years 1866–1870. Dan's clothes are from a photograph.

56   The Right Reverend William Croswell Doane, D.D., LL.D., was the first bishop of the diocese of Albany of the Episcopal Church; he served 1869–1913.

57   The Nina Pinchback dance incident was told by Christine Shoecraft Smith, who said it occurred before she met Dr. Dan, which was in 1889.

        The late Julia West Paul first told me of the Blake affair. The history of the Blake family and of Kittie May was told by Harriet L. Van Vranken, Henrietta Van Vranken Americ, and Maymie Van Vranken Gibson, all of whom confirmed Mrs. Paul's story. Harriette Kennedy Brown told me her mother (a Williams) and her father, David Kennedy, Dan's Hollidaysburg chum, knew Dr. Dan had suffered a great blow.

        Bismarck Pinchback's infatuation with one of the Blake girls was told me by Mrs. Walter Pinchback.

        St. Agnes School for Girls was founded by Bishop Doane in 1870. It originally stood near the Cathedral on Elk Street in Albany, but in 1932 was moved to the suburbs.

59   Surmises as to why Dr. Dan did not marry are stated in the article in *The Colored American*, November 11, 1893, entitled "Chicago's Pride," by M. R. Rogers-Webb.

        Dr. Dan's attendance at the Ninth International Medical Congress is determined by *Who's Who in America*, Vol. II, 1920–1921. For Mills's trip to Europe and other facts of his life, see *Portrait and Biographical Album of Rock County, Wisconsin*, Acme Publishing Co., Chicago, 1889. Persons and events connected with the Congress are taken from the published *Proceedings*.

60   Changing Chicago is described in *Architecture of Old Chicago*, Thomas E. Tallmadge, University of Chicago Press, 1941. Tallmadge mentions that Patti sang "Home Sweet Home" at the dedication of the Auditorium. That Clarence Eddy played the organ is stated in *Marquis' Handbook of Chicago, A Complete History, Reference*

PAGE
60
(*Cont.*)

Book and Guide to the City, A. N. Marquis & Co., 3d ed., 1887. Dr. Bert Anderson said Traviata accompanied Patti on several occasions.

Who's Who in Colored America, 1927, and Dr. Bert Anderson gave data about George Anderson. He was graduated from the Chicago College of Dental Surgery in 1892, at the age of thirty-seven, and did not marry until he was fifty-three. His wife was the former Ella M. Murphy. He practiced forty years in St. Louis and served as president of the Mound City Dental Society. He died in 1938 at the age of seventy-two.

Theodora Lee Purnell herself told me of Dr. Dan's gift and her reaction to it.

61

James Gordon told anecdotes of Dr. Dan's friendliness and popularity, as did Harriett Curtis Hall. "Widow Barr," mother of Elmer Barr and sister of Julia Barr (Mrs. Louis B.) Anderson, was one he advised as to her investments.

Dr. Dan's ownership of real estate at this time was recounted by Marie Hudlin whose mother rented an apartment in one of the two red brick buildings he owned in the 2900 block on Armour Avenue. See also the Rogers-Webb article, *op. cit.*

62

The late Louis B. Anderson told me how Dr. Dan attended all the churches and James Gordon mentioned the five-dollar bill at Old Bethel. Mrs. James R. White told of his attending All Souls. The church, however, has no record of membership.

Louis B. Anderson also told me of Dr. Dan's membership in the Hamilton Club, as did others. The fact is also mentioned in Watson, *op. cit.*

Dr. Dan's appointment to the Illinois State Board of Health and dates of his tenure are shown in the *Executive Register of the Governor* and are quoted in a letter from Margaret C. Norton, Archivist.

Work of the Board of Health during Dr. Dan's tenure is taken from the Annual Reports of the Board, and from

PAGE
62
(*Cont.*) *The Medical Journal and Examiner,* December 1888, article by H. A. Johnson, "The Influence of the Work of the Illinois Medical Practice Act upon Medical Education."

63   Historical aspects of disease in Illinois and methods used against it are discussed in *The Rise and Fall of Disease in Illinois,* Isaac D. Rawlings, M.S., M.D., in collaboration with William A. Evans, M.D., D.P.H., Gottfried Koehler, M.D., and Baxter K. Richardson, A.B., Vols. I and II, published by the State Department of Public Health, 1927.

    A list of health measures passed by the Illinois General Assembly during the years 1889–1893 was given me in a communication from Edward J. Barrett, Secretary of State and State Librarian.

CHAPTER VI

First Interracial Hospital, 1891

66   James Gordon, only surviving member of the original committee, told me the story of the founding of Provident Hospital, gave me the names of those connected with the task, and incidents related to it. The published annual reports of Provident Hospital for 1891–1915 were also used.

    The history of trained nursing in Chicago is drawn from: Chicago Medical Society, *History of Medicine,* etc., *op. cit.;* *A History of Nursing,* Deborah MacLurg Jensen, R.N., M.A., St. Louis, 1943; *A History of Nursing,* M. Adelaid Nutting and Lavinia L. Dock, 2 vols., New York, 1907; *A History of Nursing From the Earliest Times to the Present Day with Special Reference to the Work of the Last Thirty Years,* Nutting and Dock, 4 vols., New York and London, 1912; Mercy Hospital Annual Report, *op. cit.*

    A few pupils of the Illinois Training School for Nurses had been admitted to Cook County Hospital wards while Dr. Dan was in Chicago Medical College, but it was three years after his graduation before the Illinois Training School had adopted modern graded instruction. Mercy Hospital had had no trained nurses when Frank Pember and Dan had cared for the obstetrical wards and did not ven-

PAGE
66
(*Cont.*)

ture upon training them until 1889; the institution did not yet have its state charter in December 1890. St. Luke's had started nurses' training two years before Mercy, and Wesley had only begun this very year (1890).

See Dailey, *op. cit.*, for statement that Dr. Dan first had the idea of a hospital "four or five years after graduation," which would be three or four years before Provident was organized. Dr. Dan's own speech at Nashville (Publications No. 8) states: "Years before I was able to interest the people of Chicago in a hospital . . ."

67

Difficulties of securing hospital staff appointments are recounted in a manuscript copy of Dr. William Morgan's speech at the opening of Mercy Hospital Clinic, furnished me by Dr. Coleman G. Buford.

68

Account of Negro enterprise in Chicago at this time is from Drake and Cayton, *op. cit.*, and Harris, *op. cit.*

69

Lloyd Wheeler's niece, Mrs. James R. White, told of the marriage of her uncle to Raynie Petit. His role in race work is spoken of in Harris, *op. cit.*

Political data about Marshall, Denison, Theodore Jones, John G. Jones and Morris are found in *Negro Politicians: The Rise of Negro Politics in Chicago,* Harold F. Gosnell, Chicago, 1935.

70

The modest start of Chicago hospitals is given in Chicago Medical Society, *History of Medicine*, etc., *op. cit.*

Christine Shoecraft Smith told of meetings held in the flat of her aunt, Mrs. J. C. Plummer.

71

Indignation Jones's remark is quoted from Moxcey, *op. cit.*

72

John M. Mallet, who attended one of the early mass meetings, told of Edward H. Morris's resistance because of his real estate interests and the late Robert L. Taylor confirmed the fact.

Dr. Dan's remarks about foreigners caring for their sick is from his Nashville speech. Publications No. 8.

73

Contributions are cited in the first Annual Report of Provident Hospital.

A photostatic copy of the articles of incorporation was furnished me by the Secretary of State of Illinois.

74

The incident of the old preacher's curse is mentioned in Dr. Dan's Nashville speech (Publications No. 8). His name is given in a radioscript (undated) prepared by H. L. Fishel, which I saw in Dr. Dailey's files.

75

Lillie Smith Alexander told of the decorations and booths at the opening party. James Gordon gave the other details.

The two elderly ladies treated by J. M. Johnson were Mrs. Nellie Grant and Mrs. Georgie Anne Davis.

Jesse Binga told me of his own contributions. The Annual Reports give the rest.

76

The interest of these doctors was more than perfunctory. Isham and Billings each came twice that first year to lecture to the student nurses, while Jaggard and Starkey came four times each.

James R. White, an early Provident doctor, told me of the qualifications of Bentley and Wesley, which are confirmed in *Who's Who in Colored America*, Vol. I, 1927.

77

That Dr. Dan thought well of young Curtis was told me by his sister, Harriett Curtis Hall, who related also how the men scrubbed the operating room.

The late Mrs. George C. Hall told me her husband got his start in the red light district. Dr. James R. White said this was one reason Hall was not acceptable on the staff, but the main reason was his inferior schooling; this was also said by the late James Hale Porter. Porter sympathized with Hall.

PAGE
77
(*Cont.*)
Miss Marion Hull was principal of the training school for nurses for the first year and, according to the Trustees' Report, "deserves much praise for efficient work." The student nurses too came in for praise. Their names were Emma A. Reynolds, Lillian E. Haywood, Florence Phillips, Bertha I. Estes, Ada L. Jones, Luella E. Roberson and Lillie M. Davis. Not all seven were graduated at the end of eighteen months, though they may have been graduated later. In his Nashville speech, Dr. Dan says: "Only seven years ago, Provident sent out its first class of three graduate nurses." The Third Annual Report of Provident says: "As the term of study in the Training School is eighteen months, there have been but two graduating classes, the first consisting of four, and the last of six nurses. There are now seven pupil nurses . . ."

79
Data about the Ball was found in an invitation and a clipping from *The Appeal*, February 27, 1892, both in JNA.

Prevalence of accident cases from the stockyards was related by Dr. Isabella Garnett Butler.

Material on Robinson is drawn from an article by Victor Robinson, M.D., in *The American Journal of Clinical Medicine*, Vol. 29, No. 4, April 1922; also from *A Group of Distinguished Physicians and Surgeons of Chicago*, F. M. Sperry, compiler, Chicago, 1904, and *The Medical Fortnightly*, St. Louis, Vol. XXXVI, No. 1, July 10, 1909, article by T. G. Atkinson.

Dr. H. W. Cheney told of Dr. Dan's taking the postgraduate bacteriology course.

Dr. Dan's study with Robinson is mentioned in his paper; see Publications No 1.

80
The story of the South Side Medico-Social Society is told in Martin, *op. cit.*

The development of the treatment for appendicitis is drawn from the following: *The Cyclopedia of Medicine, Surgery and Specialties*, George M. Piersol, editor in chief,

PAGE
80
(*Cont.*)

Vol. I, 2d ed., 1939, article on Appendicitis by J. Montgomery Deaver, M.D.; *J. B. Murphy, Stormy Petrel of Surgery,* Loyal Davis, M.D., M.S., Ph.D., New York, 1938; *The Doctors Mayo,* Helen B. Clapesattle, Minneapolis, 1941; *Western Medical Reporter, A Monthly Epitome of Medical Progress,* Vol. XI, Chicago, 1889, for Proceedings of the Chicago Medical Society, November 4, 1889, paper by J. B. Murphy on "Early Treatment of Perityphlitis."

81

Fenger's article and his remarks appear in the same journals in which Dr. Dan's article appears.

82

Dr. Dan's work on the Sanitary Board for the World's Fair is mentioned in the article by Rogers-Webb, *op. cit.*

Zellie Ridgley Bennett told me of her visit with Dr. Dan's sisters to the Fair. James Gordon told of the visit of Frederick Douglass.

Various evidences of kinship between Dr. Dan and Frederick Douglass exist. Dr. Dan's nephew, the late Raphael D. Williams, told me his grandmother, Dr. Dan's mother, called Douglass "cousin." According to Alice Thornton Butler, Douglass referred to her and her sisters as "my little kinsfolk" and took them in his arms when their mother Mazie Price Thornton, a cousin of Dr. Dan and a granddaughter of Ann Wilks Price, took them up to the platform after one of Douglass's famous speeches. Mrs. Butler told me Douglass visited often in the home of Ann's daughter-in-law in Harrisburg and on one occasion took one of the children, Jennie, home with him and planned to adopt her, but Jennie grew homesick in Rochester and returned to her mother. Ann Wilks Price, Dr. Dan's grandmother, was born a slave, according to her great-granddaughter, Blanche Thornton Parnall, and was bought and freed by Henry Price, her husband. Sarah Jennings, a great-granddaughter of Peter Shorter, kin of Smith Price and Henry Price, states that the Prices "bought their wives on the Eastern Shore," which was the birthplace of Frederick Douglass. When Douglass, who had Indian as well as white and African blood, published his memoirs (*Life and Times of Frederick Douglass, Writ-*

PAGE
82
(*Cont.*)

ten by Himself, new revised ed., De Wolfe, Fiske & Co., Boston, 1892, pp. 70–71) he related, among other anecdotes of the 7000-acre Lloyd plantation where he was born, the story of William Wilks. Wilks was supposedly the illegitimate son of Colonel Lloyd by a favored slave woman. He looked so much like Murray Lloyd, the Colonel's legitimate son, and enjoyed so many favors that Murray connived until Wilks, who had first been given a gold watch and chain, was sent off to be sold at the auction block in Baltimore. There, to everyone's surprise, Wilks outbid all would-be purchasers and bought his own freedom. At the time it was supposed, says Douglass, that the hand that had presented the gold watch and chain had also provided the purchase money, but Douglass goes on to say that he later learned that Wilks had many friends in Baltimore and Annapolis who had united to save him. It now appears that these "many friends" were one man, Ann Wilks's husband, Dr. Dan's grandfather. On March 14, 1832, Henry Price manumitted a mulatto by the name of William "Wilkes," aged about forty, of "bright" complexion, raised on the Eastern Shore of Maryland. All details fit in with Douglass's anecdote. Undoubtedly Henry Price bought and set free William Wilks because he was a close relative of his wife. Undoubtedly, too, William and Ann Wilks were relatives of Frederick Douglass and perhaps through their white blood, rather than their Indian or African blood.

An account of Douglass's speech at the Fair may be read in the *Chicago Tribune* for August 26, 1893.

83

Dr. Isabella Garnett Butler and Jessie Sleet Scales told me of their training at Provident. Blanche Williams Stubbs said her sister, Mabel Williams, trained there too.

Other Provident nurses in the early classes more than fulfilled the dreams of Dr. Dan. Emma Reynolds, the occasion for the founding of Provident Hospital, went on and on and finally became an M.D. and practiced in New Orleans. Isabella Garnett became an M.D. too and with her husband Dr. Butler established a community hospital for the colored people of Evanston. Annie Schultz was another to become an M.D. All these were members of the very first classes, started on their way by Dr. Dan's vigorous training.

Hattie Curtis Hall told of bringing the lunch basket when she was a little girl.

The late Louis B. Anderson told me of Judge Barnes's influence in winning the support of George H. Webster.

CHAPTER VII

"Sewed Up His Heart!"

Date and details of the heart operation are taken from Dr. Dan's official report. See Publications No. 4.

Authorities consulted concerning the operative history of the heart and modern procedures include: *American Journal of Medical Sciences*, January 1883, quoting from *Journal de Médecine de Paris*, October 28, 1882; *Chicago Medical Journal and Examiner*, Vol. 46, January–June 1883: "Heart Puncture and Heart Sutures as Therapeutic Procedures," John B. Roberts, M.D.; *Surgery*, C. W. Mansell Mollin, F.R.C.S., 1st ed., 1891; *The International Journal of Surgery*, August 1893; *Annual of the Universal Medical Sciences and Analytical Index: A Report of the Progress of the General Sanitary Sciences throughout the World*, ed. Charles E. Sajous, M.D., Paris, and others, Vol. III, 1896, article of J. McFadden Gaston, M.D., on "Thoracic Surgery"; *British Medical Journal*, 1896, Vol. II, pp. 1, 440, Turner; *American Year Book of Medicine and Surgery*, George M. Gould, ed., Philadelphia, 1896, 1897, 1898; *Lancet*, London, 1897, Vol. I, pp. 1305–1306, also Vol. 198, 1920, pp. 1, 73, 134, "The Surgery of the Heart," Sir Charles Ballance, speech before the Royal Chirurgical Society of England, December 11, 1919, reprinted in three installments; *Medical Record: A Weekly Journal of Medicine and Surgery*, ed. George F. Shrady, A.M., M.D., New York, 1897, Vol. 51, No. 1, Whole No. 1365, pp. 304, 790; *Philadelphia Medical Journal*, 1900, Vol. V, pp. 1177 ff., "Wounds of the Heart with a report of seventeen cases of suture," L. L. Hill, and May 3, 1902, article by Nieterl; *Medical News*, Vol. LXXIX, No. 23, December 7, 1901, p. 881, article by George Tully Vaughan, M.D.; *A Manual of Modern Surgery*, John Chalmers DaCosta, 1896, 2d ed.,

PAGE
86
(*Cont.*)

1898, also his *Modern Surgery*, 4th ed., 1903; *Journal of the American Medical Association*, Vol. LII, No. 6, February 6, 1909, p. 429; article by George Tully Vaughan, M.D., "Suture of Wounds of the Heart"; Benjamin Merrill Ricketts, M.D., F.A.C.S.; *Surgery of the Heart and Lungs*, 1904, *Surgery of the Thorax and Its Viscera*, Cincinnati, 1918, also numerous articles in periodicals (Ricketts's appearance at the International Society of Surgery is mentioned in programs in his personal scrapbook now in possession of the Library of the Academy of Medicine, New York City, his appearance before the Western Surgical Association is reported in the *Journal of the National Medical Association*, Vol. 4, No. 1, January–March, 1912); *The Archives of Surgery*, Vol. XI, 1925, "The Significance of the Pericardium in Relation to Surgery of the Heart," Claude S. Beck, M.D., and Richmond L. Moore, M.D.; *Annals of Medical History*, Vol. VIII, 1926, "The Operative Story of the Heart," Claude S. Beck, M.D., pp. 224–233; *Thoracic Surgery*, Ferdinand Sauerbruch and Lawrence O'Shaughnessy, 1937.

88

Dr. Coleman Buford told me of Morgan's receiving an invitation from Dr. Dan to attend the operation, and of his own presence and reaction. Names of other doctors present are taken from Dr. Dan's official report. The presence of Mabel Williams as surgical nurse was told by her sister, Blanche Williams Stubbs.

The list of modern equipment lacking in Dr. Dan's day was given me by the late Dr. Carl G. Roberts.

92

The newspaper account of the heart operation is in the Chicago *Daily Inter-Ocean*, July 22, 1893.

93

Dr. Dan's postoperative study of the case with his students was recounted by Dr. J. W. McDowell, who said he helped abstract Dr. Dan's notes for the published report. It may have been McDowell who studied the *Index Medicus*. Examination of the *Index Medicus* for the years 1887–1899 reveals the change in editorship, the frequent lengthy delays in publication, and the inconsistent, garbled state of the indexing.

PAGE
93
(*Cont.*)
The article in the *Cyclopedia of Medicine, Surgery and Specialties* is by Arthur M. Shipley, 2d ed. rev., Vol. 3, 1944, Philadelphia.

94

Record of the case of Dalton's patient, Eugene Ludringer, was given me by the Medical Director of the St. Louis City Hospital. It was not possible to discover what happened to him after his discharge from the hospital or how long he lived.

For accounts of Dalton's operation, see *Proceedings of the Mississippi Valley Medical Association Meeting* at Hot Springs, Arkansas, November 23, 1894; *Transactions of the Medical Association* of the State of Missouri at its 37th Annual Session, Lebanon, Missouri, May 15, 1894; *The St. Louis Medical and Surgical Journal*, Vol. LXVIII, January–June 1895; *Annals of Surgery*, February 1895, Vol. XXI, January–June 1895, p. 147.

Ricketts, in his voluminous but poorly arranged and badly edited *Surgery of the Heart and Lungs*, 1904, included, besides the cases of Dr. Dan and Dalton, the following which antedates both:

"Reed R. Harvey, during the year 1887, had a case of stab wound in the left chest over the apex of the heart. He removed a section of the sixth rib and the clots in the pericardial sac and sutured the pericardium and cutaneous structures. The patient is acting as a policeman in Shelby, Ohio. (Personal communication)."

I assume that Ricketts is here referring to Robert Harvey Reed, sanitary pioneer of Ohio, who led an active professional life from the time he acquired his M.D. in 1874 until his death in 1907, and wrote and published voluminously. If he had performed so important an operation it seems he would surely have included it in his many publications; if he did, I could not find it. Ricketts, who quotes this case, in later editions dropped it along with Dalton's, and not once but again and again gives the credit for priority to Dr. Dan. In medical articles too numerous to mention and in speeches all over the country, for over a decade, he repeatedly said what he stated in his *Surgery of the Thorax and Its Viscera*, 1918, that "cardiorrhaphy was first done in 1893 by Williams, a Negro physician of Chicago, and the patient recovered." Ricketts was a charter member of the American College of Surgeons along with Dr. Dan.

PAGE
94
(*Cont.*)

In October 1892, the *Chicago Clinical Review*, Vol. I, No. 1, under the editorship of George H. Cleveland, M.D., and Albert I. Bouffleur, M.D., published an article by Bouffler concerning his case of April 18, 1891. He stated that when confronted by a stab wound of the abdomen that had penetrated upward and punctured the diaphragm, he had taken one stitch in the diaphragm which at that point coincided with the pericardial wall. He had thus stopped a serious hemorrhage and saved his patient's life. Bouffleur's operation was a transabdominal one, not thoracic, and he was not confronted with the problems of entrance into the thorax.

Argument as to priority has not usually been between claimants for Dalton versus Dr. Dan, but between claimants for Dr. Dan versus various European operators. Unfortunately neither Dalton's nor Dr. Dan's daring and successful operations were reported at the 11th International Medical Congress in Rome in 1895, as far as I could find. There Del Vecchio showed the healed wounds in the hearts of dogs following suture and this gave new impetus to European surgeons. Within a year three attempts were made on humans. Cappelen of Christiania essayed to suture a left ventricle on September 4, 1895, but in operating accidentally cut a branch of the coronary artery, probably with the needle. Two and a half days later his patient died, with the presence of pericarditis and various bacteria in the exudate. In March 1896, Farina of Rome again essayed to suture a case and again his patient died within a few days. On September 9, 1896, Rehn of Frankfort took three sutures in the right ventricle. He did not suture the pericardium but packed it with gauze and left in drains. Infection developed and, while his patient eventually recovered, it was only after prolonged illness. In 1897 Parrozzani reported two cases: one, a suture of the left ventricle, recovered; the other, a suture of the right ventricle, died on the second day due to a cut in the interventricular septum.

The complete reversal of the medical profession's negativism in Dr. Dan's day was voiced at the 1914 meeting of the American Medical Association when Dr. Axel Werelius of Chicago said: "No injury of the heart, no matter how violent, should be considered hopeless." I have been particularly happy to note the following headline in the

New York Times, November 26, 1946: "GIRL, 5, DOOMED TO INVALIDISM AT BIRTH, DANCES ON WAY HOME AFTER HEART SURGERY."

95

George Albert Cotton has been declared several times to be Dr. Dan's first heart case. His name of course does not agree with Dr. Dan's official report. I interviewed Cotton. His account indicated he was operated on in the *second* building occupied by Provident Hospital. He spoke persistently of the elevator; there was no elevator in the three-story flat building occupied 1891–1895 where the first operation was performed in July 1893. Cotton did not know the date of his operation nor even his own age. His brother, Henry Cotton, engineer at Provident for a number of years, told the late Dr. Roberts that he (Henry) was born in 1869 and his brother Albert more than two years later, that the family moved to Chicago in the year of the Fair, 1893, that he (Henry) went to the Dakotas two or more years later, and that the operation was performed on Albert while Henry was living in the Dakotas. Therefore, undoubtedly Dr. Dan operated on Cotton after his return to Chicago from Washington in 1898.

For Dr. Dan's later operations on the chest, see Publications No. 12.

Fuller's operation is reported in the *Journal of Surgery, Gynecology, and Obstetrics*, 1916, Vol. XXII, p. 747, "Surgical Repair of a Stab Wound of the Pericardium."

That operations on the heart are still hazardous was stated by Dr. N. C. Gilbert, Professor of Medicine and Chairman of the Department of Medicine, Northwestern University Medical Department, and Senior Attending Physician at St. Luke's Hospital, Chicago. Dr. Gilbert attended both Dr. Dan and his wife.

Statistics on heart operations were given by Dr. Myra Logan.

The incident of Cornish's return was related by the nurse, Jessie Sleet Scales, who was present.

CHAPTER VIII

A National Task

PAGE
97

As Republican Postmaster General ten years before, Gresham had driven the Louisiana Lottery from the mails. He was himself spoken of as presidential timber, but his convictions against the protective tariff had led him to abandon his leadership of the Republican Party and throw his support to Cleveland. He was a great prize for the Democrats and for that reason was wanted in the Cabinet. See *Dictionary of American Biography*, Vol. VII, 1931.

Gresham's suggestion that Dr. Dan apply is recounted by Dr. Dan at a committee hearing, see Senate Document 185, Vol. 8, 55th Congress, 1st Session.

See NA for the applications of Dr. Dan and others, their recommendations, correspondence and other data on Dr. Dan's injury and illness (Lillie Smith Alexander said amputation was advised), the Annual Reports of Freedmen's Hospital from 1891–1898.

In addition I drew on Howard University Catalogues for 1894, 1895, and 1896; and on *Howard University Medical Department: A Historical, Biographical and Statistical Souvenir*, Daniel Smith Lamb, 1900; on House of Representatives Report No. 776, Part III, 55th Congress, 2nd Session; on Senate Document 185, *op. cit.*; on *Black Reconstruction*, W. E. B. DuBois, New York, 1935, and other miscellaneous material in NA. Several photographs were useful.

Personal reminiscences of this period were furnished by Harriett Shadd Butcher, Zellie Ridgley Bennett, Rebecca West, the late Dr. William A. Warfield, Anna Evans Murray, Mary Church Terrell, Dr. Henry W. Furniss, Dr. Duvall E. Colley, Dr. Daniel Smith, and the former nurses – Katherine Gibson Brooks, Elizabeth Tyler Barringer, and the late Edith M. Carter.

99

There had been a scattering of colored doctors in the country even before the American Revolution. Now a few were beginning to undertake surgery – Nathan F. Mossell in Philadelphia, Ferdinand A. Stewart and R. F. Boyd in Nashville, John E. Hunter in Lexington, Kentucky. You

PAGE
99
(*Cont.*) could count them on the fingers of one hand and all were neophytes; there was no one of a caliber to recommend Dr. Dan. Some history of the Negro doctor in America may be gathered from: *The Negro in Medicine*, John A. Kenny, Tuskegee, 1912 (brochure); *Who's Who in Philadelphia: A Collection of Thirty Biographical Sketches of Colored People*, Charles Frederick White, African Methodist Episcopal Book Concern, 1912; *Negro Year Book*, 1912, Monroe N. Work, ed.; *Journal of Negro History*, Vol. I, p. 104, "Historic Background of the Negro Physician, Kelley Miller," 1916; *Southern Workman*, Vol. 63, pp. 140–142, May 1934, "The Negro Physician," H. A. Callis; *The Negro Professional Man and the Community*, Carter G. Woodson, The Associated Publishers, Washington, 1934; *Negro Builders and Heroes*, Benjamin Brawley, Chapel Hill, North Carolina, 1937; *The Negro College Graduate*, Charles S. Johnson, Chapel Hill, North Carolina, 1938; *The Negro, Too, in American History*, Merl R. Eppse, National Education Publishing Co., 1938.

102   Traviata Anderson Bentley's illness was told me by her brother, Dr. Bert Anderson, and others, and is mentioned in the Rogers-Webb article, *op. cit.*

104   For data on Jeremiah Rankin see *Dictionary of American Biography*, Vol. XV, 1935.

105   Description of Dr. Dan's quarters is from a photograph furnished by Dr. Dan's niece, Pearl Barbour Marchant.

110   The first four internes were J. Seth Hills, J. W. Mitchell, E. D. Williston and William A. Warfield. These served in the autumn of 1894 and early winter of 1895. When Dr. Dan made his first Annual Report in July 1895, the internes then serving were Jackson B. Shephard, William A. Warfield, James C. Erwin, Henry W. Furniss, and Charles I. West. Tenure was for one year. Dr. Dan made it clear that future applicants were to be chosen by competitive examination, the number depending upon the needs of the hospital.

111   A copy of Dr. Dan's circular letter soliciting enrollment of student nurses is found in BTW.

PAGE
112

The five dollars a month was not pay for services, Dr. Dan told the student nurses. As with the internes, the training given and the profession acquired were an ample equivalent, but this sum should enable any young woman without pecuniary resources, he said, to enter upon her professional career free from debt.

116

Dr. Dan argued well enough on the virtues of the trained nurse, but he might have argued even better could he have peered only a few years into the future. Freedman's first two classes alone sent trained graduate nurses to seven different states in the United States outside of the District of Columbia, one to Nicaragua and another to Canada. Within a half dozen years, graduates were extending this training to others. Three graduates were superintendents — in Kansas City, Charlotte, and St. Louis. Four were head nurses — in New York City, at Tuskegee, in Baltimore and in Washington, D.C. Three were school nurses — at Clarke University, Atlanta; at Slater School, Winston, North Carolina; and at Edward Waters University, Jacksonville. All over the country the stirring influence of the new colored trained nurse was felt. By 1902 Freedmen's no longer had to have a white superintendent; Sarah Fleetwood, graduate in the first class, came back to take over the job.

117

Dr. Shadd's young daughter, Hattie, hated Dr. Dan however. He gave her a framed quotation on Friendship; it was long and, worst of all, it was in Latin. And her father made her memorize every word of it.

CHAPTER IX

"Snatched from the Womb"

118

The account of the operation on the dwarf is drawn from Dr. Dan's published report. See Publications No. 11. The late Edith M. Carter, student nurse at the time, added other details.

119

The quotation concerning eclampsia is from *Transactions of the Gynecological Society of Boston*, 1891, Vol. 16, p. 111, and from *Obstetrics*, New York, 1900, Vol. 2, p. 92.

The brief historical remarks on the Caesarean section are drawn from the *Bulletin of the Society of Medical History of Chicago*, Vol. IV, January 1935, No. 4, p. 414; "An Inquiry into the History of Caesarean Section," Kenneth L. Pickrell.

120

Drs. U. G. Dailey and N. C. Gilbert both told me Dr. Dan observed Kelley's operations. Dr. Dan could watch Kelley operate because he was fair-skinned, and for the same reason he could take Warfield with him. A darker young man, named Kinniebrew, who wished to enroll at Johns Hopkins at this time, was refused and finally took a job as a janitor and picked up what information he could while dusting. (Letter from the late Dr. Carl Roberts.)

· The routine Dr. Dan followed in preparing his hands for the operation is taken from reminiscences of the late Dr. John A. Kenney, interne at Freedmen's soon after Dr. Dan left; see NMA Jnl, Vol. 33, No. 5, pp. 203–214, September 1941.

121

Dr. William S. Halsted of Johns Hopkins, in love with the head nurse whose hands suffered from immersion in the antiseptic solutions, saw the heavy rubber gloves brought from Germany by Dr. William H. Welch for autopsies, and had thin ones made for his nurse, later his wife. Assistants began to use the gloves too and finally surgeons did; from being a protection for the hands, these gloves became an aseptic protection for the patient. (*A Surgeon's Life*, Dr. J. M. T. Finney, 1940.)

122

The German farmer's case of tumor is taken from an old clipping furnished by Dr. Dan's niece, Pearl Barbour Marchant, and from Dr. Dan's own report; see Publications No. 7.

The operation on young Daniel Murray was recounted by Dr. H. W. Furniss and confirmed by the lad's mother.

123

The second Caesarean section, with the 18-pound tumor, is described from Dr. Dan's official report. See Publications No. 11.

124

Dr. Dan's costume is from a photograph.

PAGE
125

The late Edith Carter, former student nurse, told of Dr. Dan's uncanny diagnostic ability. The modern damage suit is taken from the *New York Times*, April 25, 1947.

Dr. Smith reported Dr. Dan's Caesarean operations at the meeting of March 9, 1898; see *Transactions of the Medical Society of the District of Columbia*, Vol. III, January–December 1898, pp. 67–69. For Johnson's remark, see *Transactions*, Vol. I, March 1896–January 1897, p. 61, meeting of April 22, 1896. Will Mayo had performed a similar successful operation in the fall of '95, though he had attempted the vaginal route first and had only performed a Caesarean section after his initial attack had failed. That same fall, John B. Murphy, in removing a fibroid tumor, found to his surprise that his patient was pregnant and had then to remove the uterus and foetus as well as the tumor. (For Mayo's case see *The Doctors Mayo*, H. B. Clapesattle, 1943, p. 302. For Murphy's case, see his paper "Fibromyoma Complicating Pregnancy; Fibroma of Vaginal Wall," *Transactions, Chicago Pathological Society*, from December 1895 to April 1897, Vol. II, p. 1.) There was no doubt that Dr. Dan stood, as Franklin Martin said, at the top of the medical profession, not only in Chicago, but in the nation — abreast of the ablest and sometimes ahead of them.

127

Dr. Dan's participation in the Medico-Chirurgical Society is found in *The First Negro Medical Society: A History of the Medico-Chirurgical Society of the District of Columbia, 1884–1939*, W. Montague Cobb, A.B., M.D., Ph.D., Washington, 1939.

The early history of the NMA and Dr. Dan's role in it was told me by the late Dr. John A. Kenney. See also Kenney's brochure, *The Negro in Medicine*, Tuskegee, 1913, and *Forty Cords of Wood*, J. Edward Perry, M.D., Lincoln University Press, 1947. The American Medical Association had ruled that national membership should be dependent upon state membership, and many state societies tried to hold back the rise of colored doctors by excluding them from the benefits of membership. The idea for the national organization did not originate with Dr. Dan, but with I. Garland Penn, Negro Commissioner in charge of the Negro Exhibit at the Cotton States and International Exposition — the same man who invited Booker Washington to give the address that launched him upon national political leadership of the race. The National Medical Association was formed in Atlanta in the closing days of the Exposition. Dr. R. F. Boyd of Nashville was the first president.

128   Dr. Duvall E. Colley (the former student barber) and William E. Cobb told of the Sunday clinics. Mr. Cobb was an ardent attender and perhaps as a result educated his son to be a doctor. At this writing Dr. W. Montague Cobb, Ph.D., M.D., is editor of the *Journal* of the National Medical Association.

130   Use of a wash boiler for sterilizer is told in Kenney's article, NMA Jnl, Vol. 33, No. 5, pp. 213–214, September 1941.

CHAPTER X
Dr. Dan's Job in Jeopardy

131   Dr. Dan told of Douglass's remarks to him in his Nashville speech. See Publications No. 8.

Date of Gresham's death is from the *Chicago Tribune* and the *New York Times*, May 28, 1895; Douglass's from the *Dictionary of American Biography*.

132   Hoke Smith's resignation from the cabinet is told in the *Dictionary of American Biography*.

The characterization of the presidential campaign of 1896 is from *The Rise of American Civilization*, Charles and Mary Beard, new edition, New York, 1936.

The Washington *Bee* throughout the winter and spring of 1897 commented continuously on the Freedmen's struggle, which may be traced in detail in NA.

134   Dr. Henry Furniss, Kate Brooks Gibson, the late Caroline Parke, Katie Johnson, and Mrs. Clarence Evans furnished the social items, while the Reverend Shelton Hale Bishop told of Dr. Dan's visit to New York and Armonk.

PAGE
135

The Reverend C. M. C. Mason's story is told in *Men of Maryland*, Rev. Geo. F. Bragg, Jr., D.D., Baltimore, 1925.

136

The Board of Medical Examiners of Maryland confirmed the fact Warfield failed to pass the Maryland examination.

137

The hearing on Freedmen's Hospital is recorded in detail in Senate Document No. 185, *op. cit.* Contemporary issues of *Harper's Weekly* proved good sources for data on the committee members, while Harriet Shadd Butcher described Purvis and told Lynch's story. His political standing was described by Emmett J. Scott.

142

According to Scott, the three important Negro political leaders at this time were Lynch, Senator Blanch K. Bruce, and James B. Mathews. Mathews had been associated with Dr. Dan's father in the early Negro conventions, and both he and Bruce were friends of Dr. Dan. Not so, Lynch.

144

Dr. DuBois remembered the European trip of Dr. Dan and Dr. Bentley because both men married shortly after and people teased them for stingily taking honeymoons *sans* the brides. Katie Johnson remembered the trip too. Attempts to discover the exact dates or the itinerary were unsuccessful. Passports were not required at that time to Western Europe and the State Department has no record of issuing Dr. Dan a passport to Russia, which was required, and examination of the *Proceedings* of the Twelfth Medical Congress held in Moscow August 7 (19)–14 (26), 1897, failed to reveal the presence of Dr. Dan. Nor could any record of a leave of absence from Freedmen's be found, but a reference to his return in June appears in a statement of Warfield to the Board of Visitors, June 27, 1898. A niece, Ada Blanche Williams, thinks he went to give some addresses; and since his official report on his famous heart operation had come out in March and was causing a stir this may have been the case, but details are wanting.

CHAPTER XI

Alice Johnson

147

Bertie Brooks Lewis told of the children's admiration of Miss Alice, and Dr. Ralph Stewart gave her ad-

PAGE
147
(*Cont.*)

dress in Southwest Washington; it was confirmed by Garnet C. Wilkinson, First Assistant Superintendent of Schools.

The following persons contributed data to the story of Isabella and Alice Johnson; Bertie Brooks Lewis, Rebecca West, the late Caroline Parke, Anna Evans Murray, Sarah Fleetwood, Nancy Atwood, Mrs. Clarence C. Evans, Charlotte Bishop Ridgley, Zellie Ridgley Bennett, Dr. Henry Furniss, Mrs. Dwight Holmes and the late Sarah Meriwether Nutter. Christine Shoecraft Smith and the late Caroline Parke told me Alice's father was Jewish. Mrs. Daniel Murray, one of Alice's closest friends, gave his name and profession. The facts of his life and background are from the following: *The History of the Jews in Richmond from 1769 to 1917*, Herbert T. Ezekiel and Gaston Lichtenstein, 1917; *The Recollections of a Virginia Newspaper Man*, Herbert T. Ezekiel, 1920; *American Jewish Historical Society Papers*, Vol. 9, p. 161; *Jewish Encyclopedia*, Vol. V, p. 319; *Sir Moses Ezekiel: An American Sculptor*, Henry K. Bush-Brown, in *Art and Archaeology*, Vol. XI, No. 6, June 1912, pp. 227 ff.; *American Art and American Art Collections*, 1889, Vol. II, pp. 803–808; *Art and Archaeology*, May 1917, article by Mrs. Lawrence Turnbull; *New York Times*, November 22, 1908, October 21, 1921; *American Art News*, March 31, 1917; *Belles, Beaux and Brains of the '60s*, T. C. DeLeon, 1909.

148

According to the U. S. Census taken in Richmond July 14, 1860, Alice was ten months old; her mother, Isabella, was twenty-three. They were living with Jane Johnson, fifty, presumably the grandmother, in a dwelling occupied by six other families — one white, four black, and one other mulatto like themselves. Jane too was mulatto and both Jane and Isabella are listed as "washwoman." While Isabella could read and write, Jane could not. If Isabella's age is correct as given, she was seven years older than Moses Ezekiel, who was then about three months short of sixteen. Twenty-three may not be correct for Isabella, since an illiterate mother might not have kept accurate count during her child's earliest years. On the other hand, Moses had had the status of a man almost four years, having worked as a bookkeeper in his grandfather's store since he was twelve. In the mores of the South at that

PAGE
148
(*Cont.*)

time, a lad's sex experiences, especially with a girl of black or mixed blood, could begin early.

Alice Johnson's mother must have been as beautiful as her daughter. Several mentioned her loveliness. Rebecca West spoke of her as slight, dainty, a lady with a sweet voice; the late Caroline Parke said she looked "Spanish"; Bertie Brooks Lewis said she had "a face like a cameo."

149   Alice Johnson's age, birthplace, residence while attending Howard University, her school record and her release from school "to go to England" are recorded at Howard University.

150   Garnet C. Wilkinson, First Assistant Superintendent of Schools, Washington, D.C., stated Alice Johnson was first appointed to teach at Mott School on October 9, 1877, and was last appointed for the school year 1897–1898.

152   Alice Parke Shadd's genealogy was told me by her daughter, Harriet Shadd Butcher.

Details concerning Mott School are from the Commissioner's reports of the period.

153   Clarence Cameron White told me the Remenyi incident.

155   The poem "To Dan" is found in *The Complete Poems of Paul Laurence Dunbar*, edited by W. D. Howells, New York, Dodd, Mead and Company, copyright 1905. It was called to my attention by Louise V. Mingo, who used to recite it.

156   Description of the welcoming reception is from JNA.

157   I visited the house at 3301 Forest Avenue (Giles Avenue), also later residences of Dr. Dan and Alice on Forest Avenue and Forty-second Street.

CHAPTER XII

Betrayal

159   The report of the Joint Select Committee was ordered to be printed March 22, 1898. It forms House of Repre-

PAGE
159
(*Cont.*)

sentatives Report No. 776, 55th Congress, 2d Session. The report of the Board of Visitors is dated June 24, 1898, but the *Evening Star* of June 28, 1898, says the report was submitted to the Secretary of the Interior "today." The Senate resolution, the Secretary's reply, and text of the Visitors' report, etc., are taken from Senate Document No. 332, 55th Congress, 2d Session.

For years there had been plain evidence that procedures for the administration of Freedmen's Hospital were loose. Four years before Dr. Dan's advent on the scene, an investigating committee from the Interior Department had declared "the surgeon in chief is emphatically an autocrat with over $50,000 public moneys annually at his disposal without any checks, balances or accountability." No correction of the situation had been made, either by Congress or the Department of the Interior. Freedmen's, it seemed, was always being investigated and nothing done about it. During Dr. Dan's regime and despite a change of the party in power, the situation continued unaltered. Appalling ignorance existed in the Interior Department of what was going on in the hospital. Almost two years before he resigned, an official of that office wrote Dr. Dan and asked him whether or not a Board of Visitors set up by the Interior Department five years before he took office was functioning. "Having heard doubts expressed," wrote the official, "whether the Board was actually in existence, I wish you would write me concerning what action it has taken, especially lately." In other words, the Interior Office asked its own appointee whether or not it was supervising him in accordance with its own established procedures. And then, once more, the matter was dropped and forgotten.

162

That Warfield enjoyed special tutelage under Dr. Dan was told by Rebecca West, Dr. J. W. McDowell, and is cited by Warfield himself in an article by the late Dr. John A. Kenney, NMA Jnl, Vol. 33, No. 5, pp. 203–214, September 1941.

Warfield is listed in the Illinois Register of Physicians for 1898 at Dr. Dan's Chicago address.

PAGE
162
(*Cont.*) The sworn testimony of Warfield, Miss Ebersole and Cordoza is in NA. Also the stenographic report of Dr. Dan's appearance with Judge Wilson before the Visitors, July 20, 1898. The report is certified as "correct" by the stenographer, but is not notarized and not signed by either Dr. Dan or Judge Wilson. Portions are jumbled and incomplete.

166   A memorandum of James H. Parker, secretary to Secretary of the Interior Garfield, in June 1908, NA, states Dr. Dan fainted at the hearing, but implies it was from a sense of guilt at being found out. Parker had his own reasons for distorting the picture. See p. 244.

171   The supplemental report of the Board of Visitors to the Secretary of the Interior, consists of fourteen typewritten pages, dated July 11, obviously an error since the report states that Dr. Dan's testimony of July 20 is included, as well as the testimony of Warfield, Miss Ebersole and Cordoza. This report mentions the presentation of the Bausch & Lomb receipts by Dr. Dan but summarizes the various testimonies in a way unfair to Dr. Dan. No recommendations for disposal of the matter are made.

McMillan's recommendation for District authority is found in Senate Document No. 1439, 55th Congress, 3d Session, ordered to be printed December 21, 1898.

172   Alice wrote to Sarah Fleetwood, her first schoolteacher, now a trained nurse and soon to be the Superintendent of Nurses at Freedmen's: "That cruel, malicious attack upon my dear husband's administration of the hospital failed in its object. Among my most cherished possessions are many letters from officials with whom my husband's duties brought him in contact, assuring him that the high opinion they held of him was in no way affected."

CHAPTER XIII

Destroying Myths

173   Dr. Charles Kahlke told of Chislett's moving out when Dr. Dan came back.

PAGE
173
(*Cont.*) Dr. Dan's neighbors included various important medical men. William Morgan was at 3100 Michigan Avenue, less than a block off. J. B. Murphy lived a few doors away, Lester E. Frankenthal had his office in the next block, and Otto L. Schmidt, Dr. Dan's former classmate, was in the one beyond. In the same building with Dr. Dan were F. O. Higbee, E. Stillman Bailey and Charles H. Kahlke.

Appointments at Provident Hospital, committee, staff and Board, are taken from published reports of the hospital.

174 James Gordon told me Clarence Darrow was a patient of Dr. Dan and in *Clarence Darrow for the Defense*, 1941, Irving Stone tells of Darrow's and Wheeler's Sunday bicycle rides.

The baseball games item is from JNA.

Dr. and Mrs. James R. White told of Jenkin Lloyd Jones's continued support of Provident Hospital.

Letters of Kohlsaat and Webster to Dr. Dan were found in his papers after his death; others from these men are in NA.

William F. Taylor, the druggist, told me of the cable cars.

Published reports of Provident Hospital state that gifts were as follows: Kohlsaat $5000 for the lot; Armour $20,000 for the building; Field $2500, Pullman $5000, and Young $500 for the adjoining properties for the nurses' home. Webster's $2500 apparently was for furnishings.

175 Description of Dr. George C. Hall, his appearance, his personality and his actions was given me by Drs. James R. White, U. G. Dailey, the late Spencer Dickerson, and the late Carl G. Roberts, among others. Emmett Scott, the late T. Arnold Hill, Dr. Herbert Turner, Dr. J. W. McDowell added details. The late John Hale Porter, who admired Hall, told me of Hall's determination to get an allopathic diploma to secure his position. Others giving a favorable

PAGE
175
(*Cont.*) picture of Hall were Alexander L. Jackson, Dr. Homer C. Cooper, and Tomietta Stokes Beckham, but I felt their testimony was outweighed by that of others. Hall's educational background is given in Mather, *op. cit.* He received his Illinois license in 1888.

176 Dr. James R. White told the recruiting incident and of Dr. Dan's appointment as major. Washington colored newspapers also spoke of Dr. Dan's appointment as colonel. It has been impossible to verify either appointment from existing War Department records.

177 The Roster of Provident Hospital Internes gives the dates and names of all internes.

Helen Brown (Mrs. James R.) White told of Hall's attempt to get White to leave Chicago. Dr. White told of Dr. Dan's encouragement of young doctors, as did others.

David McGowan told of Dr. Dan's service to the Old Folks Home, and Louise V. Mingo told of his speech at the fund-raising meeting. *The Broadax*, August 12, 1899, gives the address 610 West Garfield, and says there are eleven rooms and thirteen inmates.

178 Dr. Dan himself described the insurance scheme in a letter to Booker T. Washington (BTW). *The Broadax*, Vol. VI, No. 7, December 8, 1900, states Dr. Dan has taken charge.

180 Dr. Dan is incorrect in giving the figure 12 million. The Census for 1900 gave 8.8 million Negroes.

For Dr. Dan's medical papers see Publications.

184 Dr. Kahlke told me of his friendship with Dr. Dan.

185 Col. Phalen told me of his reaction to Dr. Dan and to Murphy and Dr. Frank Van Kirk also. Col. Phalen is the author of the article on Dr. Dan in the *Dictionary of American Biography*.

186 Dr. James Mills, Jr., and his brother Wallace Mills told of visits of Dr. Dan to their home and kindly sent me their

father's scrapbook containing many items about Chicago Medical College and Dr. Dan.

In 1906 Dr. Dan and Mills were two of twelve who attended their class reunion, enjoying "intimate pipe smoking and reminiscence." In 1913 Dr. Dan was on the reception committee for the reunion and banquet held at the Congress Hotel.

Alice's remarks are in a letter to Sarah Fleetwood, February 22, 1901. The trolley car incident was related by Mrs. J. Carlos Davis.

187   Description of Alice's costume was given by Christine Shoecraft Smith, who told me of the loss of the baby, as did the late Mrs. William T. Child. It was a case of tubal pregnancy, according to John Mallet, chauffeur for Dr. Otto Schmidt, in whose car he heard the case discussed. Mallet said DeLee took care of Alice.

188   Mrs. Bruce's visit is in *The Broadax*, Vol. IV, August 12, 1899; the talk at the Phillis Wheatley Club, same paper, Vol. V, No. 13, January 20, 1900. The clipping about the Evening with Shakespeare is from JNA.

189   Dr. Hall himself told the late Dr. Carl Roberts he was left standing in the entry and resented it.

That old friends noticed little change in Dr. Dan was apparent from conversation with the late Julia West Paul and Julia LeBeau Thompson, but Dr. U. G. Dailey gave a new picture, as stated here.

CHAPTER XIV

Moses to Negro Medicine

191   The late Dr. John A. Kenney in NMA Jnl, Vol. 33, No. 5, speaks of the brutal use of Negroes for experimental and teaching surgery.

The statement that bad conditions in Negro medical care prevailed fifty years ago should not be construed to mean conditions are good today. See *Medical Care and Plight of the Negro*, W. Montague Cobb, M.D., Ph.D., published

PAGE
191
(*Cont.*)
by the National Association for the Advancement of Colored People, August 1947. Also Dr. Cobb's article "Racial Integration in Medicine," published May 1953 in NAIRO *Reporter*, a publication of Intergroup Relations Officials, P.O. Box 163, New York 25, N.Y.; available also as a reprint from Committee for the Nation's Health, Inc., 2212 M Street, N.W., Washington 7, D.C. Also the *Negro Year Book 1952*, Jessie P. Guzman, ed., "Health and Medical Facilities," pp. 158ff.

192   Booker Washington's speech, made September 18, 1895, and reported widely in the press, pleased some whites and displeased some colored people for sentences like these: "As we have proven our loyalty to you in the past, in nursing your children, watching by the sickbed of your mothers and fathers, and often following them with tear dimmed eyes to their graves, so in the future in our humble way, we shall stand by you with a devotion that no foreigner can approach, ready to lay down our lives if need be in defense of yours, interlacing our industrial, commercial, civil and religious life with yours in a way that shall make the interests of both races one. In all things that are purely social we can be as separate as the fingers, yet one as the hand in all things essential to mutual progress." The last sentence was quoted frequently.

     The long correspondence of Dr. Dan with Booker T. Washington and Emmett J. Scott is in BTW; a few letters are in NA; and one was photostated for me by the late Dr. Bertha Van Hoosen who had presented it to the Library of the Woman's Medical College, Chicago. Dean Charles H. Thompson of Howard University Graduate School sent me copies of three letters.

     The late Dr. John A. Kenney, long on the Tuskegee staff, told me of early medical care at the Institute.

     In the spring of 1913 Tuskegee got the hospital and clinic center offered by Dr. Dan fifteen years before. George Hall was invited by Booker Washington to give the dedicatory address.

194   Hubbard's visit to Dr. Dan is told in *Meharry Medical College, A History*, Charles Victor Roman, Nashville,

1934. That Boyd and Stewart were instrumental is shown in Irene M. Gaines's article, *op. cit.* Date of the appointment is determined from a letter of Alice Williams to Sarah Fleetwood.

The dedication inscription is carved over the entrance to Meharry College, which I visited. The history of Meharry, its hospitals and clinics, is taken partly from Roman, *op. cit.*, and partly from Annual Announcements and reports of Central Tennessee College, Walden University, and Meharry Medical College for the years 1885 to 1915.

195   That Dr. Dan received only travel money and contributed that to the school was told me by Professor Emeritus John H. Holman.

Dr. Dan's brilliance as a clinical instructor was told me by Drs. Buford, Roberts, Dailey, and many others. A letter from the late Dr. M. O. Bousfield says Dr. Dan "loved to teach and give them [his internes] a chance to learn and do. Surgeons are not always generous on this score."

196   A sketch of Boyd's life is found in Kenney's brochure, *op. cit.* Dr. Dan's operations in the basement room are mentioned by Gaines, *op. cit.*

Recollections of Dr. Dan's visits were given me by Tillie Lloyd, Registrar, Professor Emeritus John H. Holman, Drs. W. A. Reed, J. A. McMillan, and F. A. Stewart, Jr., and Annie Stewart, supplemented by letters from W. H. Compton and Drs. E. A. Kendall and G. Hamilton-Francis.

197   The account of the meeting at the Phillis Wheatley Club is taken from Dr. Dan's speech. See Publications No. 8.

203   Dr. Dan's travels for the benefit of Negro doctors were recounted to me by Drs. Dailey and Perry. Also see Dailey, *op. cit.*, and Perry, *op. cit.*

204   Warfield's charges against Curtis and West are found in NA.

PAGE
205
The Dallas incident was told me by Dr. J. Carlos Davis; the Indianapolis incident, by Drs. J. H. Ward and Lawrence A. Lewis.

206
The guilty journal was *The Medical Journal,* Charlotte, North Carolina. The incident is told in detail by W. E. B. DuBois, "Possibilities of the Negro, the Advance Guard of the Race," *The Booklovers Magazine,* Vol. II, No. 1, July 1903.

For some of the results of hospital and nursing care, see the report of Hulda M. Lyttle, R.N., quoted in Roman, *op. cit.;* also *The Health and Physique of the Negro American,* W. E. B. DuBois, 11th Atlantic Conference, 1906.

The *Negro Year Book 1952,* Jessie P. Guzman, ed., records 132 Negro hospitals, but some are very small. Only 45 have 50 beds or more. In 1949, 9000 Negro nurses were integrated into the American Nurses Association with a total membership of 506,050; in that year there were 3076 Negro student nurses. The same volume estimates that in 1948 there were 3753 Negro physicians in this country. This is not the number there should be and is indicative of the educational and economic restrictions still operating against colored people. There are 3681 Negro persons in the country per each Negro doctor, nearly *five* times the ratio of total population to total physicians.

The late Dr. Kenney in NMA Jnl, Vol. 33, No. 5, gives a brief history of the rise and fall of Negro medical schools.

CHAPTER XV

History-Making Operations

207
These cases and the remarks he made are described by Dr. Dan; see his Publications No. 12.

212
Advice against operating on the spleen may be seen in John De J. Pemberton's article in *The Cyclopedia of Medicine, Surgery and Specialties,* rev. ed., 1946.

PAGE
213

Dr. Dan was a careful student. He always related his own experience to that of others. Before writing his paper, he told his listeners, he had examined thirty-three English and American surgical works. All of them advised against invasion of the chest. However, when he looked into the French and Italian writers on the subject, he found they urged immediate interference and their results, he said, showed the wisdom of their course. He himself had had twenty-six cases in eleven years and had operated on exactly half of them. All the thirteen not operated had died, while of the thirteen operated only two had died. So he sided with the French and Italian doctors.

Mrs. J. B. Beckham (née Tomietta Stokes) told me of the case of the Irish boy. She was a probationer nurse at the time and later became assistant to the Superintendent of Nurses.

214

Dr. Dailey told of the Rhode Island brakeman.

Accounts of Dr. Dan's services were given me by Mrs. Avendorph, Jessica and Archibald Anderson, Eloise Carey Bishop, Mrs. Richard Rainey, Mrs. William T. Child, Lillie Smith Alexander, Harry Branch, Dr. Marie Fellowes, Marguerite Leftlet Banks and her daughter, Helen Harris, and by Emma L. Warren-Mallet.

Jesse Binga is authority for the Mitchell "Red Devil."

216

Mrs. Richard Rainey repeated to me Dr. Dan's remark he could not charge his people much. In a letter to Booker T. Washington (BTW) in 1907, Dr. Dan said his income was $10,000 a year.

Both Dr. Dailey and Dr. Smith told me they came to Chicago to study because Dr. Dan was there. The reactions to the great man are Dailey's.

217

Dr. Booker told me about the student parties.

Dr. Fellowes told of her experience with Dr. Dan. Dr. James White told of Dr. Dan's advice and of Wilberforce's following it, while Dr. Roberts furnished details of Wil-

PAGE
217
(*Cont.*)
berforce's later life. Dr. Dan's influence on McKissick was told me by Dr. Monroe A. Majors and confirmed by Dr. Dailey.

The late Dr. Kenney told me his story. Conditions under which he operated in the South are recounted in NMA Jnl, Vol. 33, No. 5. His Appreciation was published in *The Student*, July 20, 1907. His gift of the hospital to Newark is described in a brochure, *The Community Hospital, A Brief History*, 1939.

219
Dr. Dailey told me of his relationship to Dr. Dan. Dr. McDowell and the late Dr. Roberts added comments.

222
That Murphy wore out his assistants is stated in *J. B. Murphy, Stormy Petrel of Surgery*, Loyal Davis, M.D., M.S., Ph.D., New York, 1938.

CHAPTER XVI

Alice Tries to Be a Good Wife

223
Alice wrote Booker Washington about a Miss Kelley who had achieved a position at the Art Institute but who longed to use her talent for her race, and Miss Kelley was invited to come to Tuskegee as "instructress in drawing" (BTW).

Bishop Ransom told me of his pioneering work and of his relationship to Dr. Dan and Alice, and of Alice's work for him.

BTW reveals Alice's attempts to get the Tuskegee principal to lecture, and other lecturers are found in a little brochure of the Settlement furnished me by Bishop Ransom. It was the age of formality. Alice Williams began her letters to Booker Washington: "My dear Sir" and ended them primly "Mrs. Daniel H. Williams." Later she did unbend to say "My dear Mr. Washington." She referred to her husband as "Doctor." "Doctor is well," she wrote, "and sends warmest regards to you and Mrs. Washington."

Mary Church Terrell told me of her lecture. Mary Church Terrell is a remarkable woman who has brought, said the late Carrie Chapman Catt, her friend and co-worker in the suffrage cause, honor to her college, her race, and her sex. After her graduation from Oberlin in 1884, Mrs. Terrell spent three years studying in France, Germany, Switzerland and Italy. When she spoke at the great Congress of the International Council of Women in Berlin in 1904, she was the only delegate from the United States who spoke in three languages and she was "eloquent in all three." In this country she has addressed students of most women's colleges and many men's colleges. She is a prolific writer whose work has appeared in many leading magazines and newspapers. At this writing (summer 1953) she is still active at ninety and is spearheading the movement to extend civil rights in Washington, D.C., restaurants. In 1948 she won her long campaign to open the doors of the Washington branch of the American Association of University Women to qualified members regardless of race or color.

224   The quotation from Darrow's speech is from Irving Stone, *op. cit.*, p. 170.

225   The Reverend Father Olds, of St. Augustine's Church, Washington, D.C., wrote me that church records show Sarah Price Williams died July 24, 1900, aged seventy-five, of paralysis. I use U. S. Census records and her sampler for her age, which was seventy-two. A newspaper clipping says Dr. Dan had to leave immediately after the funeral. A niece, Ada Blanche Williams, showed me the sampler, found in Dr. Dan's possessions after his death.

Dr. Dailey said Alice called Dr. Dan "Hale."

226   Emma George and Harriet George Stewart told me of the sisters' move to Pierce Place.

Among those giving me these impressions of Alice were Mary Church Terrell, Edith Fleetwood, Estelle Arnold, Eloise Carey Bishop, Harriet Curtis Hall, Rebecca West, the late Julia West Paul, the Reverend Shelton Hale Bishop, Dr. J. W. McDowell, and Dr. Arthur J. Booker.

The June 1904 reception is described in JNA. Emmett J. Scott related the event to the Republican National Convention.

PAGE
227

Julia LeBeau Thompson said the Forest Avenue neighborhood deteriorated and Eloise Carey Bishop told of the moving away of her family and of the Williamses. The addresses on East 42nd Street appear on clippings in JNA and on Alice Williams's stationery (BTW).

John Mallet told of the hate fence.

The 1903 and 1907 items about Sir Moses are from De Leon, *op. cit.*, and the 1908 item is from the *New York Times*, November 22, 1908. Christine Shoecraft Smith told me of the photograph, and Harriett Curtis Hall told of remarks about Alice's parentage.

Sir Moses died in Rome in March 1917. After the war his last statue, one of Edgar Allan Poe, was brought to America and presented to the city of Baltimore. The sculptor's body was buried in Arlington Cemetery among his Confederate comrades.

228

Theodora Lee Purnell told me of Alice's exit from the Whist Club.

Louise V. Mingo told of Alice's jealousy of Mrs. Carey, her feeling for Mrs. Wilberforce Williams, and of the luncheon party and the boat ride.

As Alice again became a recluse from society, she kept up with certain people. She exchanged the latest books with Julia LeBeau Thompson, upon whose mother Dr. Dan had operated on the dining room table at the beginning of his career. She did embroidery with Mrs. George Hancock, one of Dr. Dan's first supporters in the matter of Provident Hospital. She continued in the Women's Aid Society, and when the others paid the dues of twenty-five cents a month, she never failed, people noted, to lay down a dollar. She kept up her old friendship with Julia Barr Anderson and Mrs. Pedro Tinsley with whom she had worked so hard for the Institutional Church Settlement. She wrote back East to Caddie Parke, Maggie Vaughan, and her matron of honor, Fanny Middleton. She told Fanny she was very lax to allow her daughter, then in normal school, to go unchaperoned to the theater with a dental student. She made gifts for her nieces, the daugh-

PAGE
228
(*Cont.*) ters of Dr. Dan's sisters and brother, and was more appreciative than once she had been of the little gifts they sent her. At Christmas time she packed two big barrels and sent them to Washington. She talked of adopting the daughter of Annie, Dr. Dan's sister, but dropped the idea. When Dr. Dan's friend, J. Carlos Davis, the dentist, moved to Mexico to escape discrimination, she kept in touch with Emma Rose, his wife. "We are so interested in Mexican affairs," she wrote, "because of your presence there." She never failed to write letters of condolence when a friend lost a mother and they were letters her friends kept. "I know only too well," she wrote Emma Rose Davis, "what it means to lose a good mother." When Sarah Fleetwood died, her first schoolteacher, she wrote Edith how much she had admired her mother, "my ideal," she said, "of all that is beautiful in woman — so gentle, so refined, so cultured."

229 The late Mrs. T. G. Nutter, daughter of Mary Robinson Meriwether, and the late Dr. Roberts told me of Dr. Dan's affair with the French woman. Dr. Dailey confirmed their account.

230 Alice's visits were mentioned by Christine Shoecraft Smith and in BTW. Louise V. Mingo told of the surprise party.

CHAPTER XVII
Break with Booker T. Washington

231 The full title of *The Voice* was *The Voice of the Colored People*. It was commonly called *The Voice*.

232 Dr. J. Max Barber told me of the prairie chicken dinner and the argument over Booker Washington. The reaction of the young Negro intelligentsia is discussed by W. E. B. DuBois in *Dusk of Dawn*, 1940; and by Ray Stannard Baker in his article "An Ostracized Race," *American Magazine*, Vol. LXVI, No. 1, May 1908. Mrs. Samuel J. Evans furnished a photograph of Dr. Bentley.

This is the sort of remark made by Booker Washington which angered young Negro intellectuals: "The opportunity to earn a dollar in a factory just now is worth in-finitely more than the opportunity to spend a dollar in an opera house. . . . There is as much dignity in tilling a field as in writing a poem."

That Madden and Bentley joined the DuBois camp was stated to me by DuBois, also by Barber. That Wheeler remained in the Washington camp is apparent from BTW. These files tell the story of the newspaper dealings, the Freedmen's Hospital tragedy, and Booker Washington's choice of Hall over Dr. Dan. Details were added by Emmett Scott, DuBois and Barber.

Young Max Barber fought a losing fight with Booker Washington, who never forgave him for his criticism in *The Voice*. After an initial success in which he built the circulation to 17,000 in three years, Barber and *The Voice* fell into sore straits. In 1906 came the Atlanta riots when infuriated white mobs burned, killed and laid waste in the Negro section of the city. At no little personal risk, Barber had sent a dispatch to the New York *Tribune* presenting the Negro side of the tragic affair with unusual outspoken-ness. He had had to flee for his life. But he had re-entered the city, recovered the files of subscribers and brought them to the owners, a Chicago publishing company. Then the panic of 1907 and the subsequent use of scrip brought about a financial crisis which forced the publishers to put *The Voice* on the market. T. Thomas Fortune, maneu-vered out of *The Age* in New York by a stooge represent-ing Booker Washington, came to Chicago and bought *The Voice* but, for some reason, made nothing out of the ven-ture and soon returned East. Barber managed to get a job as editor of *The Conservator,* an anti-Washington paper in Chicago. But Booker Washington, through Dr. Dan, Louis B. Anderson and others, got control of *The Con-servator.* Louis Anderson called young Barber into his office and told him he had "made a mistake" in giving but a few lines to Washington's recent speech. And so, Barber was again without a paper. Short of funds, lecturing here and there, he traveled east. In Philadelphia he got a job as principal of the Berean Manual Training School, with a staff of seven or eight teachers to direct. "But the long arm of Washington reached out and plucked me out of that

PAGE
232
(*Cont.*)
job, too," says Barber. "I was told I would have to go, or the financial support given the school by a white real estate man, a friend of Washington's, would be withdrawn." Thoroughly discouraged after months of eking out an existence with porter jobs and the like, Barber turned to dentistry and gave up journalism.

233   History of jurisdiction over Freedmen's Hospital is recounted in Letter of the Secretary of the Interior, February 21, 1906, House of Representatives Document No. 549, 59th Congress, 1st Session.

That Warfield's political power emanated from family connections is common talk in the Negro colony. That he was mediocre in his management of Freedmen's was told me by various doctors including J. W. McDowell, the late John Kenney, by early nurses, and by Mae Irwin who served as Superintendent of Nurse Training at Freedmen's for some years. It is noticeable that both Dr. Dan and Booker Washington are careful not to mention his name anywhere in their lengthy correspondence.

237   Dr. Dan's care of Scott was told by Scott, also in BTW. Scott said he inserted the item in *The Student*.

238   Hall's status as a surgeon was given by Dailey, Scott, Roberts and others. He himself told Roberts he chose surgery for the money in it. His remark to Curtis was told by James White; his avoidance of surgical risks, by his onetime assistant, Dailey.

The Birmingham surgeon who took the knife out of Hall's hand was Dr. Ulysses Grant Mason.

240   Both DuBois and Barber said *The Age* was bought by white money to silence Fortune and give support to Booker Washington.
W. E. B. DuBois had attacked Booker Washington in the Boston *Guardian* for buying up the Negro press, and the New York *Post* had attacked DuBois for not being able to prove his accusation. All that was needed was the file of Booker Washington's correspondence with Dr. Dan, now in the Manuscript Division of the Library of Congress.

PAGE
240
(*Cont.*)

Dr. Dan was ill-fitted for the role he was now playing; he was too honest for intrigue. He urged Booker Washington to buy the *Conservator* outright and operate it, but the politician preferred his undercover methods. At the same time Washington complained piously about newspaper owners and editors who "seem to depend almost wholly upon graft rather than upon strictly business principles for success." "The main difficulty," Washington said, "seems to be that our people have such little business ability that it is almost impossible for them to carry any business enterprise to success, however much they are helped." Contrast this typical disbelief of the dictator in the abilities of others with Dr. Dan's faith in the potentialities of Negroes. "All they need is the chance," Dr. Dan said over and over.

In 1890 T. Thomas Fortune, distinguished editor and founder of the New York *Age*, contemporary of Dr. Dan and Booker Washington, had attempted to meet the menace of threatening withdrawal of Federal protection of the civil rights of Negroes. He issued a call, accepted by 141 delegates from twenty-one states, to come and found a national civil rights body. The National Afro-American League was, in a sense, the forerunner of a body of opinion that was obscured for a time by the Booker Washington philosophy and arose resurgent in the later Niagara Movement, and continued into the present in the National Association for the Advancement of Colored People. That T. Thomas Fortune and *The Age* should fall under the Tuskegee ax was tragic.

Letters of Secretary Garfield to Dr. Dan, dated November 25, 1907, and March 25, 1908, concerning appointments, were found in Dr. Dan's effects and given me by his niece, Ada Blanche Williams.

244

The Howard University plan, Purvis's plan, together with various letters of Warfield and memoranda of Parker, are in NA.

245

Accounts of the August 1908 meeting of the NMA are from files of the New York *Post* and the New York *Age*, also personal account of Dailey. A letter from Dr. Dan to Scott (BTW) says he spent $75 on slides.

Scott described to me Hall's tactics in ridiculing Dr. Dan before the NMA. The 1905 incident was told by Dr. Dudley Turner to the late Dr. Roberts who repeated it to me.

Dr. Dan's movements in the fall of 1908 are revealed in various letters to Scott (BTW). The operation upon Dunton is told in *The Age*, December 3, 1908.

Mrs. E. P. Roberts, daughter of Warren Logan, Treasurer of Tuskegee Institute, grew up on the Tuskegee campus and remembered Mrs. Hall's visits with her many trunks, cosmetics, etc.

Freedmen's threatened loss of license was related by Mae Irwin, former Superintendent of Nurses.

Dr. Dan never again asked Booker Washington to assist in anything. When President Theodore Roosevelt, before leaving office, organized a "distinguished army medical reserve corps" of "scores of the most famous doctors in America," including a dozen in Chicago, Dr. Dan was exercised that no Negro was appointed and that he himself had been left out of a list of men with whom he constantly associated professionally. He did not write Booker Washington, but he did write Emmett Scott and asked if he thought it was possible to get Booker Washington to act in the matter. He said, "Our men are the best of soldiers in time of need and should be represented in every department, especially in the killing department. I mean by this, that they should have protection and safe care by *their own* during and after the fight wherever that may be." Scott, while sympathetic, could only report that "it seems inopportune to take up this matter just as this time."

The Charity Ball invitation, listing committees, is in JNA.

The twenty-fifth anniversary banquet is described in *The Age*, May 28, 1908. The cup I saw at Provident Hospital.

The late T. Arnold Hill repeated to me Hall's accusation that Dr. Dan was undecided about race. Mrs. Hall's remark was made to me directly.

The fire bell incident was told me by Dr. Booker.

The late Dr. Roberts, Dr. Dailey and Mr. Max Gethner told me of Hall's tactics to gain power. Miss Lyon (Mrs. McMurdy) made her derogatory remarks directly to me. Dr. Booker witnessed Alf Anderson's mischievous treatment of Dr. Dan's affairs. Mrs. Ed Wright and Mrs. Richard Rainey, late patients of Dr. Dan at Provident, told of neglect of his service, as did Dr. Booker.

254

Dr. Barber told of the Bentleys' rejection of the Halls; Theodore Lee Purnell told of the Jones's rejection. The late Robert L. Taylor told the Sigma Pi Phi story as I give it here; the late Dr. Bousfield gave Hall's version.

255

The last clinic at Mercy Hospital is described in NMA Jnl, April–June 1910, Vol. II, No. 2. The first clinic at Hubbard Hospital is described *ibid.*, April–June 1911. Dr. G. Hamilton-Francis told of unveiling the portrait.

The remark about keeping Provident "alive" is in Hartshorn, *op. cit.*, item on George C. Hall.

256

Wesley's qualities were described by Dr. White, who told of the discrimination in interneships, as did Dailey; examination of the Roster of Internes confirmed the fact.

Wheeler's misfortunes were related by Mrs. White. His appointment at Tuskegee and his death are revealed in BTW.

257

Hall's upward climb at Provident may be traced in the published reports of the hospital.

Authentication of Dr. Dan's appointment to St. Luke's is given in a letter from the office of the Medical Director.

Hall's campaign to prove Dr. Dan's appointment an act of disloyalty was described by Drs. White, Dickerson, Roberts, Dailey and Herbert Turner.

The description of Webster's appearance and temperament was given by the late Dr. Roberts.

258

Minute books of the Provident Board of Trustees for 1912 have been lost and with them the account of Dr.

PAGE
258
(*Cont.*)

Dan's resignation. Dr. J. Carlos Davis, Dr. Turner and others said he offered no explanation or defense. That is true of the press notices which appeared. *The Broadax*, Vol. XVII, No. 32, May 11, 1912, states: "At a meeting of the Board of Trustees of Provident Hospital during the week, Dr. Daniel H. Williams tendered his resignation." Next week, May 18, a two-column-wide photograph of Dr. Dan was run with the caption: "Dr. Daniel H. Williams, eminent physician and advanced surgeon — one of the main founders of Provident Hospital, who resigned last week as a member of its board of Trustees." NMA Jnl, Vol. 4, No. 3, July–September 1912, said simply that "Dr. Daniel H. Williams has resigned from the Board of Trustees and the medical staff of Provident Hospital."

CHAPTER XVIII

The Record Made Straight

259

The description of Idlewild and Dr. Dan's life there is from a personal visit and talks with residents: Harry Branch, the white man who originally owned the territory, Ada Blanche W. Z. Williams, Dr. Dan's niece who inherited his property there, Mrs. Richard Rainey, young Daniel Rainey, Marguerite Banks, Mrs. Ed Wright, Mrs. Robert Hal Riffe, the late Dr. Roberts, Mrs. Edwin Elsner, postmistress for many years, Charles Grace, J. S. Royster, Dr. Isabella Garnett Butler, Mattie Herron, Dr. Ralph Stewart, Mattie Martin Gates, and Irene McCoy Gaines. In nearby Baldwin I consulted Robert Smith, Fred Bradford and Herbert Smith. I corresponded with Helen Chesnutt.

Fuller's letter was found in Dr. Dan's personal papers after his death, as were warm letters from Billings, Martin, Kohlsaat, and Webster.

260

Descriptions of the historic first convocation of the American College of Surgeons, held in the Gold Room of the Congress Hotel, Chicago, may be found in the *New York Times* of November 13, 1913, the *Chicago Tribune* of November 14, the New York *Age* of November 20,

PAGE
260
(*Cont.*) and the *Bulletin of the Chicago Medical Society*, Vol. XIII, No. 12, December 1913. The last-named publication gives the names of the Chicago men inducted. Dr. Dan's certificate of membership may be seen at Provident Hospital. Twelve hundred of the most noted surgeons of the United States and Canada were received into charter membership and made Fellows, 103 from Chicago. That night Dr. Dan wrote Emmett Scott: ". . . this recognition will ease the way . . . perhaps it may be possible to assist others." But the American College of Surgeons discriminated against the Negro surgeon for many years, despite the precedent set by its original Regents. Dr. Dan remonstrated about the situation to his friend, Franklin Martin, but was unable to effect the acceptance of other Negroes. Hall charged that he was keeping Negroes out.

261 Dr. Dan's success at St. Luke's was told me by Dr. S. C. Plummer, Dr. Arthur R. Elliott, Dr. Rufus J. Collins, Dr. James Tweedie Campbell, Dr. Louis Schmidt, Dr. N. C. Gilbert and W. H. Zabel, Chief Pharmacist.

Presentation of the bust is recounted in *The History of the St. Luke's Hospital School of Nursing*, Marie Georgette Merrill, Chicago, 1946. This item was furnished me by Carrie E. Bullock, R.N.

Mrs. Richard Rainey recounted the proposal to name a ward for Dr. Dan.

The Provident Hospital doctors named told of their experiences with George Hall.

Bentley, because of his light skin color, his office on State Street, and the professional honors that came to him from whites, was subjected to much of the same talk of disloyalty that Dr. Dan suffered. He held out until 1917 and then resigned.

262 Fall-off in patients is revealed in the published reports.

When Jeanette Lyon, Hall's ally, capped her career by marrying Judge McMurdy and retiring, Provident suffered a constant change of Superintendents of Nurses. Evelyn Kimmel, a capable woman, unsusceptible to cajolery, was the third to succeed Miss Lyon. One day, according to hospital rule, she charged Hall fifty cents for a urinalysis for an outside private patient. He was enraged. To the late Dr. Carl Roberts standing nearby he exclaimed "I'll get rid of her," and within a matter of months, he did.

Hall worked like a Trojan to save Provident. Perhaps he would have done so even had his own fate not been tied up with the only hospital in the city that offered him an arena. Mrs. Hall, as chairman of the Women's Auxiliary — entirely colored now since there was no one to maintain the contacts that had made it originally interracial — worked vigorously too. She brought in $4000 or $5000 a year. To fill gaps on the Board of Trustees, Hall brought in some capable and respected men along with some who were mediocre. A. L. Jackson, his choice for chairman, reinforced the group with outstanding graduates from Harvard, his alma mater. This made a good Board and it resulted eventually, after Hall's death, in the third and greater Provident Hospital. The 165-bed plant with good equipment serves 7500 bed and 8000 clinic patients a year. The policy Dr. Dan inaugurated of providing the highest type of education for colored doctors and nurses is now an established tradition. If white internes are seldom admitted it is because there are still so few opportunities elsewhere for the colored interne. The by-laws prohibit discrimination and during World War II Jewish refugee doctors were admitted to residencies when they could not find opportunities elsewhere that would permit them to qualify for licenses. However motivated by a desire for personal place and power, Hall gave an aggressive leadership in the civil field on behalf of the Negro. He led the drive for the Y.M.C.A., helped bring in the Urban League, was the first Negro to sit on the Library Board, and his work on the Riot Commission of 1919 was said to be important and skillful.

John Mallett said Dr. Dan walked the corridors at night.

Drs. Smith, Dailey, Roberts and Turner told of Dr. Dan's continued interest in Provident.

PAGE
262
(*Cont.*)
After all his children had grown and left home, Harry Anderson married again. His third wife was the former Julia Settles.

Dr. Bert Anderson told of his own reaction to Dr. Dan and his refusal to allow Dr. Dan to put up a tombstone.
Reaction of the various relatives was told me in person.

263
Hall's putting down his bag to fight was told by the late Dr. Roberts.

Items about Dr. Annie B. Schultz were told by Dr. Roberts and Mrs. Ed Wright.

It was Emmett Scott who said Dr. Dan "threw himself on you."

264
The birthday dinner was held January 18, 1913, at the home of Mrs. Rita Carter on Rhodes Avenue. According to the reporter, Alice Williams never appeared to better advantage, looking, people said, "like a bit of rare china."

Wilberforce University conferred the honorary degree of LL.D. on Dr. Dan in June 1909; Howard University, the degree of M.S. in June 1925. This was confirmed by the officers of these schools.

The cup, presented June 1919, may be seen at Provident Hospital.

Irene McCoy Gaines, his secretary, also Dr. Dailey, said Dr. Dan made many speeches in his sixties.

For his speech, "The Malingerer," see Publications No. 13.

265
Account of Hall's and Booker Washington's dealings is found in BTW, where appear also the letters of Robert White.

266
The faithfulness of Dr. Kenney and Emmett Scott is apparent in BTW, and was also voiced to me in person.

Dr. Kenney told of Dr. Dan's operation on his wife. Dr. Dan's letter about Kenney's brochure was published in NMA Jnl.

The incident at Camp Funston was told by Emmett Scott, also by Dr. Booker. A letter from Dr. James Mills, Jr., tells of Dr. Dan's attending his father's funeral.

The story of the commissioning of the six hundred colored officers is told in *Official History of the American Negro in the World War, Emmett J. Scott,* 1919.

Harriet Hollinger told of Dr. Dan's visits to Moses Brown's sons, and Harriette Kennedy Brown told of her husband's visit to Dr. Dan. The Wisconsin trip was told by Victoria Bishop Schuster.

David Kennedy was the child of a mulatto and a Tuscarora Indian woman. As a baby he was toted pick-a-back by his Indian grandmother. His mother died and his father grieved so much he went off and, though Negroes were not being accepted, managed to enlist in the Northern forces in the Civil War. David was just the age of Dan Williams and the two little boys became firm friends. They were playing alone together in the deserted schoolyard of the little Negro schoolhouse late one evening when word was brought David that his father had been killed. The kind white Condron family, the family for whom the Condron Opera House was named, brought up David. When he was grown he married Harriet Powell, granddaughter of Thomas Williams, Dan's father's Lewistown cousin. It was to David Kennedy that Dr. Dan confided how brokenhearted he was over Kittie May Blake.

By 1915 Dr. Dan had withdrawn almost completely from the colored medical fraternity. On a few occasions he momentarily emerged from his isolation. In 1918 he attended a dinner honoring Dr. James White on his return from service in France. In 1919, despite Hall's presence, he brought himself to attend and to speak at a dinner given for his old disciple and friend, Wilberforce Williams. Wilberforce was going abroad for the Young

PAGE
269
(*Cont.*)

Men's Christian Association, to lecture to colored soldiers. Hall could hardly stomach the acclaim given the departing doctor. "I hope the damn nigger drowns," he growled to Carl Roberts. But Wilberforce came safely home, and when he did, in January 1922, Dr. Dan again emerged from seclusion to attend a birthday dinner at his friend's home. Hall was not invited, but others susceptible to his influence were. The group was largely a medical group. On the table reposed a fine young suckling pig. The occasion was festive and the talk grew animated. Dr. Dan was led to remark that funds had been offered him from a wealthy white source with which to start another hospital, but it was specified the new hospital should be entirely staffed with colored doctors. "So," said Dr. Dan, "I refused the money, for how could we staff it?" His remark was quietly, almost carelessly made, according to Roberts, Dickerson and White; he apparently expected no reaction to it. But it was repeated outside and, as the weeks and months passed, was so exaggerated and embroidered that there was a new cry of "Disloyal!" Naturally there was keen disappointment that such an opportunity had been lost; more outlet was needed then as now for the pent-up abilities and energies of the circumscribed colored profession. The late Dr. Carl Roberts judged there were then ten or eleven men at Provident who were ready to head departments. But, even if his opinion was correct, and if Dr. Dan had pulled them all out to staff a new hospital, the new hospital would still have lacked a number of needed specialists and Provident would have been stripped of all but George Hall, for Provident would allow no man to serve on two staffs. There would have been no real gain for the race and Dr. Dan would have been subject to the accusation that he had started another hospital to ruin Hall and Provident together. As a matter of fact, the late Dr. John Kenney said: "I don't know where he could have got all the men necessary for a completely colored staff; I myself had the problem in Newark." And Dr. Dailey says: "Dr. Williams's remark was true. At that time we had no real specialists in internal medicine, no neurologist, no urologist, no obstetrician, and our specialists in eye, ear, nose and throat were only in embryo. But it was certainly an impolitic remark and was such as Dr. Williams was fated to make, but it was true."

Christine Shoecraft Smith told of the diabetes and the wood chopping, and Mrs. Beaudreau told how Dr. Dan insisted on being driven to his office when he was too weak to get there otherwise.

At sixty Dr. Dan removed a giant pyosalpinx; see Publications No. 14.

Dr. Dan's visits to Bailiff's resort at Benton Harbor were told by Hettie Mitchem Turner and confirmed by C. O. Bailiff. The late Dr. Roberts told how Hall made the place unpleasant for Dr. Dan.

Alice Williams paid her last visit to Washington in 1917. By this time she had learned to drive well and enjoyed it, as she did the resumption of her china painting. When young Reverend Shelton Hale Bishop, Dr. Dan's namesake, married Eloise Carey in 1919 she presented them with some of her handiwork, a sugar bowl and cream pitcher. Soon after she fell ill.

The nature of Alice Williams's illness was ascertained from Dr. Gilbert.

Mrs. William T. Childs and Julia LeBeau Thompson paid tribute to Alice's fortitude, as did Dr. Gilbert and others. Estelle Arnold told of Alice's rejection of a minister and Mrs. Thompson told of the reading of Tennyson's poem.

After her death, Dr. Dan was anxious, said Hugo Williams, that each of her friends should have something belonging to her. To her physician he gave a quantity of her fine Haviland.

Not until he was sixty-nine, in 1925, did Dr. Dan admit he needed help with his office patients. He asked young Dr. Leon Tancil to assist him. The arrangement was congenial and when Tancil married, Dr. Dan invited him to bring his bride, daughter of Mary Church Terrell, the noted race leader, to live with him. The house on West 42nd Street was larger than he needed since Alice had died. He had Mrs. Croker to care for him, but he wanted

PAGE
272
(*Cont.*)

company, six months of the year he would be in Idlewild. The young couple accepted, but not without misgivings. Mrs. Tancil (now Mrs. Beaudreau) writes of those days: "We had heard that Dr. Dan was difficult to get along with, but we found he was not nearly so grouchy as we were made to believe. . . . We were all like a family there and despite his reputation of being odd, we did not find him so. He used to joke about the way I ordered him around, he said no one ever had ordered him as I did, but he liked it. As he grew forgetful, he would sometimes accuse Dr. Tancil or Mrs. Croker of mislaying his books or something, but he never accused me." Dr. Dan grew weaker but was stubborn about giving up. Kahlke saw him at an Eastern medical meeting and thought he looked very ill, but Dr. Dan brushed aside Kahlke's anxious queries. At home he was less and less able to stand noise or bustle of any kind. The radio bothered him, the Tancils' two dogs bothered him, and finally the young couple, finding themselves confined to an almost hospital atmosphere, decided they must move out if they were to have a normal social life. The parting came after three years and was friendly. But now Dr. Dan was lonely indeed. He wandered back and forth between his own home and that of his old friends, Mary Lizzie and Wilberforce. And then his befuddled state led him into difficulties even with those old friends. He asked Mary Lizzie to have one of his chairs upholstered, forgot he had done so, and stormed and refused to pay the bill. In April 1929 he spent several weeks in Dailey's private sanitarium and by then Dailey confirmed the fact his mental faculties were impaired, as well as his speech. J. Carlos Davis thought his friends should ask the court to appoint a conservator and spoke to Louis B. Anderson about it, but Anderson refused to do anything for fear people would say he was after Dr. Dan's money.

Dr. Dan went off to Washington, bought a house at 1214 Park Road and took his aged sister Annie and his sister Alice to live with him. Florence had died in 1914, Sally in 1915, and Ida still earlier. Dr. Charles West cared for him, and Lily Waring Moore, an old friend of his wife's, nursed him. In May 1930, his brother Price's daughter, Ada Blanche Zaratt, came from Puerto Rico and took charge of Dr. Dan. She took him to Chicago and on to

California for the winter, where he suffered another stroke and had to be brought back to St. Luke's. Somewhat better and back in his apartment at 5942 South Michigan Avenue, he received friendly calls from Dr. N. C. Gilbert. Long before, Gilbert had delighted to listen to Dr. Dan's tales in the smoking room; now there was little he could do for the great man medically. W. H. Zabel, St. Luke's Chief Pharmacist for so many years, came too. As summer approached, Dr. Dan begged to be taken to Idlewild to die, and his niece complied with his request.

On November 12, 1930, a codicil was added to Dr. Dan's will, giving all chattel property as well as the real estate and house in Idlewild, together with one half of the residuary estate, to his niece "in consideration of her giving up her own home and affairs to live with me and to care for my remaining years." The signature, a trembling, childlike scrawl, bears no resemblance to Dr. Dan's former signature. The will is on file in the Probate Court, Chicago.

The late Dr. Minton showed me Dr. Dan's letters to him about sending his books to Mercy Hospital, Philadelphia.

Billings's letter making the dinner appointment was found in Dr. Dan's papers, along with several others expressing admiration and friendship, after his death. Dr. Ludwig Hektoen, who was at the dinner, related the engagement to the Provident Hospital drive for funds, and the late Dr. Roberts told of Billings's refusal to assist Provident after Dr. Dan's resignation and of his later acceptance of the chairmanship of the fund committee.

Dr. Dailey told of receiving the files and chair.

Obituaries appeared in the *Chicago Tribune, New York Times, Chicago Defender,* NMA Jnl, AMA Jnl, *Time* and many other papers.

The tribute in the *Lake County Star* is from the edition of August 7, 1931.

PAGE
273
(*Cont.*)

Herbert Davis, editor of the *Star*, said when I called on him that Dr. Dan's generosity was unbounded, that he educated many a boy in the neighborhood, first requiring him not to tell, and that he offered to equip a hospital in Baldwin if the townspeople would furnish the building, which they failed to do. Fred Bradford was one Dr. Dan offered to educate; he offered to set up a trust fund for his complete medical education, but Fred's mother did not want him to leave home. When Fred's brother Andy fell in a dead faint with a ruptured stomach ulcer, Dr. Dan came and stayed twelve hours by him without leaving, and visited him daily, sometimes two and three times a day, for six weeks; he saved his life and sent no bill. In gratitude the Bradfords came and put up rose trellises for Dr. Dan. At Christmas time he sent gifts to many. To Mrs. Elsner, the postmistress, besides personal gifts for herself and her husband, he sent clothing for all the needy children roundabout together with a little gift. Mrs. Elsner addressed them and mailed them out. "We remember Dr. Dan," said Mr. Davis, "with something akin to reverence up here."

274

Harry Branch's museum at Idlewild Terrace displays Dr. Dan's photograph along with some of his instruments and his razors, and displays his "card" in I. C. Harris's *Directory of Colored Chicago, 1885.*

On November 26, 1930, Mrs. Croker, his former housekeeper, a member of Father Eckert's parish, who had long been eager to have Dr. Dan baptized into the Catholic Church, sent for her priest. The rite was performed in Dr. Dan's room. In the year before his first stroke, Dr. Dan gave his religion as "Unitarian" in *Who's Who in American Medicine 1925,* Lloyd Thompson and Winfield Scott Downs, eds.

Father Eckert told me Mrs. Croker called him to come and baptize Dr. Dan and gave the date and place and said Dr. Dan was not able to walk.

The late Dr. Roberts said few colored people attended the funeral. W. H. Zabel, who attended, said the church was packed.

PAGE
274
(*Cont.*) Various persons spoke of the wreath incident at the cemetery, including Drs. Spencer Dickerson and William A. Lewis.

James Gordon told me of the failure to give recognition to Dr. Dan at the third Provident building, of his protest, and of the belated restitution. Members of the staff paid for the portrait, the National Medical Association furnished the bronze plaque. I visited Provident lobby and saw these souvenirs.

Persons Consulted

The thanks I have attempted to voice in my *Acknowledgments* I repeat here to these many persons who so patiently provided me with the detail without which this book could not have been written. They are, however, in no way responsible for the use I have made of their information.

Isaac A. Abt, M.D., James Alderson, M.D., Leonard Alexander, Lillie Smith Alexander, Henrietta Americ, Archibald Anderson, Daniel Herbert Anderson, M.D., Jessica Anderson, Louis B. Anderson, Retta M. Arnett, R.N., Estelle L. Arnold, Mrs. George Arthur, Charlotte Atwood, Nancy Atwood, Jennie L. Avendorph.

C. O. Bailiff, J. Max Barber, D.D.S., Elizabeth Tyler Barringer, R.N., Mary Terrell Tancil Beaudreau, Mrs. Beauduit, Tomietta Stokes Beckham, R.N., Zellie Ridgley Bennett, L. L. Berry, Jesse Binga, Eloise Carey Bishop, the Reverend Shelton Hale Bishop, Jennie Blackburn, Arthur J. Booker, M.D., P. C. Boomer, M.D., May Boston, M. O. Bousfield, M.D., Harry Bowser, Fred Bradford, Harry Branch, Melesenah Maine Brinkley, Kate Gibson Brooks, R.N., Charles R. Brown, Edith M. Brown, Eva Lucas Brown, Harriette Kennedy Brown, Coleman G. Buford, M.D., Carrie E. Bullock, R.N., Allan Burdick, H. W. Burnard, M.D., Mrs. Burrus, Harriet Shadd Butcher, Alice Thornton Butler, Isabella Garnett Butler, M.D.

M. Blaine Caldwell, James Tweedie Campbell, M.D., Charles W. Cansler, Archibald J. Carey, Jr., Edith M. Carter, R.N., Helen M. Chesnutt, Mrs. William T. Childs, Mrs. Robert Church, Elizabeth McCard Clark, Montague Cobb, M.D., William E. Cobb, Berta Cornell Coleman, Duvall E. Colley, M.D., Mrs. Duvall E. Colley, Rufus J.

Collins, M.D., W. H. Compton, Anna J. Cooper, Homer P. Cooper, M.D., Norman Croker, M.D., Mary Cromwell, Otelia Cromwell, Alice Williams Cuffee, Mrs. William N. Cummings.

Ulysses Grant Dailey, M.D., Herbert Davis, J. Carlos Davis, D.D.S., Mrs. J. C. Davis, Clara Demmey, Jessie Williams DePriest, Oscar DePriest, Spencer C. Dickerson, M.D., Lillie Doughty, Frederick Douglas, Kathleen Brown Douglas, W. E. Burghhardt DuBois.

Reverend Joseph Eckert, Mara Franc Edwards, Frances Middleton Elam, Arthur R. Elliott, M.D., Mrs. Edwin Elsner, Carrie Ridgley Evans, Mrs. Samuel J. Evans, Lillian Evanti, B. A. Everett, M.D.

Marie Fellows, M.D., Edith Fleetwood, Virginia Powell Florence, G. Hamilton Francis, M.D., Chester A. Franklin, Clara Belle Williams Franklin, D. Peter French, Henry W. Furniss, M.D., Sumner A. Furniss, M.D.

Irene McCoy Gaines, Alamanda Williams Garnett, Josephine Williams Garnett, Charles H. Garvin, M.D., Mattie Martin Gates, Emma George, Max P. Gethner, M.D., Maymie Van Vranken Gibson, N. C. Gilbert, .D., Roscoe C. Giles, M.D., James G. Gordon, Charles Grace, Helen Williams Ramsay Gray, Mabel Mason Greene.

Andy Hall, M.D., Harriett Curtis Hall, Mrs. Henry Hall, John B. Hall, M.D., Nina Bamen Hall, Theodocia Brewer Hall, Beatrice Fitzgerald Hawkins, Ludwig Hektoen, M.D., Franklyn A. Henderson, Mattie Herron, T. Arnold Hill, J. Seth Hills, M.D., Harriet Dennis Hollinger, John Hamilton Holman, M.D., Lucy Messer Holmes, William R. Houston, Marie Hudlin, Mary G. Hudson, Beatrice Ridgley Hume, Grace E. Hunte, John E. Hunter, M.D.

Reverend G. Lake Imes, Mae Irwin, R.N.

Alexander L. Jackson, Harry A. Jacobs, Francis Jamison, D.D.S., Sarah Jennings, Charles S. Johnson, Joseph L. Johnson, Katie Johnson, E. Kinckle Jones, Frank C. Jones, M.D., Richard Lloyd Jones.

Charles E. Kahlke, M.D., Mrs. B. Lane Kelly, Charles Kelly, John W. Kelly, E. A. Kendall, M.D., John A. Kenney, M.D., Minerva Guernsey King.

Roscoe Lane, Helen J. Lattimore, Eva Hunt LeVere, Bertie Brooks Lewis, Carrie Lewis, Charles A. Lewis, M.D., Julian Heath Lewis, M.D., Lawrence A. Lewis, M.D., Tillie Lloyd, Myra Logan, M.D., Etta E. Loomis, Grace S. Lord.

Selim W. MacArthur, M.D., J. W. McDowell, M.D., Charles McElroy, Harriet Layton McFadden, David A. McGowan, J. A. McMillan, M.D., Jeannette Lyons McMurdy, Philip McMurray, M.D.

Monroe A. Majors, M.D., Emma Lawrence Warren Mallet, John Middleton Mallet, Pearl Barbour Marchant, Mrs. E. H. Mars, Anna A. Mason, James S. Mills, Jr., M.D., Wallace C. Mills, Louise V.

Mingo, Henry M. Minton, M.D., Mrs. Henry M. Minton, Harry E. Mock, M.D., C. E. Moreland, Del Gratia Scott Moreland, Mrs. Norris Morgan, Mrs. Clifton Moss, N. F. Mossell, M.D., Eloise Palmer Mouat, Anna Evans Murray.

Sarah Meriwether Nutter.

Caroline Parke, Mrs. E. H. B. Parker, Blanche Thornton Parnall, Julia West Paul, Howard Marshall Payne, M.D., Katie B. Payne, Clarena Harris Pendleton, J. Edward Perry, M.D., James M. Phalen, M.D., Lorraine Pinchback, Samuel Craig Plummer, M.D., James Hale Porter, Theodora Lee Purnell.

Daniel Rainey, Louise Rainey, Bishop Reverdy Ransom, W. A. Reed, M.D., Curtis W. Reese, Juliana Willis Rhodes, Mary W. B. Richardson, Lottie Bishop Ridgley, Mrs. Robert Hal Riffe, Carl Glennis Roberts, M.D., E. P. Roberts, M.D., Mrs. E. P. Roberts, Mamie Roberts, Angie T. Roethe, J. S. Royster.

Jessie Sleet Scales, R.N., Louis Schmidt, M.D., Victoria Bishop Schuster, Emmett J. Scott, Howard D. Scott, James Scott, Mary Scott, Blanche V. Shaw, Christine Shoecraft Smith, Daniel Smith, M.D., Reginald Smith, M.D., Robert Smith, Anna Pounder Sorrell, Annie Stewart, F. A. Stewart, Jr., D.D.S., Harriet George Stewart, Ralph Stewart, M.D., Elizabeth Ramsey Still, Agnes Thornton Stives, Blanche Williams Stubbs, Frederick Stubbs, M.D., Charles L. Sutherland, M.D., Mrs. Orion Sutherland, Florence Prettyman Suydam.

Elizabeth Palmer Taylor, Robert L. Taylor, William F. Taylor, Mary Church Terrell, Gardner Thomas, Charles H. Thompson, Julia LeBeau Thompson, Herbert Turner, M.D., Hettie Mitcham Turner, William B. Turner.

Reverend Irvin W. Underhill.

Bertha Van Hoosen, M.D., Frank W. Van Kirk, M.D., Harriet L. Van Vranken.

Mary Louise Hall Walker, J. H. Ward, M.D., William A. Warfield, M.D., Lula G. Warlick, R.N., Esther Watson, Fannie West, Howard D. West, M.D., Rebecca West, Lola Brown Whipple, Clarence Cameron White, Helen Brown White, James R. White, M.D., Melesenah White, Walter White, Ada Blanche W. Z. Williams, Hugo Williams, O. B. Williams, M.D., Raphael Dumas Williams, Sadie Fitzgerald Wilson, Maude Hall Winnett, M.D., W. W. Wolf, M.D., Carter G. Woodson, Howard D. Woodson, Louis T. Wright, M.D., Lucille F. Wright.

William J. Yerby.

William H. Zabel.

Publications of
Daniel Hale Williams, M.D., F.A.C.S.

1. "Several Cases of Inflammation Starting in the Caecum and Vermiform Appendix," read at meeting of Gynecological Society of Chicago, March 17, 1895.
    —— *Transactions* of the Gynecological Society of Chicago for the year 1893–1894, Vol. 2, pp. 130–135.
    —— *American Journal of Obstetrics*, 1893, Vol. 28, pp. 260–281.
2. *Annual Report*, Freedmen's Hospital, July 1, 1895.
3. *Annual Report*, Freedmen's Hospital, July 1, 1896.
4. "Stab Wound of the Heart and Pericardium. Suture of the Pericardium. Recovery. Patient Alive Three Years Afterward." By Daniel H. Williams, M.D., Surgeon, Freedmen's Hospital, Washington, D.C.
    —— *New York Medical Record*, March 27, 1897, Vol. 51, pp. 437–439, illustrated.
5. *Annual Report*, Freedmen's Hospital, July 1, 1897.
6. "Uterine Fibroids," letter dated December 1, 1897, from Daniel H. Williams to Dr. E. Stillman Bailey, read as part of report by Bailey on "The Medical Treatment of Uterine Fibroids," at the Section of the Medical Diseases of Women of the Clinical Society, regular monthly meeting held December 18, 1897.
    —— *Clinique*, Chicago, 1898, Vol. 19, pp. 23–24.
7. "A Case of Intestinal Obstruction Following Ventro-Fixation." Discussion of paper by Albert Goldspohn, at meeting of the Chicago Gynecological Society, March 21, 1900.
    —— *American Gynecological and Obstetrics Journal*, 1900, Vol. 16, p. 573.
8. "Surgical Cases: An Unusual Case of Molluscum Fibrosum; Hernia of Bladder; Fibromatous Pregnant Uterus." By Daniel H. Wil-

liams, M.D., Chicago (3034 Michigan Ave.), presented at clinical meeting of Chicago Medical Society, Wednesday, December 20, 1899.

—— *Chicago Medical Recorder*, 1900, Vol. 18, pp. 43–47.

—— *Obstetrics* (New York), 1900, Vol. 2, pp. 70–72 (Fibromatous Pregnant Uterus).

—— *The Philadelphia Medical Journal*, February 17, 1900, Vol. 5, pp. 404–405 (An Unusual Case of Molluscum Fibrosum).

9. "The Need of Hospitals and training Schools for the Colored People of the South." By Daniel H. Williams, M.D., Attending Surgeon, Provident and Cook County Hospitals.

—— Reprint of paper read before the Phillis Wheatley Club at Nashville, Tennessee, January 23, 1900. 5 pages, illustrated. National Hospital Record, Detroit. No date.

10. "Ovarian Cysts in Colored Women, with Notes on the Relative Frequency of Fibromas in Both Races." By Daniel H. Williams, M.D., of Chicago, Ill., Attending Surgeon to the Cook Co. and Provident Hospitals. Read at regular meeting of the Chicago Medical Society, December 26, 1900.

—— *Chicago Medical Recorder*, 1901, Vol. 20, pp. 47–57, 100–101.

—— *The Philadelphia Medical Journal*, December 29, 1900, Vol. 6, pp. 1244–1248.

11. "A Report of Two Cases of Caesarean Section under Positive Indications with Terminations in Recovery." By Daniel H. Williams, M.D., Attending Surgeon to the Cook County and Provident Hospitals, Chicago, Ill. Read before Chicago Gynecological Society, January 18, 1901.

—— *American Journal of Obstetrics*, 1901, Vol. 45, pp. 315–322, 400–403 (illustrated).

12. "Penetrating Wounds of the Chest, Perforating the Diaphragm, and Involving the Abdominal Viscera. Case of Successful Spleen Suture for Traumatic Haemorrhage." By Daniel H. Williams, M.D., of Chicago, Attending Surgeon to the Cook Co. and Provident Hospitals. Read before Chicago Medical Society, June 16, 1904.

—— *Annals of Surgery*, 1904, Vol. 40, pp. 675–685 (illustrated).

—— *Illinois Medical Journal*, 1904, Vol. 6, pp. 384–386 (last 5 pages of article).

—— *Chicago Medical Recorder*, 1904, Vol. 26, pp. 586–591 (illustrated).

13. "The Malingerer." By Daniel Hale Williams, M.D., LL.D., F.A.C.S., Chicago. Read at 9th Annual Meeting, Surgical Associa-

tion of the Chicago and North Western Railway, Rochester, Minnesota, December 10–11, 1915.

—— *The Railway Surgical Journal*, 1915–1916, Vol. 22, pp. 445–448 (last paragraph is abridged).

—— *New York Medical Journal*, April 8, 1916, Vol. 103, pp. 684–686 (omits discussion).

14. "Unusually Large Pyosalpinx." Dr. Daniel Hale Williams, with pathological report by Mr. Kenneth Hallock. Read at regular meeting of Chicago Gynecological Society, January 21, 1916.

—— *Surgery, Gynecology, Obstetrics*, 1916, Vol. 22, pp. 741–742.

Index

Abbreviation: DHW for Daniel Hale Williams